VIKING
MEDIOLOGIES

FORDHAM SERIES IN MEDIEVAL STUDIES

Franklin T. Harkins and Mary C. Erler, series editors

VIKING MEDIOLOGIES

A New History of Skaldic Poetics

KATE HESLOP

FORDHAM UNIVERSITY PRESS

New York   2022

Copyright © 2022 Fordham University Press

All rights reserved. No part of this publication may be reproduced, stored in a retrieval system, or transmitted in any form or by any means—electronic, mechanical, photocopy, recording, or any other—except for brief quotations in printed reviews, without the prior permission of the publisher.

Fordham University Press has no responsibility for the persistence or accuracy of URLs for external or third-party internet websites referred to in this publication and does not guarantee that any content on such websites is, or will remain, accurate or appropriate.

Fordham University Press also publishes its books in a variety of electronic formats. Some content that appears in print may not be available in electronic books.

Visit us online at www.fordhampress.com.

Library of Congress Cataloging-in-Publication Data

Names: Heslop, Kate, author.
Title: Viking mediologies : a new history of Skaldic poetics / Kate Heslop.

Description: First edition. | New York : Fordham University Press, 2022. | Series: Fordham series in medieval studies | Includes bibliographical references and index.
Identifiers: LCCN 2021056770 | ISBN 9780823298242 (hardback) | ISBN 9780823298259 (paperback) | ISBN 9780823298266 (epub)
Subjects: LCSH: Scalds and scaldic poetry—History and criticism. | Poetics. | LCGFT: Literary criticism.
Classification: LCC PT7172 .H47 2022 | DDC 839/.61009—dc23/eng/20211122
LC record available at https://lccn.loc.gov/2021056770

Printed in the United States of America

24 23 22   5 4 3 2 1

First edition

CONTENTS

General Abbreviations / *vii*
Abbreviations for Poets and Poems / *ix*
Acknowledgments / *xiii*

Introduction / *1*

PART 1. MAKING MEMORIES

Rök and Ynglingatal / *15*

1. Death in Place / *20*
2. Forging the Chain / *46*

Stone—Stanza—Memory / *72*

PART 2. SEEING THINGS

3. The Viking Eye / *81*
4. Seeing, Knowing, and Believing in the *Prose Edda* / *108*

PART 3. HEARING VOICES

5. The Noise of Poetry / *135*
6. A Poetry Machine / *160*

Conclusion / *185*

Notes / *193*
References / *257*
Index / *291*

Plates follow page 78

GENERAL ABBREVIATIONS

AEW	Jan De Vries. *Altnordisches etymologisches Wörterbuch*. 2nd ed. Leiden: Brill, 1977.
CVC	Richard Cleasby, Gudbrand Vigfusson, and W. A. Craigie. *Icelandic-English Dictionary*. 2nd ed. Oxford: Clarendon Press, 1957.
EK	Klaus von See, et al. *Kommentar zu den Liedern der Edda*. 7 vols. Heidelberg: Winter, 1992–2019.
Fritzner, *Ordbog*	Johan Fritzner. *Ordbog over det gamle norske sprog*. 3 vols. Kristiania (Oslo): Den norske forlagsforening, 1883–96.
ÍF *Eddukvæði*	Jónas Kristjánsson and Vésteinn Ólason, eds. *Eddukvæði*. 2 vols. Reykjavík: Hið íslenzka fornritafélag, 2014.
ÍF 2	Sigurður Nordal, ed. *Egils saga Skallagrímssonar*. Reykjavík: Hið íslenzka Fornritafélag, 1933.
ÍF 5	Einar Ól. Sveinsson, ed. *Laxdœla saga*. Reykjavík: Hið íslenzka Fornritafélag, 1934.
ÍF 16	Ásdís Egilsdóttir, ed. *Biskupa sögur*. II. Reykjavik: Hið íslenzka fornritafélag, 2002.
ÍF 17	Guðrún Ása Grímsdóttir, ed. *Biskupa sögur*. III. Reykjavik: Hið íslenzka fornritafélag, 1998.
ÍF 23	Ármann Jakobsson, ed. *Morkinskinna*. Reykjavík: Hið íslenzka Fornritafélag, 2011.
ÍF 26	Bjarni Aðalbjarnarson, ed. *Heimskringla*. I. Reykjavik: Hið íslenzka fornritfélag, 1979.
ÍF 29	Bjarni Einarsson, ed. *Ágrip af Nóregskonunga sögum—Fagrskinna*. Reykjavík: Hið íslenzka fornritafélag, 1985.
ÍF 30	Þorleifur Hauksson, ed. *Sverris saga*. Reykjavik: Hið íslenzka fornritfélag, 2007.
ÍF 34	Finnbogi Guðmundsson, ed. *Orkneyinga saga*. Reykjavík: Hið íslenzka fornritafélag, 1965.

KLNM	Johannes Brøndsted et al., eds. *Kulturhistorisk leksikon for nordisk middelalder fra vikingetid til reformationstid*. 22 vols. Copenhagen: Rosenkilde & Bagger, 1956–78.
LP	Finnur Jónsson. *Lexicon Poeticum Antiquæ Linguæ Septentrionalis. Ordbog over det norsk-islandske skjaldesprog*. Copenhagen: Møller, 1931.
ONP	Helle Degnbol et al. *Ordbog over det norrøne prosasprog / Dictionary of Old Norse Prose*. Copenhagen: Arnamagnæan Commission, 1989–.
RGA	Heinrich Beck et al., eds. *Reallexikon der germanischen Altertumskunde*. 37 vols. Berlin: De Gruyter, 1973–2008.
SamRun	*Samnordisk runtextdatabas*, Uppsala Universitet. http://www.nordiska.uu.se/forskn/samnord.htm.
Skj	Finnur Jónsson, ed. *Det norsk-islandske skjaldedigtning. A. Tekst efter håndskrifterne. B. Rettet tekst med tolkning*. 4 vols. Copenhagen: Villadsen & Christiansen, 1912–15.
SkP	Margaret Clunies Ross et al., eds. *Skaldic Poetry of the Scandinavian Middle Ages*. 8 vols. Turnhout: Brepols, 2007–.

ABBREVIATIONS FOR POETS AND POEMS

Abbreviation	Author and Title	Edition
Anon (*FoGT*)	Anonymous, Stanzas from the *Fourth Grammatical Treatise*	Ed. Clunies Ross, *SkP* III, 570–625
Anon (*LaufE*)	Anonymous, Stanzas from *Laufás-Edda*	Ed. Gade, *SkP* III, 637–48
Anon *Líkn*	Anonymous, *Líknarbraut*	Ed. Tate, *SkP* VII, 228–86
Anon *Lil*	Anonymous, *Lilja*	Ed. Chase, *SkP* VII, 544–677
Anon *Mey*	Anonymous, *Heilagra meyja drápa*	Ed. Wolf, *SkP* VII, 891–930
Anon *Morg*	Anonymous, *Morginsól*	Ed. Clunies Ross, *SkP* III, 510–11
Anon *Mv II*	Anonymous, *Máríuvísur II*	Ed. Gade, *SkP* VII, 701–17
Anon (*Nj*)	Anonymous, *Lausavísur* from *Njáls saga*	Ed. Finnur Jónsson, *Skj* BI, 399
Anon *Nkt*	Anonymous, *Nóregs konungatal*	Ed. Gade, *SkP* II, 761–806
Anon *Óldr*	Anonymous, *Óláfs drápa Tryggvasonar*	Ed. Heslop, *SkP* I, 1031–60
Anon *Pét*	Anonymous, *Pétrsdrápa*	Ed. McDougall, *SkP* VII, 796–844
Anon *Pl*	Anonymous, *Plácitusdrápa*	Ed. Louis-Jensen and Wills, *SkP* VII, 179–220
Anon (*SnE*)	Anonymous Lausavísur, *Stanzas from Snorra Edda*	Ed. Gade, *SkP* III, 512
Anon *Vǫlsa*	Anonymous, *Lausavísur* from *Vǫlsa þáttr*	Ed. Heizmann, *SkP* I, 1089–1105
Anon *Þul Jǫtna I*	Anonymous *Þulur: Jǫtna heiti I*	Ed. Gurevich, *SkP* III, 707–22
Arn *Hardr*	Arnórr jarlaskáld Þórðarson, *Haraldsdrápa*	Ed. Whaley, *SkP* II, 260–80
Arn *Hryn*	Arnórr jarlaskáld Þórðarson, *Hrynhenda, Magnússdrápa*	Ed. Whaley, *SkP* II, 181–206
Arn *Þorfdr*	Arnórr jarlaskáld Þórðarson, *Þorfinnsdrápa*	Ed. Whaley, *SkP* II, 229–60
Árni *Gd*	Árni ábóti Jónsson, *Guðmundardrápa*	Ed. Finnur Jónsson, *Skj* BI, 440–61
Bbreiðv *Lv*	Bjǫrn Breiðvíkingakappi, *Lausavísa*	Ed. Quinn, *SkP* V
Bersi *Ólfl*	Bersi Skáld-Torfuson, *Flokkr about Óláfr helgi*	Ed. Whaley, *SkP* I, 790–95

Abbreviation	Author and Title	Edition
Bjbp *Jóms*	Bjarni byskup Kolbeinsson, *Jómsvíkingadrápa*	Ed. Lethbridge, *SkP* I, 954–97
BjHall *Kálffl*	Bjarni gullbrárskáld Hallbjarnarson, *Kálfsflokkr*	Ed. Finlay, *SkP* I, 877–90
Bragi *Frag*	Bragi inn gamli Boddason, *Fragments*	Ed. Clunies Ross, *SkP* III, 53–56
Bragi *Rdr*	Bragi inn gamli Boddason, *Ragnarsdrápa*	Ed. Clunies Ross, *SkP* III, 27–47
Bragi *Þórr*	Bragi inn gamli Boddason, *Þórr's fishing*	Ed. Clunies Ross, *SkP* III, 46–53
Bǫlv *Hardr*	Bǫlverkr Arnórsson, *Drápa* about Haraldr harðráði	Ed. Gade, *SkP* II, 286–93
Egill *Arkv*	Egill Skallagrímsson, *Arinbjarnarkviða*	Ed. Finnur Jónsson, *Skj* BI, 38–41
Egill *Berdr*	Egill Skallagrímsson, *Berudrápa*	Ed. Clunies Ross, *SkP* V
Egill *Skjalddr*	Egill Skallagrímsson, *Skjaldardrápa*	Ed. Clunies Ross, *SkP* V
Egill *St*	Egill Skallagrímsson, *Sonatorrek*	Ed. Finnur Jónsson, *Skj* BI, 34–37
EGils *Guðkv*	Einarr Gilsson, *Guðmundarkvæði*	Ed. Finnur Jónsson, *Skj* BII, 418–29
Eil *Þdr*	Eilífr Goðrúnarson, *Þórsdrápa*	Ed. Marold et al., *SkP* III, 68–126
ESk *Frag*	Einarr Skúlason, *Fragments*	Ed. Gade, *SkP* III, 151–68
ESk *Geisl*	Einarr Skúlason, *Geisli*	Ed. Chase, *SkP* VII, 5–65
ESk *Run*	Einarr Skúlason, *Runhenda*	Ed. Gade, *SkP* II, 551–59
EVald *Þórr*	Eysteinn Valdason, *Poem about Þórr*	Ed. Clunies Ross, *SkP* III, 185–88
Eyv *Hák*	Eyvindr skáldaspillir Finnsson, *Hákonarmál*	Ed. Fulk, *SkP* I, 171–95
Eyv *Hál*	Eyvindr skáldaspillir Finnsson, *Háleygatal*	Ed. Poole, *SkP* I, 195–213
Ghv	*Guðrúnarhvǫt*	ÍF *Eddukvæði* II, 402–6
Gísl *Magnkv*	Gísl Illugason, *Erfikvæði* about Magnús berfœttr	Ed. Gade, *SkP* II, 416–430
Gkv I	*Guðrúnarkviða I*	ÍF *Eddukvæði* II, 329–34
Glúmr *Gráf*	Glúmr Geirason, *Gráfeldardrápa*	Ed. Finlay, *SkP* I, 245–68
GunnLeif *Merl* II	Gunnlaugr Leifsson, *Merlínusspá* II	Ed. Poole, *SkP* VIII, 134–89
Hást *Lv*	Hásteinn Hrómundarson, *Lausavísur*	Ed. Finnur Jónsson, *Skj* BI, 91–92
HSt *Rst*	Hallar-Steinn, *Rekstefja*	Ed. Stavnem, *SkP* I, 893–939
Hamð	*Hamðismál*	ÍF *Eddukvæði* II, 407–13
HaukrV *Ísldr*	Haukr Valdísarson, *Íslendingadrápa*	Ed. Finnur Jónsson, *Skj* BI, 539–45

Abbreviation	Author and Title	Edition
Hfr ErfÓl	Hallfreðr vandræðaskáld Óttarsson, Erfidrápa Óláfs Tryggvasonar	Ed. Heslop, SkP I, 400–441
Hfr Lv	Hallfreðr vandræðaskáld Óttarsson, Lausavísur	Ed. Whaley, SkP V
Hharð Lv	Haraldr harðráði Sigurðarson, Lausavísur	Ed. Gade, SkP II, 42–46
HHI	Helgakviða Hundingsbana I	ÍF Eddukvæði II, 247–58
HHII	Helgakviða Hundingsbana II	ÍF Eddukvæði II, 270–83
Hildibrandr Lv	Hildibrandr, Lausavísur in Ásmundar saga kappabana	Ed. Jorgensen, SkP VIII, 16–20
Hjálm Lv	Hjálmarr inn hugumstóri, Lausavísur	Ed. Clunies Ross, SkP VIII, 816–42
Hókr Eirfl	Halldórr ókristni, Eiríksflokkr	Ed. Gade, SkP I, 469–85
Hróm Lv	Hrómundr halti Eyvindarson	Ed. Finnur Jónsson, Skj BI, 90
Hym	Hymiskviða	ÍF Eddukvæði I, 399–407
Hynd	Hyndluljóð	ÍF Eddukvæði I, 460–69
Ill Har	Illugi bryndœlaskáld, Poem about Haraldr harðráði	Ed. Gade, SkP II, 282–85
Ív Sig	Ívarr Ingimundarson, Sigurðarbálkr	Ed. Gade, SkP II, 501–27
KormQ Lv	Kormákr Qgmundarson, Lausavísur	Ed. Marold, SkP V
Mark Lv	Markús Skeggjason, Lausavísur	Ed. Gade, SkP III, 295–97
Oddi Lv	Oddi inn litli Glúmsson, Lausavísur	Ed. Jesch, SkP II, 614–19
Oddrgr	Oddrúnargrátr	ÍF Eddukvæði II, 365–71
Ólhv Hryn	Óláfr hvítaskáld Þórðarson, Hrynhenda	Ed. Goetting, SkP II, 658–70
Ótt Lv	Óttarr svarti, Lausavísur	Ed. Townend, SkP I, 783–86
Rv Lv	Rǫgnvaldr jarl Kali Kolsson, Lausavísur	Ed. Jesch, SkP II, 575–609
RvHbreiðm Hl	Rǫgnvaldr jarl and Hallr Þórarinsson, Háttalykill	Ed. Gade, SkP III, 1001–1093
Sigoa Lv	Sigurðr ormr í auga, Lausavísa	Ed. McTurk, SkP VIII, 663–64
Sigv Berv	Sigvatr Þórðarson, Bersǫglisvísur	Ed. Gade, SkP II, 11–30
Sigv ErfÓl	Sigvatr Þórðarson, Erfidrápa Óláfs helga	Ed. Jesch, SkP I, 663–98
Sigv Lv	Sigvatr Þórðarson, Lausavísur	Ed. Fulk, SkP I, 698–737
Sigv Nesv	Sigvatr Þórðarson, Nesjavísur	Ed. Poole, SkP I, 556–78
Sigv Víkv	Sigvatr Þórðarson, Víkingavísur	Ed. Jesch, SkP I, 533–56
Skúli Lv	Skúli Þorsteinsson, Lausavísa	Ed. Heslop, SkP III, 366–68

xii ABBREVIATIONS FOR POETS AND POEMS

Abbreviation	Author and Title	Edition
Snegl *Lv*	Sneglu-Halli, *Lausavísur*	Ed. Gade, *SkP* II, 323–32
SnSt *Ht*	Snorri Sturluson, *Háttatal*	Ed. Gade, *SkP* III, 1094–1210
StarkSt *Vík*	Starkaðr Stórvirksson, *Víkarsbálkr*	Ed. Clunies Ross, *SkP* VIII, 253–87
Steinunn *Lv*	Steinunn Refs (Dálks)dóttir, *Lausavísur*	Ed. Fulk, *SkP* V
Sturl *Hákfl*	Sturla Þórðarson, *Hákonarflokkr*	Ed. Gade, *SkP* II, 745–55
Sturl *Hákkv*	Sturla Þórðarson, *Hákonarkviða*	Ed. Gade, *SkP* II, 699–727
Sturl *Hryn*	Sturla Þórðarson, *Hrynhenda*	Ed. Þorvaldsdóttir, *SkP* II, 676–98
Tindr *Hákdr*	Tindr Hallkelsson, *Hákonardrápa*	Ed. Poole, *SkP* I, 336–58
ÚlfrU *Húsdr*	Úlfr Uggason, *Húsdrápa*	Ed. Marold, *SkP* III, 402–24
Valg *Har*	Valgarðr á Velli, *Poem about Haraldr harðráði*	Ed. Gade, *SkP* II, 300–10
Vetrl *Lv*	Vetrliði Sumarliðason, *Lausavísa*	Ed. Fulk, *SkP* III, 425–26
Vsp	Vǫluspá	ÍF *Eddukvæði* I, 291–321
Þdís *Þórr*	Þorbjǫrn dísarskáld, *Poem about Þórr*	Ed. Clunies Ross, *SkP* III, 470–72
ÞGísl *Búdr*	Þorkell Gíslason, *Búadrápa*	Ed. Lethbridge, *SkP* I, 941–53
Þjóð *Haustl*	Þjóðólfr ór Hvini, *Haustlǫng*	Ed. Clunies Ross, *SkP* III, 431–63
Þjóð *Yt*	Þjóðólfr ór Hvini, *Ynglingatal*	Ed. Marold et al., *SkP* I, 3–60
ÞjóðA *Har*	Þjóðólfr Arnórsson, *Stanzas about Haraldr Sigurðarson's leiðangr*	Ed. Whaley, *SkP* I, 147–58
ÞjóðA *Lv*	Þjóðólfr Arnórsson, *Lausavísur*	Ed. Whaley, *SkP* II, 163–76
Þhorn *Gldr*	Þorbjǫrn hornklofi, *Glymdrápa*	Ed. Marold et al., *SkP* I, 73–91
Þloft *Glækv*	Þórarinn loftunga, *Glælognskviða*	Ed. Townend, *SkP* I, 863–76
Þloft *Tøgdr*	Þórarinn loftunga, *Tøgdrápa*	Ed. Townend, *SkP* I, 851–63
Þmáhl *Máv*	Þórarinn svarti máhlíðingr Þórólfsson, *Máhlíðingavísur*	Ed. Heslop, *SkP* V
Þorf *Lv*	Þorfinnr munnr, *Lausavísur*	Ed. Whaley, *SkP* I, 845–8
Þorm *Lv*	Þormóðr Kolbrúnarskáld, *Lausavísur*	Ed. Fulk, *SkP* V
Þrk	Þrymskviða	ÍF *Eddukvæði* I, 422–27
ÞSjár *Frag*	Þórðr Sjáreksson, *Fragments*	Ed. Gade, *SkP* III, 476–81
ÞSjár *Róðdr*	Þórðr Sjáreksson, *Róðudrápa*	Ed. Gade, *SkP* I, 242–44
Þul *Jǫtna I*	Anonymous, *Jǫtna heiti I*	Ed. Gurevich, *SkP* III, 706–22
Þþyn *Lv*	Þorbjǫrn þyna, *Lausavísa*	Ed. Finnur Jónsson, *Skj* BI, 90

ACKNOWLEDGMENTS

A minor but persistent source of confusion for beginning students of skaldic poetry is the way that skalds refer to themselves in the first-person plural. "It's just a poetic convention," I tell my students, ducking the reasonable question—how did it become conventional? What is it about skaldic performance that this verbal tic responds to, in a convincing enough way to be taken up by generations of poets? I will suggest in this book that the skald's art was a profoundly dialogic and intersubjective one, circulating and competing with communal, locally anchored narratives, voicing the fears and hopes of the royal retinue, and borne on into posterity by many voices and pens. The image of the monologuing skald in a purely binary relationship of exchange with his patron is in many ways a mystification, introduced in the saga transmission to serve its own ends. It is, therefore, all the more pleasurable and personally meaningful to acknowledge my own interlocutors and supporters—though I am aware that the intersubjectivity of academic work doesn't guarantee preservation over centuries of oral transmission.

I have been enormously fortunate in my Old Norse teachers: Margaret Clunies Ross, Judy Quinn, and Geraldine Barnes in Sydney, Diana Whaley in Newcastle-upon-Tyne, and Jürg Glauser in Zurich. This book rises out of the intersection of two large projects I was involved with, the Skaldic Editing Project in Sydney and Newcastle (now *Skaldic Poetry of the Scandinavian Middle Ages*, whose editions I gratefully cite), and the Swiss National Science Foundation project *Medienwandel—Medienwechsel—Medienwissen* (Mediality: Historical Perspectives) in Zurich. These projects formed my ideas of skaldic media, and I am deeply indebted to the "Learned Ladies" (as the General Editors of the skaldic project are known) and the members of the mediality colloquium. My current department at UC Berkeley is a supportive and stimulating new home.

Margaret Clunies Ross, Klaus Müller-Wille, Karin Sanders, and Jonas Wellendorf read earlier versions of my manuscript in whole or in part and gave valuable feedback, as did members of the Townsend Fellowship group, the Medieval Studies program, and the Old Norse graduate seminar at Berkeley. I also profited from the comments of the anonymous readers for Fordham University Press. Too many colleagues to name helped with advice and materials—to them, heartfelt thanks. For help with translating, checking, proof-reading, bibliography, and indexing, I am grateful to Campbell Ewing, Nicola Barfoot, Michael Lawson, Rue Taylor, and Stephanie Ward. None of these people are responsible for those of my errors which remain despite all of our best efforts.

I have presented parts of this study to audiences in Zurich, Basel, Reykjavik, Oslo, Berkeley, Kalamazoo, Oxford, and Cambridge and to meetings of the Society for Advancement of Scandinavian Study and have benefited greatly from questions and feedback at those places. Most of Part II was written while I was a Snorri Sturluson Fellow at the Stofnun Árna Magnússonar in Reykjavik and on sabbatical at the University of Zurich. I am grateful to my hosts in both places for their hospitality and access to their excellent collections and libraries. I gladly acknowledge the financial support of the Stofnun Sigurðar Nordals and the Osher Foundation. For permission to reproduce objects in their collections, I thank the Swedish National Heritage Board, Bavarian State Library, Swedish National Museum, Dalarna Museum, Uppsala University Library, and Árni Magnússon Institute for Icelandic Studies.

Friends in Zurich and Berkeley accompanied this project through its long gestation, and, especially in the last phases of writing, offered the support which enabled it to get done. My wife, Sevgi, and daughter, Eleanor, have been remarkably patient when my book robbed them of time and attention that was rightly theirs.

VIKING
MEDIOLOGIES

INTRODUCTION

Egill Skallagrímsson, then a surly teenager, met Arinbjǫrn Þórisson on his first trip out of Iceland. Egill was impressed by the older youth, 'sought [his] friendship and followed him around everywhere.'[1] Their relationship was to last for the rest of Arinbjǫrn's life. The friends meet in Norway, England, Frisia. They give each other presents (a shipload of timber, gold rings, a sword, a decorated sail, a silk cloak, a suit of clothes made of multicolored English cloth). Egill marries one of Arinbjǫrn's cousins, Ásgerðr, and takes up the cause of another, Þorsteinn, and of Arinbjǫrn's sister Gyða. For his part, Arinbjǫrn intercedes on Egill's behalf with his royal patrons Eiríkr *blóðøx* (blood-axe) and Hákon *Aðalsteinsfóstri* (foster son of Æthelstan). Most importantly, Arinbjǫrn is a kind of muse, knowing just what to say to make his friend break into verse. His rhetorical skill extracts Egill's poetic confession of love for Ásgerðr. ("This is a case where the saying applies that you can tell anything to a friend," Egill admits.)[2] And when the two find themselves in a tight spot in York and have to persuade Eiríkr *blóðøx* to accept a poem as a "head-ransom," in lieu of Egill's life, it is Arinbjǫrn who reminds the king of the poet's command of posterity: "If Egil has spoken badly of the king [...] he can make recompense with words of praise that will live for ever (*uppi vera*)."[3] As impresario, Arinbjǫrn has an ear for what his star soloist needs to deliver:

> My advice is for you to stay awake all night and make a poem in praise of King Eirik. I feel a drapa of twenty stanzas would be appropriate, and you could deliver it when we go to see the king tomorrow.[4]

When a twittering swallow distracts Egill, struggling in his garret to eke out twenty stanzas, who sits outside on the roof all night to keep the shape-shifter at bay but Arinbjǫrn?

Egill's greatest gift to his friend is a poem. The saga reports that Egill was getting on in years and permanently settled back in Iceland when he composed a poem usually referred to as *Arinbjarnarkviða* (Poem about Arinbjǫrn). A single fragmentary medieval text survives.[5] Its central conceit is ancient: the praise of a gift.[6] Generosity is to miserliness as praise is to slander, Egill insists, right speech and action allow what is good to circulate. Or, expressed in the paradoxical way typical of this kind of poetry, Arinbjǫrn is "fierce to money" (*fégrimmr*, st. 22), ridding himself of wealth as if he hated it, and Egill, no "friend-thief" (*vinþjófr*, st. 13), repays him with the praise that is his due. Poetry is embedded in an interpersonal situation and a context of economic exchange. But the poem destabilizes these neatly balanced oppositions with another, parodic, gift to whose giver Egill is anything but grateful.[7] King Eiríkr "gives" Egill his head in the head-ransom episode, but only in the sense that he forbears from taking it, so Egill offers the recompense to Arinbjǫrn instead, in the form of an extraordinary blazon of his own head. It is a "wolf-grey hood's stump" (*ulfgrátt hattar staup*, st. 7) adorned with "dark hair" (*døkkva skǫr*, st. 3), a "voice-plane," or tongue (*omunlokarr*, st. 15), a multitude of teeth (*tannfjǫlð*, st. 9), "blackish hollows of deep brows," or eyes (*sǫkk sámleit síðra brúna*, st. 8), and "hearing-tents, gifted with listening," or ears (*hlertjǫld hlustum gǫfguð*, st. 9). Bizarrely arresting circumlocutions such as "mouth of hearing" (*hlustamunnr*, st. 6) and "handspan of audition" (*spǫnn heyrnar*, st. 19), both of which refer to the ears, center as they destabilize the most intimately felt of unities. Further body parts, the "homesteads of the halberd" (hands: *atgeirs toptir*, st. 21) and "speech-servant" (tongue: *málþjónn*, st. 25), circulate alongside both the "rings" (*hringar*, st. 22) offered by the generous lord, and material and corporeal metaphors for the poem: wood worked by the tongue, a cairn climbed by poetry's feet, or, dragging Arinbjǫrn's fame up to new heights, a "pulling-rope" (*drógseil*, st. 19) of the ears. In their willed obscurity, kennings (as these circumlocutions are called in Norse poetics) raise questions of representation with unusual insistence—in what respect is this similar to that? How far can likeness be pushed before it collapses? Those of *Arinbjarnarkviða*, with their kaleidoscopic shifts of vehicle, do so in an acute form referred to as "monstered" (*nykraðr*) or "centaured" (*finngálknaðr*) in the poetological treatises.[8] They are typical of a poetics whose metaphorical language sets the master medium of premodernity, the body, in motion among other media—gold, words, stones.

Egill's poetry about Arinbjǫrn offers a justly famous memorial image:

25. Vask árvakr,
bark orð saman
með málþjóns
morginverkum;
hlóðk lofkǫst

þanns lengi stendr
óbrotgjarn
í bragar túni.
(I was awake early,
I bore words together
with the speech-servant's
morning stint;
heaped up a praise-cairn,
one that'll long stand,
uneager to break
in poetry's homefield.)

The poet lugs words together and piles them high in imitation of another memorial technology, the cairn (*kǫstr*). Rather than simply claiming durability for the linguistic form the poet constructs, the image of the cairn, delicately circumscribed by the *litotes* of "uneager to break" (*óbrotgjarn*), suggests that poetic memorialization is shared and processual. A cairn stands because many hands maintain it. Egill's poem lives on, barely, thanks to an unending labor of repetition. Such persistent but vulnerable claims to mediate memory, presence, and praise lie at the heart of skaldic poetry.

The present book is a study of premodern media. It investigates the conditions of possibility for poetic performance in the Viking Age (c. 750–1050 CE), maps the place of poetry in the media landscape of premodern Scandinavia, explores the mediologies that key works elaborate, and reflects on media change in the Icelandic High Middle Ages (c. 1050–1300 CE). At its heart is the figure of the *skald* (poet). Skalds were the masters of poetic praise and blame at the courts of Scandinavian rulers in the Viking Age. Their poetic trademark, an intricately figured stanzaic form known as *dróttkvætt* (court poetry), was invented sometime around the beginning of this period. As the name *dróttkvætt* suggests, the skalds claimed the discursive formation of courtliness as their prerogative. But they needed to carve out a domain for themselves in competition with other media of aristocratic self-representation: visual arts, runic monuments, and the common Germanic heritage of alliterative poetry. In skaldic verses we eavesdrop as experts hammer out ideas about the power and limits of their new kind of poetry.

Mobile, hybrid, diasporic social formations—bands of raiders and traders, petty kingdoms, colonial expeditions—achieved new prominence in the

Viking Age.⁹ Skalds offered the leaders of these groups something uniquely valuable. They claimed to be able to capture communal and contingent meanings, the stuff of place-based *memoria* and embodied experience, and re-mediate them in authored, memorable, reproducible works. Like contemporary runic monuments and visual art, the *dróttkvætt* stanza held out the promise of permanence, wide dissemination, and performative force. As writing arrived in Scandinavia in the wake of Christianization (c. 1000), the media landscape shifted again. Skaldic poetry, the most conservative of Old Norse literary genres, continued in some ways in the furrow plowed by the earliest poets. Change also came to the skalds. In the poetry of the twelfth and thirteenth centuries, they adjusted to the new demands of a literate audience. At the same time, vernacular writing on poetry and rhetoric in the Icelandic High Middle Ages used the skaldic poetic tradition to explore fundamental questions about language, representation, and belief.

The "mediology" of my title is meant in two interlocking senses. Conceiving of skaldic poetry as a node in a network of medial practices, I study its place in the broader media landscape of the Viking Age and seek to describe how different media interacted in this particular historical setting. I also investigate how the poems understand their own materiality and ability to act in the world—how they are a kind of talk about media. The medial imaginary is a reservoir of thought, in Hans Blumenberg's words, "a catalytic sphere from which the universe of concepts continually renews itself."¹⁰ In Old Norse this stretches from rare explicit theorizations, through self-reflexive moments at the thresholds of texts, to a profusion of medial metaphors—talking heads, automatic verse-generators, eyes transformed into starry memorials, and the ecstatic, agonizing, memory-erasing, poetic-trance-inducing me(a)dium of poetry, wrested by the god Óðinn from the giants. Interferences, discontinuities, and impurities characterize the premodern Scandinavian media landscape, lending it enormous richness and potential.

Despite this, the dichotomy of oral versus literate transmission dominates many studies of skaldic poetry. Gripped by the nationalist passions of the nineteenth and twentieth centuries, the protagonists of the "bookprose/freeprose" debate in Old Norse studies clashed over the roles of indigenous, collective oral tradition and individual, learned authorship in the genesis of the long prose form known as the saga. This controversy left its mark on debates about other Old Norse literary genres too. In the case of skaldic poetry, it drives an implicit division of the corpus at the convenient watershed between orality and literacy provided by the conversion of Scandinavia to Christianity. And, crucially, it obscures the rich media environment in which Viking Age and medieval poets worked, both before and after the arrival of writing. In this book I aim to break with this exclusionary dualism, focusing instead on the interferences between media practices and discourses in the premodern North.

THE MEDIUM AND THE MEDIA

Media studies in its classic form concerns itself with the forms, content, history, and effects of mass media technologies: newspapers, radio, television, film, and so on.[11] From this perspective, media are communications media, and the word "medium" names the ideally neutral or noiseless channel that carries a message between sender and receiver, described in Shannon and Weaver's theory of information transfer.[12] But the concept of a medium existed long before "the media" became the word for our information-saturated contemporary lifeworld—a terminological innovation that dates from the mid-eighteenth century.[13] The idea of the medium as a third term that intervenes between two extremes has a prehistory stretching back to antiquity, as recent work has disclosed.[14] Here the key move is not "from here to there," as in Shannon and Weaver's metaphor of the channel, but suspension in an in-between-ness already signaled by the etymology of the word "medium" itself. "Medium" is ultimately derived from the Indo-European root *medhios* (radical *me- plus adverbial –dhi, the whole meaning: "in the midst"), as is the equivalent Greek expression *to metaxu*.[15] Not yet the object of a systematic theory, the premodern medium is a loose array of practices and reflections upon them in domains such as perception, religious belief, and representation.

According to premodern thinkers, the medium is what allows distant objects to actively affect the sensorium. It is thus central to explanations of perception. The visual ray, for instance, is emitted by the eye, travels through the diaphanous "in-between" (*to metaxu*) seeking its object, and returns to the soul bearing the shape and color of the percept.[16] Aristotle argues that multiple listeners can hear the same sound thanks to subtle and mysterious "affections" of the air, "not without body."[17] Ideas of mediation also explain how human beings can communicate with the divine, by the mediation of angels.[18] Christ as *mediator* joins man to God. ("For there is one God, and one mediator of God and men, the man Christ Jesus.")[19] By his dual nature Christ is in the middle (*medium*) between God and man, partaking in the essence of both.[20] Objects such as icons and relics mediate grace according to different representational schemas—the likeness, sometimes miraculous like Veronica's veil (*vera icon*), or the metonymical fragment, such as the earth from Golgotha.[21] Much premodern art and literature uses concepts of mediation to make what is absent present, whether this involves transcendent realms of faith or the ontological play of the illusion. Against the communicative focus of modern media studies, premodern ideas of mediation emphasize processes of perception and representation: how bodies apprehend the world and how signs can stand for, or make present, something else.

These two ways of conceptualizing the medium, as channel of communication and as numinous in-between, might be called in shorthand the technological and the cultural. They first meet in the work of the postwar media theorists Marshall McLuhan and Friedrich Kittler.[22] These writers draw attention to the imbrication of medium and message and the shaping force that media technologies, broadly conceived, exert on culture in general. Their insights have been developed, especially in the German-speaking world, into a highly ramified set of hyphenated *Medien-* subdisciplines (*Medien-Archäologie, -Philosophie, -Geschichte*, and so on)[23] referred to in English as "German media theory."[24] Although these theoretical endeavors gladly avail themselves of the prestige of antique roots and the notion of a "deep time" of media, the Middle Ages has until recently been something of a blind spot.[25] This is now changing, first in the German-speaking world, where this body of theory was originally at home, and more recently elsewhere too.[26]

If a definition of the medium is to encompass both the media of our contemporary lifeworld and the medieval concept of a medium—and maybe this is an impossible ask—it would have to be rather general. Semiotician Roland Posner suggests that the medium is "a system of means of communication that enables repeated communications [but] imposes certain consistent restrictions on the semiotic processes that are generated within it."[27] Although still limited to communication, his definition usefully shifts attention from semantics, the *what* of cultural meaning, to *how* cultural meaning is produced, transmitted, and received and how these meanings are conditioned by "materialities of communication."[28] Analogous moves in literary study have generated a proliferation of alternatives to critical reading: Franco

Moretti's advocacy for "distant reading," Rita Felski's celebration of "everyday reading," Eve Sedgwick's disavowal of "paranoid reading," or Hans Ulrich Gumbrecht's passion for "presence."[29] Such post-hermeneutic currents underlie interest in the mediality of medieval culture, with its potential to throw new light on both the premodern material[30] and—perhaps more importantly—on the assumptions that are brought to its study.[31]

MEDIALITY

In medieval studies, the mid-twentieth-century theorizations of oral and literate mentalities of Eric Havelock, Walter Ong, Jack Goody and Ian Watt, Ruth Finnegan, and Michael Clanchy are the best-known instances of the heuristic potential of a medial perspective.[32] Media theorists such as McLuhan (who taught Ong at Saint Louis University) and his University of Toronto colleague Harold Innis were important influences on these sociological studies of the civilizational effects of media.[33] Complementary to them, and especially influential in Old Norse studies, was the Oral Theory of Milman Parry and Albert B. Lord, with its focus on the effects of oral culture on literary creativity.[34] More recent research into premodern mediality moves beyond merely contrastive accounts of orality and literacy. Paul Zumthor's pathbreaking concept of vocality began to bring the constitutively mixed nature of medieval media into focus.[35] Studies of "cultural techniques" concern themselves with a broader range of phenomena, investigating how ensembles of signs, practices, and technologies gradually come together into new medial forms.[36] More recent work also recognizes the historical specificity of particular media constellations, something that tends to be elided in the sweeping pronouncements of scholars of orality and literacy. In Old Norse studies, this has combined fruitfully with the new philological interest in medieval manuscripts as the work of multiple hands, produced, used, copied, and rewritten in specific contexts, to produce microhistories of particular writing practices. A few examples giving a sense of the range of this approach are recent projects on the textual culture of Vadstena Abbey, the manuscripts of *Njáls saga*, or the versions of the eddic poem *Vǫluspá*.[37]

An important aspect of the historical specificity of Old Norse textual culture is the fact that it is much more committed to the preservation of pre-Christian material than are neighbor literatures such as medieval German, French, or English. In western Europe perhaps only the Celtic literatures are comparable in their wealth of vernacular texts that transmit such material. Old Norse textual culture, preserved in the main in Icelandic manuscripts, is characterized by a mixing of Latinate, learned clerical traits with a vigorous lay imagination in which elements of pre-Christian narratives and ways of looking at the world remained important well into the era of writing. Distinct temporal and representational logics are proposed in the pre-Christian mythology preserved in Old Norse texts—needless to say, most of it at a greater or lesser remove in time and framed by Christian reception. For Christian authors, mediation was an essential but temporary state of affairs. It was the only way humans could gain some knowledge of God at the present moment, but it was due to be permanently short-circuited, for the saved at least, at the end of time. Metaphors of mediated vision were important in conveying this theological truth. By contrast, eschatology seems to have been of less importance in pre-Christian Norse conceptions of time, where cyclical structures are also prominent. When the eschaton does come into view, in eddic poems such as *Vǫluspá* and *Vafþrúðnismál*, the gods are actively seeking to delay it, and humans, while not totally absent (they comprise the patiently waiting *einherjar*) do not play a very significant role. Not even the gods themselves dwell in eternity, as they are destined to die at *ragnarøkkr*. The medial strategies used for representing and communicating with the divine are also different when the gods are multiple and multiform, as the pre-Christian Norse gods are. The Norse cosmos is not Tertullian's book of nature, written by God and meant for human interpretation, but a collection of transformed body parts involved in ongoing acts of creative destruction. Its meanings are historical and particular, like the stars Þórr makes from Þjazi's eyes, in *Hárbarðsljóð*, to commemorate the defeated giant:[38]

> 19. Ek drap Þjaza   inn þrúðmóðga jǫtun,
>   upp ek varp augum   Allvalda sonar
>   á þann inn heiða himin;
>   þau eru merki mest   minna verka,
>   þau er allir menn síðan um sé.
> (I killed Thiazi, the powerful-minded giant,
> I threw up the eyes of Allvaldi's son
> into the bright heaven;
> they are the greatest sign of my deeds,
> those which since all men can see.)[39]

Indigenous notions combine in Old Norse texts, not always seamlessly, with the Aristotelean, biblical, and patristic ideas of medium and mediation common to all of Latin Christendom. The interference of the pre-Christian temporal and representational regimes briefly sketched above with these ideas could perhaps begin to be traced in the Norse reception of the concept of *figura*, a key model of the mediation of meaning for medieval Christian thinkers. Figural interpretation of the Bible proposed that the Jewish history of the Old Testament was a promise, of which the New was the fulfilment. This structure imparted a meaning to history, which played out in real events as it also transcended them in its orientation toward a future immediacy of truth, to be found in Judgement Day and the Kingdom of Heaven. The word *figura*'s roots in antique rhetoric, traced by Erich Auerbach in a classic article, lent to it as well the sense of a "shadow" (*umbra*), "the rhetorical image or circumlocution that conceals, transforms, and even deceives [. . .] a *figura* under which something other, future, true, lies concealed."[40]

The doctrine of *figura* taught that historical events were mere mediating instances for a fuller truth. Unsuitable for the Christianizing reception of pre-Christian Norse belief, and incompatible with its conception of gods who cyclically die and reappear, *figura* nonetheless retained its importance in Old Norse interpretive cultures. The two Norwegian King Óláfrs were understood in a figural sense, and the term *figura* often appears in rhetorical and poetological contexts in Old Norse.[41] Here it enters into reflections on the shadowiness of "dark figures" (*myrku fígúrur*), directly implicating the traditional means of skaldic poetics, *Lilja*'s "hidden old words" (*hulin fornyrðin*), which are also significantly referred to in fourteenth-century poetry as "wiles of the *Edda*" (*eddu list*).[42]

The idea that meaning is hidden within its mediating instance and cannot be known directly (im-mediately), key to theologically inflected thinking about the medium, is indexed in Old Norse less by *miðla*, the equivalent of "mediate," than by a range of words referring to interpretation, such as *glosa* (to gloss), *merkja* (to mark, signify), or *skýra* (to explain). Another important concept for which a vernacular equivalent needed to be found was the idea of the *integumentum* or *involucrum*, the surface or "garment" covering a deeper meaning.[43] Among the Norse words used to gloss this concept are *skrúð* (n.) and the corresponding verb *skrýða*. *Þorláks saga biskups* repeatedly uses this terminology to refer to the holy bishop's "clothing" himself in Christian virtue:

He then clothed himself anew in many virtues and most of all that virtue which David called the most needful for clerics: that they should clothe themselves with helpful counsel and righteousness.[44]

When Þorlákr dies a fellow cleric has a vision of him clad in his bishop's robes (*biskupsskrúð*), making the equation of outward form and inward virtue explicit.[45] It is perhaps not by chance that the C-redaction of the saga refers to the distribution of Þorlákr's clothes after his death using the significant word *miðla*.[46] *Skrúð* is also used in poetological contexts, to gloss words belonging to the family of *figura*; the *Third Grammatical Treatise* announces that the Greek *schema* "is called [. . .] *skrúð* in Norse."[47] Concepts such as *kenning* (suggesting a "making known," and sometimes used to mean "lesson, moral of the story") and *ofljóst* (literally "too light/clear") draw some of their paradoxical quality from *figura*, as a Christian discourse about mediated meaning gets to work on poetic practices of obscure expression with histories of their own.[48]

Taking a medial perspective on medieval culture thus calls for a historicization of the medium. "What is a medium?"—a question which presupposes a transhistorical essence—is then a less useful entering wedge than questions like how does mediation work in particular historical contexts? Which processes are conceptualized by their participants as medial? How does an awareness of mediality affect the social relations that form around certain objects or practices?

MEDIOLOGIES

The idea of a *mediology*, proposed by French sociologist Régis Debray in the 1970s, is one way to approach these interlocking questions. Debray argues that "the concept of *medium* returns inevitably to that of the *milieu* (while pointing towards a cultural ecology), and that of *milieu* to that of technical *mediation* (as emerges from the phenomenon of human evolution always in progress)."[49] The transmission of cultural meaning thus has technical, material, social, and institutional drivers, which are in turn the object of reflection in cultural texts. One instance of this is the economic element seen already in Egill's *Arinbjarnarkviða*. Circulation, exchange, and trade, ranging from barter to robbery, also structure the myth of the mead of poetry, as the poetic essence changes both forms and hands. A favorite skaldic image of the poem is that of the ship, and of its performance, a merchant voyage. Óðinn, god of poetry, is also called "cargoes-Týr" (*farma-Týr*) and has mercantile interests.[50] And the poems are filled with references to the skald's hoped-for recompense. The economic condition of possibility of the skaldic medium—the exchange of poems for gifts and patronage—thus becomes the object of poetic reflection. The "story of our tools" is crossed with "the story of our hopes and dreams."[51]

As the skaldic medium emerges in the Viking Age and is gradually transformed over the next five hundred years, three key formal features emerge. These are quatrain-based stanzaic form; the skalds' special metaphor, or *kenning*; and the internal rhyme scheme peculiar to skaldic poetry known as *hending*. Early records of the poetic form known as *kviðuháttr* (poem's meter) allow the process of becoming a medium to be traced in a particular instance. In *kviðuháttr* poetry a loose ensemble of cultural techniques—in this case, a certain subject matter, speaker position, pattern of meter and imagery, and quatrain structure— gradually becomes conventional, enabling a privileged status to be claimed for the skaldic stanza as a medium of aristocratic memory. Media-archaeological arguments of this kind cannot be made for the *kenning*, whose origins lie far back in preliterate deep time. Rather, the kenning exemplifies an oscillation between signifier and signified that is also characteristic of Viking Age visual art. Fragmented bodies are shown in the throes of transformation: as fugitive presences, such as those of the gods, which appeal to both visual and haptic sensory modes. Finally the skalds' exorbitant rhyme, most sonorously deployed in the *dróttkvætt* stanza, exemplifies the relationship between the skaldic medium and its material, the sound of the performing voice. The medium both obeys the material and experiments with it, producing sonic patterns in what Susan Stewart calls a "doubled movement of poetic production, toward mastery on the one hand and being mastered on the other."[52] The questions of the agency behind the splendid noise of poetry that this movement raises only become more urgent as the poems begin (also) to be written down.

A small-scale instance of the new view afforded by a medial perspective is provided by these very technical terms. The words *kenning* and *hending* are usually encountered as feminine substantives in modern commentary, but verbal forms are most often used in the poems and poetological commentary: *kendr* ("kenned," past participle of the verb *kenna*) and *hendr* ("rhymed," past participle of the verb *henda*). To premodern writers and performers, metaphoring, rhyming, and keeping in memory (the last often termed *hafa uppi*, to raise up) were not attributes of a piece of text but things that skalds, their rhapsodic re-performers, scribes, and audiences *did*.

In what follows, I cut cross-sections through the Old Norse poetic and rhetorical-poetological tradition. My approach juxtaposes Viking Age poetry, mostly from the Scandinavian mainland, with the medieval life of the skaldic form in the Icelandic colony and explores the roles that the embodied cognitive-sensory primes of memory, vision, and sound play in skaldic poetics. I focus on interferences between skaldic poetry and other media: landscapes of commemoration in Part I, the visual arts in Part II, and music in Part III. As the section titles suggest, the medial specificity of this poetry often lies in play on the illusory nature of its effects. The book as a whole does not follow a developmental trajectory. Rather, its arrangement in three thematic sections opens up the possibility of a new kind of literary history of the skaldic form. In my conclusion I look forward from Viking mediologies rooted in bodily presence, whether real or imagined, and ask what a *medieval* mediology of skaldic poetry might look like. I suggest that it would take account of skaldic verse as a kind of writing and bring into focus phenomena such as layout, punctuation, and, most importantly, textual variance. I hope that one result of the medial viewpoint adopted in this book is a less stable, static, and authorial, and a more dynamic, processual, and collaborative, understanding of skaldic poetry.

PART 1

MAKING MEMORIES

RÖK AND *YNGLINGATAL*

A granite monolith stands more than six feet high in the churchyard at Rök, in the province of Östergötland in central Sweden (Plate 1). Every side of it is inscribed, in a mix of short-twig runes, runes from the older *fuþark*, and no less than three runic cipher systems. At approximately 750 characters, the Rök inscription (Ög 136) is the longest in the entire runic corpus. Usually dated to the first half of the ninth century, a period otherwise poor in runestones, the Rök monument was made around one hundred years prior to the Swedish Viking Age runestone boom.[1] In the flat landscape of central Sweden, it may once have been conspicuous enough to lend its name to the place where it stands. The Old Swedish word *roker* ("haystack") may refer to the monolith.[2] Before the viewer even begins to decode the inscription, the stone bodies forth its meaning aniconically, making a conspicuous place for memory in the landscape. The inscription, carved by a certain Varin (**uarin**), is a memorial to his son Vamoð or Væmoð (**uamoþ**).[3] Despite meticulous execution the text is often ambiguous and its interpretation highly controversial.[4] According to the most generally accepted reading, it recounts a series of riddling snippets of heroic legend, including an eight-line stanza on the late-fifth-century Ostrogothic king Theoderic. The Rök stone, a long authored inscription that extravagantly displays its own writtenness, ventriloquizes the repertoire of the *þulr*, or oral performer of heroic alliterative poetry, in a novel medium. Not only in this respect, but also, as I will argue, in regard to the kind of verse it quotes, it stands on the cusp of something new.

Shifting focus some 170 miles northwest as the crow flies to Viken, the broad inlet with Oslo at its head, and about fifty to one hundred years later in time, another remarkable forerunner stands almost as isolated as the Rök stone. Carved in words rather than stone, this is the poem known as *Ynglingatal* (List of the Ynglingar). *Ynglinga saga*'s prosimetrum quotes twenty-seven stanzas of varying length, which it attributes to a poem called *Ynglingatal* by Þjóðólfr ór Hvini (from Kvinesdal). This saga is the first in the *Heimskringla* compilation, thought to have been put together in early thirteenth-century Iceland and traditionally associated with Snorri Sturluson.[5] The oldest surviving manuscript of *Ynglinga saga* is approximately one hundred years younger (Copenhagen, Den Arnamagnæanske Samling, AM 45 fol, c. 1300–25), although the text is also preserved in a number of post-medieval copies of the lost medieval vellum manuscripts Kringla and Jöfraskinna, burned in the Copenhagen fire of 1728. Finally, the most accessible editions of *Ynglinga saga* and *Ynglingatal* are those of the *Íslenzk fornrit* and *Skaldic Poetry of the Scandinavian Middle Ages* series, from 1941 and 2012 respectively.[6] While the Rök stone enables its viewer to quite literally touch the ninth-century past, in *Ynglingatal* a multilayered trans- and re-mediation of memory is written into its text at every turn.

Ynglingatal, for its part, recounts the more or less bizarre deaths of twenty-eight kings of central Sweden (the country of the Svíar, centered on Gamla Uppsala) and southern Norway. In many cases it also describes their death sites, funerals, and funerary monuments. It concludes with enigmatic praise addressed to a twenty-ninth king, the skald's patron Rǫgnvaldr. Each king is memorialized in a stanza consisting of between two and five quatrains linked together by adverbs or the conjunction "and" (*ok*). Successive quatrains often restate the same information using different kennings, giving a riddle-like impression.[7] At the stanza level, the poem's organization is driven to a significant degree by syntactical constraints imposed by its meter. The irresistible logic of the list has led most commentators until very recently to regard *Ynglingatal* as a genealogical poem, even though the line of descent is only weakly apparent in *Ynglingatal*. In what sense the poem's large-scale organization can be said to be genealogical, and what the substance is that links the kings to one another, is explored further in Chapter 2.

Both the Rök stone and *Ynglingatal*, new media of the early Viking Age, claim to capture memory of the deep past and press it into the service of their dedicatees. Not least thanks to both objects' colossal dimensions and stupendous technical mastery, they confer lasting durability on these memories. In both cases, I will argue, the powerful example of more highly organized societies to the west and south catalyzed changes toward greater social differentiation and medial complexity of their memorial practices. Much of *Ynglingatal*'s complexity is, in turn, driven by the poetic medium in which it is cast, yielding a particularly recondite form of expression. The medium and its social agency are embedded in a relationship of mutual determination.

Nonverbal memory media, most prominently graves and ruined halls, found *Ynglingatal*'s claim to reach back into the deep past. Pioneering works of memory studies touched on the question of memory's mediality, for instance those of Maurice Halbwachs and Pierre Nora.[8] As Halbwachs observed, place and ritual are key memory media, especially of religious *memoria*.[9] The rise to prominence, in recent years, of theories of cultural[10] and social memory[11]—kinds of memory that are borne by groups and expressed in cultural practices—has focused renewed attention on how memory is mediated by the material world. This work emphasizes the constructive way in which remembering subjects interact with objects and places, not as storage depots for memory, but as memory media available for reproduction and re-mediation.[12] The cultural historian Aleida Assmann contrasts a "generational place" (*Generationenort*) such as the home, sedimented with the experiences of generations of the family, with a "memorial place" (*Gedenkort*), which preserves "what remains of that which no longer exists or is in force."[13] The latter, she argues, does not bring the past into close and intimate contact with the present as the generational place does, but emphasizes the distance, the break separating past from present, and the contrast between the two.[14] Ruins, relics, and graves are particularly apposite instances of the memorial place, as they are "bridges over that abyss of forgetting which they also make manifest."[15]

The potential of graves and ruins to mediate memory was only enhanced in the course of Christianization. Rituals offer in-group identification via shared habitus, so collective rituals reinforce group solidarity.[16] In the gradual transition from paganism to Christianity in the north, "one set of rituals was exchanged for another" as "Christianity [became] part of the language of power throughout northwestern Europe."[17] As a religious practice, Christianity distinguished itself most starkly from paganism by its claim to "join Heaven and Earth at the grave of a dead human being."[18] This was no less true in the north, where Christianity's grave cult contrasted with pre-existing religious practice.[19] And on Scandinavia's southern border, Carolingian royal *memoria* was also importantly mediated by place. Carolingian history-writing is topographically structured, forming "a catena of places" in which a key mnemonic site such as Saint-Denis attracts significant events like "a gravitational mass capable of bending actions around it."[20] Uppsala plays a similar gravitational role in Scandinavian aristocratic memory. Probably composed around the year 900 CE, *Ynglingatal* is a late look back at Uppsala's Vendel Period heyday. The poet's Uppsala is a ruin, "emblematic of transience and of persistence over time [...] a physical trace of the past that expresses its own process of decay."[21]

If place-based memoria forms one side of *Ynglingatal*'s medial dispositive, explored in Chapter 1 below, the other is the new poetic form in which it is cast, a meter known as *kviðuháttr* (poem's meter). Like *dróttkvætt* (court meter), the chief skaldic meter, *kviðuháttr* almost certainly developed out of the Old Norse variant of the common Germanic alliterative meter, known as *fornyrðislag*.[22] *Dróttkvætt* quickly came to dominate skaldic encomium, comprising 65 percent of the encomiastic corpus, compared to only about 14 percent for *kviðuháttr*. While *dróttkvætt* adds a trochaic cadence to the end of regularized *fornyrðislag* half-lines, *kviðuháttr* goes in the opposite direction.[23] Its even lines are regular *fornyrðislag* with four metrical positions, but its odd lines contain only three positions arranged in catalectic variants of *fornyrðislag* patterns. Thematically, death and memory lie at the heart of poetry in *kviðuháttr*. As well as a common theme, poems in this meter share the formal qualities of catenulate structure and riddling kennings, often involving puns on proper names. The *kviðuháttr* skalds cite these generic markers with a self-consciousness that justifies approaching the poems as a group, as I will do. According to the conventional datings and attributions, the major early works in *kviðuháttr* after Þjóðólfr's *Ynglingatal* (*Yt*, c. 900) are Eyvindr Finnsson's *Háleygjatal* (*Hál*, c. 985) and Egill Skallagrímsson's *Arinbjarnarkviða* (*Arkv*, mid-tenth century) and *Sonatorrek* (*St*, later tenth century). Þórarinn's *Glælognskviða* (*Glækv*, 1030s), the earliest preserved *kviðuháttr* poem on a Christian subject, is followed by a fragmentary poem attributed to Oddi Glúmsson (mid-twelfth century) and the anonymous *Nóregs konungatal* (*Nkt*, c. 1190). Sturla Þórðarson's *Hákonarkviða* (*Hákkv*, late 1260s), finally, is the last encomiastic poem in *kviðuháttr*, clearly composed with an eye on its illustrious predecessor.[24] As the oldest extended composition in the first of the Old Norse syllable-counting stanzaic meters to emerge from the matrix of common Germanic alliterative tradition, *Ynglingatal*, in a sense, inaugurates the remarkable body of authored poetry in *dróttkvætt* discussed in the rest of this book.

The next two chapters explore these conjunctures of media, memory, and voice. In what follows, *Ynglingatal* will be read as a text that engages in a complex memorial construction of the past in the specific social and political context of early tenth-century Viken, on the frontier between the Danish kingdom and the smaller political units that would, in the course of the Middle Ages, be forged into Norway. My reading focuses on how the poem remembers the Swedish past that it looks back to. I will suggest that, rather than offering its readers tesserae that they can use to reconstruct an image of pre-Christian *Svíþjóð* (the domain of the Svíar), *Ynglingatal* presents them with ruins and is a poem as much about the *how* of remembering as it is about the *what*. In the textual culture of the twelfth century and beyond *Ynglingatal* itself becomes the object of memory-work, in bureaucratic, salvific, and emulatory modes.

CHAPTER 1

DEATH IN PLACE

What would it mean to read *Ynglingatal* as not a chronology, but a map? To follow an itinerary, rather than descend a family tree? It need not entail pursuing the Yngling kings to specific grave mounds at Uppsala or Borre, as earlier scholars aspired to do.[1] Most archaeologists now believe such identifications to be impossible and see the poem and the monuments as separate but parallel endeavors: in the words of Bjørn Myhre, "two sides of the same impulse."[2] Such an approach would, however, mean giving the places of *Ynglingatal* their full due. Not only its nineteen or so place-names, but also its natural sites—rock, river, forest, island, bay, ridge, shore, the sky—and architectural settings: hall, gallows, mound, pyre, ship. These are the places where the kings met their deaths or their bodies lie. They are organized around or, in Edward Casey's phenomenological terminology, built by bodies. "The body constitutes the crossroads between architecture and landscape, the built and the given, the artificial and the natural," he suggests.[3] And bodies build places in *Ynglingatal* and elsewhere in a still more fundamental sense. By virtue of its sheer matter the body also takes up, and so marks, a particular space.

By their presence and activity, bodies transform mere *sites* into "dwelling *places*," which "offer not just bare shelter but the possibility of sojourns of upbringing, of education, of contemplation, of conviviality, lingerings of many kinds and durations."[4] *Places* are where the natural world is incorporated into human life. *Ynglingatal* is full of such lingerings. Both the legendary Fróði and Hálfdan are said to have "dwelled."[5] Its kennings refer, unusually, to domestic animals such as dogs, horses, goats, and oxen, and everyday things ranging from bridles, straps, and a pitchfork to a baby's bottle, alongside more conventional references to the material culture of the hall: the hearth, the altar, feasts, gold rings. The martial and mythoheroic kennings typical of *dróttkvætt* memorial poetry only appear occasionally in *Ynglingatal*, whose kennings emphasize a "slow sedimentation [. . .] realized by the reenactment of bodily motions."[6] This is the memorial regime of the "generational place"

(*Generationenort*). *Ynglingatal* juxtaposes the Norse aristocratic lifeworld that these kennings evoke with the "memorial place" (*Gedenkort*) of the grave or death-site. Previous commentary has made much of the distinction between graves and death-sites in the poem, but from the perspective of *lieux de mémoire* they are equivalent, "artefact[s] created around bodily remains."[7] In her study of the memory of place in the Mälaren Valley in Sweden, Ann-Mari Hållans Stenholm finds that Viking Age (c. 750–1050 CE) graves and houses are deliberately superimposed on Migration Period (c. 375–550 CE) and Vendel Period (c. 550–750 CE) structures.[8] In this dense landscape of remembrance, ruins of both houses and graves become sites for "the creation, transfer and preservation of social memory," in a Viking Age "memory mania" that reveals both the memorially layered nature of the landscape and the multi-temporal quality of the human lives lived in it.[9] In *Ynglingatal* the kings' bodies form nodal points, occupying a middle realm between the nonhuman lifeworld and an otherworld represented in this poem by the figure of Hel, the goddess of death. The lived continuity of everyday existence is shattered by death, *Ynglingatal* suggests, but death also founds memory.

Not that *Ynglingatal* presents things and animals as benevolent or comforting. On the contrary, they are the poem's death bringers. Whereas in *dróttkvætt* memorial poetry the king is an active agent, dealing out death to the last, *Ynglingatal*'s kings are meek victims of natural or supernatural forces, whose agency is imagined in starkly material, embodied terms. The rock gaped (*gein*) at Sveigðir, the nightmare tormented (*kvaldi*) Vanlandi, the fire-dog bit (*beit*) Vísburr, fire trod (*trað*) through Ingjaldr and loosed (*leysti*) Óláfr's clothes, Hel took (*tók*) Hálfdan, and Goðrøðr was bitten (*beittr*) by treachery.[10] The rhetorical payload of passivity is a tight focus on the suffering royal body, or rather its parts: fire swallows Vísburr's breast (*byrði* [var. *byrgi*] *vilja* "ship/fortification of the will," *Yt* 4), a strap encircles Jǫrundr's neck (*at halsi, Yt* 12), Dómaldi's blood reddens (*rauða, Yt* 5) the ground, a bull's horn pierces Egill's heart (*til hjarta, Yt* 14), Óttarr's flesh dangles from the eagle's claw (*hrægum fœti, Yt* 15), Aðils' brain-sea (*œgir hjarna, Yt* 16) mixes with the mud, Hálfdan's bones (*bein, Yt* 22) lie at Skæreið, and Óláfr succumbs to a foot disease (*fótverkr, Yt* 26). These sudden, disastrous events punctuate the world of habitual action presented in the kennings. They demarcate the places where the kings' bodies are transformed into corpses.

ITINERARIES

Ynglingatal moves from one death-place to the next, stanza after stanza, in an itinerary that can still be partly traced.[11] Complicating this task is the fact that many of the poem's place-names are no longer locatable on the ground, in part due to their relative obscurity. Few of the poem's place-names, whether Swedish or Norwegian, appear elsewhere in the poetic corpus.[12] Traditions about these places were evidently borne by a medium other than poetry. In the Swedish part of the poem, only *Uppsala* (*Yt* 13, 16, 21) and *Fýri* (*Yt* 6) can be definitely located, as the settlement now known as Gamla Uppsala—on which more will be said shortly—and the river Fyrisån, which flows through Uppsala. Per Vikstrand has presented convincing arguments that the poem's *Skúta* (*Yt* 3) and *Vendill* (*Yt* 15) also refer to locations in Uppland.[13] A small stream, whose name can be reconstructed as *Skūta, runs a couple of miles south of Vendel, which Vikstrand argues is, in turn, the referent of the poem's *á Vendli* (although *Heimskringla*'s prose understands it as the better-known Vendsyssel in Jutland). Vendel is about twenty miles north of Gamla Uppsala and, like Uppsala, was the site of an impressive Late Iron Age hall, the burial mound known as Ottarshögen, and a cemetery complex.[14]

The locations of two further places, *Taur(r)* (*Yt* 9) and *Ræningr* (*Yt* 20), are even less certain. It is debatable whether *Taur(r)* in *Yt* 9 is a place-name at all. *Ynglinga saga* thinks it is, referring to a "place, to the east of Taurr and west of Stokkssund, [which] has since been called Agnafit,"[15] and recent editors of *Ynglingatal* connect it with the second element in the place-name Södertörn, but an alternative interpretation, as *taur(r)* ("(neck)ring"), is supported by two skaldic attestations, and scholarly opinion is divided.[16] The case for Ræningr as a place-name is stronger. S. B. F. Jansson seems to have been the first to suggest that it could be identified with the name *Rauningr*, mentioned on a runestone (Sö Fv1948;289) at Aspa in Runtuna parish, Södermanland, approximately seventy miles, as the crow flies, southwest of Uppsala.[17] Aspa has, like Uppsala and Vendel, an abundance of monuments to the past. It was the thing-site of Runtuna parish, and the assembly place is still identifiable by its mound.[18] An ensemble of undecorated standing stones and runestones dated, on stylistic grounds, to the late tenth or early eleventh century still stands in its original position along the road, and a river runs nearby (Plate 2).[19] The inscription on one of the stones (Sö 137) refers to the thing-site (*þingstaðr*), while two (Sö 137 and Fv1948;289) bear metrical inscriptions, and one nonmetrical inscription spans two stones (Sö 134 and Sö Fv1948;282). All these features suggest a degree of prestige for this place and its inhabitants in the tenth century if not before.[20] Stefan Brink argues that the road at Aspa formed part of the route known as *Eriksgata*.[21] According to the medieval Swedish laws, the prospective sovereign proceeded along this route to gain the assent of the provincial assemblies, starting and finishing at Gamla Uppsala.[22] The written records of *Eriksgata* date from the Middle Ages, but the roads that made it up are likely to be older—how much older is hard to say.[23] *Eriksgata* would have passed by many thing-places, both large and small.[24] Things formed natural centers for the cultivation and transmission of locally important information, including poetry, in premodern Scandinavia.[25] *Ynglingatal*'s itinerary in Svíþjóð, then, appears to follow roads, whether the *Eriksgata* or, in the case of Vendel and (probably) Skúta, the ancient road north from Uppsala known as the *Norrstig*, "a winter road that went between the royal estates along the coast of Norrland."[26]

A parallel pattern is apparent in the Norwegian stanzas. *Þotn* (*Yt* 22), the death-place of Hálfdan *hvítbeinn* (white-leg), corresponds to Toten in Oppland, some eighty miles due north of the Viken inlet. The remaining sites are strung out along the west coast of Viken. Of these, the cemetery at *Borró* (Borre), at the head of the inlet (*Yt* 24), and the estate at *Skíringssalr* (Tjølling), about thirty miles to the south (*Yt* 22), are locatable with a high degree of certainty. Like Uppsala, Vendill, and Ræningr, both these places were significant in the late Iron Age, Borró harboring a large collection of grave mounds and Skíringssalr a trading place (*kaupangr*) and royal residence. The evidence identifying *Holtar* (*Yt* 24) as Holtan, about a mile north of Borre; *Geirstaðir* (*Yt* 26) as Gjekstad, fifteen miles to the south of Holtan, the site of the Gokstad mound; and the *Vaðla* (*Yt* 23) as the river running from Farrisvannet to the coast near Larvik, about nine miles southwest of Gjekstad, is suggestive but less certain; the location of *Stiflusund* (*Yt* 25) is completely lost. As in the Swedish part of the poem, these coastal sites—Holtan, Borre, Tjølling, Gjekstad, and Larvik—form an itinerary, this time not by road, but by water. The Viken part of the poem, even more than the Svíþjóð part, leads its audience through "a landscape in which the environment offers mnemonic cues as to how to progress."[27]

Viking Age gravesites were often next to water or near roads, partly due to a desire for conspicuous memorials "by the wayside" (*brautu nær*, *Hávamál* 72) that would guarantee the posthumous fame of the dedicatees.[28] However, this simple fact cannot be the sole reason for the spatial distribution of *Ynglingatal*'s place-names. Many of *Ynglingatal*'s place-names are not burial or cremation sites, but death-sites (Limfjǫrðr, Vendill, all three instances of Uppsala, Ræningr, Þotn, Stiflusund), or places where the king lived or ruled (Holtar, for example). The very interchangeability of these categories is suggestive. Is this the itinerary taken by the poet traveling along the Swedish *landväg* or sailing along the coast of Vestfold, as he is told the stories associated with passing *lieux de mémoire*: grave mounds, gallows, monoliths, ruined halls, or the site of a royal death, marked by a wooden monument (*stafr*) that has since fallen victim to time and weather?[29] Monuments marked the route along the western Norwegian coast from the Bronze Age on.[30] The eleventh-century skald Þórðr Sjáreksson recounts a journey along the southwestern coast of Norway including sightings of no less than five coastal landmarks.[31] Less speculatively, *Ynglingatal*'s death and burial sites could be read as nodes in an *imagined* itinerary, a rhetorical wayfinding or mapping used as a basis for mnemonic recollection.

BODIES

Insular legends of martyred saint-kings recount powerful narratives of death in place. King Oswald of Northumbria, for instance, died in battle against the pagan Penda in 642 CE. Penda had Oswald's corpse decapitated and attached its arms and head to stakes. Oswald's death-site, *Maserfelth*, was marked by unusually lush grass and, as time went on, a deep hole excavated in the miracle-working earth, famed for cures of horses and other animals and protection of buildings from fire. Local relevance and performative mediality—such as healing rituals—are clear here. Shrines to Oswald were established by Oswiu, who was his brother and successor, and his niece Osthryth, at St Peter's in Bamburgh and Bardney in Lindsey, in a familial attempt to capture the prestige of the local saint-king.

Another royal martyr, St. Kenelm, son of King Cenwulf of Mercia, died sometime after 811, apparently as the result of a plot by his sister. While hunting in the forest, Kenelm's tutor beheaded him and buried the body beneath a thorn bush, from which a golden bird ascended to heaven; an ash tree rose where the doomed prince had planted his staff. Lush pasture grew and a healing spring later rose at the spot. St. Kenelm's shrine was established at Winchcombe, where his *Vita et miracula* was written in the late eleventh century. An Old English alliterative couplet predates the *vita* and demonstrates that the essential features of the *passio* were already in place much earlier:

> *In clench qu becche under ane þorne*
> *liet Kenelm kinebern heved bereved*
>
> (In Clent cow-pasture under a thorn
> lies Cynhelm king's son deprived of his head).[32]

As in the case of Oswald, localism and vernacular performance are characteristic of a cult which evidently arose long before the *vita*. The *vita* narrative itself seems to be based on local oral traditions, with a strongly topographic flavor.[33]

It has often been suggested that such legends have a folkloric quality, meaning not that they stem from the lower ranks of society, but that they draw on local, performed traditions, distant from the Latinate culture of learned churchmen.[34] Richard Green writes that "medieval aristocrats were perfectly capable of entering into the belief system of the little tradition as fully participating members."[35] John Blair argues that legends such as those of Kenelm and Oswald may be "repositories of folklore motifs captured at a relatively early date, of evidence for vernacular cult practice [. . .] even of genuine information about landscapes, sites and events."[36] He notes that the sites they describe are often linked and "mark stages along routes [that] may point to more organic origins, whether in specific journeys by individuals or in the general importance of certain lines of communication."[37]

The intention of the Anglo-Latin hagiographers, who tell many such stories, is clear.[38] In the words of André Vauchez, they seek to "salvage" traditional oral tales rooted in "lay revulsion at the injustice of [the kings'] deaths," and press them into service as narratives of origin for Christian cult.[39] Memorial narratives connecting violent deaths, resonant names, royal bodies, and significant, ruinous sites in the landscape were widespread in northern Europe and were not confined to Germanic-language traditions. The Middle Irish *dindshenchas* in the mid-twelfth-century Book of Leinster, for example, people the landscape with resonant names from myth and legend, while Flann Mainistrech (d. 1056) details the horrible fate of each member of the Irish pantheon, and the *Fianna bátar i nEmain* ("Heroes who were in Emain") of Cináed ua hArtacáin (d. 975) tallies up the graves of

26 MAKING MEMORIES

famous warriors.[40] These stories must have existed long before, but the poets did not merely transmit inherited material. They also worked creatively to augment and interpret the place-lore and traditional stories they had access to.[41] No less in Wales, Cornwall, and Brittany, "saints were the object of popular, strongly localized devotion, which involved their incorporation into myth-making, and were used to identify and explain landmarks scattered through the landscapes where their cults were based."[42] Local vernacular oral traditions preceded the adoption of these cults by royal and monastic patrons, who were often (as in the case of Oswald) family members, promoting their kin for political reasons.

The memorial function of places where royal blood has soaked the earth is clear from the insular saints' lives. *Ynglingatal* also founds memory in royal death, and its death-sites and gravesites form two itineraries, one in present-day Sweden, one in Norway. While the Viken stanzas concentrate on grave mounds, the stanzas on the kings of Svíþjóð offer a panoply of memory media: Sveigðir's monolith, the ruins of Vísburr's, Eysteinn's, and Ingjaldr's halls, the ground reddened with Dómaldi's blood, the mud thickened with Aðils' brains, Dómarr's and Óláfr's funeral pyres, Jǫrundr's and Agni's gallows, Ǫnundr's cairn. These kinds of sites were crucial to how people in Iron Age northwestern Europe related to the past.[43] Þjóðólfr himself repeatedly refers to oral informants:

6. *Ok þess opt*
of yngva hreyr
fróða menn
of fregit hafðak . . .
(And I had often asked learned men about the burial place of the prince)

7. *Kveðkat dul*, 'I call it no secret'

8. *Ok þat orð*
á austrvega
vísa ferð
frá vígi bar
(And the retinue of the leader bore the news from the fight to the east)

10. *kváðu*, '[they] said'

15. *Þau frák verk*
Vǫtts ok Fasta

sœnskri þjóð
at sǫgum verða
(I have learned that these deeds of Vǫttr and Fasti became legends for the Swedish people)

17. *með Svíum kváðu*, 'among the Swedes [they] said'

18. *Þat stǫkk upp*, 'Word spread quickly'

22. *Þat frá hverr*, 'Everyone learned that'

Such claims are noticeably more frequent in the Swedish part of the poem, but they bear no real trace of the lost Swedish Yngling poem whose existence has been repeatedly hypothesized.[44] In fact it sounds more as if Þjóðólfr's sources were not poetic. Little can rest on *sǫgur*, "legends" or "stories," as it is a broadly applicable term, but the tradition bearers Þjóðólfr mentions are not poets, and in fact not even individuals, but rather collectives: "wise men" (*fróðir menn*), the "retinue" (*ferð*), or "Swedish people" (*sœnsk þjóð*). John McKinnell suggests that the source references of *Ynglingatal* 7 and 8 are cover-ups for kings, invented by the poet as links between inherited material. He doubts that Þjóðólfr, as a Norwegian, had "personal knowledge" of the Swedish places he mentions but the Icelander Sigvatr Þórðarson seems to have made a very similar journey from Viken to Svíþjóð around a hundred years later, according to his *Austrfararvísur*.[45]

McKinnell discerns "three or four fairly distinct blocks [...] which probably reflect different oral sources" in *Ynglingatal*.[46] *Ynglingatal*'s highly regular metrical, rhetorical, and syntactical structures are a stumbling block for those wishing to argue for a diversity of literary pre-forms.[47] *Ynglingatal* is unquestionably diverse in terms of material and subject matter, and Þjóðólfr certainly worked creatively with his material—if nothing else, the concatenations of unique, elaborate kennings bear witness to that. Rather than "adapting" by "misinterpreting" pre-existing Swedish poems,[48] *Ynglingatal* in fact displays and reflects on its own re-mediation of a diverse body of oral legend. Not all of its stories are anchored in place-lore. Material anchors and place-names are absent from the stanzas about the poem's two fratricidal pairs, Alrekr and Eirekr (*Yt* 10), who kill one another with bridles, and Álfr and Yngvi (*Yt* 11), who die in a quarrel over a woman named Bera. Both sets of brothers are mentioned in Saxo's *Gesta danorum* (V.x.1–2; VIII.iii.11), and *Gautreks saga* (ch. 7) also refers to Alrekr and Eirekr. Saxo and *Gautreks saga* recount the story of Alrekr's death at the hands of his brother, and *Gautreks saga* includes the fatal bridle, but both let Eirekr survive; Saxo transmits only the names of Álfr and Yngvi. Fratricide, especially of brothers-in-law fighting over a woman, is a common motif in the Norse heroic material. Combined with the apparently non-locational nature of Þjóðólfr's information about these kings and the fact that they are known from Scandinavian literary sources independent of *Ynglingatal*, this evidence suggests that these stories may have been transmitted as alliterative heroic poetry. This kind of diversity of source material, ranging from local tale to mini-saga, would not be unexpected if *Ynglingatal* represents a relatively early attempt to gather disparate traditional material into a single work.

FROM SVÍÞJÓÐ TO VIKEN

Nine of *Ynglingatal*'s nineteen place-names refer to water. The poem mentions places by the edges of rivers and bays, on sea islands, on headlands, at the coast where fresh water runs into the sea, in water-meadows, or on gravel ridges above the water. The Baltic Sea is even personified in *Ynglingatal* 18, where it sings to King Yngvarr. Waterside memorialization has parallels in other early traditions. The first part of the *Secgan*, an Old English list of the resting-places of pre-ninth-century Northumbrian and Mercian martyrs, is also topographically focused, with a strong preference for rivers, creeks, and bodies of water such as the sea or marshes for locating the saints' resting-places.[49] Similar kinds of localized *memoria* may underlie the *Secgan* and the roughly contemporary Norse material. Artifacts also tended to be deposited in or near water in northern and western Europe, from the Neolithic to the late Middle Ages.[50] Martin Rundkvist observes that Bronze Age deposits in the Mälaren Valley tend to occur where the water does "something interesting," that is, "entry points and exits of streams [. . .] rapids [. . .] narrows in lakes and sea inlets [. . .] long narrow lakes and inlets in general [. . .] the sunlit south side of islands and promontories in the sea [. . .] the southern terminals of gravel ridges immediately above Bronze Age waters"—a list reminiscent of *Ynglingatal*'s watery sites.[51] Richard Bradley argues that water was thought of as "active, possessing a vital force of its own," potentially friendly, but also volatile and threatening.[52] His study reveals considerable continuity of find-sites across an immense period (5000 BCE–1000 AD), even where the gaps between individual deposits are so long that such continuity cannot possibly reflect memories of previous depositions. Rather, "the distinctive character of [the] sites attracted attention";[53] they reflected "general landscape rules"[54] about what kinds of places were particularly propitious. Of course, *Ynglingatal* is not describing hoard sites, still less Bronze Age depositions, but it seems to draw on a related set of landscape rules for assigning significance to places.

Place-names were freighted with associative meaning. Especially prominent in *Ynglingatal* is the famous name of Uppsala.[55] Gamla Uppsala was a place apart, with its huge mounds, extensive terracing, great hall, and specialized crafts.[56] It was undoubtedly a site of supra-regional importance in the Vendel Period, with roots extending back into the sixth century.[57] By about 800 CE, however, the character of the settlement was changing. The great hall burned around this time, and its most recent excavators argue that it was "cremated," complete with depositions and the sealing of the burned traces of the building with a layer of clay.[58] The man-made terrace upon which the hall had stood was permanently abandoned at this time, although a deposit of animal bones was made on the line of its walls some two hundred years later.[59] In the period between the burning of the great hall and the building of the current church in the mid–twelfth century, Gamla Uppsala was by no means deserted—finds indicate continued burials in boat and cremation graves, skilled craft production, and new walls and roads on the edge of the old site—but its character changed.[60] No trace has yet been found of a new Viking Age hall on the terrace or anywhere else on the site, although the site's excavators are convinced that "material evidence from the Viking Age of centralized cult [and] manifest traces of royal/elite presence and judicial meetings" await discovery, not least due to the evidence of the textual sources.[61]

The absence of a flourishing central place at Gamla Uppsala around the time *Ynglingatal* was composed is certainly awkward if we wish to read the poem as a pillar of "religious ruler ideology."[62] On this reading, the poem guarantees untroubled succession for a royal line that has Uppsala as its generational place (*Generationenort*). Svante Norr accordingly suggests that the extant version of *Ynglingatal* is the result of substantial reworking by Christian writers in the eleventh and twelfth centuries. Such a re-dating would align the poem chronologically with Gamla Uppsala's mid-twelfth-century renaissance and a consequent "new interpretation of the past."[63] Johan Ljungkvist offers an alternative way out of the bind, suggesting that investments in the place [i.e. Gamla Uppsala] in the Vendel Period had gradually created the basis for a legendary gathering site for both rulers and broader social groups, which came to seem self-explanatory. For the rulers of the Viking Age, it was apparently not necessary to continue to make the place and their own presence manifest with new monuments.[64]

The testimony of the burned hall, with its clay seal and animal offerings, complicates this picture. On the ground, the *memory* of Uppsala is preserved as a grave, or ruin: a memorial place (*Gedenkort*). The cremated hall neither disappears gradually and naturally into the past, nor participates in the continuity of power structures invoked by Ljungkvist, but leaves a scar on the landscape, a break that becomes a site for commemorative ritual.[65]

Two kings, Aunn and Aðils, die "at Uppsala" (*at Uppsǫlum*), formulaic phrasing which matches the other place-name references in the Svíþjóð part of the poem:

á beði Skútu "on the bank of the Skúta" (*Yt* 3:10)
við Fýri "near Fyrisån" (*Yt* 6:12)
til Vǫrva "to Vǫrvi" (*Yt* 8:6)
í Limafirði "in Limfjorden" (*Yt* 12:4)
at Uppsǫlum "in Uppsala" (*Yt* 13:2, 16:16)
á Vendli "at Vendill" (*Yt* 15:8)
á Lófundi "in Lófund" (*Yt* 17:4)
á Ræningi "in Ræningr" (*Yt* 20:4)

All these place-names are accommodated in the stanza's odd lines. Disyllabic names are placed at the end of bound clauses along with a finite verb in final position (e.g., *til Vǫrva kom*), while those of three syllables form a whole line with a static locational preposition and are generally placed at the end of the unbound clause that opens the stanza. This patterning is driven by the metrical organization of *Ynglingatal* itself, not by a precursor.[66] All the same, the fact that the names needed to be accommodated in two different metrical environments is some evidence that they are traditional; that they are all either death or funeral sites supports their status as memorial anchors.[67] Their very formulism makes a claim—that of transmitting the core of oral memory, the proper name. Unlike the other kings, who die or are cremated at the named places, the last king in the Svíþjóð sequence, Óláfr *trételgja* (woodcutter), is said to have "disappeared from Uppsala" (*hvarf frá Uppsǫlum*, *Yt* 21). This change in the place-name formula marks the major break in the poem, the transition from Svíþjóð to Viken. In Viken, place-names refer both to burial sites and to places or areas the kings ruled over.[68] Place-name references in Viken are more frequent (they occur in every stanza except the last), less formulaic, more flexible in their syntax, and much more detailed, adding either additional names or topographical information. The move from Svíþjóð to Viken marks a shift from remembered landscape to felt landscape, from resonant name to described topography. Greater detail and lower formulism in Viken evoke intimate, experiential knowledge. The skald's authority is based on what he has himself seen and felt:

23. *Ok nú liggr*
und lagar beinum
rekks lǫðuðr
á raðar braddi,
þars élkaldr
hjá jǫfur gauzkum
Vǫðlu straumr
at vági kømr.
(And now the inviter of the warrior [RULER] lies under the bones of the sea [STONES] at the edge of the ridge where the blizzard-cold stream of the Vaðla empties into the bay near the Gautish king.)

The poem's take on the kings themselves also shifts. For the first time, some are praised for their rule. Hálfdan *hvítbeinn* (white-leg) appears to be a settler of disputes, as he will be missed by "mediators" (*sǫkmiðlendr*).[69] Óláfr *Geirstaðaálfr* (elf of Geirstaðir) "powerfully" (*ofsa*) controls a wide territory.[70] They are laid in their mounds by grateful followers:

24. *Ok buðlung*
á Borrói
sigrhafendr
síðan fǫlu.
(And afterwards the victorious ones buried the ruler in Borre.)

The poem also makes its first explicit reference to royal succession. "Third king" (*þriðja jǫfri*) in the stanza about Hálfdan *inn mildi* (the generous) refers to the fact that he is the third king in the Viken sequence after Óláfr *trételgja* and Eysteinn:[71]

> 24. *Ok til þings*
> *þriðja jǫfri*
> *Hveðrungs mær*
> *ór heimi bauð*
> (And the maiden of Hveðrungr <= Loki> [= Hel] invited a third ruler out of the world to a meeting)

The places built by the bodies of the Viken kings are *Generationorte*. The kings are seen in life as well as death, ruling and succeeding one another, in a landscape that the skald and his audience know like the back of their hand. Ruinous memory of the deep past is succeeded by historical memory; the authority of the autopsy supplants that of oral informants. The lines "the descendants of the Þrór of strength had flourished in Norway" (*niðkvísl Þrós þróttar hafði of þróazk í Nóregi*), placed in the manuscripts at the beginning of *Ynglingatal* 26, are often suspected of being out of position, and editors have moved them to various places in the sequence. Their placement makes perfect sense if they mark a second transition point, from the historical memory of the Viken kings to the present moment of performance before the skald's patron in the following stanza.

WHY IS THE SKY BLUE?

After twenty-eight bizarre deaths, *Ynglingatal*'s praise of its last king, Rǫgnvaldr, is rather anticlimactic:

> 27. *Þat veitk bazt*
> *und blǫ́um himni*
> *kenninafn,*
> *svát konungr eigi,*
> *es Rǫgnvaldr,*
> *reiðar stjóri,*
> *heiðumhǫ́r*
> *of heitinn es.*
> (I know that nickname to be the best under the blue sky that a king might have, that Rǫgnvaldr, the steerer of the carriage [RULER], is called "High with Honours.")

Bergsveinn Birgisson sees biting irony here, proposing that Rǫgnvaldr is the name of a dwarf jester at the court of Haraldr *hárfagri*, riding into the presence of the king on a wheeled platform (*reiðar stjóri*).[72] Is this surmise necessary to make sense of this stanza? Like so much else in *Ynglingatal*, its praise of Rǫgnvaldr is indeed odd when measured against the yardstick of skaldic encomium. It avoids martial triumphalism in favor of praising the king's byname. *Heiðumhǫ́r* is a *hapax legomenon* (*heiðumhǽri*, the comparative form, is used in *Heimskringla*'s prose). The second element, *hǫ́r*, means "high." Its semantics are thus reasonably clear, even if its syntactical relationship to the first element is not; the comparative *-hǽri* of the prose sources looks like an attempt to deal with this problem. The first element is more of a puzzle.[73] *Heiðum* is grammatically a dative plural; possible glosses are *heið* (n. "clear sky"), *heiðr* (m. "honor, renown")—forms both with and without radical *r* are attested—and *heiðr* (f. "heath").[74] Of these, only *heiðr* (f.) is attested in the dative plural, and it is best attested in compounds, including names such as *Heiðabýr* (Hedeby). There are a few compounds with nom. sg. *heiðr* or gen. sg. *heiðrs-* from *heiðr* (m.) in late religious prose, but none with the plural. Bugge pointed to *sœmð* (f. "honor") as a semantic parallel that does occur in plural form.[75] This is the route taken by most recent editors, who translate *heiðumhǫ́r* as "high-with-honors." *Heiðr* (f.) would also be possible, giving "high-with (or on)-heaths" or, more elegantly, with Guðbrandur Vigfússon, "lord of the heaths." The version of this stanza in Codex Frisianus concludes with an incomplete sentence, "and the generous lord of the forest [. . .]" (*ok mildgeðr markar dróttin* [. . .]), providing a context for the gloss "heaths" for *heiðum-*. The term *heiðr* (f. "heath") suggests the uncultivated land on the edge of a settlement and would fit the geography and political status of Østfold, as I will discuss further below.[76]

The statement that Rǫgnvaldr is *bazt und blǫ́um himni* ("best under the blue sky") suggests that wordplay of a typical skaldic sort on *heið* (f. "clear sky") is also present. The phrase *und blǫ́um himni* has passed without comment in previous scholarship on *Ynglingatal*, presumably because the collocation of the sky with the color blue seems so natural. In fact, it is the most unconventional feature of the stanza. Words deriving from Proto-Germanic **blēwa*, such as OHG *blâo* and OE *blǽwen*, suggest a dark, almost blackish blue, the color of a bruise, and are never used to describe the sky.[77] This is true of Old Norse too. According to Kirsten Wolf's study of the adjective *blár* in a large corpus of Old Norse poetry and prose, this is the only certain instance where it is used to describe the sky.[78] Michel Pastoureau, in his historical study of the color blue, emphasizes the insignificance of blue in Western medieval color symbolism, writing that blue "was even absent from the sky, which most authors and artists portrayed as white, red, or gold."[79] The heavens, meanwhile, appear in multiple Germanic alliterative traditions in the merism "earth and sky above" (in Norse, *jǫrð ok upphiminn*).[80] This formula appears as part of a "creation of the world" type scene involving the contrast between high sky and low earth, the color green, and a listing of features such as grass, trees, and heavenly bodies. It is also used in eschatological contexts by several early Christian skalds.[81] Given its popularity among the poets at moments of heightened intensity, it is likely that Þjóðólfr is playing on this formula in what seems to be *Ynglingatal*'s closing stanza. There is no sign of the green earth in *Ynglingatal* 27, and also no alliterative formula; but there is the color word (*blǫr*), and the "height" motif (***upphiminn***) forms part of Rǫgnvaldr's byname, *heiðumhár*.

Þjóðólfr's version of this closing convention substitutes the blue sky for the green earth and accentuates the celestial quality of Rǫgnvaldr's renown. Pastoureau argues that the association of blue with the sky is a consequence of Christian teachings about light and clarity, and of technical advances in pigment-making. In the mid–twelfth century, Abbot Suger's glassmakers perfected cobalt blue glass, and in the thirteenth dyers discovered how to dye cloth a colorfast bright blue.[82] The Virgin Mary began to be clad in blue in the twelfth century, and royal blue became a color of kingship in heraldry, iconography, and dress.[83] Prior to this, blue was rare, absent from fabrics, stained glass, the system of liturgical colors, and, for the most part, from manuscript illumination. Carolingian luxury books were an exception, and one that Scandinavians would have been familiar with.[84] The best blue pigment, made from lapis lazuli mined in Afghanistan, was as expensive as gold, and its presence signified a valuable book.[85] Carolingian illuminators used blue as a background in portraits of rulers and in representations of Christ in majesty and the hand of God, as "a celestial color signifying divine presence and intervention," images that are a compelling visual counterpart to *Ynglingatal*'s claim that Rǫgnvaldr is "best under the blue sky."[86] Charles the Bald is shown enthroned in the Codex Aureus of St. Emmeram (Plate 3), an opulent gospel book whose binding was perhaps the most sumptuous produced in the entire Middle Ages. On the facing recto is a heavenly vision of the Adoration of the Lamb. Both Charles and the Lamb are placed against a deep blue heavenly canopy. It has been suggested that the layout of the two facing pages mimics the interior of the Palatine Chapel at Aachen, where Charles's throne was placed in the gallery and the Adoration was depicted in mosaic on the dome: "the two-page spread emulated the emperor's actual place in the celebration of the Mass in his palace chapel."[87]

Further information on Carolingian visual culture is provided by Ermoldus Nigellus's poem *In honorem Hludovici*. Its description of the painted decoration of the *aula regia* at Ingelheim has been proposed as an influence on skaldic ekphraseis such as Bragi's *Ragnarsdrápa*. Russell Poole has recently argued that Ermoldus's use of *tmesis* was significant too, concluding that "tmesis is most characteristically in Carolingian usage a linguistic play upon naming [. . .] Naming, gifting, dedication—these are central moments of interpellation and transaction where, if anywhere, cultural transfer from Empire to the northern kingdoms might have occurred."[88] Danish royals were frequent visitors in Carolingian courts in the late eighth and ninth centuries, with Haraldr *klakk*'s baptism by Louis the Pious in 826 (the main subject of Ermoldus's poem) only the best-known example. In the next generation, the Danish ruler Rorik was received by no less than three Frankish rulers (Lothar I, Charles the Bald, and Louis the German), converted to Christianity, and became all three kings' *fidelis*. Godfrid, a leader of the Viking Great Army that crossed the Channel in 879 to ravage northern France, was given the illegitimate daughter of Lothar II in marriage by Charles the Bald and a benefice in Frisia to go with it.[89] There was also contact between aristocratic and royal Danish milieux and the Franks during diplomacy, missions, and luxury trade.[90] Cultural encounters are not, however, enough to prove that Latin influenced skaldic poetry, and in fact there are several objections to such a conclusion. No source says there were poets in the entourages of Danish royal visitors to Carolingian courts, although this is not to say that there were none. A more substantial problem is the sophisticated Latinity that would have been required to understand and imitate the complex verse of Ermoldus and his contemporaries. There is no other evidence for skalds having been well-versed in Latin before the priest-poets of twelfth-century Orkney and Iceland, and it is hard to see how and, even more, why they would acquire such a competency. Poole's point as to the importance of "naming, gifting, dedication" is well-taken, however, and suggests a key locus of ideological display, namely imperial iconography. Carolingian coins, royal titles, portraits, seals, and monograms spoke a common "symbolic language of authority" that was echoed in Charlemagne's new Rome at Aachen.[91]

Virtually all Carolingian churches were lavishly decorated with wall paintings and mosaics.[92] This visually arresting display of royal authority, in media stretching from the monumental to the portable, would doubtlessly have impressed and attracted the rulers of small southern Scandinavian polities and was also accessible to those without Latin.

Ermoldus's description of the palace at Ingelheim is particularly resonant when drawn into dialogue with *Ynglingatal*.[93] According to Ermoldus, the palace was decorated with images of seven pagan rulers from distant times and places, their stories most likely taken from Orosius's *Historiæ adversus paganos*. They are depicted in paintings showing shocking deeds and horrible deaths. Tomyris, queen of the Massegetai, for instance, stores Cyrus's severed head in a blood-filled goatskin. These images are succeeded by those of five kings who "gloried in ancestral deeds and in the pious faith of more recent times."[94] In the group of five pious kings (Constantine, Theodosius, Charles Martel, Pippin III, and Charlemagne), Ermoldus observes that "the amazing deeds of the Franks are joined to those of the caesars of the great seat of Rome."[95] Perhaps this is a sample of the kind of art talk that could have been heard by Danish visitors? Despite its Virgilian echoes, Ermoldus's account of the decorations of the *aula regia* is usually thought to be historically accurate and is supported by finds of plaster fragments with painted figural decorations from the contemporary palace at Paderborn, and the relatively well-preserved frescoes of the abbey church of St. John in Müstair, Switzerland.[96] The sequence of kings is not merely an artifact of Ermoldus's poem, for excavations at Ingelheim reveal a hall between whose windows images of the pagan kings could have been placed, along with a terminal apse with space for the five pious kings, an architectural framing that would have underlined the sequential nature of the decorative program.[97] A longer series of bloody and disastrous foreign kings followed by a shorter sequence of five exemplary "ancestral" rulers corresponds neatly to *Ynglingatal*'s pattern of the rulers of Svíþjóð followed by Rǫgnvaldr's five predecessors in Viken.

"GENEROUS-MINDED LORD OF THE BORDERLAND"

Recent scholarship has almost unanimously returned to the early dating of *Ynglingatal* implied by *Heimskringla*, and the currently suggested dates cluster around the end of the ninth century and the beginning of the tenth.[98] The most important dissenting voices are those of Sophus Bugge and Claus Krag.

Bugge dated the poem to the late tenth century, on two grounds: the implausibility of the then-conventional mid-ninth-century date (selected by Gustav Storm so as to make space for Rǫgnvaldr before Haraldr *hárfagri*'s presumptive ascendancy in Vestfold in the 860s), and influence from the Hiberno-Norse kingdom of Dublin.[99] Claus Krag re-dated the poem to the twelfth century as part of a revisionist effort aimed at the conventional wisdom that the unification of Norway proceeded outward from Viken and was achieved by Haraldr *hárfagri*, from whom all subsequent Norwegian kings drew their legitimacy as "Ynglingar."[100] Krag's attack on the idea of Haraldr as unifier of Norway has been largely successful, with recent historiography seeing him as a petty king in western Norway.[101] Krag's re-dating of *Ynglingatal* on the basis of supposed anachronisms has not found favor, however. Most recently, Christopher Sapp and Klaus Johan Myrvoll find that *Ynglingatal* shares so few metrical characteristics with inarguably late poems in *kviðuháttr*, such as the late twelfth-century *Nóregs konungatal* and Sturla Þórðarson's mid-thirteenth-century *Hákonarkviða*, and so many with the poetry composed in that meter by Eyvindr Finnsson and Egill Skallagrímsson, that a late dating is not credible.[102] If the traditional identification of the man buried in the Gokstad mound as Óláfr *Geirstaðaálfr* is to be believed, it gives a dendrochronological *terminus ad quem* for *Ynglingatal* of around 901, as Rǫgnvaldr is said in *Ynglingatal* to be Óláfr's son.[103] Besides Rǫgnvaldr, *Skáldatal* lists Þjóðólfr as having composed for five other rulers. Þorleifr *inn spaki* (the wise) Hǫrðu-Kárason is thought to be the Þorleifr mentioned in the refrain of Þjóðólfr's *Haustlǫng* (Autumn-Long). No poetry is extant for Hákon jarl Grjótgarðsson, Strút-Haraldr jarl, and Sveinn jarl.[104] The names Strút-Haraldr and Sveinn suggest Danish connections on Þjóðólfr's part. Sveinn is unidentifiable, but the name was popular among Danish aristocrats, while Strút-Haraldr ruled over Skåne in the later tenth century.[105] Poetry for only one Swedish ruler has been preserved, but Edith Marold argues that the memorial poetry in *fornyrðislag* on Viking Age runestones is evidence for skaldic composition in Sweden.[106] The stanza on the Rök stone is an even closer parallel, as I will argue in the conclusion to Part I, below. Its existence implies that skaldic-like poetry was already being composed in the East Norse area in the mid–ninth century.

Although nothing more is known about Rǫgnvaldr than what *Ynglingatal* reports, the strong focus of the Norwegian part of the poem on the region around Viken makes it most likely that he ruled in this area. Viken in the late ninth and early tenth centuries was border country. Its western side, Vestfold, seems to have been a small regional political unit, with shifting patterns of rulership. Viking raiders who struck Aquitaine in 843 called themselves *Wesfaldingi*, bearing witness to this local identity.[107] Vestfold was a wealthy area with good access to the natural resources of the hinterland, an ancient and prominent memorial site at Borre, and a significant early town, Kaupangr in Skíringssalr. Its eastern side, now called Østfold, was by contrast said by the late-ninth-century traveler Ohthere to belong to a larger political unit, namely *Denamearc* (Denmark). The exact nature of *Denamearc* in the obscure period between the mid-ninth-century heyday of "poachers [and] gamekeepers"[108] on the northern border of the Frankish realm and the triumph of Harald *blátǫnn* (bluetooth, d. c. 985 CE) is hard to pin down. A recent analysis of Danish ethnogenesis concludes that

> Just what form the Danish kingdom, or kingdoms, took in the later ninth and early tenth centuries is impossible to say, but by the time of Ohthere and Wulfstan at least the name Denmark had become established. This came about as nobles in various parts of what would later constitute the kingdom of that name, through various kinds of alliances whose full complexities are lost to us, sought to establish their claim as the rightful heirs to the legacy of the kingdom on the Frankish border that had contended with Charlemagne.[109]

Østfold is thought to have been important to the Danish kings as a conduit for Norwegian iron exports, and the emporium at Kaupangr may have been under Danish control. The Danish character of the area can be traced in its place-names.[110] Østfold's generally simpler burials, as well as one of Norway's rare chamber graves, have been interpreted as signs of influence from southern Scandinavia and the Continent.[111] The comparatively restrained mortuary practice of the ninth-century Danish kings may also reflect their relatively secure and unchallenged power, compared to the anxious contestation among the rulers of Vestfold as manifested, especially, in intense activity at Borre.[112] When Danish power began to decline at the beginning of the tenth century, leading to Kaupangr being given up by the 950s, the Tune mound and the two large mounds at Rolvsøy were erected on the other side of the fjord in Østfold.[113]

Viken was a crossroads, where routes to the North Sea and the Baltic met, and archaeological investigations reveal not only large numbers of insular artifacts, but also objects showing clear connections to the Frankish empire.[114] Particularly interesting are the Carolingian-style sword fittings, riding gear, and other prestige goods, both of Frankish manufacture and local imitations, found in the graves at Gokstad, Hoen, and Rolvsøy. Birgit Maixner reads these as evidence that Danish ruling families "in the name of a stabilizing self-presentation borrowed material culture and practices from the partner culture [i.e., the Carolingians], as it was experienced as superior."[115] Danish rulers displayed and imitated the regalia and signs of rank of their Carolingian competitors, often modifying the objects, for instance by drilling holes in them, to enable different uses from those intended by their original makers. In the dynamism of such processes, Hermann Kamp suggests, a "productive appropriation of the other" took place, in a dialectic between acculturation and the building of Scandinavian identity.[116]

Images of kingship that drew on the Carolingian iconography of the sovereign could have been useful insofar as they were directed at opponents, the Danish rulers of Østfold, who were themselves impressed by such trappings. As I will explore in Chapter 2, *Ynglingatal*'s kings are very different from the kings of other tenth-century praise poetry. They are the victims of evil schemers, or the defenders of their people, rather than leaders of Odinic war-bands. They die notable deaths and live on in the landscape and in collective memory. Rǫgnvaldr, their heir, rules under heaven—as God rules above, an idea that becomes commonplace for the poets composing for Knútr *inn ríki* (the great) a hundred years later. This heaven is blue, perhaps in imitation of the iconographic use of that color in Carolingian miniatures. Decorative programs in Frankish palaces, as described by Ermoldus for Ingelheim, could have provided a model for the "broken chain" structure of *Ynglingatal*, whose list of kings presents "them" being succeeded by "us." The hypothesis that complex rhetorical structures were visually mediated interculturally is more persuasive at this early date than the notion that Norse-speaking oral poets attended performances of Latin poetry, became connoisseurs, and emulated it in their own work. Óðinn appears only once in the poem, as the beneficiary of trollish witchcraft, hardly a positive representation of the chief god of late paganism. Could the Rǫgnvaldr for whom *Ynglingatal* was composed, the "generous-minded lord of the borderland," in fact have been a Danish ruler of Østfold rather than one of the *Wesfaldingi*?[117]

Þjóðólfr's central claim, as poetic speaker of *Ynglingatal*, is one of mediation. He describes himself as capturing local legends of ancient kings, hitherto preserved in monuments, landscapes, songs, and stories, and linking them to his patron, Rǫgnvaldr. *Ynglingatal* marks the emergence, as far as we can tell from the surviving sources, of the first-person skaldic speaker from a ruinous and inscrutable matrix of folk legend and monumental commemoration, which he—to be briefly anachronistic—"privatizes" in the new medium of stanzaic poetry, as a verbal monument to his aristocratic patron. The rhetorical move of anchoring memories of the dead in the landscape was to prove durably useful for later poets composing in *kviðuháttr*.

DEATH IN PLACE IN THE TRADITION OF *KVIÐUHÁTTR* POETRY

The *kviðuháttr* poems that follow *Ynglingatal* also circle around the grave. The speaker awaits Hel on the *nes* (headland) at the end of *Sonatorrek*, according to *Egils saga* the location of the family cemetery. *Háleygjatal* makes repeated reference to memorial sites, and as I discussed in the Introduction, Egill's *Arinbjarnarkviða* closes with the image of a memorial cairn (*lofkǫst*). The *Gesta danorum* of Saxo *grammaticus* offers intriguing evidence for similar traditions on Danish soil.[118] Saxo reports that upon the death of King Frotho III, the Danes drew his corpse around his kingdom on a wagon for three years, until its advanced state of decay could no longer be ignored. They entombed him beside the bridge Værebro in Zealand and, as he was thought to have no successor, offered the royal scepter to the man who could "attach" (*affigeret*) a poem to Fróði to his newly erected gravemound, thereby giving a good account of the king for posterity. A certain Hiarnus (Hjarni) composed a verse in the vernacular, "a distinguished verbal memorial," for which he was duly rewarded with the kingdom. Saxo includes a translation of "the general sense of its four lines" (*cuius intellectum quatuor uersiculus editum*):[119]

> *Frothonem Dani, quem longum uiuere uellent,*
> > *Per sua defunctum rura tulere diu.*
> *Principis hoc summi tumulatum cespite corpus*
> > *Aethere sub liquido nuda recondit humus.*
> (Because they wished to extend Frothi's life, the Danes
> > long carried his remains through their countryside.
> This great prince's body, now buried under turf, is covered
> > by bare earth beneath the lucent sky.)[120]

DEATH IN PLACE 41

The similarity of Saxo's elegiac distiches to *Ynglingatal*'s quatrains and, still further back, to the Rök stanza is striking. The four lines of Hjarni's poem correspond to the quatrain structure of *kviðuháttr*. Hjarni's verse places the king's name prominently in initial position, as do the Rök verse and many of the verses of *Ynglingatal*. It also strongly contrasts "then" and "now"—an often-noted point of similarity between *Ynglingatal* and Rök—and includes a bizarre anecdote about the king's death. Even the imagery of the verse, juxtaposing sky, earth, and corpse, is similar. *Ynglingatal* 19, on Ǫnundr, is particularly close:

Varð Ǫnundr
Jónakrs bura
harmi heptr
und Himinfjǫllum.
Ok ofvæg
Eistra dolgi
heipt hrísungs
at hendi kom.
Ok sá frǫmuðr
foldar beinum
Hǫgna *reyrs
of horfinn vas.

(Ǫnundr was killed by the pain of the sons of Jónakr [STONES] beneath Himinfjǫll. And the crushing hatred of the bastard [STONES] came upon the enemy of the Estonians [= Ǫnundr]. And that wielder of the reed of Hǫgni [SWORD > WARRIOR] was surrounded by the bones of the earth [STONES].)

Heimskringla interprets this stanza as describing Ǫnundr's death in a rockfall, but "killed" is a rather loose translation of *heptr*, which usually means "impede, hinder, fetter, thwart," and it is more likely that it records his inhumation.[121] The *Gesta* stanza's combination of a bizarre anecdote—the story of a rotting corpse being driven around the country—with gravesite *memoria* resembles *Ynglingatal* very closely. Although nothing can be said about the meter of Hjarni's stanza, its pragmatics and poetic form are reminiscent of skaldic poetry.[122] According to Saxo, Hiarnus himself was buried on the small island of Hjarnø off the east coast of Jutland. As no other source mentions him, he is most likely a fiction, his name derived from that of the island, which lay close to important sailing routes and boasted an unusual type of ship setting for Denmark.[123] Saxo's story of Hiarnus's grave is in the final analysis an instance of the kind of place-based storytelling proposed above for *Ynglingatal*.

Christian skalds also availed themselves of *kviðuháttr*'s discourse of death in place. The *Glælognskviða* (*Sea-Calm Poem*) of Þórarinn *loftunga* (praise-tongue), composed in the early 1030s for Sveinn Alfífuson, is the first poem to celebrate Óláfr Haraldsson's sanctity.[124] It is also the earliest surviving *kviðuháttr* poem to use locational *memoria* in a Christian context. By presenting Óláfr as *rex perpetuus Norvegiæ*, able to grant rule over Norway to the Danish prince Sveinn, it argues that Sveinn's succession to the throne is legitimate. The conventions of *kviðuháttr* memorial poetry helped the skald make this point. *Glælognskviða*, like its forerunners, affirms the fact of its subject's death ("he departed to the heavenly kingdom," *hann hvarf til himinríkis, Glækv* 3) and the location of his memorial, "in Trøndelag, there where Óláfr previously dwelt, and there became enshrined alive" (*í Þrandheimi . . . Þars Óleifr áðan byggði . . . ok þar varð kykvasettr, Glækv* 2–3), from where his successor, Sveinn, will "always rule the settlements throughout his life" (*æ ævi sína . . . byggðum ráða, Glækv* 2). St Clement's Church in Trondheim is a waterside site, as in earlier *kviðuháttr* poetry, but for the first time the dead person is entombed at the heart of the settlement, a notorious Christian innovation.[125] The postmortem activities of the pre-Christian dead among the living could be the cause of anxiety.[126] St Óláfr, by contrast, is praised as a "mediator" (*sættir; Glækv* 4) between God and man. The bulk of Þórarinn's poem is taken up with a sensual evocation of the miraculous new media of communication between heaven and earth that Christianity offered the believer: bells (*Glækv* 6), candles (*Glækv* 7), and books ("sacred nail of the language of books," *reginnagla máls bóka, Glækv* 9; the referent of this, the poem's only elaborate kenning, is disputed). They mediate the healing power of heavenly grace, manifest in the bodies of believers:

8. Þar kømr herr,
es heilagr es
konungr sjalfr,
krýpr at gangi.

En beiðendr
blindir sœkja
þjóðir máls,
en þaðan heilir.
(A host comes there, where the holy king himself is, [and] bows down for access. And people, petitioners for speech [and] the blind, make their way [there], and [go] from there whole.)

It has been suggested that Þórarinn chose *kviðuháttr* because Sveinn, a native speaker of English, would find this comparatively simple meter easier to understand.[127] The associations of *kviðuháttr* with gravesite *memoria* must have been at least as important to Þórarinn's poetic choice.

Another verse epitaph allows this tradition of gravesite *memoria* to be traced through the sparse poetic records of the twelfth century. The skald Oddi *inn litli* (the small) accompanied the Orkney jarl Rǫgnvaldr on a crusade to the Holy Land in the 1150s.[128] His comrade Þórbjǫrn died at Acre, and Oddi composed two stanzas in *kviðuháttr* about him. It is not known whether they once formed part of a longer poem:

Bǫru lung
lendra manna
fyr Þrasnes
Þórbjǫrn svarta.
Trað hlunnbjǫrn
und hǫfuðskaldi
Áta jǫrð
Akrsborgar til.
(The vessels of landed men carried Þórbjǫrn svarti ('the Black') past Þrasnes. The roller-bear [SHIP] trod the ground of Áti <sea-king> [SEA] to Acre beneath the chief skald.)

Þar sák hann
at hǫfuðkirkju
siklings vin
sandi ausinn.
Nú þrumir grund
grýtt of hǫnum

sólu birt
á suðrvegum.
(There I saw him, friend of the prince, sprinkled with sand at the chief church. Now stony ground, brightened by the sun, lies still over him in southern parts.)

The skald names the deceased and the place of his burial and affirms that he has seen it with his own eyes. Appropriately for a crusader, Þórbjǫrn is buried at the chief church. The final quatrain expands on this statement with the literally gritty detail beloved of poets composing in *kviðuháttr*, juxtaposing the stony, sandy ground with the brightness of the sun.[129] While this is credible as an eyewitness report of Levantine geography, it most likely has theological significance too. The liturgy for Ash Wednesday included the phrase "remember, man, that you are dust and to dust you will return" (*Memento, homo, quia pulvis es et in pulverem reverteris*, Genesis 3:19), and the symbolism of the sun as God and its beam as Christ is omnipresent in medieval Christianity.

* * * *

While Hjarni's stanza demonstrates the presence of skaldic gravesite *memoria* on Danish soil, *Glælognskviða* and Oddi's stanzas from Acre show that the associations of *kviðuháttr* with death in place were strong enough to make poetry in that meter still a compelling medium for poets drawing on a Christian idea of the afterlife. Of course, *Ynglingatal* also has its prehistory— the traditional association between acts of commemoration and places in the landscape, which I have sketched above. By marking so strongly the shift from remembered name to experienced place as bearer of memory in the break between the Svíþjóð and Viken sections of *Ynglingatal*, Þjóðólfr makes a claim about the poet as mediator and poetic authority. He moves from the artful reshaping of traditional oral knowledge, tied to the proper name as memorate, to the rather different authority of the autopsy. *Ynglingatal*'s information about the Viken kings can be trusted, the poem suggests, because its speaker has seen the mounds in which the kings lie and knows about their dwellings and spheres of influence. The distinctive memorial role of *dróttkvætt* in the poetic economy of the Viking Age was its capacity to preserve events of the recent past as models of praise- and blame-worthy action.[130] Skaldic encomium gives a lasting form to memories of the recent past. The deep past of cultural memory, on the other hand, was preferentially mediated in *fornyrðislag*, a poetic practice characterized by connections with the past (as its name suggests), folkloric patterning, traditional Germanic alliterative meter, collective and perhaps even participatory modes of performance and recomposition, and profound time-depth, evidenced by its preservation of ancient lexical material. Lacking the authorization by shared cultural memory enjoyed by the eddic performer, the skald needed to emphasize his own poetic agency as guarantor of the truth of his utterance. It is in *kviðuháttr*, the earliest surviving form of skaldic-like poetry (authored, highly complex, syllable-counting), that this agency emerges as a certain poetic persona of the skald, and a certain claim, namely to the ability to forge a link between past and present for his royal patron.

CHAPTER 2

FORGING THE CHAIN

> After the death of her husband this Åsta was joined in marriage to Sigurd Sow, a king from the mountain region. Sigurd Rise (the Giant), Harald Fairhair's son, had sired Halvdan, the father of Sigurd Sow. Åsta bore him Harald, a man of deep perspicacity, a great expert in the science of warfare, and from him, as if along a thread descended the glorious Norwegian royal line in its genealogical pattern up to the present (*de quo quasi quodam filo textus genealogie regum Norwegie hucusque protelatus gloriose descendit*). (*Historia Norwegie*, XV)

Searching for a metaphor for his genealogical construct, the anonymous author of the late twelfth-century Latin history of Norway known as *Historia Norwegie* hit on the image of the thread. Vernacular kings' sagas further enriched the repertoire of imagery for lines of descent with the tree metaphor, ubiquitous in the Middle Ages due to its favorable implications of rapid ramification from a single root, improvement over time, and expansiveness.[1] Less conventional is a dream of Hálfdan *svarti* (the black) reported in chapter 1 of *Fagrskinna*:

> It seemed to him that he was naked, with his hair hanging in thick locks (*hár hans allt í lokkum*). Some of these reached to the ground, others to the middle of the leg or of the calf, or to the knee, or the middle of his side, but in some places it was no longer than to his neck, and in some only sprouted from his skull like short horns. And his locks were of many different colors (*hverskyns litr*), but one lock surpassed all the others (*einn lokkr sigraði alla aðra*) in fairness, beauty and brightness [...] people believe that that lock signified (*jartegnaði*) the blessed Óláfr, who of all kings of Norway is the holiest and brightest (*helgari ok bjartari*) in heaven and on earth.[2]

A head of hair, strange as it may seem, was a fitting metaphor for the Norwegian royal line as presented in the kings' sagas, not just because one of the uppermost ancestors, Hálfdan's son Haraldr, bore the byname *hárfagri* (fine-hair).³ It was also a good match for the complex genealogical construct of the Norwegian royal house. The early history of the line as presented in the kings' sagas is not an unbroken patriline descending through the generations from father to son. Rather, first a few of Haraldr *hárfagri*'s sons reigned in succession, individual hairs sprouting from the crown of the head, while other hairs started out small and peripheral but went on to produce beautiful locks, still others never got anywhere much—and St Olaf is the shiniest curl of all. There are grounds for thinking that the royal line that these sagas construct, from Haraldr *hárfagri* to St Olaf, is a fiction.⁴ Convenient dreams set the seal of divine approval on a myth of origin whose kinks were all too apparent. They bear oneirically vivid witness to the importance of genealogical data in the written historiographical tradition, arranged according to *Genea-Logik*.⁵ As Gabrielle Spiegel observes, by means of this logic "the human process of procreation and filiation [became] a metaphor for historical change."⁶

Alongside threads, trees, and hairs, the rhetoric of medieval memory held other metaphors ready. An important one was the chain. The Latin word for chain, *catena*, gave its name to a commentary constructed by hooking together patristic commentaries, verse by verse, in the same order as the text itself. Thomas Aquinas is said to have composed his gospel commentary *Catena aurea* ("Golden Chain," 1263) from texts committed to memory over the course of a long and peripatetic life.⁷ Memory is deeply inscribed in the chain metaphor. One link hooks into and draws up another, just as one commentary links and leads to another. The form known as "drawings" (*drǫgur*, from *draga*, "to drag"), the *Háttatal* commentary explains, mandates that "the word that is first in [the] stanza is the last in the preceding one, and thus the second is "drawn" from the first."⁸ This particular pattern is little attested in extant Old Norse poetry, but catenulate structures of other kinds are prominent in the skaldic corpus, most of all in poems in the meter known as *kviðuháttr*.

Like most Old Norse metrical terms, *kviðuháttr* is first attested relatively late, and its meaning is obscure.⁹ The earliest secure instance of a poem name ending in *kviða* (f. "poem") is *Glælognskviða* ("Sea-Calm Poem"), first recorded in *Óláfs saga helga*, conventionally dated to the 1220s. A link between *kviða* and the verb *kveða* ("to speak, recite") seems obvious at first glance (cf. *kvæði* n. "poem") but the difference in stem vowels is difficult to explain. Elias Wessén instead connected *kviða* with *kvíða* (vb. "to feel sorrow, anguish"). Germanic cognates such as *cwīðan* (vb., OE, "to lament, bewail") and *quīthian* (vb., OSax., "to lament") offer support.[10] At least once *cwīðan* clearly denotes a retrospective performance. Beowulf recounts the festivities in Heorot prior to the arrival of Grendel's mother. At times, he says, stories of the early days were told, at times there was harping, at times fantastic tales, and

> *hwīlum eft ongan eldo gebunden*
> *gomel gūð-wiga <gioguðe> cwīðan,*
> *hilde-strengo; hreðer inne wēoll,*
> *þonne hē wintrum frōd worn gemunde.*
> ([That great-hearted king,] gray-bearded old warrior wrapped in his years, at times began to speak of his youth again, his battle-strength; his heart surged within him when, old in winters, he remembered so much.).[11]

Taking its place in a panorama of oral genres, the particular force of *cwīðan*, in this instance, is to name a performance that looks back on the past and elicits a powerful emotional charge.[12] Wessén sees the relationship between *þylja* (vb. "speak, recite") and *þula* (f. "rhapsody") as a parallel for the sound change from *kvíða* (vb.) to *kviða* (f.)[13] Originally, he suggests, a *kviða* was a mourning song, especially for the death of a hero, but its meaning shifted over time:

> It turned into a memorial poem, the hero's deeds were embellished and survived in heroic legend, the epic element became ever stronger, and finally the narrative poem emerged, as we know it from the *Edda* and from German and Old English heroic poems.[14]

The parallel pair *þylja* and *þula*, and the presence of a cognate in other Germanic languages that denotes a particular kind of poetic performance, strengthen the case that the term *kviða* is fairly old and connected, like *þylja*, with a particular kind of performance. The *þylja/þula* word-group includes an element missing from the *kvíða/kviða* one, namely a word for the practitioner, *þulr* (m. "wise man"). In the conclusion to this part, I will argue that the corresponding practitioner for *kviða* is the skald.

Finnur Jónsson rejected Wessén's idea, on the grounds that there is no evidence for *kviða* having this nuance of meaning (although the bulk of surviving poetry in *kviðuháttr* could constitute such evidence) and that modern Icelandic pronunciation guarantees the short *i* in *kviða* (f.), an objection met by Wessén with the *þylja/þulr* pairing.¹⁵ Erik Noreen was uncomfortable with the idea of the gradual emergence of a genre from collective performance, but his argument for derivation from Greek via Gothic **qiþa*, involving "general reasoning about the intelligence and cultural significance of the Goths," is no less dated and involves a series of complex cross-linguistic interactions.¹⁶ Edith Marold recently rejected Wessén's theory on the grounds that not all poems in *kviðuháttr* are tragic; rather, she thinks they are all genealogical.¹⁷ It is true that neither of these absolute demands are satisfied by the corpus of poetry in *kviðuháttr*. This is not altogether surprising: other Norse genres exhibit the pattern of a core group, sharing all proposed generic characteristics, plus a penumbra of outliers, sharing many but not all of them.¹⁸ As I will show, the anonymous author of *Nóregs konungatal* (Enumeration of the Kings of Norway) and Sturla Þórðarson, in his *Hákonarkviða* (Hákon's Poem), still see themselves as participating in a genre founded by *Ynglingatal*, even though the social and cultural practices that support it had changed enormously in the intervening 250 years.

In what follows, then, I will ask what the substance is that forges the links in *kviðuháttr* poetry. In other words, is the chain also a metaphor of *Genea-Logik*? How far back can the genealogical interests so clear in *Nóregs konungatal* be traced? As explored in Chapter 1, *Ynglingatal* is a poem of death and ruins rather than generation, continuity, and succession. Its view of the experience of death and the world of the dead stands in stark contrast to the near-contemporary works *Háleygjatal* and *Sonatorrek*, a difference with certainly a rhetorical, and possibly a religious dimension. The change in religion and medium which separates this poetry from the codex culture of the twelfth century and later is another watershed. Nonetheless, aspects of *kviðuháttr*'s traditional memorial poetics persist right through to Sturla's *Hákonarkviða*, the latest work composed in this meter, showing that *kviðuháttr* remained a viable medium of royal memory well into the thirteenth century.

"SAD STORIES OF THE DEATH OF KINGS"

The heroic vision of the warrior's death in battle and everlasting fame is omnipresent in *dróttkvætt* encomium. *Ynglingatal*, by contrast, is dominated by the goddess of oblivion Hel. She is mentioned six times in the poem, usually in kennings linking her to Loki and Fenrir, while Freyr appears twice and Týr and Óðinn once each. *Ynglingatal* is conventionally read under the sign of Freyr, because the Svíar are thought to have a special affinity for this god, but it would be closer to the truth to call it Hel-ish. Not only that: *Ynglingatal*'s kings meet their ends in ways that are drastic, but unheroic. They die due to accidents, treachery, illness, supernatural malevolence, or suicide, or they are punished for crimes; all that is told about two kings is that they die in a fire.

This is all rather odd, and in a paper originally presented at the 1982 Saga Conference in Toulon, Lars Lönnroth suggested a solution. He proposed that *Ynglingatal* is a satire, intended to "make fun of the Ynglings, at any rate the Swedish ones."[19] Although Lönnroth only briefly mentioned this possibility—whose appeal to an ironical Swedish student of Old Norse literature is easy to imagine—the idea of *Ynglingatal* as satire has been taken up enthusiastically in subsequent scholarship. Much recent commentary on the poem takes the kings' unheroic deaths as a sign that the poem is satirical, grotesque, or even carnivalesque.[20] To some extent this interpretation relies on reading *Ynglinga saga* into *Ynglingatal*. Edith Marold has recently argued that some of *Ynglinga saga*'s most flagrant bizarreries are consequences of its misunderstanding the verses.[21] But an undeniable residue of weirdness remains and is even commented on by the skald:

10. Fráat maðr áðr
eykja greiði
Freys afspring
í folk hafa.
(No one has heard before of an offspring of Freyr [= Swedish king] using riding gear in battle.)

"I heard" (*frák*) is the usual formula for a skald introducing an account of his patron's brave deeds. Using its negation in emphatic line-introductory position suggests that *these* kings' deeds are *a*typical, unexampled. The claim of the *Ynglingatal*-as-satire school that the poem diverges from encomiastic norms is to that extent justified. If we assume that *Ynglingatal* was composed as praise of the dedicatee's ancestors, as most commentators prior to the 1980s did, then the kings' disastrous or ignoble deaths are troubling. For readers who see the poem as ironic, on the other hand, the putative absurdity of the kings' deaths is not a problem; rather, it is the only evidence for their argument. Ironic readers must also explain how a poem that was understood as satire when it was composed and performed, around 900 CE, had already become an influential model for "straight" compositions such as Eyvindr Finnsson's *Háleygjatal* a mere eighty years later and was able to form the backbone of *Ynglinga saga*'s historical narrative. Proponents of the ironic reading have no explanation for this rapid and complete inversion of the poem's pragmatics in the course of memorial transmission.

SACRAL KINGS?

The most popular alternative is that *Ynglingatal*'s royal victims are precious evidence of a pagan Germanic institution of sacral kingship. Although among the latest sources, Scandinavian material has loomed large in the theory of sacral kingship. Recent studies have shaken faith in such conceptual pillars as sacred marriage between the ruler and the land (*hieros gamos*), ritual sacrifice of kings, and royal luck (*gipt, gæfa*).[22] Advocates of sacral kingship now espouse a weaker version that Olof Sundqvist calls "religious ruler ideology."[23] This comprises a belief in the ruler's "close relation to the mythic world" (amounting to the kings being divinely descended and going to the gods after their death), a leading role for kings in pre-Christian religious ritual, both performing and controlling cult, and rulers' use of religious symbols, broadly defined. The centralization of cult under the control of the ruler and rulers' use of religious symbols can be substantiated by contemporary evidence.[24] The ideological content of this putative institution, however, such as beliefs in divine descent and posthumous deification, can only be supported by textual sources. These bring with them serious problems of dating and interpretation. *Ynglingatal*'s evidence for descent from the gods is distinctly equivocal, as I will show. Without such beliefs, the theory is left merely with the king as cultic performer—not enough to sustain the idea that pre-Christian kings enjoyed hereditary sacral legitimation.[25]

How, then, does Þjóðólfr remember *Ynglingatal*'s kings? Many are victims of treachery. Vísburr, Alrekr and Eirekr, and Álfr and Yngvi are attacked by their closest male relatives: Vísburr is killed by his sons, while the two sets of brothers slaughter each other. Aunn kills his own descendants, if this is what the unparalleled kenning "reddener of kinsmen" (*ǫttunga rjóðr*) means.[26] Dómaldi and Guðrøðr are killed by their followers. If the mysterious "Tunni" is a personal name, as *Ynglinga saga* claims, Egill's death also results from insubordination, as Egill has to flee before "Tunni's power" (*Tunna ríki*), although the instrument of his death is a monstrous bull. Óttarr and Yngvarr die in battle against traditional enemies of the Svíar: Óttarr, "before Danish weapons" (*fyr Dana vǫpnum*), and Yngvarr, at the hands of "Estonian troops" (*herr eistneskr*). The use of the ethnonym in both cases frames these deaths as defense of the land and people of the Svíar against a hostile *gens*.

Other kings die in settings evoking the aristocratic good life in the hall. Fjǫlnir dies at Fróði's court in some connection with beer (*Ynglinga saga* says he falls drunkenly into a vat); Agni is killed with his retinue (*herr*), at the behest of a woman called Skjǫlf and in connection with a gold ring (*með gollmenni*); the Swedish Eysteinn is burned alive in a hall with his entourage. That the kings die during celebrations in the hall makes treachery likely here too, and the stanza on Skjǫlf's killing of Agni condemns the female scheming that causes the death of an innocent king: "I call it a wonder if Skjǫlf's plans seemed to the liking of Agni's troop" (*Þat telk undr, ef rǫ́ð Skjalfar þóttu her Agna at skǫpum*). *Ynglinga saga* and *Historia Norwegie* believe that these stanzas describe betrayals. According to them, Skjǫlf is Agni's wife, and Eysteinn burns in a hall where he is enjoying hospitality. *Historia Norwegie* calls Eysteinn's killers Gauts (*Gautones*), local rivals of the Svíar.

Negative evaluations mainly refer to the kings' killers. Álfr, the fratricide, is "envy-ridden" (*ǫfundgjarn*) and the brothers act "out of jealousy" (*af afbrýði*), but the real villain of the piece is the woman Bera, who incites (*hvetja*) them. "That was not right" (*Vasa þat bært*) says the skald, in an unusually clear condemnation. The plotters against Guðrøðr include the woman Ása and a servant, and they and their "plot"(*umráð*) are ferociously condemned as "treacherous-minded" (*inn lómgeði*) and "hate-filled" (*heiptrœkt*); their triumph is a morally suspect "hidden victory" (*launsigr*). The kings' violent deaths call into question Sundqvist's assertion that "continuity of power" and "smooth succession" are the political messages of *Ynglingatal*. These evaluative phrases lay bare the unjust and undeserved nature of those deaths. Regarding the kings as "ignoble" or "grotesque" *per se* is therefore rather reductive.[27]

ÓÐINN CONTRA HEL

Scarcely less prominent in *Ynglingatal* than the innocent victims of injustice, treachery, and the enemies of the *gens* are kings who are bested by magical or supernatural agents. Many death-bringers are female. Vanlandi is killed by a nightmare (*mara*) and Aðils by a sorceress. Of Yngvarr, killed by the Estonian troop, Þjóðólfr reports that:

18. [. . .]*austmarr*
jǫfri sœnskum (var. *fǫllnum*)
Gymis ljóð
at gamni kveðr.
([. . .] the Baltic sea sings the songs of Gymir <sea-giant> to the delight of the Swedish (var. fallen) ruler.)

It has a close parallel in *Ynglingatal* 22, the final quatrain of which runs:

22. *Ok Skæreið*
í Skíringssal
of brynjalfs
beinum drúpir.
(And Skæreið mourns over the bones of the mailcoat-elf [WARRIOR] in Skíringssalr.)

Just as Hálfdan's burial site is presented in pathetic terms, the land of Skæreið grieving for Hálfdan as it droops (*drúpir*) over his bones, so the waves crash to comfort Yngvarr in his watery grave. Waves are gendered as female, and the word *gaman* usually has sexual overtones, so the idea of the sea-goddess Rán's erotic enjoyment of dead sailors is not far away.[28] Land and sea enclose Hálfdan and Yngvarr in a well-disposed embrace.

Hel has her way with four of *Ynglingatal*'s kings. She "chooses" (*kjósa*) Dyggvi, "takes" (*taka*) Hálfdan *hvítbeinn*, and "invites" (*bjóða*) Hálfdan *inn mildi* out of this world, while Eysteinn, ruler of Vestfold, "goes" (*fara*) to her "because of a sailyard" (*fyr ási*). The grave is imagined as Hel's realm, a bower where she enjoys the dead kings.[29] Hel's name, which probably derives from Proto-Germanic **helan* (to cover), implies she is identified with the concrete physical space of the grave.[30] Here she is personified, while eddic poets usually depicted *hel* as a place.[31] In *kviðuháttr* poetry Hel is described by means of her kin relations, often using a special type of circumlocution called *ofljóst* (too clear) in the *Prose Edda*. This involves the replacement of a noun with a kenning for its homonym. Loptr, for example, an alternative name for the god Loki, can be referred to using a kenning for Loptr Sæmundarson, the father of the dedicatee of *Nóregs konungatal*:

*áðr * lǫfðung*
lífi at ræna
ǫðlings kom
einkadóttir.
(the only daughter of the chieftain [= Loptr Sæmundarson, and so by *ofljóst* Loptr/Loki, whose daughter is Hel] came to rob the ruler of his life.)[32]

Hilda Ellis Davidson saw the skaldic personification of Hel as a literary conceit without religious significance, a view with which Abram concurs.[33] It would be ill-advised to import the view from the *Prose Edda* that references to Hel suggest the kings have died bad deaths. Rather, the place-based *memoria* of *kviðuháttr* licenses a poetically productive oscillation between a proper name Hel and a place *hel*. Such *ofljóst* kennings are part of the stylistic signature of *kviðuháttr*.[34]

Another important complex of ideas around death, Óðinn's hall Valhǫll, its complement of dead warriors (*einherjar*), and the looming final battle (*ragnarøkkr*), is almost completely absent from *Ynglingatal*, a surprising omission in a poem otherwise so doomy. Óðinn is only mentioned once in *Ynglingatal*, when the "creature of charms" (*véttr vitta*) kills Vanlandi by means of a nightmare, causing him to visit the brother of Vili, that is, Óðinn (*Yt* 3). The figure who sends Vanlandi to Óðinn is "troll-descended" (*trollkundr*), undoubtedly a pejorative term.[35] Óðinn, master of *seiðr* and shape-shifting and teacher of magic, is this being's patron, and going to him via nightmare seems considerably less pleasant—the verb used is *kvelja* ("torment")—than enjoying Hel's embraces. In striking contrast, Eyvindr Finnsson's *kviðuháttr* poem *Háleyjgatal* (*Hál*), composed some eighty years after *Ynglingatal* in praise of Hákon jarl Sigurðarson of Lade in northern Norway, is obsessed with Óðinn.[36] While the surviving stanzas of *Háleygjatal* include one tragic death after the manner of *Ynglingatal* (*Hál* 9–10), they are otherwise a frantic display of Odinic martial protagonism. The jarls, to whom Eyvindr offers Óðinn's drink, or poetry, in *Háleyjgatal*'s opening stanza, are Óðinn's descendants (*Hál* 2), kinsmen of Freyr (*Hál* 7) and Týr (*Hál* 10).[37] They fight in Óðinn's storm (i.e. battle, *Hál* 6) and Óðinn's din (also battle, *Hál* 8), feed blood to Óðinn's swans (i.e. ravens, *Hál* 9), sail their ships into battle (*Hál* 11) and conquer territory, referred to as "bride of the slaughter-god" (*brúðr valtýs*), that is, Óðinn's concubine Jǫrð, and so by *ofljóst jǫrð*, or "earth" (*Hál* 12); the poem itself is described as "ale-feast of the gods" (*jólna sumbl*). Fully one-third of *Háleygjatal*'s kennings refer to Óðinn, and its ideal ruler is the war-leader and conqueror of territory, the same ideal that dominates *dróttkvætt* encomium and—in Christian guise—the skaldic portrayals of kings such as Óláfr Haraldsson and Magnús Óláfsson.

It is difficult to say whether the female-centered imagery of death in *Ynglingatal* is a marked deviation from an otherwise Odinic norm. Conceptions of death in pre-Christian religions of the North were quite varied. Old Norse heroic poetry frequently represents death as an encounter, often sexual, with a supernatural female being such as the sea-goddess Rán, Hel, a valkyrie, or Freyja.[38] Arab travelers among the Rus' say that rape was part of pre-Christian Scandinavian funeral ritual, and their accounts find some support in the archaeological evidence.[39] Whether *Ynglingatal*'s interest in Hel reflects religious belief or merely poetic play, the strenuous Odinism of *Háleygjatal* suggests that centering this god was an important element of Eyvindr's counter-discourse. In this, as in its version of the *catena* discussed below, *Háleygjatal* presents a polemical alternative to the earlier poem. This also extends to its revision of *Ynglingatal*'s female-dominated, subterranean, and submarine worlds of death. *Háleygjatal* does mention burial sites, but it swerves away from the grave, and its kennings evoke the shining, Odinic, aerial world of renown most beautifully expressed in the eddic poetry on Helgi *Hundingsbani*, the quintessential Viking warrior-hero:

> *Mál er mér at ríða*　　*roðnar brautir*
> *láta fǫlvan jó*　　　　*flugstíg troða*
> *skal ek fyr vestan*　　 *vindhjálms brúar*
> *áðr Salgofnir*　　　　*sigrþjóð veki.*
> ("It is time for me to ride along the blood-red roads,
> to set the pale horse to tread the path in the sky;
> I must cross the bridge in the sky-vault,
> before Salgofnir awakens the victorious people.")[40]

Terry Gunnell has recently suggested that veneration of Óðinn was especially associated with "a new southern Scandinavian military, aristocratic elite which had increasingly nationalistic ambitions of territorial rulership extending beyond the local clan, tribe or family."[41] The relationship between *Ynglingatal* and *Háleygjatal* (and *Sonatorrek*, another significantly Odinic *kviðuháttr* poem) complicates this picture, suggesting that Odinism is at home in northern Norway and Iceland, but not in the royal milieu of southern Scandinavia to which *Ynglingatal* belongs.

GENEALOGY AND THE SUBSTANCE OF RELATION

Catenulate structure is fractal in *kviðuháttr* poetry, dominating not only each stanza, which heaps up kennings for the same object, but also the poems in their entirety, which tend to be organized as lists. Lists have clear mnemonic implications and are characteristic of both oral transmission and of the earliest stages of literacy.[42] *Háleygjatal* and *Nóregs konungatal* are structured as genealogical lists, and the latter even comments, with wry mock-modesty, on the length of its list of forefathers:

2. *Róa skal fyrst*
fjarri reyði,
* *koma þó niðr*
nær, áðr lúki.
(One must first row far from the whale, yet come down close before it is finished.)

The verb *telja* ("reckon up, count, tell") is strongly associated with the memorial practice of listing.[43] It appears not only in the names of several *kviðuháttr* poems, but also in their texts, for instance in *Sonatorrek*:

5. *Þó munk mitt*
ok móður hrør
fǫður fall
fyrst of telja
(But yet I will first tell of the death of my mother and the fall of my father.)

10. *Mik hefr marr*
miklu rœntan
grimt es fall
frænda at telja
(The sea has robbed me of much; it is cruel to tell of the fall of kinsmen.)

Egill's *Arinbjarnarkviða* claims to have "twofold and threefold" praise to recount of its dedicatee.[44] The claim in the four-line *kviðuháttr* fragment attributed to Þorvaldr *blǫnduskald* (?poet of Blanda) to "have included many things" also implies that the lost poem to which it belonged was list-like.[45] In contrast to *Háleygjatal* and *Nóregs konungatal*, none of these references to listing are explicitly genealogical. What about *Ynglingatal*?

The answer may, at first glance, seem obvious. For most of the 750 or so years of critical engagement since *Heimskringla*, *Ynglingatal* has been described as a "genealogical poem." The consensus has lately been showing some cracks. The poem's most recent editors choose a cautious formulation, noting that "some scholars justifiably doubt" this generic identification, and that *Heimskringla*'s mention of "death and burial-places" (*dauða- ok legstað*) "might encourage a view of the poem as a mnemonic or an enumeration" instead.[46] Beate Kellner, in her fundamental study of genealogical models in medieval texts, writes that "origin and continuity reveal themselves as the two central issues of every genealogical construct."[47] *Ynglingatal* has strikingly little interest in either the origin of its list of kings or its continuity. Earlier scholarship proposed that there were once several stanzas at the beginning of the poem that linked the king list back to Óðinn, a hypothesis which is both possible and unprovable.[48] Whether or not these stanzas once existed, the recent editors' observation that "the line of descent has almost no relevance within the poem" is borne out on closer reading. Two kings are called "descendant" (*ǫttungr*) of the gods Týr or Freyr (Egill: *Týs ǫttungr*, *Yt* 14; Aðils: *Freys ǫttungr*, *Yt* 16), and one of them, Egill, is also said to descend from the Skilfingar (*Skilfinga nið*, *Yt* 14).[49] As *Dusla konr* (*Yt* 2), King Sveigðir is either a descendant of a certain Dusli (?"Shabby") or a member of a group of Duslar, also unknown. Alrekr and Eirekr are called "kinsmen of Dagr" (*Dags fríendr*, *Yt* 10; Dagr is the subject of *Yt* 8 and, according to *Ynglinga saga*, the brothers' grandfather), while Dómarr is "descendant of Fjǫlnir" (*niðr Fjǫlnis*, *Yt* 6). These last two instances are the only references to names that occur earlier in the poem's sequence and may simply have satisfied the needs of alliteration. Explicit genealogical references are confined to the beginning of the poem—if that is what they are, rather than merely being alliteratively convenient markers of affinity, as "descendant of the kindred of rulers" (*áttkonr kyns lofða*, *Yt* 21), that is, "ruler," clearly is.[50]

Skalds rarely go further back than one generation: "son" (*sonr*) is by far their favorite genealogical term. Even terms such as *arfi*, *arfvǫrðr* (inheritor), which allow longer-range links, are almost invariably combined with the name of the father.[51] Jan Vansina's model of the "floating gap" in oral tradition offers a convincing explanation.[52] Memory is relatively precise for the *sæculum*, encompassed by individual memory and chronological reckoning. Memory dims as it stretches further back in time and forms of chronology fail, only to acquire clarity again in the unchanging mythic epoch of the origins. The memory-gap "floats" as time passes and the leading edge of forgetting progresses forward. In accordance with Vansina's theory, the ancestors that the skalds refer to using such vague kinship terms as *niðr* ("descendant"), *kind* ("offspring"), or *konr* ("kinsman") belong to the legendary deep past: King Ælle of Northumbria; Vǫlsungr, eponym of the Vǫlsungar; or the sea-king named Heiti. Runic inscriptions referring to family relations of a greater time-depth than a single generation on either side of *ego* are also rare.[53] The main exceptions are two Viking Age stones, the Malsta stone, from Hälsingland in northern Sweden (Hs 14), which goes back seven generations, and the stone from Norra Sandsjö in Småland (Sm 71), which traces a family line back five generations. Both these genealogies proceed backward in time from *ego*, following the male line. The Malsta stone commemorates a rich and powerful landowner and was perhaps intended to make a legal claim.[54] This may also be the case for the Sandsjö stone.[55] The importance of genealogy in legal contexts is clear in the early provincial laws and in eddic poems such as *Hyndluljóð*, but runic inscriptions and skaldic poetry do not seem to have been important media for genealogical knowledge more broadly.

The sole unequivocal instance of genealogical organization in the early *kviðuháttr* poetry is Eyvindr's *Háleygjatal*. It lists the ancestors in the male line of Hákon jarl Sigurðarson back to their mythical origins in the union of Óðinn and a giantess named Skaði. Only four generations between Óðinn and Hákon appear in the fragments that survive, but the genealogical plan is clearly stated in the opening stanza, where the skald asks for a hearing "while I reckon his [Hákon's] lineage back to the gods" (*meðan hans ætt til goða teljum*). Its relationship of "rivalry and appropriation" to *Ynglingatal*, perhaps spiced with the hostility signaled in Eyvindr's byname, "skalds' despoiler" (*skáldaspillir*), makes *Háleygjatal* a complex witness to the putative genre of genealogical poetry.[56] Þjóðólfr and Eyvindr's poetic relationship is a parallel to the rivalry of Hallfreðr *vandræðaskáld* and Halldórr *ókristni* around the time of Óláfr Tryggvason's militant missionizing.[57] Eyvindr's claim that the jarls of Lade were descended from Óðinn may reflect a competitive intensification of *Ynglingatal*'s vague references to divine kinship. This polemical edge is sharpened if, as argued above, *Ynglingatal* belongs to a less intensely Odinic milieu than *Háleygjatal*.

The kings' saga prose that transmits *Ynglingatal*, by contrast, is fascinated by genealogy. Ari Þorgilsson's *Íslendingabók* (Book of the Icelanders, c. 1122–25) and *Historia Norwegie* include genealogies going back to Yngvi and the gods, which substantially overlap with *Ynglingatal*'s king-list. Ari devotes a great deal of space in *Íslendingabók* to establishing a chronology for the history of Iceland. Chronology is also a concern of the *Historia de antiquitate regum Norwagiensium*, composed c. 1180 by Theodoricus *monachus* ("monk"). Theodoricus is too cautious to include the kings before Haraldr, saying that

> because it is clear that no established succession of the royal line existed in this land before the time of Haraldr Fair-hair, I have begun with him; and I have not done this because I doubted that before his day there were in this land men who, by the standards of the present age, were distinguished by their prowess.[58]

Understandably more focused on Norway than is Ari, Theodoricus goes to some trouble to establish a chronology for his kings, based on regnal years:

> Haraldr Fair-hair, son of Halfdan the Black, became king. He first drove out all the petty kings, and alone ruled all Norway for seventy years before he died. (Theodoricus, *Historia*, Ch. 1)

> Haraldr was succeeded by his son whose name was Eiríkr . . . He ruled Norway for three years. (Theodoricus, *Historia*, Ch. 2)

> Hákon, fosterson of Æthelstan and son of Haraldr, ruled for twenty-five years. (Theodoricus, *Historia*, Ch. 4)

> His [Óláfr Tryggvason's] father was of royal lineage—he was the son of Óláfr, son of Haraldr Fair-hair. (Theodoricus, *Historia*, Ch. 4)

Historia Norwegie, by contrast, lacks regnal years altogether, and it includes the pre-Haraldr kings that Theodoricus found too dubious. Even if the establishment of a plausible chronology is outside its purview, it is nonetheless keen to display the historical logic of filiation, as it counters *Ynglingatal*'s loose paratactic sequence with a series of unambiguous genealogical statements:

60   MAKING MEMORIES

> King Yngve, who according to a great many was the first ruler of the Swedish realm, became the father of Njord, whose son was Frøy ... Frøy engendered Fjolne ... His son, Sveigde ... He sired Vanlande ... He was the father of Visbur ... [etc.]

(*Historia Norwegie*, Ch. IX, "On the lineage of kings")

Ynglinga saga, too, deploys descent as one of a series of techniques for converting the fragmentary, discontinuous series of *Ynglingatal* into a chain that exhibits both genea- and narrative logic.[59] As does *Historia Norwegie*, it makes the father-son links explicit. Bizarre and darkly comical though the *Ynglinga saga* narrative often is (this king befriending a sparrow, that one swept overboard by the boom of his own ship), it works hard to generate a sense of history as the "genealogy of events."[60] This is sometimes couched in moral terms:

> Vísburr, son of Vanlandi, leaves his first wife, the daughter of Auði *inn auðgi* "the Wealthy." When petitioned by their young sons, he refuses to return her *mundr* "bride-price, bridal gift," which comprises a precious neck-ring and three large estates (*Yt* 4);[61]

> a bull that should have been sacrificed escapes into the forest, turns mad and becomes a great danger to the people (*Yt* 14);

or in the feud patterns familiar from the sagas of Icelanders:

> Guðrøðr, the son of Hálfdan, asks King Haraldr of Agðir (Agder) for his daughter Ása in marriage but is refused. He therefore attacks the king's residence; Ása's father and brother die in the struggle and she is carried off and married to Guðrøðr. A few years later, while the king is anchored in Stíflusund, Guðrøðr is murdered by a servant of Ása as he departs drunk from a feast (*Yt* 25).

The saga text also attempts to provide a chronology, or at least a sense of the passing of time:

> When after ten years [Vanlandi] does not come back to her as promised, Drífa commissions a sorceress to perform a spell which will either bring him back or kill him (*Yt* 3);

> King Dómaldi succeeds his father Vísburr. The Swedes, plagued by famine, stage a sacrificial ceremony in Uppsala three years in a row (*Yt* 5).

And the poem's jumps from place to place are rationalized by stories of visits to the Winter King:

> King Vanlandi, son of Sveigðir, stays the winter in Finnland with the prince Snjár inn gamli ("Snow the Old") and marries his daughter Drífa ("Snowstorm") (*Yt* 3);

and Viking campaigns:

> Jǫrundr and Eiríkr, the sons of Yngvi, encounter Guðlaugr, king of Hálogaland (Hålogaland), while raiding in Denmark (*Yt* 12); Yngvarr, son of King Eysteinn, becomes ruler of Sweden. Having made peace with the Danes, he goes raiding in the Baltic. On a foray to Eistland (Estonia), he is attacked by a large Estonian force near Steinn and killed in battle (*Yt* 18).

The foregoing comparison of *Historia Norwegie* and *Heimskringla* with *Ynglingatal* demonstrates just how little interest the poem has in fatherhood, sonship, and the logic of filiation, in contrast with the prose texts. This difference is obscured for us in part by our belief that "blood is thicker than water." As David Schneider puts it in his *Critique of the Study of Kinship*, "this assumption makes kinship or genealogical relations unlike any other social bonds, for they have especially strong binding force and are directly constituted by, grounded in, determined by, formed by the imperatives of the biological nature of human nature."[62] A belief in the primacy of blood kinship underlies our own culture's understanding of relatedness. In what became the founding work of the New Kinship Studies, Schneider argues that such an understanding is tied up in the "biologistic" biases of western culture.[63] Although he does not discuss the Middle Ages, it is obvious that these biologistic biases are also temporally specific and do not necessarily apply to western medieval thinking. Christopher Johnson and his coauthors accordingly write that "the time has come to engage more directly with the New Kinship Studies and to explore ideas of 'relatedness' and offer an historical, critical account of the ways 'substance' [. . .] has been employed in the European past to make connectedness."[64]

Such a "historical, critical account" could not assume *a priori* that the substance that joins the links of *Ynglingatal*'s chain is the same as that in the historiography of the twelfth century and later—nor that the latter is the same as what links us to our forebears. An obvious difference is the role of religion in the Middle Ages. For medieval Christians, in the words of Gabrielle Spiegel, "genealogical histories are [. . .] from a structural point of view, narrative mimeses of the creation of life itself and as such acquire a genuinely paradigmatic character as imitations of the supernatural order upon which the social order of the human community is based."[65] What made genealogy important for medieval thinkers was not human agency, based in the primal biological substance of blood. Rather,

> genealogies were accounts of carnal origins, whose chains marked the generational progression of history and bore witness to the continuity of God's promise in the world, most obviously in the unbroken line of descent from Adam to Jesus, but also in the successions of kings, emperors, judges, priests, and bishops. Because they were carnal, they took the form of Matthew's genealogy of Jesus's carnal birth, beginning at a point in the past and descending from generation to generation to the present, either by filiation, succession, or an interweaving of both.[66]

From this perspective, the emphasis on genealogy that we see in the twelfth- and thirteenth-century Norse historiographical tradition is driven by a desire to discern "the visible patterns of divine order embedded in the material chaos."[67] Carnality interwove with typology, joining human beings into a chain of succession that demonstrated the unfolding of God's plan, through time, in the world. The idea that all subsequent kings of Norway held the country in fief from St Olaf, *perpetuus rex Norwegie* (*Historia Norwegie*, XV, 5), and in turn were descended from the line of pre-Christian kings going back as far as Haraldr *hárfagri*, or even further still, is the significant content of these Norse genealogical constructs. The historiographic texts seek to demonstrate the working out of this divine plan. As Sverrir Jakobsson observes,

> A notable difference between [twelfth- and thirteenth-century Norse historiography] and the evidence gained from the eleventh century sources is the fact that the claim of Harald Sigurdsson to the throne of Norway no longer rests on his being the brother of St Olaf, instead he is a claimant because of his descent in a straight male line from a ninth century King Harald, who happens to be his namesake. In fact, the genealogy in *The Book of the Icelanders* demonstrates that the claim of King Harald rests on the same foundation as that of Olaf Tryggvason and St Olaf. The fact that they share a name further illustrates the connection between the eleventh century Harald and his putative ninth century ancestor who emerges in this text as the progenitor of the Norwegian royal line.[68]

In the Old and Middle Irish versified royal pedigrees and necrologies, no less than in the Anglo-Saxon royal genealogies, the lineages are learned constructs, with the Bible, Jerome, and Eusebius as models.[69] These Irish poetic genres arose in the seventh century but did not become dynastic (that is, lists of the deeds of a line of kings in succession) until some two hundred years later. Chronology, Peter Smith suggests, did not become an important concern before the tenth century.[70] This development is paralleled in the Norse material. There, too, a change in medium goes hand in hand with one of religion. Because the advent of writing was so late in Scandinavia compared to Ireland and England, the precursors that supplied the historiographers with their material, such as *Ynglingatal*, can still be glimpsed in the written sources. As argued above, this does not license a further move back in time, beyond the period of oral memory contemporary with Þjóðólfr, into the dim prehistory of Svíþjóð. Rather, the material Þjóðólfr re-mediates is, for the most part, local, contemporary, orally performed place-lore, of a kind that existed both before and after the advent of writing and the conversion to Christianity. What the comparison with the Irish and insular cases does reveal, however, is the illegitimacy of the assumption that this material was genealogically formed. In the Norse setting too, an interest in genealogy and chronology is associated with Christian learning and the growing importance of writing.

Háleygjatal's explicit *Genea-Logik* may be the earliest evidence of such interests. Its dedicatee, Hákon jarl, owed his power to the patronage of the missionary king of Denmark, Haraldr Gormsson, by whom he had been baptized. If Eyvindr's byname *skáldaspillir* can be taken in a positive sense, it may record the ways in which *Háleygjatal* does not merely copy, but outdoes its exemplar *Ynglingatal*.[71] Where *Ynglingatal* claims divine *affinity* for its kings, whom Þjóðólfr calls the gods' "offspring" (*afspringr*) and "descendant" (*ǫttungr*), "like the gods" (*goðum glíkr*), *Háleygjatal* asserts that Hákon is the lineal *descendant* of Óðinn and his consort Skaði, carnally linked to the gods and giants.[72] Although only fragments of *Háleygjatal* are preserved, the first two stanzas present the first bud on the family tree, as Óðinn and Skaði generate an unnamed jarl who is identified in the prose frame as Sæmingr, Hákon's ancestor. The nature of Eyvindr's commitment to pre-Christian religion is an open question: is it sincere, ambivalent, strategic?[73] Scholarly indecision indexes the genuine complexity of the religious situation in late-tenth-century northern Norway. From whatever perspective he did so,

Eyvindr evidently wished to turn his powerful predecessor in a new direction. Were Hákon and his circle perhaps already aware of the importance of filiation in Christian mythology, and so of genealogy as a structural device, and is *Háleygjatal* best seen as a splendid piece of syncretic propaganda?

The anonymous poem that Flateyjarbók calls *Nóregs konungatal* (Enumeration of the Kings of Norway) is an unmistakable instance of genealogical interests in the medium of *kviðuháttr*. Composed around 1190 at Oddi in Iceland, and so approximately contemporary with the early historiographic prose, this poem interweaves two subjects. The first is the prominence of the kin of Haraldr *hárfagri* among the rulers of Norway. The second is praise of Jón Loptsson, genealogically linked to these almost thirty princes via his mother, Þóra, a daughter of King Magnús *berfœttr* (bare-leg). Its 664 lines contain more than twenty-five kennings adumbrating family relationships within the putative kindred of Harald *hárfagri*. Harald is called "Hálfdan's son," Olaf *inn kyrri* (the quiet) is "Magnús' father," Magnús in turn is "Eysteinn's father," and so on. Forced to break the chain after Magnús Óláfsson, who was succeeded by his father's half-brother, Haraldr *harðráði* (hard-ruler), the poet conscientiously points out that he is doing so. The poem's concern with chronology extends as far as supplying regnal years for its monarchs. In this it is a perfect reflection of the twelfth-century Icelandic genealogical tradition. It even includes a footnote to the now lost king-lists of Sæmundr *inn fróði* (the wise), Jón Loptsson's grandfather:

> 36. *Nú hefk talt*
> *tíu landreka,*
> *þás hverr vas*
> *frá Haraldi.*
> *Inntak svá*
> *ævi þeira,*
> *sem Sæmundr*
> *sagði inn fróði.*
>
> (Now I have enumerated ten sovereigns, each of whom was descended from Haraldr. I recounted their lives just as Sæmundr *inn fróði* (the learned) said.)

Neither burial places nor dates are recorded for the poem's Icelandic subjects. Instead the Oddi lineage who were Jón's ancestors are described as exemplary magnates, worthy of their place at the apex of Icelandic society. They are leaders (*hǫfuðsmaðr*, st. 72), upholders of institutions (st. 69

describes their skill in the law), kinsmen and friends of kings ("king's kinsman" [*konungsfrændr*], st. 70), "confidant of the king" (*konungs spjalli*, st. 75), generous ("distributor of pure gold" [*deilir vella*], st. 70), "much-bountiful" (*margnýtr*, st. 73), and popular (*vinsæll*, st. 70; "Loptr had no enemy born beneath the flame of clouds," st. 71). The concern of *Nóregs konungatal* with quantifiable, detailed information, such as dates, lines of succession, and source references, is worlds away from *Ynglingatal*. It reflects the "bureaucratic mind" apparent in king-lists dating to the early days of writing, from Ireland to Ancient Egypt and Sumeria. Writing, as Haicheng Wang observes in his comparative survey, makes population and territory "legible" for early states, an aspiration also visible in Iceland in a work such as *Landnámabók*.[74] The quite different medial environment in which *Ynglingatal* and other early poems in *kviðuháttr* came into being means that *Nóregs konungatal* is an unreliable guide to the generic norms governing *Ynglingatal*. The powerful echoes of *Ynglingatal* continue to make themselves felt, however, not only in *Nóregs konungatal*, but also in the last royal encomium in *kviðuháttr*, Sturla Þórðarson's *Hákonarkviða*.

"WOULD-BE REVIVER OF AN OLD PERISHED FASHION"[75]

Sturla Þórðarson's *Hákonarkviða* (*Hákkv*), probably composed around 1270, is dedicated to the Norwegian king Hákon Hákonarson (r. 1217–63), grandson of King Sverrir. It is transmitted in the prosimetrum of *Hákonar saga Hákonarsonar*, a royal biography commissioned from Sturla by Hákon's son and successor, King Magnús *lagabœtir*. Although Hákon's death is not mentioned in *Hákkv*, Kari Gade argues that the lack of apostrophes to him indicates that the poem was composed after news of the king's death, in Orkney in 1263, had reached Norway.[76] It is thus also a memorial work. The poem recounts Hákon's flight from the Vik region to Trondheim at the age of two, his struggle with his cousin Skúli Bárðarson for the Norwegian throne, and his coronation feast in 1247, and it ends with a diplomatic expedition to Sweden in 1249. No other encomiastic poem in *kviðuháttr* is biographical. This may reflect the influence of the *ævikviða*, or of his uncle Snorri Sturluson's *Háttatal*, a poem Sturla knew well.[77] All the same, Sturla incorporates much traditional *kviðuháttr* imagery. Rather than describing Hákon's death and burial, he stages that of his great rival Skúli. A fierce battle in a churchyard, described with a profusion of *ofljóst* kennings (*á grænni málu geir-Týs*, "on the green wife of the spear-Týr" [= Óðinn > = Jǫrð (*jǫrð* "earth")]," *Hákkv* 18; *dísir hlýrna mans Högna*, "*dísir* of the sun and moon of Hǫgni's girl [= Hildr (*hildr* 'battle') > SHIELDS > VALKYRIES]," *Hákkv* 22), ends with Skúli's forces decimated. Hel takes them to the underworld:[78]

21. *Ok þar felt*
feigum hausi
Gjallar mans
greypri hendi
Fenris nipt
fylkis dólga
í hjörgöll
heiptar blóði.

(And there Fenrir's sister [= Hel] hooded the doomed heads of the leader's enemies with the blood of hatred by the gruesome hand of Gjǫll's girl [= Hel] in the sword-din [BATTLE].)

Skúli and the remains of his party take refuge in the monastery of Elgeseter in Trondheim, but his enemies set fire to the building and they are killed as they escape:

23. *En nafnfrægt*
nøkkvi síðar
í náreið
á Niðarbakka
við leygför
leggja knátti
rausnarlíf
ríkr hertogi.
24. *Ok þar gekk*
á Gjallarbrú
ræsis mágr
fyr riðusóttum
bauga bliks,
er boðar fellu
elda vers
of afarmenni.

(And a little later, the powerful duke placed his renowned, splendid body on the bier on the banks of Nidelven because of the raging of fire.

And there the in-law of the ruler stepped on Gjallarbrú because of the fevers of the gleam of shield-bosses [SWORD] when the offerers of the fires of the ocean [GOLD > GENEROUS MEN] fell around the proud man.)

Like the twelfth-century kings Eysteinn and Óláfur Magnússon (Anon *Nkt* 48), Skúli rests *á Niðarbakka*. Whereas their corpses are interred in Kristkirken, memorial church of the Norwegian kings, Skúli is killed in front of the burning monastery of Elgeseter, on the river's banks. Rather than being dynastic, as Eysteinn's and Magnús's deaths were, Skúli's death-scene looks back to the tragic ends of the kings of earlier *kviðuháttr* tradition. The bier his body lies on is called a "corpse-wagon" (*náreið*). As a noun this compound is unique, but it is closely paralleled by *Háleygjatal*'s adjective "corpse-bearing" (*náreiðr*, Eyv *Hál* 5), referring to the tree that bears Guðlaugr's body, and the echo is probably deliberate. Gade observes that "this reference to the pagan realm of Hel is rather curious [. . .] The stanza does not seem to imply that Skúli was going to rest peacefully in heaven after his death since he was imagined to be on his way across Gjallarbrú."[79] As shown above, there is nothing surprising about meeting Hel in a *kviðuháttr* poem. This reference draws Skúli into the company of Egill Skallagrímsson and the kings of *Ynglingatal*, whose journeys into death involved encounters with her.

Guðrún Nordal suggests that Sturla's language in *Hákkv* presents Skúli as a man of the legendary past in contrast to Hákon, whose coronation by the papal legate is described in the following stanza.[80] The contrast the text draws between the two men is still more far-reaching. Writing about the conflict between Skúli and Hákon involved a delicate balancing act for Sturla. His own family's sympathies lay with Skúli, who was a personal friend of his uncle Snorri Sturluson. Sturla's patron King Magnús was both the son of Hákon and the grandson of Skúli on his mother's side.[81] The eulogy for Skúli in *Hákonar saga* ch. 242 accordingly blames his fall on his bad luck: "men would have said, if that unlucky year had not come over him that he last lived, that no man had been born in Norway who had shown himself a better man of those who have not come in the direct line of the kings."[82] The theme of Skúli's ill-luck is foreshadowed, some forty chapters earlier, in a stanza from *Hákkv* marking the moment when Skúli is acclaimed king at the Eyraþing:

9. Þat er skröklaust,
at Skúli var
frægðarmaðr

í frömu lífi,
þótt hvarbrigð
á hann sneri
aldar gipt
auðnu hvéli,
þá er ofrausn
öfgu heilli
randa rjóðr
reisa knátti,

(It is not a lie that Skúli was a famous man in his outstanding life, although the fickle luck of mankind turned the wheel of fortune on him, when the reddener of shield-rims [WARRIOR = Skúli] raised an excess of heroism with adverse luck.)

Sturla skillfully embeds the traditional *kviðuháttr* theme of tragic, undeserved death in the up-to-the-moment motif of the wheel of fortune. Old wine appears in new bottles elsewhere in the poem too, literally so in the description of Hákon's coronation feast in *Hákkv* 28–29, where wine is both a healing balm (*heilivágr*), as it is in the romances, and skaldic surf that crashes into gum-skerries (*gómsker*) and drenches the mind-ship (*geðknörr*). The trope of unheroic death, so memorably established in *Ynglingatal*, is echoed in *Hákkv*'s depiction of Skúli's death in battle as an illness, "fever of the gleam of shield-bosses" [SWORD] (*ríðusótt bauga blíks*, *Hákkv* 24). The traditional compositional resources of *kviðuháttr* enabled Skúli to be portrayed as a blameless victim, and Hákon to be relieved of any agency in bringing about his death. This was no doubt welcome to Sturla as he went about his tricky task.

Hákonar saga's prose depicts Hákon as a near-saintly figure. He is surrounded by quasi-miraculous events, keen to come to terms with antagonistic bishops, and loath to violate the sanctity of churches with killings.[83] *Hákkv* uses the traditional topos of the king as bringer of prosperity and good harvest (*ár ok friðr*), updated with references to fruit trees and songbirds (*Hákkv* 4) and the four elements (*Hákkv* 5), to describe him. His good fortune is attributed to divine favor and implicitly contrasted to Skúli's ill-luck:

25. *Sú kom gipt*
af guðs syni
yfir Hákon

heilli góðu.
(That luck came by good fortune upon Hákon from the son of God [= Christ].)

Another difficult point for Sturla to negotiate was that Hákon's illegitimate birth made his claim to the throne weaker than Skúli's by the 1163–4 Law of Succession.[84] At the ceremony of Skúli's acclamation at the Eyraþing, a speaker declaimed his ancestry back to St Olaf (ch. 199). The saga therefore bolsters Hákon's claim by a pattern of spiritual kinship with the two Olafs. Like Óláfr Tryggvason, he was smuggled to safety under his enemies' noses as a young child (ch. 3). *Hákkv* refers to this event as him "pushing his noble head" (*drepa tírarhǫfði*) into Óláfr Tryggvason's "line" (*ætt*, *Hákkv* 1), oblique phrasing that leaves open precisely what kind of kinship is being claimed. The other Olaf intervenes more actively in the saga's plot. Skúli and Hákon attempt, on separate occasions, to swear on St Olaf's shrine in Nidaros, but both are hindered. In Hákon's case, the church's canons, who are members of the opposing party, bar the door (ch. 17). In Skúli's, the shrine sticks fast when his supporters lay hands on it, and his son Pétr needs to administer a shove with his knee to get it moving (ch. 198). St Olaf himself rejects Skúli's claim of rightful succession, and so of "[bearing] witness to the continuity of God's promise in the world."[85] On his deathbed, Hákon has first saints' lives, then "the tale of the kings from Halfdan the black, and so on of all the kings of Norway, one after the other," and finally *Sverris saga* read to him (ch. 329). This, the saga's last scene, centers the kinship that mattered most in the high medieval setting of *Hákonar saga:* the spiritual family of God and the saints, framing "the tale of kings," the carnal medium in which God's plan plays out.

* * * *

The late-fourteenth-century compilation Flateyjarbók is perhaps the largest and most splendid of all medieval Icelandic codices. It was written by two priests, Jón Þórðarson and Magnús Þórhallsson, in the closing years of the fourteenth century. Recent close studies of the manuscript by Kolbrún Haraldsdóttir and Guðvarður Már Gunnlaugsson suggest that the manuscript was written in two main campaigns.[86] The first was in 1387, when Jón wrote *Eiríks saga víðfǫrla*, *Óláfs saga Tryggvasonar*, and the beginning of *Óláfs saga helga*, and Magnús completed *Óláfs saga helga* and added after it *Nóregs konungatal*, *Sverris saga*, and *Hákonar saga Hákonarsonar*. In a second writing campaign, in late 1390, Magnús framed this material with additional texts. At the beginning of the codex he added genealogical material, including the poems *Geisli* and *Hyndluljóð*, and, at the end, hagiographic texts and some annals.[87] This re-dating makes it less likely that the book was originally intended as a present to Óláfr IV Hákonarson, the last Norwegian king of Norway (1370–87).[88] Rather than being a royal gift, the manuscript was probably written for its commissioner, the wealthy Icelandic farmer Jón Hákonarson.

The weightiest evidence is the gap in Flateyjarbók's otherwise comprehensive account of Norwegian history. No sagas for the period between 1030 (the end of *Ólafs saga helga*) and 1177 (the beginning of *Sverris saga*) are included, probably because Jón owned another manuscript with these sagas in it, the kings' saga compilation *Hulda*.[89] One function of *Nóregs konungatal* in Flateyjarbók is to bridge this temporal gap. The poem covers all the kings from Haraldr *hárfagri* on, and Sverrir reigns in the poem's present (*Nkt* 65). In its praise of the Oddaverjar in the terms used for the *rex iustus*, *Nóregs konungatal* holds up a flattering mirror to the late medieval Icelandic aristocracy, of which Jón Hákonarson was a part. The memory-supporting, catenulate structure of *Nóregs konungatal* was probably an important factor in its inclusion too. *Nóregs konungatal* summarizes the chronological sequence of kings before *Sverris saga* begins, and in this way it functions as a preface to it.[90]

History as "the genealogy of events" has a competitor in *Flateyjarbók*, namely the nonchronological design of salvific history. Kolbrún demonstrates how Flateyjarbók reorganizes the *Separate Saga of St Olaf*, in comparison to the redaction in AM 62 fol, by moving the accounts of Olaf's burial, his translation, the building of his church, and his miracles out of chronological order and placing them at the end of the saga to make a miracle collection. These are the very topics focused on in *Geisli*, the twelfth-century skaldic praise poem on St Olaf that Magnús adds to the beginning of the book. *Geisli* provides a digest, in highly memorable poetic form, of the miracles of this king chosen by God, from whom all subsequent Norwegian rulers were said to hold the realm in fief. The *catena* of filiation in *Nóregs konungatal* is supplemented by *Geisli*, at the beginning of Flateyjarbók. *Geisli* shows how God's plan plays out in the world of human, fleshly engendering, which operated in the generations down from Haraldr *hárfagri* to produce Norway's saint-king, whose relationship to those who come after him is not merely carnal, but also spiritual and feudal.

This leaves unexplained the presence of *Hyndluljóð*, an eddic exercise in mythic and legendary genealogy recounted by the giantess Hyndla to the goddess Freyja and her protégé Óttarr. Why on earth did Magnús decide to include it, as the last of three poems in his frame? In the course of *Hyndluljóð*, Óttarr turns out to be related to absolutely everybody who's anybody in heroic legend, and Hyndla's repeated assurance that "all of that is your family, silly Óttarr!" ("*allt er þat ætt þín, Óttarr heimski*") starts to sound almost embarrassed.[91] *Hyndluljóð*'s expansive genealogies push the claim of fleshly kinship to the point of absurdity. Carnality, rather than blood, was the key metaphor of kinship for medieval Christians.[92] Like blood, flesh implies generation, but also ruin, decay, and death. In *Ynglingatal* the king's dead flesh is a nodal point tying narrative to the landscape and the ruins of human habitation. For Christian believers, the significance of the flesh lay in its transcendence by spirit. Flesh alone could never triumph over the ravages of time; a Norwegian homilist quotes the biblical commonplace that "every flesh is as grass" ("*hvert hold er sem gras*").[93] Jón Þórðarson says, in his epilogue to *Eiríks saga víðfǫrla*, that the Norsemen's pagan ancestors, living before the revelation of God's truth, have only earthly fame, while Christians

> when they have gone forth through the door of death, common to all, as no flesh can avoid, they will have come into possession of their reward, that is to say, eternal rule without end with almighty God.[94]

Allt er þat ætt þín, Óttarr heimski!—all that, but nothing more.

I have argued in this chapter against the received opinion that *kviðuháttr* poems such as *Ynglingatal* and *Nóregs konungatal* belong to an ancient and deep-rooted Germanic genre of "genealogical poetry." Both poems are catenulate, as is most poetry in *kviðuháttr*, for reasons I explore in the conclusion to Part I below. But their links are forged from different substances. *Ynglingatal* constructs a spatial mnemonic, where the kings' dead bodies make sites of memory and live on in local place-lore. *Nóregs konungatal* shares an interest in filiation and chronological reckoning with the emerging written historiographical tradition. In its fourteenth-century transmission context in Flateyjarbók, *Nóregs konungatal* works as a *précis* of the material that comes before *Sverris saga*. There its logic of genealogical filiation is subsumed in Magnús's larger frame, within which the merely carnal relatedness of the pagan legendary heroes of *Hyndluljóð* perishes at that door of death which "no flesh can avoid," while the spiritual kinship of Christian believers endures.

STONE—STANZA—MEMORY

The inscription on the Rök runestone resists the intelligence of modern interpreters, almost successfully. In 2003 Helmer Gustavson listed forty previous interpretations, and another half dozen have appeared since.[1] When Gustavson was writing, a consensus had formed around Elias Wessén's 1958 construal—there was, at least, agreement on the transcription of the runes and order in which they should be read.[2] Most commentators also agreed with Wessén's view that the inscription consisted of a series of compressed, riddling references to heroic narrative.[3] In the mid-2000s the Swedish linguist Bo Ralph, and following him Per Holmberg, attempted to upset this applecart, how successfully is not yet clear.[4] According to them the inscription is self-referential and consists of a single extended riddle about the conditions under which its signs can be read, with no stanza and no references to heroic legend: "exit Theoderik," Ralph concludes.[5] The entering wedge for the Ralph school's attack is that the standard interpretation assumes Rök is different from every other runestone and so offends against the convention-driven pragmatics of inscriptional communication. However, Rök is self-evidently different from other runestones—as discussed above, the inscription is unique in its length and technical complexity.[6] Another, more serious, objection to their construal is that Ralph and Holmberg ignore its similarities to *Ynglingatal*. From Henrik Schück on, parallels in phrasing have been taken to indicate that the Rök inscription bears witness to a Swedish poem on the Ynglings, from which *Ynglingatal* also derives more or less directly.[7] As is by now apparent, I do not believe it is feasible to reconstruct literary pre-forms for these monuments in any detail, and my view on their possible precursors is also different from Schück's. Nonetheless, I agree with the conventional wisdom that *Ynglingatal* and Rök are alike in many ways, some of which I will now explore.

In the reading order proposed by Wessén, the Rök stone's inscription steadily increases in complexity from beginning to end. Its script shifts from short-twig runes in the sixteen-character *fuþark*, to the archaic twenty-four-character *fuþark*, then alphabetical and numerical ciphers. Its layout morphs from parallel lines on the front face, through a frame or spiral layout on the back, to cipher runes arranged in cross shapes uppermost. The inscription also increasingly departs from conventional runestone formulae. It begins with a raiser formula, carved in larger runes, but soon opens out into a highly complex prosimetric text of a kind unparalleled in any other runic inscription. All who have studied the stone concur on its exceptional complexity and challenge, and the supreme technical skill shown by its carver. In an arresting phrase, Gun Widmark calls the stone "a kind of robot," a *þulr*-golem intended to repeat its praise of Vamoð automatically throughout eternity.[8] The new medium's ability to transform transient, embodied oral performance into colossal, eternal material form must have seemed almost magical to its first audiences.[9]

Pressure from more sophisticated and highly organized societies to the west and south may have played a role in Rök's quantum leap in complexity compared to the curt, anonymous utterances of the earlier South Scandinavian runestone tradition.[10] A similar emulation of Frankish memorial practice has been argued to have played a decisive role in an earlier step-change in funeral practice on the frontier. In the early seventh century, barrows, some richly furnished, were constructed in England, the Rhineland, southern Scandinavia, and northern Switzerland. These are often interpreted as vigorous assertions of pagan identity in the face of advancing Christianity, but John Blair proposes instead that assimilation and imitation of the monumental architecture of Francia—in particular, of the church, that impressive, memory-safeguarding innovation in funerary practice—were the driving forces behind this change:

> Both the date and distribution of these barrows are important: they appeared around the fringes of Christian Francia, and they did so well after the adoption of church burial by royal and some noble Franks. So they are not relics of entrenched pagan practice, even if one purpose of them was to manufacture links with an imagined past suggested by prehistoric barrows. Rather, they share with other signs of the times a striving for a monumental expression of status, achieved in more developed cultures by means of funerary churches, above-ground sarcophagi, and tomb-sculpture.[11]

By virtue of its sheer size and prominence, the monolith at Rök mediates memory, building a place in the landscape for the person for whom it was erected, in the same way *Ynglingatal*'s ruins, stones, and mounds did. Rök is, to use Blair's terms, a "monumental expression of status" in the crowded memorial landscape of central Sweden, and as such a worthy successor to the barrows of Gamla Uppsala. Like *Ynglingatal*, it makes a powerful claim of mediation: to be able to gather oral memories from near and far, link them to prestigious memory places, and claim them for its dedicatee.[12] Unusually, the Rök inscription begins with the person to be commemorated, Vamoð: "After Vamoð stand these runes" (*Aft Vamoð standa runar þar*).[13] *Ynglingatal*, at least in the form we have it, ends with Rǫgnvaldr. The dedicatee is emphasized at the threshold of both works. The claim of mediation acquires a cutting edge in these dedications, revealing the radical nature of the maker's move to affix communal memories to the name of his patron.

The stanza on the Rök stone is thought by most recent commentators to refer to the equestrian statue of Theoderic the Great, moved from Ravenna to Aachen by Charlemagne in the year 801—a material link to the Carolingian world:[14]

> (first line on front side) **raiþiaurikʀhinþurmuþistiliʀ**
> (second line on front side) **flutnastrąntuhraiþmaraʀsitiʀnukarurą**
> (third line, on right edge) **kutasinumskialtiubfatlaþʀskatimarika**
> Reð Þioðrikʀ
> hinn þormoði,
> stilliʀ flutna,
> strandu Hraiðmaraʀ;
> Sitiʀ nu garuʀ
> a guta sinum,
> skialdi umb fatlaðʀ,
> skati Mæringa.
> (Theoderic, bold leader of sea-warriors, ruled over the coast of the Hreið Sea; now he sits on his (Gothic) horse, with shield fastened, prince of the Mærings.)[15]

Walahfrid Strabo's poem *De imagine Tetrici* (829 CE), in part a highly complex ekphrasis of the statue in Aachen, represents the clerical view of Theoderic as heretical persecutor of orthodox believers, but this cannot have been how Charlemagne understood him. Although no other Carolingian text mentions the statue—perhaps because it clashed with the negative clerical image of Theoderic—the fact that Charlemagne had it transported and erected before his palace suggests that he understood Theoderic as an ideal.[16]

For the emperor, who named one of his illegitimate sons Theoderic, the Gothic king probably exemplified ancient kingship in the heroic mould of the legendary Dietrich of Bern, whom a lively vernacular narrative tradition identified with Theoderic. This tradition was dominant in Scandinavia, and its echoes are preserved in *Karlamagnús saga* and *Guðrúnarkviða III*. The sculpture also connected Aachen with Rome, where an equestrian statue thought in Charlemagne's time to represent Constantine stood before the Lateran palace, and with Constantinople, where an equestrian statue of Justinian stood on the Augusteion between the Chalke gate and Hagia Sophia.[17]

Rök's stanza continues this citational chain: just as the equestrian statue enabled Charlemagne to connect Aachen and Rome, so did Rök's stanza link Östergötland with Francia, evoking both the heroic past and the impressive monumental ensemble at Aachen. It has often been compared to *Ynglingatal* due to its contrastive rhetoric of past versus present. Poem and runestone also share the rhetorical move of anchoring memories of the distant past in material objects. As the Rök inscription tells us, the stone is a surface on which pre-existing memorial practices are gathered, whose medium was oral performance and which were remembered and performed by the group (if the reading **sakumukmini**, "We tell a folk-memory," is correct).[18] In the robotic voice of Varin, the stone claims to re-mediate these traditions, capturing and enclosing traditional material in a discourse which is emphatically noncollective, authored, and associated with the praise of a particular contemporary figure.

For Rök, this new medium is runic writing, on the brink of exploding into ubiquity in Viking Age Sweden, while for *Ynglingatal* it is authored, stanzaic poetry. By another strange overlap between these two *sui generis* objects, the link may be still closer than that. For Rök's stanza, often cited as the earliest extant piece of *fornyrðislag*, has been suggested by several metrists to in fact be in an incipient form of *kviðuháttr*.[19] This would make the Rök stanza the earliest attestation of a syllable-counting meter in Scandinavia. Kari Gade argues that *kviðuháttr* originated from the regularization of already existent patterns in common Germanic alliterative meter, under the pressure of the phonological changes that took place in Proto-Nordic.[20] The Rök stanza, with its mixture of forms, parachutes us into this lengthy process of phonological change somewhere near its end.[21] Syncope, or the deletion of short unstressed vowels (e.g. "garuʀ" < *gǫrr*, "sitiʀ" < *sitr*), was a particularly consequential change from the point of view of prosody, as it vastly increased the language's inventory of monosyllabic words. Line 1 (in Old Norse normalization, *Réð Þjódrekr*) is clearly trisyllabic, and line 5, *Sitir nu garur*, would be trisyllabic after syncopation (*sitr nú gǫrr*), while the remaining lines are tetrasyllabic, in *fornyrðislag* patterns.[22] If this analysis is correct, it means that the lines emphasized by catalexis are those at the beginning of each quatrain. In an orally performed poem, Christoph März suggests, the opening line has an equivalent function to the title or preface in a written text, as a given metrical form recalls earlier works in the same meter and so suggests a particular content: "every form communicates, so to speak, with its own past."[23] The first and fifth lines also mark the building blocks of the stanza. The stanza is most commonly realized in *fornyrðislag* and *kviðuháttr* as a sequence of quatrains.[24] It represents a key innovation of the Old Norse poetic system in relation to the common Germanic alliterative tradition.[25] Quatrain organization is stringently observed in *Ynglingatal*.[26] Put together, syllable-counting plus stanzaic organization make up a formidable mnemonic technology, and as such mark decisively the potential of the new medium.

The Rök inscription thus represents, in compressed form and inscriptional medium, a comparable historical nexus to *Ynglingatal*, another early colossus exquisitely conscious of its own innovativeness. This nexus consists of, in the first place, a new kind of speaking voice, enabled by a new medium, that acts as guarantor of the statements made. In *Ynglingatal*, this is the first-person speaker, *ek*, the skald, in the tradition given the name of Þjóðólfr, who acts as a conduit for information from distant times, places, and performers. In the Rök inscription, it is the voice of the stone. Secondly, both stone and poem claim to mediate cultural memory of the deep past, in *Ynglingatal* via references to local legends of "death in place," in the Rök inscription by the repeated element **sakumukmini** ("We tell a folk-memory" or "we say to the young men"). And thirdly, both refer to commemorative monuments as the material anchors of this mediating process: in *Ynglingatal*, the grave mounds, death sites, and funeral sites, and in the Rök inscription, the statue of Theoderic. By numbering its sections, the Rök inscription also signals that it sees itself as a *tal* (list). The substance that binds the chain of stories together is memory itself. The poet's aspiration to claim these memories for a particular patron is what links *Ynglingatal*'s kings together, rather than genealogy.

Many aspects of the Rök inscription are surely destined to remain obscure. The inscription's immense time-depth, stretching from the past that it remembers, through the changes in the monolith's status, use, and surroundings over the past thousand or so years, guarantee that—as, still more, does its maker's active desire to produce an enigma. Yet even stripped of references to Theoderic, Aachen, "folk-memory" and all the rest, a basic similarity to *Ynglingatal* is evident. At a minimum, stone and poem can be understood as ambitious early claims to capture collective memories in a durable medium and put them to work for a particular person. Because, from our perspective, *Ynglingatal* and Rök stand at the beginnings of their traditions, it is impossible to know with certainty what kind of material their makers drew on. Only the uses that later skalds and rune carvers made of these early innovations are clear. In the cultural practices that follow in their wake, of the skald as eyewitness guarantor of communicative memory, and the runestone raiser as focus of the inscription, the novel claims that *Ynglingatal* and the Rök stone make become normalized and transparent.

Plate 1. Rök runestone, Östergötland, Sweden (Ög 136), 9th century. The stanza on Theoderic begins in the horizontal lines at the bottom of the front face.

Plate 2. Viking Age stone setting at Aspa, Södermanland, Sweden.

Plate 3. Portrait of Charles the Bald. Codex Aureus of St Emmeram (BSB Clm 14000, c. 879, Munich, Bayerische Staatsbibliothek), fol. 5v.

Plate 4. Round silver niello brooch decorated with puzzle pictures from Jämjö, Öland, Sweden, Viking Age (cat. no. SHM 13534).

Plate 5. Wooden sculpture, probably of Saami origin, from Sundborn, Dalarna, Sweden, c. 1500 (cat. no. DM 4650).

Plate 6. Gylfi's encounter with High, Just-as-High and Third. Codex Upsaliensis (DG 11 4to, c. 1300-1325, Uppsala, Uppsala universitetsbibliotek, fol. 26v).

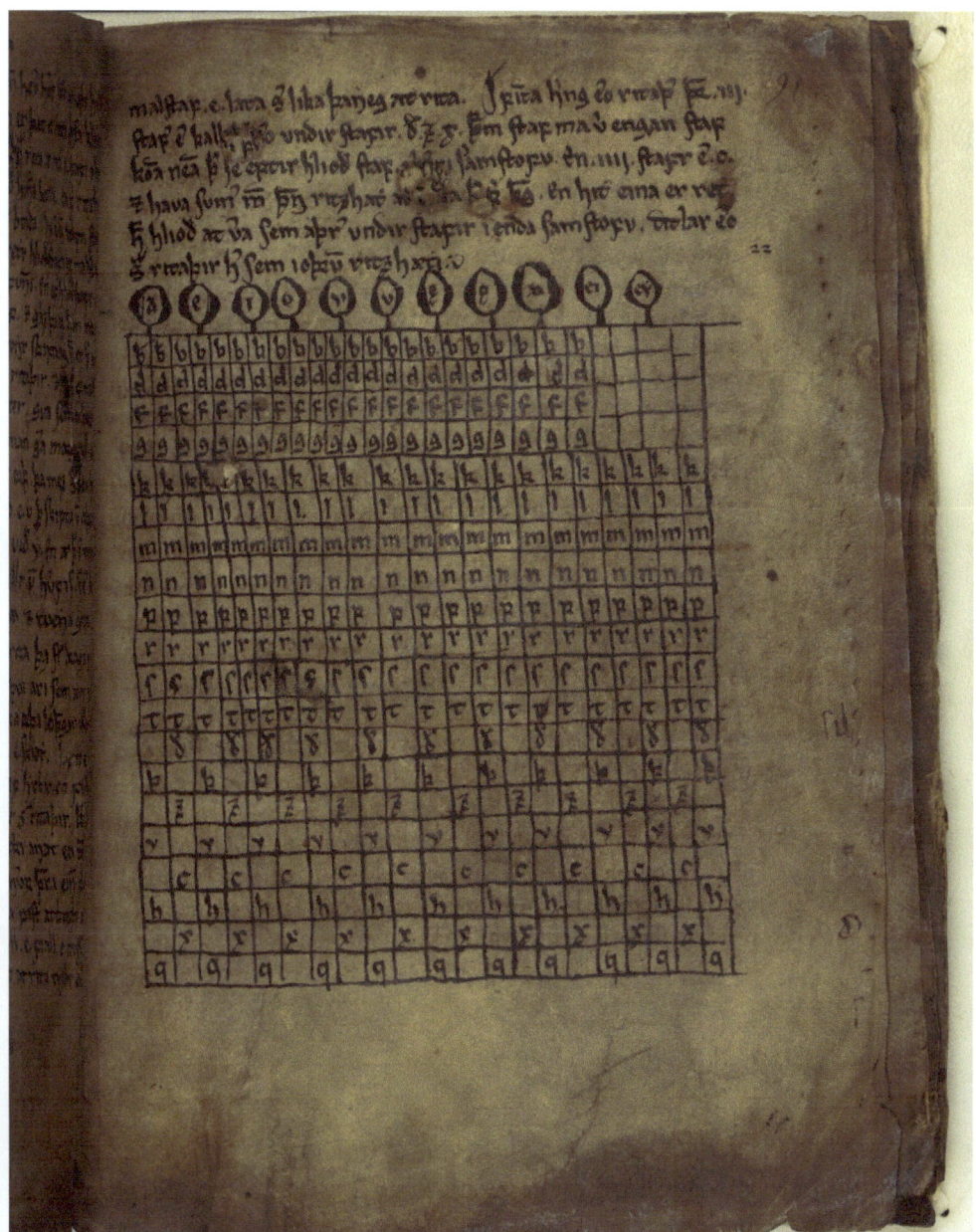

Plate 7. The rectangular diagram from the *Second Grammatical Treatise*. Codex Upsaliensis (DG 11 4to, c. 1300–1325, Uppsala, Uppsala universitetsbibliotek, fol. 46r).

Plate 8. The circular diagram from the *Second Grammatical Treatise*. Codex Upsaliensis (DG 11 4to, c. 1300–1325, Uppsala, Uppsala universitetsbibliotek, fol. 45r).

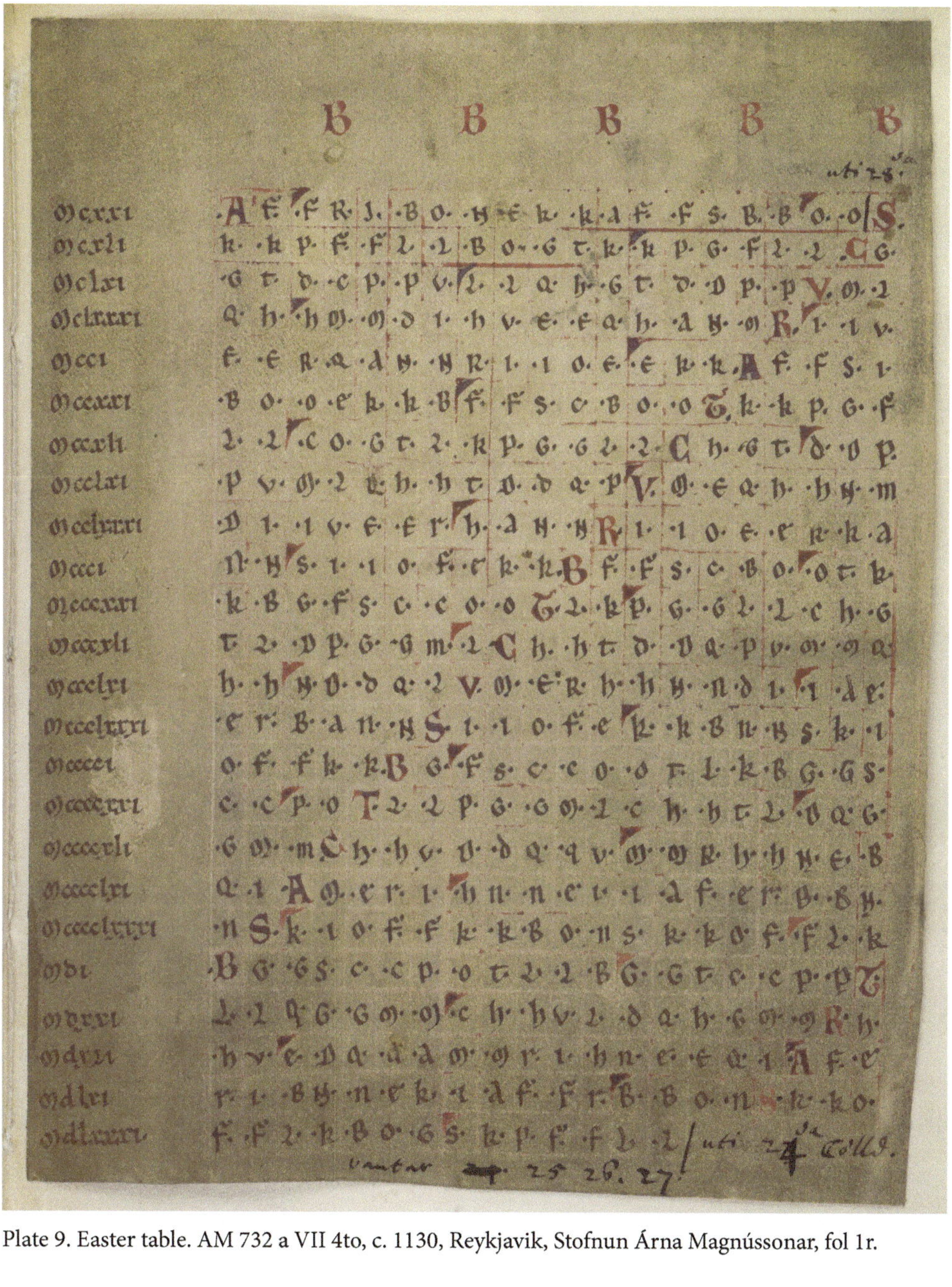

Plate 9. Easter table. AM 732 a VII 4to, c. 1130, Reykjavik, Stofnun Árna Magnússonar, fol 1r.

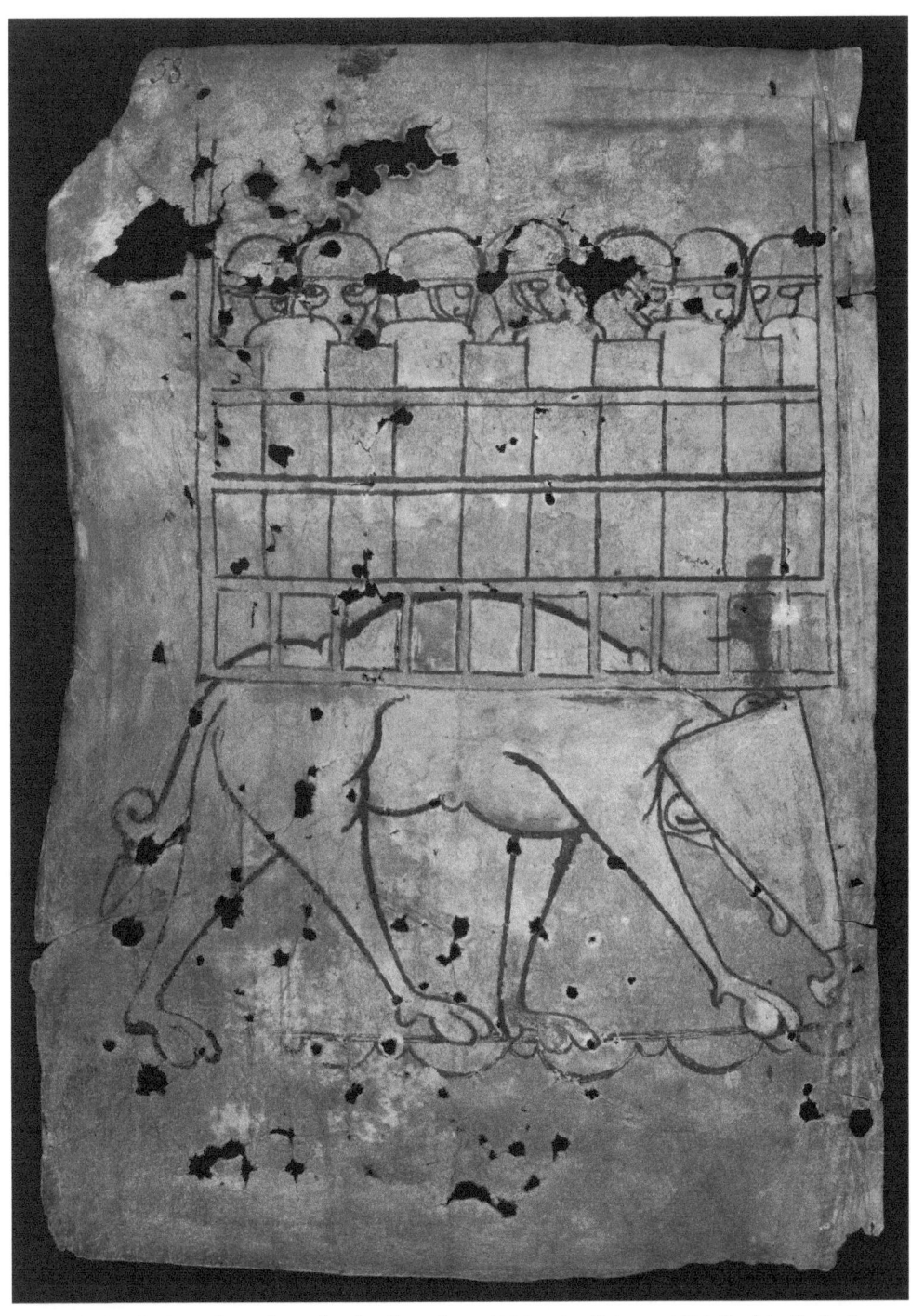

Plate 10. The elephant from the Icelandic *Physiologus* (AM 673 a II 4to, c. 1200, Reykjavik, Stofnun Árna Magnússonar, fol 7v).

PART 2

SEEING THINGS

CHAPTER 3
THE VIKING EYE

Mental images—percepts, visions, memories—feature prominently in the next two chapters. There is a practical reason for this: no figurally decorated shield like those apparently described in skaldic picture poems survives from premodern Scandinavia. Rather than bemoaning this absence, I propose shifting the points and traveling on a new track, by asking instead what *mental* images these poems summon up. Any sense of such mental images must, of course, be based on actual objects, but I will argue that the skaldic picture poems are more revealing of Viking Age practices of visual interpretation than they are of images on lost shields.

Media support and convey images; they are what enable images to be transmitted to the mind. No mere interchangeable supports, certain media are closely correlated with certain kinds of images. According to the art historian Hans Belting, learning to discriminate between the image and its medium is one of the competencies that founds the cognitive activity of looking.[1] This is also true of the specific case of reading. Acquiring information from a codex demands a learned ability to segment the physical space of the vellum page and draw distinctions between the skin and what is inscribed on it. It is an allied practice to looking at a picture, where the viewer must also learn to distinguish figure from ground. In Scandinavia, the advent of writing and the rise of the narrative image seem to be contemporary phenomena, as I have argued elsewhere.[2] This suggests that readings of the picture poems should focus on the Viking Age media contemporary to the poems, which typically bear descriptive, not narrative images.[3] Media also enable a politics of the image, because "mediality usually is controlled by institutions and serves the interests of political power."[4] It is not by chance that the things skaldic picture poems describe are media of power: shields, warships, and halls in secular skaldic poetry; shrines, churches, and crosses in the Christian devotional material. Finally, the entanglement of image, text, and medium implies that the mediality of the vellum page, and the hierarchically structured paratextual system that assists in its decoding, are vital elements of the meaning of these poems in a manuscript culture, as will become clear in Chapter 4.

Sight enjoyed high status in medieval western Europe, as a sensory modality closely linked to knowledge and, in the visionary experience of "seeing God," to the divine.[5] Well-documented shifts over time in the classification and hierarchy of the senses demonstrate the historical distinctiveness of sensory regimes.[6] While the physiological underpinnings of the senses are biologically determined and so may be taken as cross-culturally universal, the way that sense perceptions are experienced, described, and interpreted is not. This distinction can be expressed as a contrast between "vision" and "visuality," which "signals a difference within the visual—between the mechanism of sight and its historical techniques, between the datum of vision and its discursive determinations—a difference, many differences, among how we see, how we are able, allowed, or made to see, and how we see this seeing or the unseen therein."[7] Reading premodern poetry that represents visual experience thus involves reckoning with a historically situated visuality, what might be termed the "Viking eye."[8]

SKALDIC PICTURE POEMS

The *Ragnarsdrápa* (Ragnarr's Poem, 9th c.), attributed to Bragi Boddason, is thought to be the oldest of a group of *dróttkvætt* poems known as "picture-describing poems" (*billedbeskrivende dikt*).[9] Ten stanzas are preserved in *Skáldskaparmál*, as two extended quotations, and attributed there to a poem named *Ragnarsdrápa*, by Bragi, about Ragnarr *loðbrók* (hairy-breeches).[10] The first set describes the death of the Gothic king Jǫrmunrekkr and has a refrain stating that this story is depicted on a shield. The second concerns the legendary princess Hildr and her role in the Everlasting Battle, or *Hjaðningavíg*, and also includes a refrain mentioning a shield. Two further half-stanzas are attributed to Bragi elsewhere in *Skáldskaparmál* to exemplify shield-kennings and are included in *Ragnarsdrápa* by editors. A further six half-stanzas (*helmingar*), edited separately from *Ragnarsdrápa* under the title *Þórr's fishing* in the most recent edition, concern Þórr's fishing up of the Midgard Serpent.[11] They are cited individually in *Skáldskaparmál* to exemplify kenning types and do not specifically refer to a shield or any other visual representation. They do share formal features such as a strong emphasis on seeing and the presence of the keyword *kenna* with the stanzas that *Skáldskaparmál* attributes to *Ragnarsdrápa*. Possibly they are indeed part of the same poem, as earlier editors took them to be.

Þjóðólfr of Hvin's *Haustlǫng* (Autumn-Long, c. 900) is also quoted *in extenso* in two sets of stanzas in *Skáldskaparmál*.[12] One set recounts Óðinn, Hœnir, and Loki's encounter with the giant Þjazi. The other describes Þórr's fight with the giant Hrungnir. Each group of stanzas includes at least one instance of the refrain, which mentions a gift of a shield.

A third skaldic picture poem, Úlfr Uggason's *Húsdrápa* (House Poem, c. 980), is a later, Icelandic production, and apparently about a decorated hall rather than a gift of a shield.[13] It is also the only one of these three poems whose performance is described in a medieval source. *Laxdœla saga* reports as follows on a building project of Óláfr *pái* (peacock) Hǫskuldsson at Hjarðarholt in western Iceland in the late tenth century:

> That summer Olaf had a fire-hall built at Hjardarholt which was larger and grander than men had ever seen before. On the wood of the gables, and the rafters, excellent tales were carved. It was so well crafted that it was thought more ornamental without the tapestries than with them [. . .] Geirmundr was then engaged to Thurid, and their wedding was held later that winter at Hjardarholt. A great number of people attended the feast as the fire-hall was finished by that time. Among the guests was a poet, Ulf Uggason, who had composed a poem about Olaf Hoskuldsson and the tales carved on the wood of the fire-hall which he recited at the feast. It is called House Drapa and is a fine piece of verse.[14]

Laxdœla saga does not quote from *Húsdrápa*, or indeed from any of the other skaldic long poems it mentions. As is the case for the other two poems, the stanzas assigned by editors to *Húsdrápa* (twelve half-stanzas and one full stanza) are transmitted only in *Skáldskaparmál*, cited piecemeal in lists exemplifying kennings and *heiti*. The resulting poem has three subjects: Þórr's fishing up of the Midgard Serpent, the funeral of Baldr, and Heimdallr's fight with Loki at Singasteinn. *Skáldskaparmál*'s prose notes that Úlfr composed "a long section" and "for a long time" (*langt skeið/langa stund*) about Baldr and about Heimdallr's fight with Loki at Singasteinn respectively, but (as is the case for *Ragnarsdrápa*) it does not say anything about the *helmingar* on Þórr, leaving it to editors to decide whether this material is part of the poem.[15]

The fact that all three compositions are cited in *Skáldskaparmál* suggests that they were thought to be important works, suitable to exemplify the skaldic art for young poets—a point to which I will return in Chapter 4. Perhaps their reflections on the imagistic potential of the skaldic form were also already appreciated in the thirteenth century. The Norwegian philologist Hallvard Lie recognized this self-reflexive aspect in his studies of the skaldic picture poems.[16] *Ragnarsdrápa* forms the centerpiece of Lie's argument that *dróttkvætt*'s complexly interwoven syntax had its origins in "a certain culturally and historically determined will to form [*kunstvilje*]" that is also reflected in the interlace style of Viking Age animal art.[17] Lie's idea of *kunstvilje* is indebted to the Austrian art historian Alois Riegl, who in his influential book on the late Roman art industry conceived of *Kunstwollen* as the symptomatic imprint of a particular age across multiple artistic forms.[18] Lie espoused the idea of *kunstvilje* against the then-popular claim that *dróttkvætt*'s involuted style was little more than a side effect of its extreme metrical demands. Rather, he argued, interlace is a formal goal of a particular historical moment, common to different art forms and realized in the medium specific to each. Part of his argument concerns visuality, and as such opens a rich field of enquiry, which I will explore—along a different line than that of interlace—in this chapter. Lie's claim that a certain Viking Age *kunstvilje* explains the riddle of the skaldic form's origins, on the other hand, is so abstract as to be unfalsifiable, and his work has tended to be mentioned respectfully, rather than taken up, in subsequent research.[19]

In search of an explanation for the phenomenon of skaldic picture poems, recent researchers have instead adopted the term "ekphrasis." Until the mid-twentieth century this word appeared only in discussions of Hellenistic and Byzantine rhetoric, usually in footnotes, but its popularity rapidly increased and reached escape velocity in the early 1990s.[20] An immense secondary literature now exists, discussing ekphrasis in fields of literary study ranging from ancient Greek and Roman epic and oratory, through medieval epic and romance, classical Arabic lyric, early modern art criticism, the novel, and Romantic and Modernist poetry, as well as in art history and interarts studies. Old Norse has not been left out, with a flurry of publications in the 2000s. These focused on three main themes: the possible influence of Carolingian ekphrastic poetry on skaldic texts, comparison between the picture poems and other textual and visual evidence for the same narratives, and the pragmatics of the skald-patron interaction.[21]

These studies rely, more or less explicitly, on J. A. W. Heffernan's definition of ekphrasis as "the verbal representation of graphic representation."[22]

Ekphrasis is then illustration in reverse, and its scholarly interpretation involves "match[ing . . .] the iconographic particulars of an image with the details of a text."[23] This procedure is driven by a "logocentric assumption that the visual can be reduced to the verbal—that an image can communicate a text, and that a text can unlock the meaning of an image."[24] This both renders the poem epiphenomenal—why would a patron value such a verbal equivalent?—and elides thinking about visuality in favor of textual interpretation. Circularity threatens too, as the poems are compared to the *Prose Edda*'s versions of mythic and legendary narrative, several hundred years younger than the poems and partly based on information drawn from them. In studies of classical Greek and Roman material, a preoccupation with the reality of the artworks that ekphraseis purport to describe is the hallmark of nineteenth-century positivism, and few now attempt to reconstruct these objects.[25] Earlier reckonings with the skaldic picture poems used hypotheses about visual sources to explain away textual cruces and proposed lost stanza-sequences based on ideas of symmetry, or how many images would fit on a shield-board.[26] Such arbitrary arguments have been abandoned in more recent research, but the new interdisciplinary study of skaldic ekphrasis remains committed to a referential mode of reading focusing on shields and halls.[27]

IN SEARCH OF LOST SHIELDS

As well as these methodological issues, a referential reading of the ekphraseis confronts a practical problem. We know next to nothing about the notorious shields. Iron bosses, handgrips, and rims from Viking Age shields have survived, but the shield boards themselves, made of vulnerable wooden planks, are rare finds. The little that has survived of the shields' decoration, which was painted or incised on the shield board or its leather cover, bears witness to geometric rather than figurative ornament.[28] Fragments of a ninth-century shield from Ballateare, Isle of Man, are painted in a pattern of red dots and black stripes parallel to the rim on a white ground.[29] Around sixty shields, painted alternately black and yellow, were preserved along the rail of the Gokstad ship (850–900 CE).[30] A tenth-century shield found at Trelleborg, Denmark, has holes around its edge for securing a cover, and tiny fragments of leather with traces of red and white pigment survive.[31] Perhaps the most promising find is from a mid-tenth-century equestrian chamber grave from Grimstrup in Denmark. It includes an organic layer covering the deceased from cranium to pelvis, and bearing small fragments of a narrow interlaced-band pattern with dotting in black, gray-green, white, and red pigments, which could be interpreted as a shield board. The excavators urge caution, however, noting that they found no traces of a shield rim or boss, that shields are rare in equestrian graves, and that the shape and dimensions of the organic layer could have resulted from partial decomposition of a painted ceiling.[32]

Nor does the iconography of shields in art from the period include, as far as I know, a single instance of a figurally decorated shield.[33] Virtually none of the shields mentioned in eddic and skaldic encomiastic poetry have decoration more complex than a single color, usually white or red.[34] Figurally decorated shields appear often in sagas, on the other hand. The verbs used in these prose ekphraseis are drawn from a rich lexis denoting writing, inscribing, image-making, and committing to memory: *skrifa* ("write, draw, paint, embroider, carve"), *fá* ("inscribe, draw, paint"), *ríta/rita* ("write, draw"), *rísta/rista* ("carve, engrave"), *draga* ("paint, decorate, overlay"), and *marka* ("draw, fix, mark with an emblem, impress upon the mind"). This pattern bears witness to a culture in which images and texts are analogized in many diverse ways but rarely diametrically opposed to one another in the way that Heffernan's definition would demand.

In a tirelessly cited passage, Egill Skallagrímsson receives a shield "adorned with legends, and between the carvings [...] overlaid with gold and embossed with jewels" (*skrifaðr fornsǫgum, en allt milli skriptanna váru lagðar yfir spengr af gulli, ok settr steinum*; *Egils saga* ch. 81) from his fellow poet Einarr skálaglamm (scale-tinkle), and decides to kill him to avoid composing a poem about it.[35] More restrained shields appear in *Færeyinga saga*, where three men in a raiding party carry a particolored (*hálflitr*) dark blue and yellow shield, a red shield, and a red shield "with a person painted on it" (*dreginn á mannfái*) respectively. Bevers, the Norse version of Bevis of Hampton, carries a shield adorned (*skrifut*) with a lion (*Bevers saga* ch. 7; one redaction adds "in gold"), as does Kári Sǫlmundarson (*Njáls saga* ch. 92), although the verb used is again *draga*. In romances whole booksful of learned history can be portrayed on the hero's shield. *Alexanders saga* reports that Darius' shield is seven layers thick, "[over]laid" (*lagðr*) with the obligatory gold, and adorned (*skrifaðr*) with the deeds of his ancestors (except for the shameful ones), including the building of the Tower of Babel, Nebuchadnezzar's expedition to Jerusalem, and Balthasar seeing the writing on the wall.

The romance hero Vilhjálmr *sjóðr* ("pouch") receives a shield, from a giant, decorated (*skrifut*) with the stories of Jason and Alexander; like Egill's, it is "[over]laid with gold and set with gems" (*gulli lagdan og gimsteinum settann*; *Vilhjálms saga sjóðs* ch. 7), albeit more lavishly: "a thousand marks of gold were on the shield, and gemstones worth yet more." Sigurðr *Fáfnisbani*, as befits his status and well-developed iconography, bears a shield that is particolored, gold-plated, and decorated with his *own* heroic deeds: "His ornamented [*var.* multilayered] shield was plated with red gold and emblazoned [*skrifaðr*] with a dragon. Its top half was dark brown and its bottom half light red [...] the dragon was illustrated [*markaðr*] on all his arms, so that when he was seen, all who had heard the story would recognize him as the one who had killed the great dragon called Fafnir by the Væringr."[36] Hildibrandr in *Ásmundar saga kappabana* (ch. 9) also bears this autobiographical kind of shield, "on which are marked (*markaðir*) as many men as he had killed." The same shield is mentioned in a verse quoted in the saga (Hildibrandr *Lv* 3), where the verb used is, exceptionally, "counted" (*eru þar taldir*), and we are told that the victims number eighty. It is interesting that Hildibrandr's verse, probably the earliest source for the motif, does not specify a pictorial representation, but rather suggests tally-marks or notches. Saxo exuberantly embroiders the description of Hildibrandr's shield, reporting that the "Swedish shield" (*clypeus Sueticus*) displays the unfortunate dead warriors "depicted in colorful art" (*multicolor pictura notat*), surrounding a portrait (!)[37]

Saga shields are kin to the emblematic objects of Continental romance, many of them also shields, and like them they function as "text-internal projection screens" that reflect and concentrate the narrative in a smaller compass.[38] The similarity of Egill's shield to romantic confections such as Vilhjálmr's provokes skepticism about the reliability of the shield description in *Egils saga*. The former's painted decorations soon disappear from view in any case. After reluctantly composing a poem (whose single surviving stanza I will discuss below), Egill takes the decorated shield with him on a trip where it gets damaged and is thrown into a whey-vat. Only the mounts survive, and Egill has them removed and valued for their weight in gold (a mere twelve ounces). Dissolved soon after the first performance of the poem that describes it, *Egils saga*'s legendary shield stands metonymically for the artworks described in the picture poems.

Focusing on what appeared on the vanished shields is not only methodologically questionable; it is also impractical. Yet if not by means of comparison, then how to give the visual its due? What makes a picture poem different from one that simply narrates the Hjaðningavíg, or Þórr's fishing trip? In other words, what is ekphrasis for? This question will have varying answers in different epochs and genres. As mentioned above, ekphrasis in medieval romance has a distinct, emblematic purpose. Carolingian Latin ekphrasis, although close to the skalds in time and space, is composed in a very different medial and social context and is not strongly reminiscent of skaldic poetry. Ekphrasis in modernist poetry—John Ashbery's 1975 meditation on Parmigianino's *Portrait in a convex mirror*, for example—has a different set of concerns again, the poetic speaker responding to the innovation of a fellow artist, eruditely reflecting on art-historical tradition and questioning the idea of authentic self-representation.

To use a concept like ekphrasis it thus needs to be historicized. I propose doing so in two steps. The first is to examine the accounts of ekphrasis in antique Greek and Roman rhetorical theory. Ekphrasis is not mentioned in the Norse grammatical treatises, so reflective statements on it must be sought elsewhere.[39] Discussions of ekphrasis in ancient rhetorical handbooks offer an obvious starting point for analyzing the skaldic picture poems, because Viking Age skalds, like antique forensic orators, worked in a highly competitive performance culture that valued the ability to persuade, although it is likely that non-Western traditions of orally performed poetry—medieval Arabic, for example—would also yield illuminating comparative data.[40] The second step is to interrogate the historically situated visuality of Viking and medieval Scandinavia, or "Viking eye."

WHAT WAS EKPHRASIS FOR?

The Greek verb *ekphrázein* simply means "to describe [*phrázein*] completely [*ek-*]."[41] The *Progymnasmata*, preliminary exercises for Greek students of rhetoric of the first to fifth centuries CE, admitted a wide range of subject matter for ekphrastic description, including people, places, times, battles, plants, animals, and festivals. What made ekphrasis distinctive for ancient rhetoricians was not its relationship to the visual arts, but its effect on its audience, summed up in the word *enargeia* ("clarity, vividness"). Quintilian defines *enargeia* in his *Institutio oratoria* ("The orator's education," first century CE) as a quality "by which we seem to show [*ostendere*] what happened rather than to tell [*dicere*] it; and this gives rise to the same emotions as if we were present at the event itself."[42] It animates speech, making it seem "as if alive."[43] According to Quintilian, descriptions imbued with *enargeia* "penetrate the emotions" and "display [the subject] to the mind's eye."[44] There is, furthermore, a close association between visualization and memory: memories can take the form of visual images, and imagination has memorial images as its raw material. The subject matter of ekphrasis is only subject to limitation insofar as it is able to foster the desired vividness: "in order to be effective [...] enargeia, and thus ekphrasis itself, must [...] be a re-presentation of familiar and accepted material—it is this very familiarity which gives the speech its evocative and emotive power."[45] The forensic orator using ekphrastic techniques "prompt[s] his audience to re-enact internally the act of seeing such a sight, and therefore to achieve an approximation of what an actual witness might have felt."[46]

Three main points can be taken from the ancient rhetoricians' account of ekphrasis. The first is their emphasis on effect on the audience. *Enargeia* is the goal of ekphrasis: a discourse that penetrates the listener's mind and "produces a viewing subject."[47] It is a technology of the emotions, serving the persuasive aim of the orator. The second is that ekphrastic performance aims to evoke a subject-matter, not a particular artwork. Culturally central narratives bore significance that went far beyond any single representation of them made by a craftsman.[48] An audience member listening to an ekphrasis *envisions* in their mind's eye the conventional imagery associated with a canonical subject. The highly conventional nature of visual representation before the era of art means that "the extent to which [the poetic speaker] rhetorizes a particular viewpoint [is] all the more conspicuous to a reader acquainted with visual representations of the myth."[49] A space opens between narrative and image, into which the skald can insert himself. The third is that ekphrasis' lively evocation of visuality—the shape, color and movement that the skaldic picture poems stress in their refrains—made it well-suited for evoking the presence of the supersensory, or the divine. The oscillation between representation and presence at the heart of epiphanic experience was a trademark of antique ekphrasis.[50]

So much for comparison. It is time to turn to the medieval Norse texts and see how they can help in the task of historicizing ekphrasis. What do saga descriptions of viewing suggest about discourses around perception in premodern Scandinavia, and about the social contexts of ekphrastic description?

SAGA VISUALITY

Chapter 85 of *Orkneyinga saga* describes how Jarl Rǫgnvaldr and his Icelandic skalds Ármóðr and Oddi amused themselves one Christmas. First Rǫgnvaldr gave Ármóðr a gold-inlaid spear and asked him to make a verse in return, in an instance of the gift-exchange context for ekphrasis that is centered in scholarship on the shield poems. Ármóðr's verse praised the spear in seasonally appropriate imagery as "the best blood-candle, made bright with gold."[51] The holy season continued, and one day, as the jarl and his men contemplated (*hugðu at*) some tapestries, the jarl instructed Oddi, "Make a verse about the deeds of that man who is there on the tapestry, and don't finish your verse any later than I do mine. Don't have any of the words in your verse that I do in mine either."[52] Russell Poole has convincingly analyzed the verses, which the saga quotes, as versions of the story of Starkaðr's clash with Ingeld's Saxon bride.[53] The prose frame implies that viewing is a cognitive process, as shown by the verb *hyggja*, and that a single image can give rise to two competing verbal versions, Rǫgnvaldr's and Oddi's.

The *Orkneyinga saga* episode has a pendant in a famous passage in *Sneglu-Halla þáttr*.[54] Among many poetry-related jokes, several of them ekphrastic, the *þáttr* tells the story of a smith, a tanner, and a skald.[55] King Haraldr *harðráði* (hard-ruler) and his entourage hear the smith and the tanner fighting inside a house. Haraldr tells his skald, Þjóðólfr Arnórsson, to compose about their dealings (*deild*). When the skald protests, Haraldr tells him that the task is more difficult than he thinks. Þjóðólfr is to make of them other men than they are (*gøra af þeim nǫkkvat aðra menn en þeir eru*), first Geirrøðr and Þórr, then Sigurðr and Fáfnir, each of whom he is to "characterize [*kenn*] by his trade." Þjóðólfr composes two verses whose kennings take their base words from mythic narratives and their determinants from the tools of smithing and tanning.[56] Here again a percept, this time an aural one, is interpreted twice. In a parody of the "competition of skalds" motif, the roguish Icelander Sneglu-Halli is asked whether he could have performed as well, and he replies "'I am not as good a skald as Þjóðólfr, least of all when I am not present.'"[57] More explicitly than in *Orkneyinga saga*, this anecdote claims that skill in poetry is a matter of *seeing as*, making things other than they are. The keyword *kenna* marks the gap between sense perception and poetic response.

The cognitive side to perception is also highlighted, and a shield at last comes into view, in the *Great Saga of Olaf Tryggvason*. In chapter 74 of the saga the missionary Þangbrandr is given a decorated shield by Hubert, bishop of Canterbury, because, the bishop says, "you have the manners of a knight, although you are a cleric."⁵⁸ Þangbrandr re-gifts the shield to King Óláfr:

> When Óláfr saw the shield he carefully contemplated (*hugði hann at vandliga*) what was marked on it, and found it very significant. He said to Þangbrandr, "Whom do you Christian men venerate, tortured on the cross?" Þangbrandr replied, "We venerate our lord Jesus Christ." The king asked, "How did he transgress, that he was so tortured?" Þangbrandr explained all about the passion of our lord and the token of the cross. Then King Óláfr asked to buy the shield, but Þangbrandr gave it to him.⁵⁹

As in the previous examples, the ambivalence and open-endedness of the visual medium is thematized, giving rise to a doubling of possible interpretations. Not, of course, of what is represented, for the crucifix is surely the prime instance in Christian visual culture of an unambiguous image. By virtue of its materiality, however, the shield is double, signifying both knighthood and clerical vocation, as Bishop Hubert points out. This ambiguity means that its reception demands careful thought, *at hyggja*.

SEEING DOUBLE

These saga anecdotes are suggestive, but to see through Viking eyes it is necessary to turn to skaldic encomium. Þjóðólfr Arnórsson composed a group of verses (ÞjóðA *Har*) on the voyage of Haraldr *harðráði*'s fleet to the Battle of the Niz River in 1062.⁶⁰ Ekphraseis of ships are fairly common in skaldic verse, usually focusing on the splendor of their gold decoration, and occasionally comparing the ship to an animal.⁶¹ Þjóðólfr's sequence begins with three verses describing anonymous female viewers' responses to the spectacle of the fleet's departure. The first runs as follows:

> *Skeið sák framm at flœði,*
> *fagrt sprund, ór ǫ hrundit;*
> *kennd, hvar liggr fyr landi*
> *lǫng súð dreka ins prúða.*
> *Orms glóa fǫx of farmi*
> *frǫ́n, sízt ýtt vas hǫnum*
> *—bǫru búnir svírar*
> *brunnit goll—af hlunni.*

(I saw the warship, beautiful lady, propelled out of the river onto the ocean; look where the long side-planking of the splendid dragon-ship lies offshore. The gleaming manes of the serpent [dragon-ship] shine out above the cargo, since it was launched from the rollers; the decorated necks bore burnished gold.)

The first half-stanza counterpoints the skald's perception of a "warship" (*skeið*) with the lady's of "the proud dragon" (*dreki inn prúði*). The distinction the stanza draws between the skald's seeing, denoted by *sjá* (cognate with English *see*), and what he instructs the lady to observe is based on the same word as in the challenge to Sneglu-Halli: the verb *kenna*, here in its imperative form. *Skeið* ("warship") is the usual word for ship in the skaldic corpus and also appears several times in runic inscriptions, while *dreki* ("serpent," i.e., "dragon-ship") is a poetic conceit rather than a technical term.[62] The presence of two observers brings this stanza into the orbit of the saga anecdotes, where a single visual stimulus sparks proliferating interpretations. Competition, the ground bass of poetic interaction, sounds out clearly in *Orkneyinga saga* and *Sneglu-Halla þáttr*. Here, perhaps because the second observer is female, a different set of conventions is activated: the skald becomes a privileged interpreter of the visual realm, able to offer the silent female observer an enhanced experience of the percept.

The rest of the stanza sequence maintains this double vision. Although the female focalizer drops from view, the poem's perspective on the ship continues to shift back and forth. At times the speaker focuses attention on the ship's materiality and made-ness, marked with past participles. The ship has "tarred sea-gear" (*sortuð sæfǫng*, Har 3) and "planed stems" (*skafnir stafnar*, Har 5), is "nailed with iron" (*neglðum með járni*, Har 4), and is "armored around the oarports" (*hábrynjaðr*, Har 5). On the figurative level the ship is presented as animate, in powerfully affective terms: the oars feel "anguish" (*sorgar*, Har 4) at hard rowing, ships "get shelter" (*eigu skjól*) and "let the headland protect them" (*láta sér eið hlýja*, Har 5), while the seabed "gnaws at the stout anchor-fluke" (*gnegr af gaddi digrum*, Har 6). Þjóðólfr uses none of the animal-based kennings for ships. He prefers to explicitly contrast the materiality of the ship and its poetic figuration, so that his verses oscillate between a "seen" ship, splendidly made and skillfully rowed, and a "kenned" animal, whether dragon, hunted quarry, or eagle. When the ship is under oars, he says, looking out from inside is "like seeing an eagle's wing" (*sem líti arnarvæng*, Har 4).

The most commonly attested shield decoration, too, is stylized imagery of fierce animals, celebrating the exemplary martial fervor of the aristocratic male and offering him the protection of numinous powers in battle.[63] Raptors, serpents, and sea monsters represent the warrior's ability to wield violence and triumph against the odds. In Þjóðólfr's ship stanzas, images of fierce animals express the war band's resolution, sharpened by an undercurrent of anxiety, as they hurtle toward "a meeting, owed to the raven" (*fundr, hrafni skyldr*, Har 7). *Enargeia*'s explosive emotional tenor, a mixture of pride, aggression, and fear, projects the feelings of the listening retinue (*drótt*) onto the main tool of its trade, the longships which terrorized the North Atlantic and Mediterranean. Using the flexible and multivalent image of the animal, the skald can explore deeper emotional resonances of his audience's shared experience of war. These include the first stanza's display of martial splendor and the wealth that it brings, something which, the skald assures his listeners, undoubtedly impresses any woman who happens to be watching—a masculine, sexualized prowess. But the terrifying possibility lurks of becoming prey rather than predator, hunted animal rather than hunter. *Dróttkvætt* poetry's ability to voice such anxieties, in the context of a social group constituted by the collective exercise of violence, is perhaps one of the keys to its compelling power.

Skaldic double vision has a visual counterpart in the puzzle picture (*Vexierbild*). Puzzle pictures consist of interlocking motifs that can be combined in different ways to yield contrasting images, usually of human faces and animal bodies. They can be traced over a long period in Germanic animal art.[64] In a series of thought-provoking studies, archaeologist Michael Neiß has argued that puzzle pictures can be equated with skaldic style along various axes: for instance, that compositions combining human and bird forms are reflections of poetic *heiti* such as "eagle-head" (*arnhǫfði*) for Óðinn.[65] Most of the objects decorated with such compositions are relatively small and can easily be held and rotated in the hand, facilitating the cognitive process of switching between the different images. Among the most spectacular puzzle pictures are those on brooches (Plate 4). Women's dress included three brooches, two oval-shaped ones permanently worn at the shoulders to hold the garments together, and a third, usually circular, trefoil, or equal-armed in shape, which could be removed. The puzzle pictures appear only on the third brooch, suggesting that it was taken off, held, and perhaps passed around a group, "a shift of function from the mundane into the sphere of feast and cult."[66]

Brooches decorated with puzzle pictures imply that an interpretive practice involving oscillation between contrasting motifs, triggered by looking at and handling highly wrought manufactured objects, was an important part of aristocratic sociability. The saga anecdotes show that the production of competing interpretations continued to be a favored way of responding poetically to visual artworks well into the Middle Ages. Howard Williams writes that the "ocular art" of Sutton Hoo "challenges the viewer to see."[67] A similar challenge, I will suggest, is at the heart of *Ragnarsdrápa*'s aspiration to make its audience "recognize" (*kenna*) the narratives on the shield.

KENNA BEFORE *KENNING*: PREHISTORY OF A MEDIAL CONCEPT

That Viking shields are round is a banal observation. Nonetheless, as Roberta Frank observes, roundness is what Bragi emphasizes in his kennings for the shield that is *Ragnarsdrápa*'s subject.[68] Bragi calls his shield "wheel of Hǫgni's girl" (*Rdr* 2), "moon of the chariot of Rær" (*Rdr* 7), or "Óðinn's hall-penny" (*Rdr* 12) and compares it to a leaf, "brightly planted with color" (*Rdr* 1). These metaphors keep the round surface of the shield, animated with color, before the mind's eye. Key objects in the poem's narratives are also denoted by kennings that emphasize roundness. The ring Hildr offers her father, Hǫgni, is called *halsbaugr* (*Rdr* 8), *men* (*Rdr* 9), and *svíra hringr* (*Rdr* 10), all of which mean "neck-ring." The World Serpent Þórr fishes up is called "ring of the ship's road" (Bragi *Þórr* 4). And as Hamðir and Sǫrli launch their attack on King Jǫrmunrekkr, his warriors protectively "encircle" (the verb used is *gyrða*, ["gird with a band or hoop"]) his "vat of the floor-steed," a kenning for a bed (*Rdr* 5). The rarity of the base word *sár* ("vat") in the skaldic corpus confirms that the focus on round objects is not accidental. Equivalences based on shape are an important way to create likeness within the figurative system of the *kenningar*. Coordinating the shield and its narratives draws attention to the logic of difference within likeness that is a key feature of the skaldic metaphorical system. The skalds had a technical term for this special medial potential of their poetry: they called it *kenna*, meaning "to make known," "to perceive," or even "to touch."

The core meaning of the word *kenna* is "come to know." The dictionary definition includes the glosses "know," "recognize," "acknowledge," "impute," "feel," "taste," "scent," "touch," "call," "teach," and "tell."[69] *Kenning*, a noun derived from *kenna*, is used in the thirteenth-century poetological and grammatical literature as the name for the skaldic technique of circumlocution.[70] The verb *kenna* occurs around fifty times in the skaldic corpus. Many are references to teaching, whether in Christian contexts or in encomiastic poetry where *kenna* is used in a similar way to *minna* ("remember, remind,") as the victorious war-leader "teaches" or "reminds" his enemies of their subjugation. There are also a number of instances in which *kenna* denotes perception. Any of the senses may be involved: smell (Hfr *Lv* 18); taste (Anon *Pét* 3); touch (Anon *Mey* 4, RvHbreiðm *Hl* 24, Anon *Lil* 81), including sexual contact (KormQ *Lv* 5); and sight (Þorm *Lv* 6). Often multiple sensory inputs, and memory as well, drive the processes of recognition denoted by *kenna* (e.g. Anon *Vǫlsa* 3, BjHall *Kálffl* 1). It is especially clear in poems on Christian subjects that no firm boundary can be drawn between the domain of the senses and more abstract notions of recognizing or acknowledging, when *kenna* refers to acknowledging a saint's power as manifested in a miracle (EGils *Guðkv* 38), recognizing the fact of Christ's incarnation (Anon *Lil* 69, Anon *FoGT* 42), or accepting the new faith (Anon *Pl* 53). Medieval people well understood that sense perception is not merely a matter of acquiring data via the external senses, but also of the interplay of this data with mediating psychological processes that created their own mental images.

For Bragi, the appeal of *kenna* seems to have lain in its conjunction of multiplex sense perception and psychological insight. *Kenna* occurs three times in the poetry attributed to him. The simplest instance is in *Þórr's fishing*, where it marks the climactic moment when Þórr lifts his hammer against Miðgarðsormr, the Midgard serpent:

3. *Hamri fórsk í hœgri*
hǫnd, þás allra landa,
œgir Ǫflugbarða,
endiseiðs of kenndi.
(The terrifier of Ǫflugbarði <giant> [= Þórr] lifted the hammer in his right hand, when he recognized the boundary-saithe of all lands [= Miðgarðsormr].)

Kenna with a genitive object (here "boundary-saithe," *endiseiðs*) denotes touch: Þórr feels Miðgarðsormr on the line.[71] In the prose version of this narrative in *Gylfaginning*, it is the serpent who feels Þórr, or rather his fishhook (*er ormrinn kendi þess*, ch. 44). In both cases, the nuance "recognize" is also present. In *Gylfaginning*, Miðgarðsormr recognizes, when he feels the hook, that he has been tricked (*ginti*), while the sense of Bragi's stanza must be that Þórr recognizes already from the strong pull on his line, without seeing the serpent, that this is the "test of strength" (*freisti afls*, Bragi Þórr 1) he seeks.[72]

In *Ragnarsdrápa* 4 Hamðir and Sǫrli have just completed the first phase of their revenge on Jǫrmunrekkr by cutting off his hands and feet, with bloody results:

Flaut of set við sveita
sóknar alfs á golfi
hræva dǫgg, þars hǫggnar
hendr sem fœtr of kenndu.
(Dew of corpses [BLOOD] flowed over the bench together with the blood of the elf of attack [WARRIOR = Jǫrmunrekkr] on the floor, where people recognized hewn arms and legs.)

Who perceives? There is no explicit subject, only a third person plural verb (*kenndu*). Both intra- and extradiegetic audiences are possible. In the other extant poetic telling of the story, the eddic poem *Hamðismál*, Jǫrmunrekkr is commanded to look at *his own* severed limbs in a moment of ironic horror typical of heroic legend: "*Fœtr sér þú þína, / hǫndum sér þú þínum / Jǫrmunrekr, orpit / í eld heitan*" ("You see your own feet, you see your own hands, Iormunrekk, hurled into the hot fire").[73] Jǫrmunrekkr no longer has proprioception of his severed hands and feet, the organs of touch. They are horribly alienated from his body, rendered the thing-like objects of sight, smell, and taste, like roasted joints of meat. *Ragnarsdrápa*'s use of *kenna* relies instead on the ekphrastic ability to make the audience into eyewitnesses. The ambiguous reference of *kenna* melds the audience of the poem with the viewers in Jǫrmunrekkr's hall. The potential of poetic envisioning to conjoin text-internal observers with the visualizing audience makes ekphrasis a powerful way of producing a viewing subject. As I will show in Chapter 4, the Christian skald of *Líknarbraut* (Way of Grace) was well aware of the force of this rhetorical move.

Kenna appears a final time in marked position in the frame of *Ragnarsdrápa*, as part of the poem's refrain:

12. Þá má sókn á Svǫlnis
salpenningi kenna.
Ræs gǫfumk reiðar mána
Ragnarr ok fjǫl sagna.
(That attack can be recognized on the penny of the hall of Svǫlnir <Óðinn> [Valhǫll > SHIELD]. Ragnarr gave me a moon of the chariot of Rær <sea-king> [SHIP > SHIELD] and a multitude of stories.)

Here *kenna* marks a difference between the material object of perception and its poetic representation. Bragi's claim is double: that his poem enables the audience to envision the narrative of the Hjaðningavíg, and that its shield resembles something else, namely a penny. The coin, a sign of political and economic authority, was also the most widely available Viking Age object decorated with anthropomorphic imagery.[74] Horst Bredekamp argues that "the intimacy of contact with the fingers" potentiates the connection the coin makes between subject and ruler.[75]

Þjóðólfr Arnórsson's verses on Haraldr's fleet opposed *kenna* to *sjá* in order to contrast the facture of the ship, its materials and madness, with its metaphorical animation: its shape, motion, and affective power. For Bragi too, *kenna* was the word that came to mind when reflecting on the power of his medium. "Sight" is not the semantic center of *kenna*, and in fact in modern Icelandic this verb has nothing to do with vision, instead denoting smell and taste. That poets chose *kenna* as the marker of poetic difference suggests that they saw poetic cognition as a multisensorial process, involving other senses alongside vision. Touch seems to have been especially important. The haptic aspect of skaldic imagination is manifested in many metaphorical kennings: people are like trees because both are smooth-skinned elongated forms standing perpendicular to the ground; the cold steel of a sword is like an icicle, shields are rings, and so on. The skalds' use of *kenna* suggests an understanding of skaldic poetics, prior to *Skáldskaparmál*, as a matter of *grasping*: Bragi's penny as something turned in the fingers, round, shining, decorated, like the shield is.

ANTIFEMINIST *ENARGEIA*

When telling well-worn stories such as the Jǫrmunrekkr narrative, the poet attempts to persuade the audience of his own perspective on the narrative by using vivid language charged with *enargeia*. *Ragnarsdrápa* offers an overwhelmingly negative portrayal of Hildr, female protagonist of the Hjaðningavíg story. She is malevolent, sorcerous, and deathly. As "desiring-Rán of the excessive drying of veins" (*ósk-Rǫ́n ofþerris æða, Rdr* 8), she lusts after the combatants' blood, and as "curing-Þrúðr of bloody wounds" (*bœti-Þrúðr dreyrúgra benja, Rdr* 9), she heals them only so they can fight again. She is hostile (*fárhugr, Rdr* 8) and malicious (*fyllda bǫls, Rdr* 8), and while she behaves as if she is hindering the battle—her father and her lover are the combatants, after all—she actually spurs the fighters on.[76] Through her sorcery (*fordæða, Rdr* 11) she destroys the good things ("booty," *feng, Rdr* 11) that are the hoped-for outcome of war and consigns warriors to the company of voracious and deathly females: Rán, a sea-goddess who lusts after drowned sailors; Fenrir's sister Hel, goddess of the underworld ("the sister of the complete monster of a wolf," *lifra algífris ulfs, Rdr* 9); and Hveðra, a troll-woman who personifies the hungry mouth of the battleaxe (*Rdr* 11).[77] In our last glimpse of this terrifying figure before *Skáldskaparmál*'s quotation breaks off, she has the battle in her hands (Hildr "took control on the island," *nam ráða í holmi, Rdr* 11). In this desperate situation the exemplary martial *habitus* of the fighters, who "went forward quickly, enraged" (*gekk framm brǫðum, reiðr, Rdr* 11), will be of little use to them.

None of this vivid horror is apparent in the conventional gestures of greeting performed by the female figures on the Gotland picture stones Lärbro Stora Hammars 1 and Stenkyrka Smiss I—if these scenes do indeed depict Hildr.[78] Fuglesang emphasizes the difficulty of interpreting the "woman between warriors" motif, saying of the Oseberg wagon's image of a woman grasping the wrist of a male figure, "whether she is holding him or egging him on remains an open question."[79] *Ragnarsdrápa*'s claim that Hildr "continually behaved as if she was hindering the battle, although she was inciting the princes" (*lét ey, sem letti orrostu, þótt etti jǫfrum, Rdr* 9) could be read as the poem's acknowledgment of the conventional iconography of the "woman between warriors" motif. Against this visual tradition Bragi's viewpoint stands out in high relief. The poem's demonic imagery is strikingly different from the visual motif, a distance from conventional imagery that opens a space for the poetic speaker's own perspective. Aðalheiður Guðmundsdóttir argues that "Hildr may stand for the woman who has lost loved ones; who wishes for power over death; who lives on and mourns."

This may be true of the later prose versions, but describing Bragi's Hildr as being "uncomfortable with the consequences of war" misses the powerful note of condemnation in *Ragnarsdrápa*.[80]

Eddic heroic poetry preserves a number of variations on the theme of the hero's valkyrie lover. Although these depict different valkyrie-warrior pairings, the stories of Sigrún/Sváva and Helgi in the Helgi poems maneuver their protagonists into the same dead end as Hildr, where the woman's closest male relatives kill each other over her. Helgi himself draws a comparison with the Hildr story, saying that Sigrún has been "a Hildr to us" ("*Hildr hefir þú oss verit*").[81] In the *grand-guignol* ending of the *Second Poem of Helgi Hundingsbani*, where Sigrún visits the undead Helgi in his grave mound, she describes herself as

43. [. . .] svá fegin   fundi okkrum
sem átfrekir   Óðins haukar,
er val vitu,   varmar bráðir,
eða dǫgglitir   dagsbrún sjá.
([. . .] so glad, at our meeting
as are the greedy hawks of Odin
when they know of slaughter, steaming flesh,
or, dew-gleaming, they see the dawn.)[82]

Skalds usually take the winner's perspective. The victorious warrior feeds carrion animals with the corpses of his enemies, or gladdens them, or dulls their hunger, or breaks their fast, and so on in endless variations. Here this trope is suddenly inverted. No longer the open-handed feeder—a role which mirrors the conventional imagery of the good ruler's generous provision of food—the warrior becomes food, whether for an animal (here a raven) or, yet more terrifying, for a supernatural eater, a giant or valkyrie. What on the picture stones is indistinguishable from a scene of greeting, and in the Helgi poem is a metaphor for the frustration of sexual desire by death (it is Sigrún's greedy longing for Helgi's body that keeps him from passing on to the afterlife), is presented as grisly reality in *Ragnarsdrápa*. Bragi's perspective on the story of the hero and his valkyrie lover is that what she really desires is the warrior's blood and his delivery into the hands of female underworld beings, to become the object of "endless predation by the demons and monsters of the underworld."[83]

SEEING THE GODS

There are significant systematic gaps in our knowledge of Viking Age imagery. Especially conspicuous by its absence is anthropomorphic wooden sculpture. While such figures survive in large numbers from prehistoric times, and again from the High Middle Ages on, none has yet been discovered from the Viking Age.[84] There is no reason to assume that longstanding practices of image-making, stretching thousands of years into the past, suddenly came to a halt. Recent metal-detector finds, such as the silver figurine from Lejre showing a person seated on a throne, demonstrate that figural sculptures in the round were produced in this period.[85] Other explanations for the gap are not difficult to imagine. These images most likely had religious significance to believers in the pre-Christian religions of the north. In the course of religious rituals, the devout consigned them to marshes or other bodies of water, or buried them in the foundations of structures, where wet earth preserved wooden objects to the present day.[86] Sagas of the Norwegian kings of the conversion period describe how Óláfr Tryggvason, St Óláfr, and their followers destroyed sites of pagan worship and toppled, smashed, and burned idols.[87] Prohibitions on the public exercise of pre-Christian cult would have inhibited believers from ceremonially depositing any objects that survived the missionaries' attacks. What the images embodied (supernatural presences venerated in pagan cult), their conspicuous dimensions (the *Astgabelidole*, figures made from forked branches, are often many meters tall), and their material (wood, which needed special conditions to survive) must all have contributed to their disappearance. The tradition of anthropomorphic wooden sculpture in the round can be traced again once the new religion has become established and such artifacts, now depicting beings with Christian significance, are again the objects of care and protection.

Most saga accounts of Þórr mention images of the god or artifacts such as high-seat pillars (*ǫndvegissúlur*) associated with him.[88] The high-seat pillars with their "holy nails" (*reginnaglar*) have been compared to early modern accounts of Arctic cult practices involving wooden posts or statues decorated with nails.[89] Schefferus's *Lapponia*, from 1673, quotes an anonymous manuscript account of the Saami cult of Hovrengaellis, where sparks were part of the ritual and understood to be the work of the thunder god: "They drove a steel nail or spike and a piece of flint into the idol's head, so that Thor should make fire with it."[90] According to Samuel Rheen (1671), the Saami statues were made from the inverted trunk of a birch, whose roots formed the head and bole the body; the statue held a hammer in its hand.[91] A similar carving was found in 1929 in a marsh near Falun in Dalarna, Sweden.[92] It was recently C14-dated to 1500 CE and connected with the cult of either Sáráhkká or Hovrengaellis, practiced by the Saami people who lived in the forested parts of Dalarna at that time.[93] A simple, massive form some 1.2 meters in height, with its head carved from the tree's root and its body and legs from the branches, it is quite unlike the idols described in the saga accounts (Plate 5). This is only to be expected, as the saga authors were reconstructing these long-vanished objects on the basis of learned literature.[94] Their desire to present the missionary kings as the successors of a long line of Christian destroyers of idols determines the way they present these artifacts, rather than any aspiration to documentary realism. The sculpture from Sundborn may, after all, be the closest thing we have to a Þórr idol.

Þórr enters *Haustlǫng* with a bang. As he drove to the mound of Grjótún, swelling with rage, "the path of the moon resounded beneath him" (*vegr mána dunði und hǫnum*, *Haustl* 14).[95] Cosmic clamor is not uncommon in descriptions of Þórr's journeys: in *Þrymskviða* "the mountains split asunder, the earth flamed with fire" (*bjǫrg brotnuðu, brann jǫrð loga*, *Þrk* 21) when Þórr drove to giantland. Smashing, clanging, shattering, and crushing are how Þórr gets the job done. Verses in *Kristni saga* on the missionary Þangbrandr's shipwreck off eastern Iceland in the late 990s describe how Þórr shook (*hristi*), smashed (*beysti*), flung (*laust*), broke (*braut*), and wrecked (*kneyfði*) the ship.[96] His preferred blunt instruments, hammer and fists, produce sounds usually rendered using the verbs *bella* "clang" and *skjalla* "ring." In *Húsdrápa* 6, Þórr "let his fist slam (*skjalla*) against the serpent's ear," while in Eysteinn Valdason's fragmentary poem on the same subject (EVald *Þórr*), the god's fists banged (*skullu*) on the gunwale of Hymir's boat; the litany of Þórr's giant-killings by Þorbjǫrn *dísarskáld* (lady's poet) begins "there was a clang on Keila's crown" (*ball í Keilu kolli*, Þdís *Þórr* 2), and the narrator of *Þrymskviða* observes with relish the comeuppance of the giantess: "striking [*skell*, from *skjalla*] she got instead of shillings" (*Þrk* 32). *Hymiskviða* reports that when Þórr lifted Hymir's kettle "the handle-rings jingled at his heels" (*enn á hælum hringar skullu*, *Hym* 34), again using the verb *skjalla*; the same verb is used in *Gylfaginning* to describe the effects of hammer and fists.[97] It is hard to imagine how a visual artist might have depicted sound absent the conventions of superhero comics. Rather, these examples demonstrate the multisensorial vividness striven after by ekphrastic poets. Skalds imagining Þórr conceived of his divine efficacy and presence as a matter of nonsemantic, ringing sound. Óðinn, by contrast, is associated with verbalizations such as spells (*galdr*) and sorcery (*seiðr*). This association brings Þórr, as many things do, into the orbit of the giants, whose names often refer to noise.[98]

Haustlǫng then opens out to an awe-inspiring vision of the god:
15. *Knǫ́ttu ǫll, en Ullar,*
endilǫg, fyr mági
grund vas grápi hrundin,
ginnunga vé brinna,
þás hofregin hafrar[99]
hógreiðar framm drógu
—seðr gekk Svǫlnis ekkja
sundr—at Hrungnis fundi.
(All sanctuaries of hawks, low from end to end [SKIES] were burning, and the ground was battered with hail in front of the kinsman of Ullr [= Þórr], when the goats drew forward the temple-deity of the comfortable chariot [= Þórr] to a meeting with Hrungnir; the widow of Svǫlnir <Óðinn> [= Jǫrð (*jǫrð* "earth")] split asunder at once.)

The expression "temple-deity" (*hofregin*, nom. *hofreginn*) for Þórr here is remarkable.[100] The first element, *hof*, means "sacred place, temple" and is consistent with a number of saga accounts associating Þórr with such places.[101] A compound *hofreginn* is not otherwise attested, but similar compounds in prose such as *hofgoði, -gyðja, -blót* ("temple-priest, -priestess, -sacrifice") suggest that it could be interpreted as a genitive compound denoting a feature or person associated with the temple, rather than a kenning; the genitive *hógreiðar* "of the comfortable chariot" can be construed both with *hofreginn* and with the goats (*hafrar*) which pull Þórr's chariot. The god is disclosed or "drawn forward" (*framm drógu*), his presence signaled by the signature effects of thunderous noise, flames, and violent weather.

Ekphrasis shades into epiphany as the text wavers between representing (a representation of) Þórr and staging the transcendent experience of the god's presence. Þórr is the only deity for whom poems addressed in the second person are preserved.[102] This hymnic poetry testifies to performance settings in which worshippers experienced the god as present, inhabiting his cult objects.[103] The divine archetype is not merely represented and available to the worshipper in immaterial form, but materially imbues his image.[104] The reports of sparks being struck from statues of Hovrengaellis are very suggestive here, as they bear material witness to the god's magical efficacy. Such an experience of cultic viewing could form the background to the command to see (*sér*) in *Haustl* 14.

The refrain of *Haustlǫng* calls its shield a "quivering cliff of the shield-boss [SHIELD], decorated with moving stories" (*bifkleif baugs bifum fáða*, Haustl 13, 20). *Bifum* is dat. pl. of a noun whose gender and form (masc. *bifr*, fem. *bifa*, or neut. *bif*) are uncertain. It is related to the verb *bifa(sk)* ("tremble, falter"). This verb is used to describe people trembling in affective response (usually fear, occasionally religious enthusiasm), or people or things physically moving in response to a force. *Bif-* is often prefixed to kenning base words in skaldic poetry, where it turns an inanimate base word toward an animate referent, or suggests the lively motion of a wielded weapon, as *bifkleif* does here. *Bifum* is another matter. What does this word suggest the shield is "decorated" (*fáða*) with? It is tempting to translate it as "movies": the decoration moves, that is, it produces affect, but it also (seems) *to move*, recalling both the long history of technological attempts to simulate animation and the medial oscillation of the puzzle picture.[105]

EYE TO EYE

Húsdrápa's account of Þórr fishing up the Midgard serpent emphasizes the eyes of god and monster. One *helmingr* is devoted to depicting the gaze of each of the adversaries:

3. *Innmáni skein ennis*
ǫndótts vinar banda;
óss skaut œgigeislum
orðsæll á men storðar.
(The interior-moon of the forehead [EYE] of the hostile friend of the gods [= Þórr] shone; the praise-blessed god shot terror-beams at the necklace of the earth [= Miðgarðsormr].)

4. *En stirðþinull starði*
storðar leggs fyr borði
fróns á folka reyni
fránleitr ok blés eitri.
(And the flashing-eyed stiff cord of the earth [= Miðgarðsormr] stared at the tester of the peoples of the bone of the earth [ROCK > GIANTS > = Þórr] below the ship's side and blew poison.)

Þórr's gaze weaponizes the ancient optical theory of extramission, further discussed in Chapter 4. Extramission taught that visual perception was effected by beams emitted from the eyes that touched the seen object. Þórr's eye shot out "terror-beams" (*œgigeislar*) that made physical contact with his enemy. The serpent is by nature flashing-eyed (*fránleitr*; the brightness of serpents' eyes is proverbial), but although it stared (*starði*) back at Þórr, it emitted poison rather than media of vision, an emanation from lower in the sensory hierarchy.

What "typified image" did this description summon up in the minds of its audiences? Þórr's fishing is well represented in such visual sources as the Viking Age Altuna (U 1161) and Hørdum (NJy 30) runestones, but all extant images lack this tense interchange of glances. *Húsdrápa*'s text takes care to describe how the two opponents meet face-to-face. *Fyr borði* (*Húsdr* 4), translated above as "below the ship's side," strictly means simply "before, by the ship's side." The etymology of *ǫndóttr* ("hostile") is debated, but it is possible that the first element is *and-* ("opposite, against.")[106] The same word marks the climax of Þórr's encounter with the giant Þrymr in *Þrymskviða*:

27. *Laut und línu   lysti at kyssa,*
enn hann útan stǫkk   endlangan sal:
'Hví eru ǫndótt   augu Freyju?
þykki mér ór augum   eldr of brenna.
(He bent under the head-dress, he was keen to kiss her,
instead he sprang back right along the hall:
"Why are Freyia's eyes so terrifying?
It seems to me [fire] is burning from them.")[107]

Here again it is a matter of an exchange of glances between two faces in intimate proximity. Þórr's eyes emit a dangerous light, dramatized by the backward leap of the unwitting Þrymr. Miðgarðsormr is a cooler customer, and *Húsdrápa* takes a Þórr's-eye view. As the next verse reveals, Þórr is surrounded by enemies. His giant fishing companion Hymir is also in the boat as Þórr pulls up the "mighty draught" (*megindrǫttr, Húsdr* 5). In the *dénouement*, Þórr takes action in symmetrical fashion, clouting Hymir over the ear (*við eyra, Húsdr* 6) with one fist while wielding his hammer in the other to knock the "ground of the ears" (*hlusta grunn, Húsdr* 6), or head, off the shining serpent. The extant visual images of Þórr's fishing depict the moment of greatest dramatic tension in the narrative, as Þórr raises his hammer to attack the monster, but they are not at all interested in this exchange of glances.

The importance of eyes in these lines of *Húsdrápa*, and the way Þórr is positioned between two enemies, suggests a rather different visual intertext. This is the ancient compositional schema of the beastmaster (*Tierbezwinger*), consisting of a warrior between two animals or monsters.¹⁰⁸ The Vendel Period helmet patrix from Torslunda, for instance, shows two creatures (usually identified as bears) attacking a half-naked warrior from either side. The bears stare at the warrior with large round eyes, their muzzles close to his head, as he drives a sword into one and holds a dagger ready for the other. Another patrix from Torslunda shows a half-naked warrior turning toward a single zoologically indeterminate monster; in one hand he holds a chain, in the other hand, which is apparently gloved, an axe. Again, the warrior gazes at the beast in his moment of triumph, as is shown by the unusual three-quarter profile representation of his face. The beastmaster motif is widespread in Germanic art and may derive from late Roman and Byzantine images of gladiatorial combat.¹⁰⁹

Þrymskviða and *Húsdrápa* both capture the terrifying sensation of being in the crosshairs of Þórr's glare, but *Húsdrápa* goes a step further by evoking this visual formula and confronting Þórr with not one but two monsters, the giant and the Midgard serpent. He batters both into submission, underscoring his heroic prowess in the defense of gods and men. Did *Húsdrápa*'s audience, like the hapless Þrymr, nonetheless spring back as they felt themselves raked by the god's "terror-beams"?

* * * *

The point of calling the skaldic shield poems "ekphrastic," it seems to me, is to open up a wider range of potential comparators than a field-internal term like *billedbeskrivende dikt* does. Such openings prove productive. They reveal that detailed prose accounts of decorated shields conform to the emblematic convention of medieval epic ekphrasis, whereby an image frames and reflects the larger narrative into which it is inserted. Such accounts probably do not describe actual Viking Age shields, the nature of whose decoration remains elusive. Classical ekphrasis also earns its keep as a comparator. It encourages consideration of further poetic descriptions (of ships, women, and nuts, for example) alongside the retellings of myths and legends that make up what is usually thought of as the genre of skaldic ekphrasis.¹¹⁰ Rejecting the model of equivalency ("verbal representation of graphic representation") focuses attention instead on the rhetorical force of ekphrastic description. Vividness makes audiences into eyewitnesses, rapt with the story's emotion, while the skald's interpretive tour de force (*íþrótt*) opens a gap between conventional, well-known visual motifs and the poetic narrative. One example of how *enargeia* can be sparked in the gap between traditional representations and the poet's narrative art is the complex of ideas around animals and food.[111] The hunger of predators for human corpses is a cliché in Germanic heroic poetry, and the equation of warriors and their weapons with fierce animals is widespread and ancient. These *topoi* acquire new pointedness in Bragi's depiction of Hildr as a monstrous, demonic eater, and Þjóðólfr Arnórsson's of the dragon-ship as hunted animal. Finally, a poetics of epiphanic sensual immediacy, encompassing touch and hearing as well as sight, allows the audience to see and be seen by the gods. Although Þórr idols are no more prominent in the archaeological record than painted shields are, I have argued that such idols did once exist, and that late medieval and early modern Saami sculptures give a sense of a shared northern world of cultic experience also reflected in *Haustlǫng*.

A last question remains. What were the skaldic picture poems *for* in their social contexts of performance and transmission? In a stimulating contribution published almost forty years ago, Edith Marold argues that the skald-shield-patron triangle has an additional vertex: a second skald, the speaker's competitor.[112] The Hrafnketill who is asked to hear the poem in the opening of *Ragnarsdrápa* is no shield delivery boy, she suggests, but rather a fellow poet against whom Bragi is competing. As she notes, Saxo's description of the battle of Brávellir includes both a Brahi and a Rankil—a pair of skalds. The fondness of storytellers for tales of poetic contention of all kinds would have preserved such poems even once their visual sources were long gone.

Such a performance situation might be inferred from the two fragmentary shield poems attributed to Egill Skallagrímsson. Only one stanza of each survives, combining calls for a hearing and references to the poem's occasion with praise of the skald's own prowess. In *Berudrápa* (Shield Poem) the call for a hearing is addressed to a "retainer of the king" (*þegn konungs*). No other skaldic bid for a hearing describes its addressee in such modest terms. According to the saga Þorsteinn Þoruson is the donor of the shield, but as he is in Norway the address would have to be indirect. The most recent editor suggests that the shield delivery boy, a sea captain named Þormóðr, is to "learn the poem by heart (or possibly have it carved on a rune stick) and recite it to Þorsteinn when he returned to Norway."[113] Could not the "king's retainer" be a fellow skald, Egill's competitor? The nameless poem referred to by editors as *Skjaldardrápa* (Shield Poem) that Egill composes about Einarr's notorious gold- and gem-encrusted shield also interposes a delivery boy between donor (Hákon jarl, the original giver of the shield) and performing skald. Here the saga tells us he is another poet, namely Einarr *skálaglamm* (scales-tinkle). Egill's poem on this shield opens as follows:

> *Mál es lofs at lýsa*
> *ljósgarð, es þá*k, barða*
> *—mér kom heim at hendi*
> *hoddsendis boð—enda.*
> (It is time to proclaim the shining fence of ships [SHIELD], which I have received, with the end of praise [PRAISE POEM]; the message of the treasure-sender [GENEROUS MAN = Einarr *skálaglamm*] came to me at home.)[114]

The elaborate scenario presented in *Egils saga*'s prose looks rather like it was constructed on the basis of this stanza. Its note of urgency ("it is time," *mál es . . .*) could be the reason for the saga's information that Einarr awaited Egill's return for the socially acceptable maximum of three days before leaving the shield behind, while Einarr's absence would explain why the shield is, rather oddly, referred to as a "message" (*boð*). These phrases could alternatively be explained by the supposition that it is time for the speaker of the stanza to take his turn, now that his opponent's verbal challenge (*boð*) has "c[o]me to me at home."[115]

Contemporary puzzle pictures, like later saga descriptions of poetic competition, suggest how such a competition might have played out. The puzzle picture heightens the fertile ambiguity of the visual realm and shares significant features with skaldic ekphrasis: multisensorial appeal to both vision and touch, foregrounding of the moment of cognitive breakthrough (one of the glosses of *kenna* is "recognize"), and the role played by an undecidable oscillation between different interpretations. The prominence of puzzle pictures in the art of the Viking Age and before suggests that visual interpretation involving the optic and haptic grasping of highly worked, playfully ambiguous material objects was a valued part of courtly sociability.

CHAPTER 4

SEEING, KNOWING, AND BELIEVING IN THE *PROSE EDDA*

In chapter 20 of the Old Norse translation of the *Elucidarium* of Honorius Augustodunensis, the student expresses a wish to be like St Peter. His master remonstrates with him:

> If you wished to be Peter, you could not, because you would wish to be someone other than you really are. But no one will have more glory there than he deserves, just as a foot here on earth does not want to be a hand, nor does an ear want to be an eye.[1]

The master's hierarchy dominates ancient and medieval thinking about the senses.[2] Plato and Aristotle placed sight above all other senses. Plato claims in the *Timaeus* that "the supreme benefit for which sight is responsible is that not a word of all we have said about the universe could have been said if we had not seen stars and sun and heaven" (47a–c).[3] Aristotle says that "we prefer seeing (one might say) to everything else. The reason is that this, most of all the senses, makes us know and brings to light many differences between things" (*Metaphysics*, 980a).[4] There are differences of emphasis here—for Plato, vision allows subjects to discern the truth of the natural world, while Aristotle stresses its powers of differentiation—but the message is clear. Above any other sense, vision brings knowledge.[5]

An allied understanding is reflected in the semantics of vision in the Indo-European languages. Verbs of seeing often have abstract senses connected to knowledge and wisdom. The IE root **ueid-* ("to see") for example, yields Latin *videre* ("see"), Greek *eidénai* ("know") (the source of the English word "idea"), Germanic *wise*, *vit* ("wit"), *wissen* and *vita* ("to know"), and Iranian *fios* "knowledge." The equivalence between seeing and knowing may have its origin in the way that sight, more than any other sense, is able to focus on a single stimulus among many.[6] Isidore of Seville writes that the sense of sight "is called vision (*visus*) because it is more vivid (*vivacior*) than the rest of the senses, and also more important and faster, and endowed with greater liveliness, like memory among the rest of the faculties of the mind. Moreover, it is closer to the brain, from which everything emanates. . . ."[7] The primacy of vision, and its link to knowledge, is a central pillar of premodern ideas about the senses. Even the smallest move away from this pillar discloses a complex landscape.[8] What counts as a sense? How many senses are there? Is their hierarchy stable? Do they passively receive or actively seek out impressions? How do sense perceptions enter consciousness, imagination, and memory? What links seeing and envisioning? And—an especially pressing question for vision—can sense perceptions be trusted?

The idea that the external senses are five in number, and their treatment in the order "sight, hearing, smell, taste, touch," is already found in Aristotle's discussion of the senses in the second book of *De anima*.[9] It dominates the Western medieval vernaculars. The collective word for the senses in Old Norse seems to have been *vit* "wit," as it is in premodern English (the "Five Wits"). Alongside references to "all the wits" (*ǫll vit*), the Old Norse prose corpus preserves the notion of five (bodily) wits (*fimm líkamsins vit*), often in the form of lists of the senses.[10] Such lists, usually in the order *visus, auditus, gustus, olfactus, tactus* (sight, hearing, taste, smell, touch) were common in homiletic literature across Europe and drew upon various Latin sources.[11] Norse homiletic literature is no exception, and it offers rich material for an exploration of Norse ideas of sense perception and cognition.[12] Lists of the senses in Old Norse (almost) invariably begin with sight and hearing and end with touch, but there certainty ends.[13] *Vit* can also refer to the eyes and ears alone, or to the senses excluding those of the mouth (*af munni hans ok vitum*). The sequence of the inner items of the list is fluid, and both what counts as a sense and the words used for them vary considerably. Speech, for instance, sometimes appears, as in a Norse homily drawing on Bede's *In Octava Nativitatis*, where the homilist admonishes his audiences to purify "eyes, hearing and speech, smell and touch" (*augna, heyrnar og máls, ilmingar og kennisemi*).[14] In *Arinbjarnarkviða* 7–8 Egill itemizes what he has gained in receiving his head from Eiríkr. His list too emphasizes the organs of speech: eyes, mouth, teeth, tongue, ears (but no nose!). The inclusion of speech among the senses, while foreign to our own intuitions, does not lack for parallels in medieval texts. It reveals the active, extramissive quality attributed to the senses in premodernity.[15]

The stable sensory hierarchy presupposed by the "Five Wits" topos is further shaken by the fact that touch, reliably to be found at the end of the list, also has a privileged association with knowledge. Sweetser finds the semantic link between touch, manipulation, and intellection to be "absolutely pervasive" in Indo-European languages. The same word is often used to mean both "grasp with the hand" and "understand, think," for example Latin *comprehendere*, Greek *katalambáno*, and Norse *halda* ("hold, insist"). Touch is an important channel for knowledge, particularly knowledge of the divine, in early medieval accounts of devotion to the cross, "reveal[ing] a deep pessimism about the potential of corporeal sight, the use of eyes alone."[16] The Old Norse homily for Candlemas (*Purificatio Sancta Mariae*) recounts the story of Simeon the God-Receiver:

> And when Jesus was borne into the temple, then Simeon took him in his arms. Great is the mercy of God, that he gives us more than we might know to ask for. Simeon asked for this: that he might be able to see Christ. But to him was also granted that he could touch him with his hands. Simeon took in his hands the weakness of mankind, and he recognized [*kenndi*] the power of divinity in humanity.[17]

Simeon's cult was widespread in the Middle Ages and centered on relics of his arms, so the Norse homilist is in the mainstream of theological interpretation when he understands the core of the Simeon story as the immediate experience of the God-man via the sense of touch. His exegesis is also an early instance of the abiding interest of the Norse tradition in how sensory perceptions, in particular sight and touch, enable (re)cognition.[18] This epistemological potential of the senses, beyond mere registration of a sense impression, is encoded here by the keyword *kenna*. Etymologically a causative form of *kunna* ("to know"), its root also appears in one of the terms for the sense of touch, *kennisemi*.[19] As shown in Chapter 3, the skalds too were alert to the valence of *kenna* as a second-order activity, involving the mental reprocessing of a percept. This sensory aspect of *kenna* has been largely neglected in discussions of *kenning* as a poetological term, in favor of theories of language and memory. The homiletic and poetic accounts of *kenna* bring the body back into the semantics of the kenning and reveal the way it marks the gap between embodied perception and the deeper meanings vouchsafed by spiritual or poetic envisioning.

The centrality of the body to premodern conceptions of mediation cuts across the divide of Christianization. Metaphors expressing one sense in terms of another, for example, were popular with patristic authors and skaldic poets alike. Origen writes of "inner [...] nostrils" and "internal ears," and Augustine of the "hand of my heart" (*Conf.* x.8.12), "ears of my heart" (*Conf.* iv.15.27), and "hand of my tongue" (*Conf.* v.1.1).[20] Old Norse prose offers "mind's ears" (*hugskots eyru*) and "mind's hands" (*hugskots hendr*), while the skalds are closer to Augustine's exuberance, with metaphors such as "hasty mouths of hands" for touch (*hrapmunnar handa*, Eil Þdr 18) and "mouths of ears" for hearing (*munnar hlusta*, Egill Arkv 6). Such metaphors gesture in the language of embodied perception at a generalized notion of mediation allied to the "common sense" (*sensus communis*), which I will discuss further below.

This chapter will sketch some high points of the itinerary of sight, knowledge, and belief in premodern optical and cognitive theory, first counterpointing medieval learning with Norse homiletic reflections, then pursuing the impact of these theories on the account of ancient poetry given in the *Prose Edda*. I will show how ideas about sight and its reliability are central to the *Edda*'s arguments about how their pagan ancestors came to have knowledge about the world and, in a more playful mode, to its key image of the *sjónhverfing* or optical delusion. Analysis of manuscript transmission of the work known as the *Prose Edda* in the late Middle Ages reveals differences in how the various skaldic picture poems were put to use in the evolving practice of the poetic handbook, while later medieval religious poetry shows the continued usefulness to poets of the visionary techniques of ekphrasis.

RAY VS. SPECIES: MEDIA OF VISION

Sight and touch are united not only in the homilist's exegesis of the Simeon story, but also in one of the main premodern understandings of the physical workings of vision, namely the theory of extramission.[21] Extramission proposes that vision is enabled by a sensory medium emitted by the eye, which touches the object seen and returns the percept to the cornea for further processing. The eye thus emits its own light, understood by the Pythagoreans as a fiery beam and by Galen as the result of an interaction of psychic pneuma, the animating medium of all brain functions, with air pneumatized by light. Theorists of extramission elaborated a model of visual rays defining a cone with the eye at its apex. The mathematics of ray geometry could then be used to explain visual phenomena ranging from the rainbow to puzzling aspects of the perception of size, distance, and shape.[22] This lent the theory considerable explanatory power.[23]

The competitor theory, intromission, whereby vision is mediated by simulacra or *species* emitted by the object seen, was repeatedly espoused (for instance by Aristotle in *De sensu*) but did not make much headway prior to the late Middle Ages, as it offered no comparably convincing mathematical model. Intromission remained secondary in western European optical theory until the assimilation of the more sophisticated geometrical analysis of Arab scientists such as Alhacen.[24] This shift can be traced in late medieval Icelandic devotional poetry. The late fourteenth or early fifteenth-century *Máríuvísur II*, for example, recounts how a statue (*skrift*) of Mary cured a woman's barrenness after her tearful intercession. Offended by the woman's absorbed gaze at her newborn son (*má hún varla af sjá*, Anon *Mv II* 11), which causes her to neglect her devotions, Mary allows him to die of an illness. The woman returns to the statue and implores it to look upon the corpse of her son ("look here at the beautiful child," *líttu hier á barn frítt*, Anon *Mv II* 16), whereupon he comes back to life. Intromission lends new importance to the exchange of gazes between the beholder and the sacred object, as the species the latter emits become bearers of numinous power.

Extramission was not decisively refuted until the late sixteenth century, and it remains intuitively appealing. It has always dominated the discourse of magic, in which powerful, materially effective emissions from the eyes are omnipresent, ranging from the deadly blasts of the evil eye to the fascinating arrows sent out by the eyes of lovers. Both of these ideas are well represented in Old Norse literature. Many sagas describe a practice of covering a condemned sorcerer's head with a bag, thought to originate in fear of the evil eye. In *Laxdæla saga* the doomed Stígandi nonetheless manages to blast a field with his evil eye, thanks to an unluckily placed hole.[25] Kormákr's poetry on Steingerðr plays extensively on topoi of vision, including the unseen beloved and her "aggressive eye": "the bright lights of both cheeks of the woman blazed upon me," Kormákr says.[26] In skaldic verse the aggressive eye was not confined to the female beloved, as it is in Arabic and Provençal love poetry.[27] In the anonymous poem *Morginsól*, for example, the (presumably male) speaker's eyes shoot lightning bolts at the beloved: "I do not often raise forehead lightning [EYES] from the shard of the fire of the wave [WOMAN]."[28]

Also in extramission's favor was the support it offered for a theology of light, in which "the corporeal vision of physical objects 'by the visual rays that shine through the eyes and touch whatever we see' served as a model for understanding how the 'mind's gaze' (*acies mentis*) actively reaches toward and achieves intellectual knowledge or spiritual understanding of intelligible objects such as God.".[29] If the senses were understood as active, turned out into a world from which they eagerly sought impressions and into which they emitted sensory media, they needed stern discipline; to be "hidden from the world's pleasure and enjoyment," as *Gregors saga* enjoins. The tongue was particularly vulnerable. The Norse homily *Jn dedicatione tempeli*, known as the "Stave-church homily," interprets the door of the church's main entrance tropologically as "control of the tongue" (*tungu stilling*). Sight, on the other hand, is enabled by divine light and so, for the homilist, is inherently godly. Windows illuminate the church, as God illuminates all who believe in him ("því at droten sialfr lysir alla þa er inn ganga í tru h*ans*"), and they admit the brightness of the Christian message ("liost [. . .] boðorð drotens"), by virtue of which men see: "that illuminates our eyes" ("lysir *þat* augu vár"), he says.[30] This is in perfect accordance with the Galenic theory of extramission. God's light transforms air into a medium of vision, into which the psychic pneuma is emitted by the eyes.

Whether the light, eyes, and seeing that the homily refers to are spiritual or corporeal remains unclear. The gap between divinely inspired, spiritual vision and earthly seeing with carnal eyes was a constant concern of patristic reflections on seeing. It was brought to the point in the question of whether, and if so how and when, the faithful might see God, and what role images had to play in this process.[31] Augustine, for example, contrasts "true Light, [which] is one, and all who see and love it are one" with "the physical light [that] spices up the life of this world with a seductive and perilous allure for those who love it blindly," and also with the curiosity that "masquerades as a craving for knowledge and understanding," which he calls *concupiscentia oculorum* or "visual desire."[32] If insufficiently well-guarded, he suggests, sight is liable to go astray.

HUGSKOTS AUGA: SEEING WITH THE INNER EYE

The transition from physical sight to the "spiritual" or "inner" sight of the "eye of the mind" (*oculus mentis*) or "eye of the heart" (*oculus cordis*), known in Old Norse as the heart's (*hjartans*), soul's or mind's (*hugskots, hugar*), or thought's (*hugsunar*) eye, intersected not only with theological and moral issues, but also with epistemological concerns around the reliability of vision that stretched back into antiquity.[33] In Mark Smith's words, the crucial question for premodern optical theory is "how do we pass from the perception of physical particulars to an understanding of them, and how can we be sure that this understanding is veridical?"[34] Premodern optics, Smith argues, is as much interested in psychological as it is in physical processes; it is literally a matter of "worldview," of ascertaining whether reality conforms to the image of it that our minds construct.[35] Antique and medieval thinkers conceived of the *oculus mentis* as a sense no less than the others, in fact more powerful and significant than the external senses. To get a clearer sense of what is at stake in references to the *hugskots auga*, it is necessary to follow the itinerary of sense perceptions into the brain.

Augustine's influential model of the mental dimension of perception is, to a great extent, a synthesis of pre-existing antique tradition. He describes how a percept produced by the external senses is first subject to the monitoring of the "inner sense" (*sensus interioris*), a self-reflexive and directive faculty similar to Aristotle's "common sensibility" (*koinē aisthēsis*). According to antique and medieval thinkers the "common sense" (*sensus communis*) is the first stop of the percept on its way from the external senses to the higher faculties of the brain, and it performs a number of important tasks. It enables the subject to apprehend the Aristotelean "common sensibles" of motion, rest, figure, magnitude, number, and unity, which require multiple senses for their perception. The common sense also combines and discriminates between the inputs from different senses, each of which has its "special sensible" (for example, color is the special sensible for vision). And the common sense is a meta-sense: it is what enables the subject to realize they are sensing, or to perceive their own perception.[36] Augustine is the first Latin writer to call the common sense "inner sense" and, at times, he uses *oculus mentis* as a metaphor for it.[37] His model, in broad strokes, suggests that the percept then passes into memory as a *similitudo,* or likeness, from where it is accessible to reason, *ratio*, which processes it into knowledge. A further step (*gradibus ascendens*, *Confessions* x.8) explains how it is possible for a product of a mere sensory perception, no matter how veridical, to yield insight into spiritual matters. By virtue of grace, Christ acts as the soul's teacher and God illuminates the knowledge generated from sense impressions, enabling the subject to discern (albeit vaguely) the underlying truth.[38]

Sensory perception is freighted with awesome responsibilities. It is clear that a lot could go wrong. In his *Confessions* (x.30–34), Augustine worries about his senses being tempted toward unsuitable objects: sexual fantasies that creep up when he is asleep; the pleasures of food beyond what is needful for sustenance, and alcohol in any quantity; scents (fortunately only mildly tempting); singing, also in church; pleasing shapes, beautiful colors, and even, if used for pleasure, light itself. To these failures of the will can be added the unreliability of the medium, whether ray or species, which raises the troubling question of whether "the mediator provide[s] access to knowledge, or does the imperfection of its transmission make it a barrier to clear and perfect knowledge?"[39] Finally, there are the representational processes involved in the doubling of the outer senses by the common sense.

Many aspects of the reception of this complex body of theory in the medieval North remain unclear. The poor preservation of Latin texts from medieval Scandinavia means it is hard to tell how much of this material reached there. The vernacular textual culture, especially that of Iceland, was more assiduously preserved and leaves an incomparably richer archive, but it presents its own problems. Its discussions of topics such as the senses and mental faculties tend to be concrete, contextually specific, and unsystematic, and often appear in narrative rather than expository contexts, making the study of terminology, for example, a challenge. Religious literature is one place where Old Norse ideas about the external and internal faculties can be glimpsed. A Lenten homily in the *Íslensk hómilíubók* outlines a relatively sophisticated model of human psychology, combining the faculty psychology handed down from antiquity with orthodox Christian doctrine on the inner and outer man and the tripartition of human being into body, soul, and spirit:

> And that is not foolishness if a man should know what he is or of what divisions his being consists. One is called 'body', the lowest and outermost part of the man. And the other is called 'soul' [*önd*], which is both more inward and higher. And the other is called 'spirit' [*andi*], greatest by far and most noble and innermost. The body is the visible part, but the soul is invisible. Growth and touch, taste and smell, sight, and hearing: all these things are given to [the body] by the soul. And all [the body's] life is thanks to [the soul's] help and power and motions. And both of them [together] are one being and are called the outer man. Because although [the soul] be invisible and counted among those things which are spiritual [*andligr*], yet it is aware of that which is corporeal and lustful, and also of that which is godly. The third part is called 'spirit', which is much the noblest and innermost and highest in a man. It gives to man ingenuity [*hugkvæmi*]

and discernment [*skilning*], wisdom to judge [*dómspekt*] and memory, speech, and reason [*skynsemi*], quickness to learn belief in God, and free will. It is called the inner man, or angel. Under its protection is all the management of the man.[40]

The sources of this intriguing text have not yet been identified. In it the soul, *önd*, takes up a mediating position between body and spirit. It is similar to the Augustinian common sense insofar as it monitors (*ávita þess*) the activities of the senses, discerning between the worldly and the godly; it is also the origin of the body's sensory powers. The soul is decisively set off from the spirit, *andi*, to which is ascribed a list of higher mental faculties. The first of them is given a name which occurs only here, *hugkvæmi*, translated above as "ingenuity." The more common adjective *hugkvæmr*, literally "freely coming to mind," is used both to mean, of people, "ingenious" and, of things, "recurring to the mind," a combination of characteristics that reflects medieval understandings of imagination as being based in memory.[41] Probably, then, *hugkvæmi* is used here as an equivalent to *imaginatio*. The remaining faculties present fewer problems to the translator, but the homilist's brevity and disinclination either to locate the faculties physically or to expand on their capabilities make it difficult to identify this passage with any one of the many variants of the list of internal faculties.[42] Nevertheless, it is evidence for sophisticated and well-informed reflection, already in one of the earliest preserved Old Norse texts, on the role of the senses in cognition. Particularly interesting are the link proposed via the soul between the bodily senses and the internal faculties; the emphasis on the soul's powers of discrimination, suggesting a differentiated model for the processing of sense data; and the rhetorical topos of the list itself, reminiscent of the lists of (quasi)-synonyms in *Skáldskaparmál*. These features form a beachhead for a consideration of vision and visuality in the *Prose Edda*, and the role of the so-called skaldic ekphraseis in that textual setting.

VISUALITY IN THE *PROSE EDDA*

Recent scholarship concurs that the *Prose Edda* (traditionally dated to the first half of the thirteenth century; oldest manuscripts from the first quarter of the fourteenth century) combines local knowledge, especially mediated by poetry, with structures and explanatory models drawn from the grammatical, rhetorical, and encyclopedic learning of the medieval schoolroom.[43] Bound up in this insight is a recognition of the importance of the *intentio scribendi* that is disclosed to the audience in the address to young poets near the beginning of *Skáldskaparmál*.[44] This passage implies that the *Prose Edda* can be read—the obvious caveats imposed by its compositional looseness and complex redactional history will be investigated in what follows—as a composition "written to serve a particular purpose."[45] No mere scholarly archive of myths, the *Prose Edda* artfully coordinates (*setja saman*) its heterogenous material within a narrative frame.[46] It can thus be read, like any other narrative, hermeneutically. Naturally the question of what the *Edda* text means has received widely differing answers: for instance, that it propounds "a coherent view of the relationship between poetic language and religious thought" (Clunies Ross); that it espouses an "Óðinn theology," whether positively (Beck) or negatively (Holtsmark) valorized; that it coordinates the euhemerized Norse gods into the framework of salvific history (Weber); or that it is a text "characterized by a certain skepticism about language and poetry . . . [that] stages uncertainty, on the thematic as well as the discursive level" (Glauser).[47]

With the exception of Clunies Ross, these studies focus on *Gylfaginning*; and even Clunies Ross's book largely ignores the skaldic quotations in *Skáldskaparmál* in favor of a consideration of the terminology and structure elaborated in that work's prose. In what follows, I will suggest that an important goal of the complete redactions of the *Prose Edda* is epistemological; that it is interested in the question of how humans know. This claim appears more familiar in the quickened, communicatively urgent form in which it is expressed in the *Edda* text: how and what did our ancestors know, and how can we understand and use that knowledge? This question plays out in the first two parts of the text, the *Prologue* and *Gylfaginning* ("Deluding of Gylfi"), which contrast knowledge of God and his works with knowledge of pagan mythology. *Skáldskaparmál* ("Language of Poetry"), the third part, explicates the pre-Christian epistemology evidenced in skaldic poetry and demonstrates how contemporary poets can learn about the cultural capital of the past, so that they can use it in the present. As I will show, the way quotations from the so-called skaldic ekphraseis are presented in *Skáldskaparmál* contributes to these goals. *Háttatal* ("List of Meters"), finally, the most derivative part of the *Edda*, imparts to young poets the structured, technical knowledge of Old Norse metrics and rhetoric already treated in the Orkney *clavis metrica* known as *Háttalykill* ("Key of Meters"). Reading the *Edda* as an epistemological project, I will argue, reveals the centrality of the senses, especially sight, to its theory of knowledge.

AT THE THRESHOLD:
OPTICAL ILLUSIONS AND THE NAME OF GOD

Gylfaginning and *Skáldskaparmál* both open with scenes of vision.[48] In *Gylfaginning*, King Gylfi of Sweden (calling himself Gangleri) sets out to visit a tricky bunch of incomers, the "Æsir-people" (*Ásafólk*), who have established themselves nearby:

> When he [Gylfi] got to the city he saw there a high hall, so that he could scarcely see over it [. . .] In the doorway of the hall Gylfi saw a man juggling with knives, keeping seven in the air at a time [. . .] He saw there many apartments and many people [. . .] He looked around and thought many of the things he saw were incredible [. . .] He saw three thrones one above the other, and there were three men, one sitting in each.[49]

Skáldskaparmál describes how a being called Ægir (elsewhere described as a giant) heads for Ásgarðr, again to visit the Æsir:

> He [Ægir] set out to visit Asgard [. . .] And in the evening when they were about to start the drinking, Odin had swords borne into the hall and they were so bright that light shone from them, and no other light was used while they sat drinking [. . .] Everything there seemed to Ægir magnificent to look at. The wall-panels were all hung with splendid shields.[50]

At these two textual thresholds, a stranger arrives at the court of the (euhemerized) gods. Gylfi *sees* the hall, so high it almost cannot be *seen* over; a man in the doorway; many apartments and people; and, *looking around* and scarcely believing what he *sees*, the triple throne immortalized in the famous drawing in Codex Upsaliensis (Plate 6). In preparation for Ægir's visit, the gods decorate their hall with swords that *shine* so *brightly* that no other *light* is needed, and with *splendid* shields, all of which strike their visitor as noble to *look at*. Both Gylfi and Ægir are about to engage in the dialogical form of wisdom transaction known as *frœði*, when the dominant sense will shift from sight to hearing, and, in *Skáldskaparmál*, vanish altogether as the frame of "Bragi's discourse" (*Bragarœður*), is abandoned. Nonetheless, the beginning of their knowledge is visually mediated.

The *Prologue* to the *Prose Edda* recounts how postdiluvian humans forgot the name of God and so ceased to tell stories about him:

> After Noah's flood there lived eight people who inhabited the world and from them generations have descended, and it happened just as before that as the world came to be peopled and settled it turned out to be the vast majority of mankind that cultivated desire for wealth and glory and neglected obedience to God, and this reached such a pass that they refused to mention the name of God. But who was there then to tell their children of the mysteries of God? So it happened that they forgot the name of God . . .[51]

Mankind's path to acquiring knowledge of their creator by learning and passing on stories about him is barred. Their disobedience turns on their failure to listen: they *afræktusk guðs hlýðni*, literally "neglected obedience to God," where *hlýðni* (f. "obedience") is a nominal form of *hlýða* ("to listen"). Listening to the word of God is the origin of faith; "not wanting to hear means rejecting an offer of salvation."[52] Fortunately, God left humans a loophole. It establishes the new primacy of seeing in their attempts to acquire understanding:[53]

> But even so God granted them earthly blessings, wealth and prosperity for them to enjoy in the world. He also gave them a portion of wisdom so that they could understand all earthly things and the details of everything they could see in the sky and on earth. They pondered and were amazed [. . .].[54]

In a striking parallel to the antique accounts of seeing at the beginning of this chapter, the power of sight to draw distinctions among natural phenomena suffused by divinely mediated wisdom (*miðlaði hann ok spekina*) is the origin of knowledge for postdiluvian humanity. Not only do these people think, they also, like Gylfi and Ægir, *undrask* (wonder) at what they see. The idea that *admiratio* or wonder is the beginning of knowledge is a commonplace: "It is owing to their wonder that men both now begin and at first began to philosophize."[55] Vincent of Beauvais writes that stupefaction of the mind follows from observing Creation: we see the effect but cannot comprehend the cause and are moved thereby to praise the Creator, "but we also marvel at the *varietas*, and we are moved by such experience, which sight best gives us, to understand causes."[56] The *Prologue*'s postdiluvian humanity is unable to learn about God because they have forgotten his name. By observing his created world they arrive at a measure of understanding of his power and dominion, even if "they understood everything with earthly understanding, for they were not granted spiritual wisdom" (*alla hluti skilðu þeir jarðligri skilningu þvíat þeim var eigi gefin andlig spekðin*).

Gylfi and Ægir, by contrast, see the gods. The image in Codex Upsaliensis carefully aligns eyes and pointing hands, emphasizing the exchange of glances between Gylfi and the Æsir. As readers, however, we are clued into the true nature of their perceptions.[57] The narrator imparts that the Æsir "prepared deceptive appearances for [Gylfi]" (*gerðu í móti honum sjónhverfingar*) and "[Ægir] was given a great welcome, though many things had deceptive appearances" (*var honum fagnat vel en þó margir hlutir með sjónhverfingum*), before Gylfi's and Ægir's acts of seeing are described. The word *sjónhverfing* ("turning of sight") indicates that these are *optical* illusions, and both take place in halls, in a setting of aristocratic hospitality. Isidore explains in his *Etymologies* that the entertaining "illusion" (*praestigium*) is the invention of Mercury, and so called "because it dulls (*praestringere*) the sharpness of one's eyes."[58] The court magician whose "prestiges" combine supernatural illusion, sleight of hand, and marvels of engineering is a stock figure in romance.[59] Such magicians appear in *riddarasögur*, for example in *Clári saga*, which shares the "vanishing-castle" motif with *Gylfaginning*.[60] In this saga, the magician Master Pérús of Arabia produces a *sjónhverfing* by means of which his protégé becomes king, marries, and rules for three years, all in the time it takes to roast a chicken—illusion as narrative, narrative as illusion. He is also a conjurer, exiting the saga by climbing a rope into the sky. The technology that enabled a magician to fill the king's hall with water, as the protagonist of *Magus saga* does, was most likely unavailable in medieval Iceland, though such wonders were staged at early modern courts. Ben Jonson's *Masque of Blackness*, performed at Whitehall for Queen Anne on January 6, 1605, included a stage setting by Inigo Jones, with a wooded landscape and an artificial sea "raised with waves which seemed to move [. . .] The masquers were placed in a great concave shell like mother of pearl, curiously made to move [. . .] and rise with the billows."[61]

Whether ocular delusions relied upon magical transformations or were the result of sleight of hand was a question that intrigued premodern commentators. A *locus classicus* of visual illusion is the story of Pharaoh's serpents in *Exodus* 7. God sends Aaron before Pharaoh to demonstrate a miracle: he is to throw his rod on the ground, where it will miraculously turn into a serpent. When he does, Pharaoh's sorcerers react by throwing down their own rods, which also become serpents. Premodern reception of this tale involved "endless debates over whether [the sorcerers] substituted real serpents for real rods by sleight of hand, or made non-real serpents appear by ocular delusion, [turning] a biblical episode into a series of perceptual and epistemological puzzles."[62] The Old Norse version in *Stjórn* comes down on the fake snake side: citing Peter Comestor, it reports that "the magicians made a foolish deception and ocular delusion [*sjónhverfing*] of the eyes of those men who were looking on there."[63] By calling the Æsir's tricks *sjónhverfingar* the *Prose Edda* suggests that they too are magical, even as the presence of the juggler hints at the alternative explanation that they are conjurers' tricks, put on to amaze and amuse visitors to a royal court. Although Gylfi's and Ægir's external senses are deceived, this does not, in itself, demonstrate hostile intent, as the romance parallels show. Indeed, while *sjónhverfingar* are frequently devilish, they are not inevitably so; sometimes they are even saintly.[64]

The *Edda*'s *sjónhverfingar* are best not moralized, but read as "perceptual and epistemological puzzles": signs at the entrance warning the reader that the *Prologue*'s model of acquiring wisdom via visual mediation may not apply. Reflections on the veracity of sight were an integral part of mainstream medieval thinking about visual perception, especially in homiletic discourses contrasting corporeal with spiritual vision. Such ideas percolated out into narrative genres such as the ghost story. The *Konungsannáll* in *Flateyjarbók* for the "year of wonders" 1118 reports that:

> In a certain village in Worms, people saw a large number of armed knights ride from a mountain all at once, and at nones back into the mountain. Then one of the local men, well signed with the cross, dared with trembling to go near them and adjure one of that folk to him, to say what kind of men they were. He said the following to him: "We are not ocular delusions [*sjónhverfingar*], as you think [*hyggit*], and not a party of knights, as we seem to be [*sýniz*] to you, but rather the souls of those knights who fell shortly before. The weapons and gear which in life were our tools of misdeeds are now our means of repentance, and all is fiery that you have seen [*sét*] of us, although you may not distinguish it with corporeal eyes [*líkamligum augum*]."[65]

This passage draws a ternary distinction between the percepts of the external senses, marked by the verb *sýna* ("seem"), the product of reflection on these in the *ratio*, marked by *hyggja* ("think"), and the religious truth which cannot be distinguished by the external senses but only seen (*sét*) by spiritual insight. The binary distinction between truth and delusion propounded in the accounts of *sjónhverfing* is complicated here by a theological discourse about the psychology of vision. This emphasizes that the percepts of the corporeal eyes are both subject to internal processing, and extended by spiritual vision, by virtue of which human beings can see through the phantasms that comprise earthly experience.

The accounts of the internal, or spiritual senses in Old Norse hagiographic and homiletic literature transmit significant currents of thought about perception to the North. They reflect the preoccupation of medieval theologians with the difference between visual and spiritual perception, and the possibility of the supervention of this difference in the beatific vision. In the Old Testament, God's invisibility is absolute, while in the New Testament it is temporary and provisional, due to be resolved at the second coming. Vision thus "comes to represent a mode of eschatological finality," by which God becomes visible at the end of time.[66] This is an idea with powerful repercussions in skaldic devotional poetry, as I show below. Gylfi and Ægir, however, perceive the gods with their corporeal eyes. They realize the dream of every Christian, but calling their vision *sjónhverfing* invites the audience to consider its mediated, ludic quality—the ways in which it falls short of the immediacy, promised in 1 Cor. 13:12, of the face-to-face encounter with the divine. Inside the frames of *Gylfaginning* and *Skáldskaparmál*, ocular delusion appears as a courtly "prestige," a sign of a good party. For the audience of the text, it describes the process going on in the mind of the reader as he or she imaginatively enters the pre-Christian world of the "chief skalds" (*hǫfuðskáld*).

ØRMJǪT. SIGHT IN *SKÁLDSKAPARMÁL*

All the medieval manuscripts of the *Prose Edda*, despite considerable rearrangements and abbreviations of material, include similar lists of kennings for the parts of the human body in *Skáldskaparmál*. This part of the treatise evidently continued to work well for its users and required no great revision.[67] It constitutes valuable evidence for medieval Icelandic understandings of the body and its senses, not least because the nature of the source material means it straddles any divide between pre-Christian and Christian intellectual worlds.

Skáldskaparmál's list of body kennings proceeds in something close to the order of the Five Wits: first come terms for the head, then eye, ear, mouth, teeth, tongue; then beard and hair. As in Egill's blazon of his head in *Arinbjarnarkviða*, the nose is missing, but even this lack is made good in the version in *Litla Skálda*.[68] Then come the heart, breast, and thought—linked by the idea that the breast was the seat of the internal faculties—and finally the hands and feet. The *heiti* for the eye are listed as follows:

> Eyes are called sight and glance or look, aimers. They may be referred to by calling them sun or moon, shields and glass or jewels, or stone of eyelashes or eyebrows, eyelids or forehead.[69]

The proposed kenning base words indicate an underlying conception of the eye as round and shining with light. This matches antique and medieval visual theory, according to which the eyes emitted beams like the heavenly bodies do and were round, clear, and lustrous. The only opaque item in the list of *heiti* is the final one, "aimers" (*ørmjǫt*), a *hapax legomenon*. Its first element could be either "completely" (*ør-*) or "quickly" (*ǫr-*).[70] Whatever the case, the underlying visual model is extramissive: the visual ray actively extends into its environment.

A fragmentary text known as *Orms Eddu-Brot* in Codex Wormianus offers a substantial rearrangement of material from *Skáldskaparmál*. A number of items are added to the eye-kenning list, arranged in alliterating pairs: picture, light, air, stars, gold, beam, "and everything bright."[71] Picture (*skript*) is especially intriguing, as it suggests that by the mid-fourteenth century the intromissive concept of the visual *species* had begun to influence concepts of seeing.[72] Other items confirm the importance of luminosity, color suffused with light, in late medieval visual art and accounts of vision.[73] The redactor of *Orms Eddu-Brot* includes a florilegium of skaldic quotations on the eyes: half-stanzas by Einarr Skúlason (exemplifying the kenning "heavenly bodies of the brain," *himintungl heila*), Egill Skallagrímsson ("sunken place of the brows," *sǫkk brúna*), from the anonymous poem *Morginsól* ("forehead lightning," *ennileiptr*), and from *Húsdr* ("inside-moon of the forehead," *innmáni ennis*). In comparison to the innovative prose list in this redaction—of the added items, only stars and gold are attested in surviving poetry—its selection of poetic quotations is largely traditional. With the exception of

Morginsól, which appears nowhere else, all these skalds are also cited in *Skáldskaparmál*.

Neither the list of possible kenning base words in *Skáldskaparmál* nor the one in *Orms Eddu-Brot* matches the corpus of the poetry of the chief skalds whose usage *Skáldskaparmál* sets out to explicate. The moon (*máni, tungl*) is the most common eye-kenning base word in this poetic corpus, followed by stars (*merki, stjarna*), while the sun is not attested prior to the fourteenth century.[74] Poetry attributed to Egill describes the eyes as part of the landscape of the face, "joined plains of eyelids" (*hvarma hnitvellir*) or "sunken place of brows" (*brúna sǫkk*), but no eye-kenning in the verse of the *hǫfuðskáld* uses "stone" (*steinn*) in its literal sense. "Stone" (*steinn*) and the corresponding verb *steina* often denote color, either because of the use of minerals in pigments or the bright colors of gems, and an association between the eye and color likely underlies the inclusion of "gem," "stone," and perhaps even "shield" in *Skáldskaparmál*'s list. This would be in keeping with color's role as the "special sensible" of vision in Aristotle.[75] The conceit of the eye as a jewel indeed first appears in skaldic verse fairly late, for example in the verses attributed to Ragnarr *loðbrók* in his saga. In general, these lists of eye *heiti* owe more to high medieval learning about vision than to old poetry. Another innovation is the addition in *Orms Eddu-Brot* of a list of kennings for tears after the eye-kennings. Tears express emotion, for instance in the fourteenth-century devotional poetry addressed to Mary, in which weeping is frequent and abundant. The importance of the later redactions of *Skáldskaparmál* as handbooks for writers of Christian devotional poetry, suggested by the inclusion of a collection of such poems at the end of the B redaction, begins to come into view here.

DO THE GODS KNOW *HAUSTLǪNG*?

There are significant differences between the redactions of *Skáldskaparmál* as regards their treatment of extended quotations from skaldic poems, a category that includes, alongside *Ragnarsdrápa* and *Haustlǫng*, another Þórr-poem, *Þórsdrápa*.[76] As Finnur Jónsson demonstrated, the redactions can be divided into two groups according to their selection and ordering of kenning categories and narratives in *Skáldskaparmál*: RWTC versus UAB.[77] The same groups appear in their treatment of the extended quotations. *Ragnarsdrápa* and *Haustlǫng* are cited *in extenso* in the R version of *Skáldskaparmál*, with each poem broken into two runs of stanzas. W also includes the extended quotations, though it does not contain the Vǫlsung narrative and so lacks the first block of stanzas from *Ragnarsdrápa*. Both the divergent redaction of the entire *Prose Edda* in U, and the versions of *Skáldskaparmál* embedded in new compilatory contexts in A and B, omit all the extended poetic quotations. Finally, the C manuscript is defective and includes only parts of *Skáldskaparmál*, including the first run of stanzas from *Ragnarsdrápa*. It is impossible to know whether C once contained the other extended quotations as well. The closeness of its redaction to the R version, both as regards wording and sequence of sections, suggests as much, but on the other hand it seems never to have included *Háttatal*.[78]

Most of the medieval redactors of *Skáldskaparmál* evidently agreed that some or all of the extended skaldic quotations could safely be omitted from the text. The function of these quotations is thus specific to the version of the *Prose Edda* preserved in the RW redaction. It could be hypothesized that the extended quotations from poems are omitted in U because the compiler expected the audience to supply them from memory. This is less likely in the case of A and B, where the poems are not even mentioned. These manuscripts simply had no use for these lengthy quotations. When *Skáldskaparmál* was transmitted separately from the other parts of the *Edda* compilation, as it is in A and B, it seems to have been understood as a handbook for composers of royal encomium and/or Christian devotional poetry, for whom narrative poems about the pagan gods were of little relevance. The beginnings of this shift are already discernable in U. By moving the narratives about Þjazi, Hrungnir, and Geirrøðr into the end of *Gylfaginning*, the compiler of U creates a new context for *Haustlǫng* and *Þórsdrápa*, which are named but not cited, that is, the eddic mythological poetry staged in *Gylfaginning* as a medium of cultural memory. Lacking the stanzas with their present-focused references to the context of performance, *Haustlǫng* and *Þórsdrápa* appear in U as names of mythic narratives of the deep past, different only in point of authorship from eddic poems like *Vǫluspá* and *Vafþrúðnismál*. *Skáldatal*, placed in U between the extended *Gylfaginning* and a reorganized version of *Skáldskaparmál*, reframes *Skáldskaparmál* as a textbook for composers in the great tradition of royal encomium. In a nutshell, U mythologizes *Haustlǫng* and *Þórsdrápa* and secularizes *Skáldskaparmál*.

The redactions in R and W preserve *Haustlǫng* and *Þórsdrápa* as integral parts of *Skáldskaparmál*. Features of page layout and prose framing act to bring these two texts closer together and differentiate them from *Ragnarsdrápa*, which is also quoted *in extenso* in both redactions. Although it is not easy to discern a clear hierarchy in R and W's use of initials, there are traces of distinct treatment. The first word of the second *Haustlǫng* quotation in W (sts. 1–13), and the incipit of the first *Haustlǫng* quotation in R (sts. 14–20) are marked with the large initials that the scribes usually use to mark a new section. (The other quotations, *Haust* 14–20 in W and *Haust* 1–13 in R, are not similarly distinguished, however.) The incipit of *Þórsdrápa* in both manuscripts is (or was) also marked with a two-line initial, and in R this initial is decorated, placing it close to the top of the manuscript's structural hierarchy.[79] The *Ragnarsdrápa* passages receive no such distinction, simply beginning in the middle of the page without initials. Care was taken by the scribe of R to ensure that *Haust* 1–13 appears on a single page. The preceding page has 37 lines, rather than the 36 customary in R, enabling the scribe to begin the *Haust* quotation at the top of the next page, and the final half-line of the prose conclusion that immediately follows the poetic quotation is written in the bottom margin, so the next page can begin with a new section. These paratextual signals suggest that *Haustlǫng* and *Þórsdrápa* have a distinct status within the text of *Skáldskaparmál*, whereas *Ragnarsdrápa* takes its place, at least where layout is concerned, alongside the other *helmingr-* or stanza-long skaldic quotations that pepper the text.

Albeit to a lesser degree than *Gylfaginning*, *Skáldskaparmál* too intersperses its encyclopedic, list-like presentation of poetic material with dialogic moments imitative of the back and forth of oral conversation. The god Bragi and the giant Ægir, the partners in *Skáldskaparmál*'s discontinuous frame dialogue, largely vanish from the text after the address to young poets and are only reintroduced for the Hrungnir narrative. The Hrungnir story culminates with the first quotation from *Haustlǫng*, which is thereby lent a peculiar status, suspended between evidential citation and performance. Does Ægir's awestruck response, "Hrungnir seems to me to have been very mighty," suggest that he was the audience for a performance by Bragi of these stanzas?[80] Do the gods know *Haustlǫng*? The prose frame, with its emphasis on the effect of Bragi's story on Ægir, seems designed to invite such (unanswerable) questions.

The moment of medial transition, where the material is given poetic form, is marked for all the extended quotations by an incipit describing them as "based on this story" (*eptir þessi sǫgu*). The introductory prose before the citations of *Ragnarsdrápa* also emphasizes the place of (the poet) Bragi's composition within a poetic tradition.[81] At the end of its swift retelling of the Vǫlsung legend, R's impersonal narrator observes: "most poets have composed poetry based on these stories and have used various elements of them," before launching into the first *Rdr* quotation.[82] The second quotation from *Ragnarsdrápa* comes at the end of the story of the Hjaðningavíg, where the narrator notes that "it says in poems that the Hiadnings must thus await Ragnarok"; the incipit and then the quotation from *Ragnarsdrápa* follow.[83] Unlike *Haustlǫng* and *Þórsdrápa*, which loom as solitary monuments out of *Skáldskaparmál*'s prose, *Ragnarsdrápa* is presented as just one of many skaldic poems on such themes.

In the case of the Vǫlsung narrative, we know this claim is true.[84] Leaving aside the accuracy of these introductory phrases as literary history, they also present *Ragnarsdrápa* as a "cultural text" in Aleida Assmann's sense, offering still-valid models of collective identification in the warrior heroics of Hamðir, Sǫrli, and Heðinn and the bloodlust of Jǫrmunrekkr and Hildr.[85] In contrast to *Haustlǫng*, *Ragnarsdrápa* is presented as being productive for new connections and reworkings: a "classic."[86] Envisioning remained a central plank of devotional poetry right up to the end of the skaldic tradition, but the subject matter of *Haustlǫng* and *Þórsdrápa* made them literally inimitable. Epiphanies of the pagan gods were a dead end for thirteenth-century skalds seeking to compose poetry for contemporary rulers or pious audiences of believers. In *Skáldskaparmál* they represent "cold remembering": hieratic textual monoliths which resist being made useful for imitative textual production.[87] *Ragnarsdrápa*, on the other hand, offered an example of how to yoke vivid narratives about heroes of the past to praise of contemporary addressees, and as such could be used as a model by young skalds. Two of the manuscripts that contain *Skáldskaparmál* also preserve experiments in this genre, known as "history poems" (*sǫgukvæði*).[88]

If, as the balance of internal evidence suggests, the *Þórr's fishing* stanzas were originally part of *Ragnarsdrápa*, then the model of cold vs. hot remembering offers an explanation for why *Skáldskaparmál* cites these stanzas not as an extended quotation, but as single *helmingar* in the lists exemplifying kennings. The compilers of the manuscripts of *Skáldskaparmál* evidently knew large amounts of poetry about and to Þórr. A piecewise method of citation enabled poems about the pagan gods, whose subject-matter made them unsuitable as models for encomiastic poetry, to be broken down into their still useful component parts, namely kennings and *heiti*, and made to serve the didactic ends of *Skáldskaparmál*. The stanzas from *Húsdrápa* were also cited in this way, as a quarry for the raw materials of kennings. The fashion for *sǫgukvæði* appears to have been relatively short-lived. Alongside *Jómsvíkingadrápa* (c. 1200) and *Íslendingadrápa* (date unknown, but perhaps a twelfth-century composition), Þorkell Gíslason's *Búadrápa* (possibly the twelfth century) and Rǫgnvaldr jarl and Hallr Þórarinsson's *Háttalykill* (first half of the twelfth century) are the main other compositions of this sort. As noted above, the collection of poems on Christian themes in the B redaction of *Skáldskaparmál* indicates the dominant thematic direction that the skalds of the thirteenth and fourteenth centuries followed instead.

VISIONS OF DEVOTION: FROM LIGHT TO SIGHT

Sight, both corporeal and spiritual, was ascribed immense value in late medieval Christian accounts of the ways in which living humans could experience grace.[89] Skaldic poetry offers ample evidence that these ideas were well-known in Iceland. Einarr Skúlason's *Geisli* ("Light-beam," 1153) and the anonymous *Líknarbraut* ("Way of Grace," late thirteenth century) place light and sight at the center of their sensory evocations of the divine.[90]

In the opening stanzas of *Geisli*, a memorial *drápa* of seventy-one stanzas for Óláfr Haraldsson, saint-king of Norway, Einarr calls Christ the beam of the sun of mercy, the light of the world who destroys darkness, bright sun from a bright star (Mary, *stella maris*), and the sun of righteousness, while Óláfr, whose canonization was soon to be confirmed by Pope Alexander III, is said to shine with miracles. The dazzling profusion of light imagery in *Geisli*'s opening stanzas is especially appropriate for a poem on Óláfr, whose death in the battle of Stiklestad some 120 years earlier was traditionally associated with a solar eclipse. Sight, on the other hand, plays a decidedly subordinate role in the poem. Einarr imagines the martyred St Óláfr enjoying the *visio pacis* "vision of peace" (named in a Norse calque as *friðarsýn* in *Geisl* 63), the sight of heavenly Jerusalem granted to the saints. But he stops short of prescribing or even evoking visionary experience for his audience. They perceive divine grace only with their corporeal eyes: the saint's "clear signs" (*bjǫrt tákn*, *Geisl* 51) take the thoroughly material form of victory in battle, and worshippers are encouraged to meditatively gaze upon the rood, ornamented with silver and gold, that was set up in Kristkirken in Óláfr's memory (*Geisl* 34), as well as his shrine (*Geisl* 64) and relics (*Geisl* 50).

Líknarbraut is preserved in the collection of Christian devotional poetry at the end of the B redaction of *Skáldskaparmál* and is thought to have been composed late in the thirteenth century. By this time visionary experience had become a key element of Norse religious practice. The poem, fifty-two *dróttkvætt* stanzas long, consists of a nine-stanza exordium, a survey of salvific history (incarnation, passion, harrowing of hell, resurrection, and last judgement, *Líkn* 10–29), an adoration of the cross (*Líkn* 30–46), and a six-stanza conclusion. It draws extensively on Latin and Old Norse texts from the liturgy, hymns, and exegetical and homiletic literature. After describing in his exordium how God's "wholly radiant light of love" drove out the "blindness of [his] despondent mind" (*Líkn* 4), the anonymous poet sets out to rouse imaginative sympathy for Christ's passion by the textbook methods of *enargeia*. He proceeds through evocations of hearing and touch ("High clanging was heard from hammers," *Líkn* 16; "Certainly the highest woman [Mary] bore cheeks wet from weeping," *Líkn* 18) to an appeal to the sense of sight in *Líkn* 25–28, in the exact middle of the poem. These stanzas are full of familiar iconography.[91] Christ is depicted as Pantocrator in *Líkn* 25 (he "holds in his hand mightily his creation all at once"), and the general resurrection is depicted in *Líkn* 26 ("each tree of the sword-meeting [BATTLE > WARRIOR] shall hasten quickly from out of the ground"). In *Líkn* 27, the climax of the ekphrasis, the cross and the *arma Christi*, or instruments of the passion, appear before resurrected mankind at the last judgement:

> *Kross mun á þingi þessu*
> *þjóðum sýndr með blóði*
> *—uggs fyllaz þá allir*
> *aumir menn—ok saumir.*
> *Líta seggja sveitir,*
> *svípur ok spjót á móti*
> *sér ok sjá með dreyra*
> *sjálfs Krists viðir Mistar.*

(At this assembly the Cross will be shown to the people with blood and nails; all wretched men will then be filled with terror. Hosts of men look, and the trees of Mist [warriors] see before them the whips and spear with the blood of Christ himself.)

The intercalary clause in ll. 3–4 ("all wretched men will then be filled with terror"), parallels similar parenthetic statements in *Líkn* 26 ("fear comes then") and 28 ("grace will not fail then") and supplies an exemplary affective content for this apocalyptic vision. The present-tense verb "look" (*líta*) fuses the intradiegetic witnesses of the last judgement with the poet's audience, who are invited to envision the scene the text describes.

This is clear at the end of the *adoratio crucis*, when Christ himself speaks directly to "each man on earth" (*maðr hverr á hauðri*, *Líkn* 43) and commands them to look upon his suffering. The last stanza before the conclusion instructs the audience in an embodied practice of compunctive visualization that mirrors the vision enjoyed by the resurrected in *Líkn* 27:

46. Leiðum hörð á hauðri
hjarta várs með tárum,
systkin mín, fyr sjónir
siðgætis meinlæti.
(My brothers and sisters, let us bring the hard torments of the faith-guardian [= God (= Christ)] on earth before our heart's eyes with tears.)

The "brothers and sisters" (*systkin*) who are the poet's audience see with their "heart's eyes" (*hjarta sjónir*). The Last Judgement is when the saved enjoy the beatific vision, the face-to-face sight of God, and the damned see the torments of hell. *Líkn* 27 depicts this eschatological moment, when what is usually the domain of visionary seeing is visible to resurrected bodily eyes. The audience in the present moment of the poem must make do with their heart's eyes, nourished by the images in the text. Ekphrasis becomes a tool for awakening compunction and faith in the souls of the audience by giving them a sneak preview of the divine sights awaiting the saved at the end of time. It enacts the community of believers in the form of a shared vision.

* * * *

The epistemological function attributed to sight in the *Prologue* is relativized in the introductory chapter of *Gylfaginning*, where the *evidentia* presented to Gylfi by the Æsir take the form of *sjónhverfingar*, or ocular delusions. The lifting of the delusion at the end of *Gylfaginning*, when the Æsir's hall vanishes and Gylfi/Gangleri finds himself alone on a plain, is marked by a surround-sound boom (*því næst heyrði Gangleri dyni mikla hvern veg frá sér*). The illusion leaves a paradoxical trace behind, the reverberation of something which is not. In the complete redactions of the *Prose Edda*, *Þórsdrápa* and *Haustlǫng* provide powerful and memorable examples of how the "chief skalds" went about producing poetic moments of vision. They fascinate the thirteenth-century audience with their face-to-face encounters with the divine and allow readers to draw the conclusion that this was also a goal of pre-Christian poetry. The optical delusions of the framing prose fence in these pagan epiphanies, however, reminding the audience of the illusory status of the knowledge that the pagan poets claim to confer. Only the "light of the sun of holy faith" (*ljós sólar heilags siðar*, Geisl 3) can be relied upon to dispel "the darkness of the world" (*heims myrkr*, Geisl 2).

At the same time, *Haustlǫng* offers an answer to one of the *Edda*'s central epistemological questions: how can a thirteenth-century audience come to know the achievements of the past? *Haustlǫng*'s shield, material bearer of narratives, is a text from a time before text, a prehistorical authority that deepens the *Prose Edda*'s reach into the past. Saga authors are fond of suggesting that storied weapons long outlived their first bearers and carried their fame into posterity; shields and swords decorate Valhǫll, although we are not told whether Þórr and Hrungnir are pictured on them. Emplaced into just two of the six medieval redactions of the *Prose Edda*, *Haustlǫng*'s shield (if it ever existed) only narrowly survived its second remediation, from oral poem to writing. The evidence of the manuscript paradosis is that this poem was relatively quickly eliminated from the canon. By the time the B redaction was written, around 1400, the complexly mediated visions of *Líknarbraut* had supplanted *Haustlǫng*'s ekphrastic epiphany in the exemplary repertoire of the *Prose Edda*, but sight continued to mediate the central truths of human existence. Whether in the reading of a text, or through the perceptions of the inner eye, for late medieval Christians it was clear that "seeing, of all senses, makes us know."

PART 3

HEARING VOICES

CHAPTER 5

THE NOISE OF POETRY

Skaldic encomium is a body of exquisite, intricate poetry almost entirely devoted to the celebration of violence. The skalds tirelessly describe their protagonists' battles, often in an up-close style that emphasizes the handicraft of slaughter. "Strife is seen as the normal condition of humanity and peace an accidental lull," Roberta Frank observes; the peaceful reign of King Óláfr *kyrri* (the quiet) meant his skalds had trouble finding anything to say about him.[1] Even when skalds do describe praiseworthy activities other than fighting,

> ferocity and aggression are so integral to the conceptual and lexical frameworks of skaldic poetry that even noble generosity can be figuratively represented in those terms. A munificent lord will reward his followers, often by 'destroying' or 'flinging' gold. He is 'cruel' or 'fierce' to rings or riches. Conversely the word *mildr* 'generous, benign' can be applied to violence, as in *mildr ógnar* 'generous with battle or terror.'[2]

To the twenty-first-century reader, the celebration of brutality in skaldic battle poetry is hard to stomach, but to avoid it altogether; to consider it in purely formal terms; to search, mostly in vain, for a critique of violence; or to hope for Christian amelioration are inadequate as responses to the skalds' most highly prized poetry. One way out of this impasse could be to accept that skaldic encomium does, indeed, praise violent acts, and to consider what kind of ethics a poetics of violence could be propounding. For the poetry to be preserved in oral transmission over hundreds of years, it needs to be a message which appealed to a broad social group, not just sycophancy. I suggest that this ideal was that of glory.

In her 2014 book *Knowing What To Do*, moral philosopher Sophie Grace Chappell describes glory as the distinction that arises from outstanding performance in a culturally valued practice.[3] It manifests itself in a wide range of historical contexts, ranging from Homeric poetry, through Greek philosophy, through the Allied war effort in the Second World War, to modern sporting, artistic, and cultural performances. Glory, she suggests, is "a kind of radiance."[4]

This phrase recalls eddic descriptions of Sigurðr as a "jewel" (*jarknasteinn*, *Gkv I* 18), shining with "fire of the serpent's bed," or gold (*eldr ormbeðs, Gkv I* 26), or the young hero Helgi as a hart whose antlers "glow right up to the sky" (*glóa við himinn sjálfan, HH II* 38).[5] The idea of radiance is also reflected in the aural and visual brightness and clarity that dominate skaldic kennings for weapons, ships, and battle: a weapon is a "clash-gleam" (*gnýljómi*, Þmáhl *Máv* 5), the golden decoration of ships dazzles, mailcoats jangle, spears sing.

Chappell situates the nugatory nature of many glory-producing activities (her main example, cricket, is persuasive) in the context of philosopher Alasdair MacIntyre's idea of a practice:

> a practice creates its *own* standards of worthwhileness and goodness, standards which are internal to the practice and irreducible to any kind of external standards. The practice opens up for its practitioners ways of excelling, and so of flourishing, which would not exist—would not even be describable—without it.[6]

From the glory-focused perspective that the skalds take on their main subject, the ruler at war, external standards such as the political consequences, wisdom, morality, or even success of his actions are irrelevant. Defeats are memorialized in the same glorious terms as victories. Hallfreðr's memorial poem for Óláfr Tryggvason (Hfr *ErfÓl*), defeated at the Battle of Svǫlðr (c. 1000 CE), stresses how the king's words live on (*ErfÓl* 3), that his prowess is widely known (*ErfÓl* 4, 26), his retinue was the best (*ErfÓl* 14–16), he gave his all to the fight (*ErfÓl* 12), and no more outstanding king can be found (*ErfÓl* 11, 26, 27). The skalds' evaluative language pertains solely to the issue of renown: whether the fighting in question was excellently done, whether these martial deeds are widely known, whether they will be remembered (especially by the conquered), whether anyone else will ever be as excellent a warrior as the king is. Moral evaluation is only occasionally hinted at, as when rulers are praised for killing bad actors such as thieves or looters.[7] When rulers are criticized from a moral standpoint, for example in Sigvatr Þórðarson's *Bersǫglisvísur* (Plain-speaking verses), it is in relation to royal activities such as law-giving, not their prosecution of war. The issue of whether violence should ever be condemned thus rarely arises, in contrast to eddic heroic poetry, which is quite interested in this question.[8] The attitude taken to violence seems to have little to do with whether the poet was Christian or not.[9] Christian skalds, and skalds composing for Christian rulers, praise warlike exploits in the same terms pre-Christian ones do. Rather, this attitude to violence results from the poets' single-minded concentration on the glory achievable via prowess in battle.

Inextricably intertwined in the ideal of glory with the criteria of excellent performance and a valued practice, Chappell argues, is a third essential element, that of merited praise. Excellent performance is only glorious if it receives the approbation it deserves:

> Think of the fantastic goal that is scored—but in an empty stadium; or the marvellous opera that is composed—but never performed; or indeed, somewhat closer to home, of the wonderful philosophy book that is written—but no one ever reads it. [...] The kinds of activity in which we seek glory have a reference to an audience—in some cases perhaps only a single person, in other cases necessarily more—constitutively built into them.[10]

This third essential element is what the poem provides.[11] The *Prose Edda* gives as a list of synonyms for "skaldship" (*skáldskapr*) "rhyme and praise, rhapsody, encomium, eulogy" (*bragr ok hróðr, óðr, mærð, lof*).[12] *Lof* simply means "praise" (cf. *lofa*, Ger. *loben*), while *hróðr* means "glory" (cf. OE *hræð*, OSax. *hrōð*, Goth. *hrōþeigs* "glorious") and *mærð* is related to *mærr* "famous" (cf. Lat. *maior* "great," OIr. *mār* "large"). The noun *bragr* also means "best, chieftain," although the relationship between *bragr* as a term for poetry and *bragr* "best, leader" is rather unclear. *Óðr*, finally, seems to be related to words meaning "rush, fury." This is often connected with the name Óðinn and the ecstatic experience of composing poetry, but it could just as well refer to the poem's effect, as the other terms in the list do. The semantic field of glory dominates this insider's view of what poetry is for: the list could be translated more simply (if less elegantly) than Faulkes does as "poetry and glory, rush, fame, praise." The skald himself, as eye- or ear-witness (*sák, frák*) is the most immediate audience of the warrior's performance, and the important role played by women as intradiegetic audiences has been explored in several contributions.[13] But another, larger, audience is also listening in.

Dróttkvæðr háttr, usually translated "court meter" (Ger. *Hofton*) is the verse-form used more than any other in skaldic encomium. In this form, to quote the *Dictionary of Old Norse Prose*, "pairs of lines (generally containing six syllables and ornamented with internal rhyme) are linked by alliteration in two quatrains to form an eight-line stanza." The word *dróttkvæðr* is used many times in *Háttatal*, and occasionally in the grammatical treatises, to denote the commonest skaldic verse-form. The second element, *-kvæðr*, is an adjective formed from the verb *kveða* ("to speak").[14] The first, *drótt-*, refers to the retinue, the tight-knit group of followers of a Viking Age chieftain that was succeeded as a social institution, during the Middle Ages, by the larger and more differentiated "court" (*hirð*).[15] Although the nature of the semantic relationship between the two elements of the compound is obscure, it is clear that the verse-form is especially associated with this group of people.[16] The *drótt* is the audience whose merited admiration of the ruler's prowess in war the poet seeks. The members of the *drótt*, assisted by the fixed form of *dróttkvætt*, ensure that after both king and skald are dead, the ruler "will always be extolled while the world is peopled" (*mun æ uppi meðan heimrinn byggvisk*, Arn *Hryn* 15). Chappell writes on this point that

> glory is constitutively interpersonal, not only in the sense that there are two parties (agent and audience), but also because, at least in many cases, the (proper) audience is irreducibly a plurality of people, and the individuals in this plurality are reacting not only to the agent, but also to each other.[17]

The plurality of the bearers of the *dróttkvætt* tradition is sometimes obscured by the skald's insistence on a personal, ideally reciprocal, relationship with his patron.[18] Nonetheless, as the name *dróttkvætt* suggests, this is poetry performed *before* the *drótt*, and also *for, about,* and *by* that group. In the small pre-state societies of the Viking Age, the retinue was bound to its leader by personal emotional ties—kin relationships, friendship, loyalty—and by the hope of financial gain. Monetary rewards could be substantial, as runic inscriptions and silver hoards attest. The leader's success in war was crucial to maintaining these preconditions of group solidarity. It was the main source of his charisma, and of his ready cash.[19] *Dróttkvætt* poetry acted to form a collective identity for the group, centered on the leader's and his retinue's prowess in battle. Its survival over hundreds of years of nonliterate transmission can only be explained by the hypothesis that it was memorized, performed, and passed down by the members of this social group, as a form of what Horst Wenzel calls "courtly education."[20] Runic inscriptions offer a terse version of the system of values and behavioral norms embodied in courtly *habitus*. One example is the topos "he fled not," which appears in skaldic verse and runic inscriptions as the epitome of warrior-like behavior.[21] The skaldic form allowed poets to move far beyond this minimal negative exhortation. Their ethical ideal of glory as radiant "hurrahability" (to use Chappell's term) is a model of virtue that goes beyond the exigent endurance of fear, suffering, and death—topics which the skalds avoid.[22] The skalds present battle as an exhilarating peak experience given sensual presence, memorable form, and significant meaning by the technical resources of *dróttkvætt*. I will argue that the heightened sonority of *dróttkvætt* made it a powerful medium through which Viking warbands could collectively relive the rush of fighting, commit their leaders' glorious words and deeds to memory, and reproduce them long after all the participants in the original performance were dead. Battle as speech without words, a favorite theme of skaldic encomiasts, is reflected in their poetry on the phenomenal level, as resounding words which approach the condition of music.

THE SOUNDSCAPE OF BATTLE

It is a historiographic cliché that the nineteenth- and twentieth-century soldier's experience of mechanized warfare was one of overwhelming noise.[23] Soldiers described their sonic experiences vividly. "I felt that if I lifted a finger I should touch a solid ceiling of sound," wrote a Canadian soldier at Vimy Ridge. Another soldier catalogued for the *Cornhill Magazine* in 1916 "the 18-pounder's ear-splitting crack"; the German 77 mm like "the banging together of two planks in a courtyard where there is some echo from the walls"; the "intermittent, hollow, rushing sound" of a heavy howitzer, "with an ever-deepening note which dies away"; the "whirr" of shrapnel splinters and "miaow" of flying bullets; "the loud 'clump clump clump' of the bursting 'Archies.'" War poets and authors emphasized the immersive, oppressive quality of what Ernst Jünger called the "terrific tornado of noise" to which they were subjected. Nauseating and psychologically damaging, noise was blamed for shell shock and was undoubtedly responsible for an epidemic of burst eardrums caused by the pressure waves from exploding munitions.

Such accounts remind the modern reader, stupefied by the glorious drone of the skalds, of visceral experiences of battle's soundscape as a source of pain and fear. Trench warfare is, in most ways, incommensurable with Viking Age hand-to-hand combat between small groups armed with traditional weapons. Still, in a time and place when waterfalls, thunderclaps, and breaking surf would have been the loudest sounds people heard in the course of their daily lives, it is not surprising that battle had a distinctive sonic signature in poetry.

Depictions of the ocean are the other major place where skalds describe sound. Alongside poetological reasons such as the role of the sea in the myth of the poetic mead, Michel Serres's point that "we never hear white noise better than when at sea [. . .] this marine noise is the original one" should not be forgotten.[24]

During the First World War, "fragments and noise were [. . .] integrated into the cultural sound system" in artistic movements such as Futurism and Vorticism.[25] Noise became "a musical resource [with] the capacity to generate new sonic sensations [. . .] a source of aesthetic reinvigoration and revitalization."[26] The testimony of *dróttkvætt* encomium is that traditional oral poets also found the sonic experience of the battlefield fruitful for their innovative poetic of "fragments and noise."[27]

"WHERE THE LOUD CLASH OF WEAPONS COULD BE HEARD"

Swords, shields, spears, bows, and axes *gjalla* ("resound"), *þjóta* ("roar"), *hvína* ("whistle"), *bresta* ("crack"), *glymja* ("ring"), *dynja* ("clatter"), and *gnesta* ("clash") in skaldic battle scenes. The English translations of these verbs are rather arbitrary, and in the translations in this chapter (mainly taken from *SkP*) the lack of standard equivalents is readily observable. No systematic work seems yet to have been done on the Old Norse lexis of sound. This lacuna bears out the claims of sound studies scholars that "for twenty-five centuries, Western knowledge has tried to look upon the world," and it is past time to listen to it.[28] Old English and Old French battle scenes also resound with the din of spears and shields. The beasts of battle typescene in Old English, in which ravens, eagles, and wolves eagerly anticipate slaughter, is often accompanied by descriptions of their "noisy exultation," making the beasts into prophetic heralds of war.[29] Sometimes the animals cry or yell (*giellan, hropan*); their sounds are also often described in terms of speech or song.[30] In the Old English Exodus, the sound of trumpets and horns is added to this battle soundscape, perhaps because of their prominence in the biblical source material. Its poet was doubtlessly influenced by such scenes as the awesome blast that heralds the appearance of God on Mount Sinai (Exodus, 19:16–19) and the mighty blare of voices and horns before the walls of Jericho (Joshua, 6:20):

> then the old rams' horns began to blow
> and the trumpets began to sound;

Joshua commanded the men to shout
and the walls came tumbling down.[31]

The Exodus' trumpets are associated with courage, well-marshalled forces, and glory—fitting accompaniments to Moses' laws, whose fame is praised in the opening of the poem, "Let him hear who will!"[32] Musical instruments are rare elsewhere in Old English battle poetry, but important in battle descriptions in Old French. In the *Chanson de Roland*, human vocalizations and the sounds of horns and trumpets are ever-present. The Franks are identified by their battle cry of *Monjoie*, in contrast to their opponents' *Precieuse*, and the Saracens' vocalizations are depicted as bestial braying, neighing, and yelping. Roland's horn, the *olifant*, dominates the *cors* and *grailles* of the rest of the army, and his final blast on it secures his glory "at the price of his life [as it] serve[s] to blare the repute of its owner."[33]

As the skalds describe it, battle is largely devoid of sounds produced by the human or animal vocal apparatus, or by musical instruments. Skaldic beasts of battle are usually silent.[34] Sometimes the cries of animals appear as part of a general battle soundscape, but there are few parallels to the Old English use of animal cries as harbingers of battle or props in creating an elegiac atmosphere.[35] Instead battle is "where the loud clash of weapons could be heard" (*þars knátti heyra hátt vápnabrak*, Sigv *Nesv* 8). Descriptions of battle noise have a practical usefulness for the composing skald trying to fill the middle part of the *helmingr* with intercalary lines or phrases:

brandr gall á Írlandi, "a sword rang out in Ireland," Anon (*Nj*) 3:2

— *brandr gall* — *á Írlandi*, "the sword rang out—in Ireland," Anon *Óldr* 6:6

brandr gall á Englandi, "the sword shrieked in England," HSt *Rst* 4:6

— *brandr gall við brún* —, "the sword rang against the brow," ESk *Run* 9:7

— *gall brandr við slǫg* — (*randa*), "the sword resounded against weapons (of shields)," HSt *Rst* 17:2

Ben svall; brandr gall, "A wound swelled; a blade resounded," RvHbreiðm *Hl* 78/1:1

Skalds also use descriptions of sound along with the colors white and red to evoke a general sensory impression of battle, often as the opening stanza of a more detailed account:

Brǫkuðu broddar,   brotnuðu skildir,
glumruðu gylfringar   í gotna hausum.
(Points clanged, shields burst, swords clattered in men's skulls.)³⁶

Dregr él yfir   ógnar ljóma
gerir drjúgan dyn   dýrra malma
Gnýr es á glæstum   Gǫndlar himni
ok í hǫrðum hlam   Hlakkar tjǫldum.
(A blizzard of the light of terror [SWORD > BATTLE] is blowing; it causes a mighty din of precious weapons. There is a clashing on the shining heaven of Gǫndul <valkyrie> [SHIELD] and a thudding against the tough awnings of Hlǫkk <valkyrie> [SHIELDS].)³⁷

Vér drifum hvatt, þars heyra
hátt vápnabrak knátti,
— rǫnd klufu roðnir brandar —
reiðir upp á skeiðar.
(We pressed, enraged, keenly up on to the ships, where the loud clash of weapons could be heard; reddened blades split the shield.)³⁸

As well as these (and many more) discursive descriptions of the sounds of battle, there is a large body of battle-kennings that employ noise-words.³⁹ Battle is the din of points, spears, swords, shields, the helmet; of the valkyries Gunnr, Gǫndul, and Skǫgul; of iron, steel, the raven, and Óðinn. The most common noisy base word, by far, is *gnýr*, followed by *brák, dynr, glymr, hljómr, hlymr, róma, rymr, þrima, þruma,* and *þrymr,* while *glaumr, rimma, jalm, gǫll, gnaustan,* and *sveimr* occur a handful of times. These simple kennings are highly stereotyped. Rudolf Meissner notes that their determinants are mostly prosaic words for weapons such as *vápn* ("weapon"), *geirr* ("spear"), *sverð* ("sword"), *rǫnd* ("shield"), and *oddr* ("point").⁴⁰ The utility to the composing poet of a formula like *geirs/geira gnýr* ("spear's din"), attested no less than eight times, is immediately apparent. What is the effect of these profuse but unostentatious kennings?

The similar sonic profile of many of these noise-words (e.g., *glymr/hlymr/rymr/þrymr*) suggests that sheer sound is an important part of their point. Not quite onomatopoeic, they are instances of what Leanne Hinton and her coauthors call "conventional sound symbolism."⁴¹ *Glymr* and its rhyming siblings share an *-ym-* element which appears to be associated with low-pitched, resounding noise. Word elements showing "analogical association[s] of certain phonemes and clusters with certain meanings," known in linguistics as phonaesthemes, are attested in many languages.⁴² A well-known instance is the association of the *gl-* onset in English with sight, light, and brightness (*glint, glimmer, glance, glitter, gleam, glow*, etc.). Phonoaesthemes are also used in many languages to represent movement: "the rhythms of sound and the rhythms of movement are so closely linked in the human neural system that they are virtually inseparable."⁴³ *Háttatal*'s story that a meter it calls "the old shivering one" (*in forna skjálfhenda*) was invented by a shipwrecked sailor on a skerry is an instance of such a link between poetic rhythm and bodily movement. Not just a description of battle, then, but the phenomenal experience of being in the midst of the fight rings out in these kennings, and the poem becomes a sound recording medium. Writing of the "sweet sound" (*süßer Klang*) of the *Minnesänger*, Susanne Köbele observes that "sound is on the one hand thematized on the object level of the poetry; on the other hand, and more importantly, sound becomes (euphonically, euphorically) audible in the poem."⁴⁴ The *dróttkvætt* encomium *Glymdrápa* ("Clangour-Poem") is an instance of this double potential in skaldic poetry.

SONIC PATTERNING IN *GLYMDRÁPA* ("CLANGOUR-POEM")

Nine whole and half-stanzas are attributed in *Heimskringla* to a poem that it calls *Glymdrápa* and says is by Þorbjǫrn *hornklofi* (horn-cleaver). The stanzas describe the battles of a ruler who is addressed as "Haraldr" in st. 9 and identified in the saga prose with Haraldr *hárfagri* (finehair). If their conventional dating to the last quarter of the ninth century CE is correct, they are the earliest instance of regular *dróttkvætt*.⁴⁵ According to the prose of the various kings' sagas in which they are transmitted, they recount Haraldr's career up to his victory at the battle of Hafrsfjǫrðr (c. 885–90). Three of the *helmingar* are quoted in the *Prose Edda*, and *Egils saga* and *Skálda saga* in Hauksbók locate Þorbjǫrn in Haraldr's retinue. Þorbjǫrn's place in the Icelandic reception of skaldic poetry is thus assured, but almost nothing more is known about him. His byname is yet to be satisfactorily explained, and his patronym and place of origin are unknown.

The title *Glymdrápa* suggests that the poem's soundscape—the sounds it describes, and its "euphonic, euphoric" audibility—was salient to premodern audiences. The most obvious aspect of this is *Glymdrápa*'s extra internal rhymes, over and above the *dróttkvætt* norm. *Dróttkvætt* adds two types of internal rhyme, *skothending* (consonantal rhyme) and *aðalhending* (full rhyme), to alliteration in a regularized version of the pattern found in *fornyrðislag*. In regular *dróttkvætt*, *skothending* occurs between two syllables in odd-numbered lines and *aðalhending* between two syllables in even-numbered lines. *Glymdrápa* combines this with echoic effects involving additional full and consonantal rhymes. *Glymdrápa's* sixth stanza gives a sense of its densely patterned soundscape:

Grennir þrǫng at gunni
gunnmǫ́s fyr haf sunnan
(sá vas gramr) ok gumnum
(goðvarðr) und sik jǫrðu.
Ok hjalmtamiðr hilmir
holmreyðar lét olman
lindihjǫrt fyr landi
lundprúðr við stik bundinn.
(The feeder of the battle-gull [RAVEN/EAGLE > WARRIOR] forced the land and people under himself in battle south across the sea; that ruler was god-protected. And the splendid-minded ruler, used to the helmet of the island-salmon [SNAKE], had the fierce mast-hart [SHIP] moored to a stake before the shore.)[46]

In the first couplet, the same word (*gunnr*, "battle") occurs at the end of line 1 and the beginning of line 2. The second couplet exhibits only the conventional *dróttkvætt* pattern, that is to say, ll. 3 and 4 are linked by alliteration (*gramr* / *gumnum* | *goðvarðr*), while the rhymes of the two lines are self-contained (*gramr* / *gumnum* | *goðvarðr* / *jǫrðu*). In the third and fourth couplets, consonantal rhyme of distinct words links ll. 5 and 6 (*hjalm*- "helmet" / *hilm*- "ruler" | *holm* "island") and 7 and 8 (*lindi*- "mast" / *landi* "shore" | *lund*- "mind").

Both these echoic patterns recur elsewhere in the poem. Odd lines are linked to even ones by repetition of the same word in *Gldr* 8:1–2 (*marg*- "many, much") and *Gldr* 8:3–4 (*sand*- "shore").[47] Linking via rhyming sounds in distinct words appears in *Gldr* 1:1–2 (*réð* "commanded" / *heiði* "heath" | *-skíð* "plank") and 3:1–2 (*hrjóðr* "clearer" / *tíðar* "time" | *-ráðr* "ruling").[48] Further patterns involve echoes between words that are not part of the line-internal rhyme scheme, and on one occasion, triple rhyme:

5. *Háði gramr, þars gnúðu,*
geira hregg við seggi,
— *rauð fnýsti ben blóði* —
bryngǫgl í dyn Skǫglar.
(The king fought a storm of spears [BATTLE] against men where mail-shirt-goslings [ARROWS] roared in the din of Skǫgul <valkyrie> [BATTLE].)

Here the conventional scheme (consonantal rhyme of **rauð** / **blóð**- in l. 3, full rhyme of -**gǫgl** / **Skǫgl**- in l. 4) is combined with triple rhyme linking lines 3 and 4 together (**ben** | **bryn**- / **dyn**). In line 4 this yields an alternating double-rhymed pattern that *Háttatal* calls "completely rhymed" (*alhent*) when extended across an entire stanza.[49] Echoes resound, intensifying and prolonging the poem's sonic effect. In the *hjalm-hilm-holm* and *lind-land-lund* sequences, the sequence steps down through a sequence of minimally varying syllables, while the repetition of declined forms of the word *gunnr* in the first two lines is sonically identical (leaving aside such unrecoverable aspects of skaldic performance as differential stress at line ends). This polyptoton has a close parallel in Hallfreðr's well-known "sword" stanza, which begins

11. *Eitt es sverð, þats, sverða,*
sverðauðgan mik gerði
fyr svip-Njǫrðum sverða [. . .]
("There is one sword among swords that has made me sword-rich before brandishing-Nirðir <gods> of swords [WARRIORS] [. . .]")[50]

Hallfreðr's polyptoton emphasizes what the stanza is about. In *Glymdrápa* 6, too, it is more than mere chance that the repeated word is *gunnr* ("battle"). Is digging deeper in an attempt to extract thematic significance from *Glymdrápa*'s "shimmering of signifiers" justified?[51] The name of *Glymdrápa*, almost entirely isolated in its reference to sound rather than subject matter, suggests that this text has been raising such questions for a long time.[52]

". . . WORD-WISE GODS OF THE IRON-VOICE"

On the object level too, *Glymdrápa* is a noisy poem. Battle is the "noise of the battle-plank" (*þrima hjaldrskíðs*, *Gldr* 1) and the "din of Skǫgul" (*dyn Skǫglar*, *Gldr* 5), the ruler a "noise-increaser" (*gnýstœrandi*, *Gldr* 1) and "din-Þróttr" (*gný-Þróttr*, Gldr 2), who causes weapons to "clamour" (*glymja*, Gldr 2, 7); in the fight, the skald says, the sword "resounded" (*gall*, Gldr 5) and the "roar" (*rymr*, Gldr 7) of the retinue's axes swelled. The ruler and his retinue set weapons in motion, yielding a soundscape of dinning and clanking. Such kennings play battle sounds straight, expressing "a real function, an actual relationship."[53] Intertwined with this conception in *Glymdrápa* is another common skaldic conceit, that weapons themselves speak or sing.

Sometimes this takes the form of an extended metaphor where the sword is a tongue (*tunga*), yielding a full or half rhyme with *sungu* ("sang") and *syngva* ("sing") respectively:

> *þars svaltungur sungu,* "there where cool tongues [of swords] sang" (Bersi Ólfl 2:3)
>
> *gyltar sungu hjalta tungur,* "gilded tongues of hilts [SWORDS] sang" (Ólhv Hryn 10:8)
>
> *slíðrtungur lét syngva,* "made scabbard-tongues sing" (Glúmr Gráf 4:5)

In the last of these instances, the tongues of swords in the second *helmingr* are counterpointed with the swords of poets in the first:

> 4. Austrlǫndum fórsk undir
> allvaldr, sás gaf skǫldum
> — hann fekk gagn at gunni —
> gunnhǫrga slǫg mǫrgum.
> Slíðrtungur lét syngva
> sverðleiks reginn — ferðir
> sendi gramr at grundu
> gollvarpaða* — snarpar.
>
> (The mighty ruler, who gave many poets strikers of battle-temples [SHIELDS > WEAPONS], subdued eastern lands; he gained success in war. The god of sword-play [BATTLE > WARRIOR] made keen scabbard-tongues [SWORDS] sing; the prince sent troops of gold-throwers [GENEROUS MEN] to the ground.)[54]

As this instance suggests, the trope of battle as song or speech invites self-reference—the skald's performance is also a kind of "battle-song"—and reflection on the relationship between the sound that is being described and the phenomenal ringing out of the poem itself.

In *Glymdrápa*, Þorbjǫrn calls battle the "chant of the standard-road" (*galdr vébrautar*, Gldr 1), the "incantation of the sword" (*seiðr lǫgðis*, Gldr 8), and the "song of flight-driven spears" (*sǫngr flugbeiddra vígra*, Gldr 7), suggesting that the noise of battle is an organized, meaningful sound, in contrast to grinding or clashing, *gnýr* or *dynr*. Gldr 4 deepens this contrast:

> 4. Ok allsnœfrir jǫfrar
> orðalaust at morði
> – endisk rauðra randa
> rǫdd—dynskotum kvǫddusk.
> (And the very vigorous rulers greeted each other wordlessly with din-shots at the battle; the voice of the red shields [BATTLE] sufficed.)

The rulers' wordless greeting is to let shots clatter on to shields. As the intercalary sentence says, they let their weapons do the talking for them, a topos in skaldic descriptions of battle.[55] Reading this comparison back into the earlier references to weapons singing and casting spells reveals an implicit contrast between words and violence that runs through the poem. In Gldr 4, the question of whether the wordless greeting of weapons wins out over verbal performance is held in suspension by the verb *endisk*, the reflexive form of *enda*, which can mean both "to suffice" (as in the translation above), and "to come to an end."[56] The polysemousness of *enda* raises the question of whether the speech of weapons is more suited to the task of establishing dominance than human speech is, or less.

The backdrop against which such a question can be framed is the pervasive link between battle and verbal performance in the skaldic corpus. A substantial group of encomiastic battle-kennings combines *heiti* for weapons or names of valkyries with words related to verbal arts, including:

> *dómr* "judgment"
> *eiðr* "oath"
> *galdr* "chant"
> *hermðarspjǫll* "anger-words"
> *kveðja* "greeting"
> *messa* "mass"
> *níð* "slander"
> *ríkismál* "sovereign speech"
> *salmr* "psalms"

sannyrði "true words"
seiðr "incantation"
senna "quarrel"
spá "prophecy"
sǫngr "song"
vers "verse"

These base words let both non-Christian (*spá, senna, galdr, seiðr, níð, sǫngr*) and Christian (*messa, salmr, vers*) vocal magic be heard.[57] Neutral expressions for speech or words, such as *mál, orð, and spjall*, seem to be eligible as battle-kenning base words only with additional elements to bolster their performative force (*hermðar-, ríkis-, sann-*), a revealing difference from the otherwise similar use of such words in poem titles.[58]

When weapons speak, then, it is in a performatively heightened language. The efficacy of their speech is often magical: "it sang grievously at the meeting of swords" (*sǫng sárla at þingi sverða*, Tindr *Hákdr* 2), "the prince caused the beginning of a chant of Gunnr [BATTLE]" (*gramr valda upphǫfum galdrs Gunnar*, Sigv *Víkv* 4), and warriors are "word-wise gods of the iron-voice" (*orðvísa Ása* [acc.] *jarnraddar*, Anon (*LaufE*) 6). It can also be legislative: "monsters of shields [AXES] proclaimed the laws, enough for the doom of warriors" (*gǫlkn hlífa sǫgðu upp lǫg, gnóg til feigðar gumna*, Hfr *ErfÓl* 8). Or even prophetic:

Knǫttu, hjalmi hættar,
hjaldrs á mínum skjaldi
Þrúðar vangs ins þunga
þings spámeyjar syngva.
(Prophetesses of the heavy meeting of the plain of the Þrúðr <goddess> of battle [VALKYRIE > BATTLEFIELD > BATTLE > ARROWS], dangerous to the helmet, sang against my shield.)[59]

A French soldier in the trenches of the First World War described how "we listen for an eternity to the iron sledgehammers beating on our trench [. . .] Amid this tempest of ruin we instantly recognize the shell that is coming to bury us. As soon as we pick out its dismal howl we look at each other in agony."[60] On one interpretation of *Gldr* 4, the message of these speech-metaphors for battle is that of the sound which is death, the "dismal howl" of the weapon with your number on it. The voice of red shields is enough (*endisk*); the kinds of laws that axes proclaim carry out the sentence without procedural detour; the prophecy of arrows does not merely predict violence—it performs it. But the polysemy of *endisk* unavoidably opens up a space for other interpretations.

Battle is a crossover point in the poetic system, where the "object level" of the poem's description of events and the phenomenal level of its perceptibility as sound come into contact. On one reading, *Gldr* 4 could suggest that the "voice of red shields" (*rauðra randa rǫdd*) fades out (*endisk*) as the skald's voice takes over. Verbal battle-metaphors bring the audience's attention back to the present moment of the poem's performance and emphasize its capacity to let past aural experience resound again. The wordless noise of battle contrasts with the wordy clamor of the verse. Encompassing and re-mediating phenomenal sound is an impressive achievement of the poet's linguistic art, but it also raises the question of the agency of nonsemantic sound in poetic language. Skalds' claims of mastery are potentially undercut as they are themselves mastered by "the imperatives of rhyme and repetition."[61] A sense of the body's enthrallment by the noise of poetry can also be detected in another skaldic term of art: *hending*.

"LIKE SOUNDS WHICH SIGNIFY DIFFERENTLY": PUNS, RHYMES, SOUND, AND SEMANTICS

Syllabic rhyme is the sonic feature which most clearly distinguishes *dróttkvætt* from the eddic meters, which exhibit only consonantal rhyme of the beginning of the word, or alliteration.[62] Rhyme is rare cross-culturally: "most of the world's 4000 languages lack or avoid rhyme."[63] The origin of syllabic rhyme, or *hending*, in the Norse cultural area is a much-debated topic. Earlier scholars proposed influence from Old Irish poetry or from Latin hymn meters.[64] Recently Kristján Árnason has argued that no external influence need be posited.[65] As he sees it, the crucial factor is the syllable-based nature of skaldic meter. This made word-internal boundaries visible to the metrical system and so available for sonic patterning.

The names *aðalhending* and *skothending* are given to *dróttkvætt*'s two kinds of internal rhyme in the vernacular grammatical literature of the thirteenth century.[66] In contrast to *kenna*, discussed in Chapter 3, the verb *henda* ("to catch") plays no great part in skaldic diction and does not seem to occur there in reference to poetry.[67] It is usually suggested the internal rhymes were thought of as "catching" on to one another.⁶⁸ The verbs used for acquiring skaldic verse aurally (that is, learning or memorizing it) are close semantic cousins of *henda*, for instance "take" (*nema*) and "fasten" (*festa*). Once Arinbjǫrn has chased the shape-shifting bird off in ch. 59 of *Egils saga*, Egill is able both to compose (*yrkja*) and to memorize (*festa*) *Hǫfuðlausn* in the course of a single night. In *Óláfs saga helga* the king's skalds perform encouraging stanzas before the battle of Stiklestad, and we are told that "men memorized (*námu*) those verses straightaway," in a phrase that also captures the role of the *drótt* in the oral transmission of skaldic poetry.⁶⁹ Arnórr's *Þorfinnsdrápa* preserves a similar locution in verse: *Nemi drótt, hvé* [...] ("Let the retinue take in how [...]," Arn Þorfdr 15). *Hending* probably has memorial implications, like *nema* and *festa*. Rhyme "catches" the ears, and so the memory, although in contrast to the *kenning*, with its parallels in rhetorical teachings on memory-images, rhyme (or the equivalent *homoiteleuton*) plays no role in classical *ars memorativa*.⁷⁰

Speaking *í hendingum* ("in rhyme") is a divine achievement, shared by Óðinn, who "spoke all in rhyme, like the way what is now called poetry is composed" and a nameless eleven-year-old shepherd boy healed of ergotism by the Virgin Mary, who had the Old Testament down pat, read aloud from the New like a second David, and "spoke all in rhyme, as quickly as if he were reading from a book."⁷¹ The Norse word *hending* is also used of the non-quantitative verse-form known in Latin as *rithmus* or *rithmica*, which came to include end-rhyme. *Clári saga* says that the source of Jón Halldórsson's translation is a Latin text "in the form that they call *rithmos* and we call *hendingar*."⁷² The word "rhyme" appears to be etymologically related to Lat. *rithmus* via OFr *rime*, and Old Norse *ríma* (f. "rhymed poem,"), medievally attested in the rubric to *Ólafsríma* in Flateyjarbók, is clearly akin to the Continental vernacular words *rime* and *rîm*, while *hending* is not.⁷³ In fact, little evidence supports the assumption that *hending* is an indigenous technical term with deep roots in the language of the skalds prior to the advent of writing. Unlike *drápa* (cf. Þloft *Tøgdr* 8:4), it does not appear in a skaldic poem. The earliest poem to bear a name in *-henda*, Arnórr Þórðarson's *Hrynhenda*, is instead called *Hrynjandi* ("Rushing one") in its oldest manuscript (Holm perg 2 4to, c. 1250–1300), probably referring to its eight-position line, which tends to fall into a trochaic pattern. Titles of poems are notoriously unstable in manuscript transmission, and the use of *Hrynhenda* for Arnórr's poem in later manuscripts may reflect the growing popularity of *hending* terminology in the grammatical literature. *Háttatal*, for example, adds another dozen metrical classifiers in *-hent* to the six attested in *Háttalykill*. While there is no reason to doubt the antiquity of rhyme as a constitutive feature of *dróttkvætt*, as the Karlevi runic inscription from c. 1000 already shows the familiar pattern of alternating internal rhyme, it seems advisable to be cautious about the implications of the word *hending*. Its connections with memory, compositional facility, and the god Óðinn may be products of analogies drawn within thirteenth-century grammatical learning between *dróttkvætt* as rhythmically intricate, rhyming poetry, and the contemporary Latin and vernacular practice of *rithmus*.[74]

Thirteenth-century commentators equated skaldic rhyme with the figure of paronomasia, or the pun. Óláfr Þórðarson writes in the *Third Grammatical Treatise* that:

Paronomasia setr saman likar raddir, þær er ójafnt merkja, sem hér er kveðit:

Heldr vill hilmir
herja en erja.

Þetta kǫllum vér aðalhendingar í skáldskap ok taka af þessi fígúru upphaf þeir hættir, er með hendingum eru samansettir, ok breytiz þat á marga vega, sem finnaz man í Háttatali því, er Snorri hefir ort.
(Paronomasia puts together like sounds which signify differently, as is said here:

The ruler would rather raid (*herja*) than plough (*erja*).

We call this *aðalhendingar* [full rhymes] in poetry, and those metres which are composed with rhymes have their origin in this rhetorical figure, and it is varied in many ways, as may be found in that *Háttatal* which Snorri composed.)[75]

Margaret Clunies Ross argues that Óláfr is led astray by the poor fit between classical categories of rhetorical analysis and Norse poetry, and that "the analogy between *paronomasia* and *aðalhending* is quite misleading and fails to establish the central importance of full internal rhyme to Norse poetics," but possibly this judgment is too stern.[76] Óláfr's language of origins ("beginning" or "cause" are other possible translations of *upphaf*) signals the centrality of the play of sound to *dróttkvætt* using a conventional medieval figure of thought, whether or not it is correct as a literary-historical claim. The deeper affinity of rhyme and pun lies in how both invite the hearer to reflect on the relationship between the phonic and the semantic and to heed, in Jonathan Culler's words, "the call of the phoneme."[77] Jean Paul agrees with Óláfr on the priority of puns, writing in the *Vorschule der Ästhetik* that the pun is "the older brother of rhyme, or its beginning."[78]

Scholarly discomfort with Óláfr's identification of *paronomasia* and *aðalhending* is perhaps at bottom due to his claim that something as trivial as a pun could offer insight into the nature of *dróttkvætt*. When met in daily life, puns tend to be greeted with a groan, "viscerally [...] reaffirming a distinction between essence and accident, between meaningful relations and coincidence."[79] Their presence in Shakespeare has been called *ekelhaft* ("disgusting"; C. M. Wieland) and "effeminate" (William Empson); puns are Shakespeare's Cleopatra, says Samuel Johnson. Despite scholarly distaste, premodern European literatures are rife with puns. Vernacular languages were highly productive of homophony due to sound changes such as the falling together of unstressed vowels. No dictionaries yet existed to demarcate individual words as "discrete semantic units [...] circumscrib[ing] their potential for meaning."[80] Pronunciation and orthography tended to be variable and unfixed; parts of speech and syntax were more fluid.[81] And authoritative works such as Isidore's *Etymologies* lent their stamp of approval to uses of language which "served to blur the distinction among words of similar sounds rather than differentiate them with an origin and history of their own."[82]

While Jurij Lotmann argued that "phonic coincidence only accentuates semantic difference," Susan Stewart leaves the nature and effect of the relationships that rhyme founds undecided, stating that rhyme's "relation to semantics remains both under- and overdetermined, for rhyme can endow meaning with greater depth or empty it of its syntactical or context-bound force."[83] Köbele agrees, calling rhyme a "game of sound" that enhances the stanza's cohesion and, "in a way difficult to capture in analysis, [is] disencumbered from semantics without being non-semantic, unthematic or in any way nonsense."[84] Brogan and his coauthors' formulation misses this disencumbering effect but notes the potential for a gap between sound and semantics:

> rhyme depends less on the structure of the language than on the semantic field presently relevant in the poem: only some of the available rhymes

for a given word are possible candidates for use in a poem on a given subject.[85]

A significant but little-remarked effect of the kenning is its expansion, almost but not quite uncontrollable, of the semantic fields of potential rhyming words. Some of the rhyme-words in *Glymdrápa*'s extended patterns do shore up a single semantic field, such as *hrjóðr* ("clearer") / *tíðar* ("time") | -*ráðr* ("ruling"), which pertain to the ruler's authority, or *hjalm-* ("helmet") / *hilm-* ("ruler") | *holm* ("island"), which describe the physical setting of the battle. Rhyme can also juxtapose semantic discordance with sonic concord: *gǫgl* ("goslings") does not obviously have much to do with the word it rhymes with, the common valkyrie name Skǫgul.[86] Viewed from the other end of the telescope, that is from the perspective of the homonymous play of sound rather than its resolution into meaning, the synonymous wordplay of *ofljóst* ("too clear") is revealed as the extreme end of a spectrum of semantic proliferation enabled by *dróttkvætt*'s loosened syntax and acoustically driven lexis.

The line announcing Skírnir's arrival at Gerðr's court in *Skírnismál* 14 marks the outermost limit of punful potential, *figura etymologica*:[87]

Hvat er þat hlym hlymja   er ek hlymia heyri nú til?
(What is that noise of noises that I hear now making a noise?)[88]

Semantics, rhyme, and the sound symbolism of the words *hlymr* and *hlymja* all reinforce one another: the "noise of noises" thunders phenomenally in the performance of the poem. Semantically, on the other hand, the construction is fairly empty. Perhaps the sonorous threefold repetition and resultant "play of sound" is the point: "what's that hlym of hlyms that I hear hlymming there now" may, after all, be the best translation. *Glymdrápa* 2:4, where *hlymrœks* ("of the noise-promoter") rhymes with the verb *glymja* ("clamor"), also plays on this aural effect, as does 7:2, *rymr—knǫttu spjǫr glymja* ("roar—spears could resound"). Rhymes on *hlym-/rym-/þrym-* and *glymja* often signal battle elsewhere in the skaldic corpus, including a verbatim repetition of *Glymdrápa* 7:2 in Hallfreðr's *Erfidrápa* for Óláfr Tryggvason:

hlymþél við mǫl glymja, "din-file [SPEAR] against the gravel resound" (Eil Þdr 7:6)

rymr; knǫttu spjǫr glymja, "roaring; spears could resound" (Hfr ErfÓl 7:4)

hlymr, veðrvitar glymja, "roars, weathervanes resound" (ESk Frag 15:4)

In the fragment by Einarr Skúlason it is a matter of the ocean resounding, rather than battle, while *Þórsdrápa* combines the associations of battle and water in its portrayal of the god Þórr crossing the river and adds an additional *skothending* on *þél/mǫl* ("file"/ "gravel") for good measure. Phenomenal sound makes intense, perilous experience present for the audience.

The repetition of Þhorn *Gldr* 7:2 as Hfr *ErfÓl* 7:4 suggests it was a well-known pattern; perhaps the poem's name even rests on the prominence of *glymja* in rhyming position. *Glymdrápa* 2:4 is more rebarbative. This line is another of *Glymdrápa*'s many textual cruces: should the first word in the line, whose second element the manuscripts spell as "-ræks," "-rœks," and "-reks," be read as *hlymrœkr* ("noise-promoter") and so (via various construals) "warrior"? Or should this word be taken as an adjective, "noise-making," modifying one of the nouns in the *helmingr*? Or is it, in fact, *Hlymreks* ("of Limerick"), the place of origin of the "thieves" (*hlennar*) mentioned in l. 3? Despite the best efforts of the poem's editors, who are obliged to produce a single text and so to argue for the superiority of one of these readings, it is not easy to decide which interpretation to prefer. It seems unlikely that it was easier in a live performance setting. The skald may have offered interpretive aids via gesture or voice, but we cannot reconstruct these. The audience's first impression of the stanza, then as now, is one of powerfully cohesive sonic patterning contrasting with semantic proliferation—no fewer than seven different construals of *Glymdrápa* 2 have been proposed. The popularity of the poetic genre of *rímur* ("rhymes"), whose derivative subject matter and reduced kenning repertoire contrast with an extraordinary productivity of meter and rhyme, show that it was the skalds' soundscape which retained its appeal over the centuries.

RECORDING AND ECHO: POETRY ON ÓLÁFR TRYGGVASON

Skalds like to claim they can get speech on tape. Hallfreðr captures Óláfr Tryggvason's words before the battle of Svǫlðr in his memorial poem for the king (Hfr *ErfÓl*):

3. *Geta skal máls, þess's mæla*
menn at vápna sennu
dolga fangs við drengi
dáðǫflgan bǫr kvǫðu:

baðat hertryggðar hyggja
hnekkir sína rekka
— þess lifa þjóðar sessa
þróttarorð — á flótta.
(One must mention the speech which men reported the deed-mighty tree of the tunic of strife [MAIL-SHIRT > WARRIOR] addressed to the warriors at the flyting of weapons [BATTLE]: the confounder of the army's security [WARRIOR] did not ask his men to think of flight; the forceful words of this bench-mate of the people [RULER] live on.)[89]

The density of references to speech in this stanza is remarkable. Where *Glymdrápa* 4 opposed the rulers' wordless greetings to the speech of weapons and, implicitly, to the speech of the skald, this stanza sets up a complex verbal relay based on distinctions between individual and collective; past, present, and future; and battle-noise, speech, and poetry. Amid the "flyting of weapons" (*vápna senna*), the king speaks (*mæla mál*, another *figura etymologica*), espousing a key tenet of the retinue's military habitus, the prohibition on flight. This was collectively reported (*kvǫðu*) to the skald, who in turn mentions (*geta*) it in the poem's present, so that the ruler's "forceful words" (*þróttarorð*) live on into the future. The rhyme of *þróttarorð* with *flótta* echoes and recuperates that of *drótt* and *flótta* elsewhere in the poem (*ErfÓl* 1), where the flight of "men from Trøndelag" (*þrœnzkar drengir*) is reported as *mǫrg kom drótt á flótta* ("many a band took to flight"): there shame, here glory. *ErfÓl* 3 emphasizes the role of the retinue as bearers of collective memory and transmission. They hold the king's words in mind and pass them on to the skald, getting them back in future-proofed form.

In the famous stanzas where Hallfreðr weighs the rumors that Óláfr survived the battle (*ErfÓl* 18–23), the relationship between the poet's performance and the retinue's collective memory is more fraught. Here too the link is pointed up by an echo between rhyming syllables. In stanza 15 the relay between retinue and skald is still in working order:

15. *Gótt es gǫrva at frétta*
— gunnr óx fyr haf sunnan —
— sverð bitu feigra fyrða
fjǫrrǫnn — at því mǫnnum:
hvern rakkligast rekka
randláðs viðir kvǫðu

— Surts ættar vinnk sléttan
sylg — Óleifi fylgja.
(It is good for people to ask searchingly about this — battle swelled south of the sea; swords bit life-halls [BREASTS] of fated men —: which of the champions did trees of the rim-land [SHIELD > WARRIORS] say supported Óláfr most bravely; I make the smooth drink of the family of Surtr <giant> [GIANTS > POETRY].)

It is good (*gótt*) to ask (*frétta*) which warriors conformed to the ethical ideal of glory. The retinue's battlefield reporting is fulfilling its function. Accordingly, the skald's poem, "smooth drink of the family of Surtr" (*slettr sylgr Surts ættar*) is humming along nicely.

Three stanzas later the relay has already begun to break down:[90]

18. Veitkat hitt, hvárt Heita
hungrdeyfi skalk leyfa
dynsæðinga dauðan
dýrbliks eða þó kvikvan,
alls sannliga segja
— sárr mun gramr at hvǫru —
— hætts til hans at frétta —
hvárrtveggja mér seggir.
(I do not know whether I am to praise the hunger-soother of the gulls of the din of the gleam of the beast of Heiti <sea-king> [(lit. 'hunger-soother of the din-gulls of the beast-gleam of Heiti') SHIP > SHIELD > BATTLE > RAVENS/EAGLES > WARRIOR] dead or, after all, alive, since men tell me both as the truth; the lord must be wounded either way; it is risky to enquire about him.)

It is now risky (*hætt*) rather than good (*gótt*) to ask (*frétta*) about the king. Embedded reporters on the battlefield have become unreliable, and the skald can no longer easily compose his poem. The first *helmingr* presents his dilemma as one of poetic genre. Is he composing an encomium or a memorial; should he praise (*leyfa*) a living king or a dead one? The second *helmingr* begins to search for an answer. Its keywords are *sannliga* ("true"), *segja* ("to say"), and *sárr* ("wounded") in ll. 5–6, and *seggir* ("men, warriors") in l. 8. The first three are the alliterating staves of ll. 5–6, while the third adds a distant echo of the *s* sound in the stressed but non-alliterating penultimate syllable of l. 8. These words resound in the succeeding stanzas, moving in and out of metrically marked positions in a "shimmering of signifiers" that underscores the text's exploration of the conditions of possibility of linguistic mediation: misinformation, partiality, vacillation.

Sagðr vas mér—né meira "was said to me—no greater" (19:1)

oddbragðs—hinns þat sagði "of point-thrust—who said that" (20:2)

menn geta máli sǫnnu | [. . .] *ferri* "people guess things [further] from the truth" (20:7–8)

Enn segir auðar kenni "Still tells to the master of riches" (22:1)

seggr frá sǫrum tyggja "warrior about the wounded ruler" (22:3)

Nús sannfregit sunnan "Now is truly heard from the south" (22:5)

This intricate game of sound keeps in the front of the audience's mind the topic of what is surely (*sannr*) spoken (*segja*) by the soldiers (*seggir*)—do they report the king to be dead or merely sore (*sárr*)? The technique used to highlight the relevant lexical items is reminiscent of the alliterative collocation that has been proposed for eddic poetry and other alliterative traditions, enriched in *dróttkvætt* by the additional resource of rhyme.[91]

The possibility of the king's death is raised in *ErfÓl* 18 by the plain adjective *dauðan* ("dead"), in apposition to the baroque kenning "hunger-soother of the gulls of the din of the gleam of the beast of Heiti," with no less than six elements one of the longest in the entire corpus. Immediately thereafter it becomes unspeakable, as words for death vanish until stanza 22 of the poem. Oddr Snorrason writes that the king, known for his aquatic skills, swam underwater to a waiting ship, which took him to the Holy Land to live out his days in a monastery.[92] The story, unlikely to be true, is an aftereffect of the gripping performance of doubt in the *Erfidrápa*. The payoff comes in the second *helmingr* of *ErfÓl* 22:

Nús sannfregit sunnan
siklings ór styr miklum
(kannka mart við manna)
morð (veifanarorði).
(Now the slaying of the king is truly heard of out of the south from the great battle; I do not care much for vacillating words of men.)

Beginning with the emphatic *nús* ("now is"), and the claim to have news that is *sannfregit* ("truly heard"), this *helmingr* announces that the time for *veifanarorð* ("vacillating words") is past. The keyword here is, of course, *morð* ("slaying"), foreshadowed for the attentive listener or rhapsode by the anticipatory *m* of *miklum* ("great") in stressed but non-alliterating penultimate position in l. 6. Alliteration on *m* in l. 7 makes a word beginning with *m* at the apex of l. 8 inevitable, but the blunt monosyllable still packs a punch. It must have been a dramatic moment in performance. *Morð* n. is cognate with English "murder," but in skaldic verse it usually lacks the pejorative overtones of the legal term, which refers to a killing that has been concealed rather than announced as it should have been; a fitting gloss for the word in Hallfreðr's poem.[93]

* * * *

Sonorous echoes and repetitions inhabit skaldic poetics on every level, from the internal rhyme of the line, through the alliterative pattern of the couplet, to the "intertextual" echo of verse lines from skald to skald. Figures of speech which render the subject matter (battle) in terms of the medium (speech) encourage close identification between what the skald is describing and the audience's present experience. The *Prose Edda*'s designation of *ofljóst* as a kind of kenning suggests that poets and their audiences were alert to the semantic potential of sonic correspondences. Hallfreðr's *Erfidrápa* for Óláfr Tryggvason, for example, uses rhyme and alliteration to link and contrast significant words both at the level of a line or stanza and across multiple stanzas. Perhaps most importantly, rhyme and alliteration "craft from repetition *in* poetry a figure for the repetition *of* poetry: by supporting memory, sound repetitions ensure that the poem will be remembered and repeated."[94] The prosimetrum of the Runby stone (U 114) makes this point with all the clarity one could wish for, switching from a prose prayer for the dedicatee's soul, to an older memory technology, *fornyrðislag*, to express a wish for the repeated voicing of poetic praise into perpetuity:

Kristr hialpi sālu þæiʀa. Þæt skal
      at minnum manna   mēðan mænn lifa.
(May Christ help their souls. That shall [live]
      in memory of the men as long as people live.)[95]

Adding rhyme to alliteration, *dróttkvætt* redoubles the formal repetition that grounds renewed voicings. Powerful coordinating and affective forces are set to work by the performance of patterned language, and the shared rush elicited by rhythmic speech must have thrilled the listening retinue. Hans Ulrich Gumbrecht suggests that poetic patterning also makes language easier to memorize by reducing the number of unique syllables, words, and sentences that the listener has to keep in mind.[96] Recent research on aphasic stroke sufferers indicates another, more deeply rooted mechanism for the memorability of rhythmic language. The involvement of motor processing areas of the brain in formulaic and rhythmic speech triggers automaticity, easing articulation, because repetition drains words of semantic meaning and switches neural processing to pathways associated with music.[97] This effect becomes stronger, rather than weaker, with repetition, as Diana Deutsch's "speech to song illusion" suggests. When her experimental subjects heard a strongly rhythmic spoken phrase a number of times, their perception of it shifted from hearing it as speech to hearing it as song.[98] Deutsch argues that this closeness demonstrates that speech and music evolved from a protoform of communication with elements of both media.[99] On the more modest timescale of Old Norse poetics, a move toward the condition of music can be traced from the beginnings of *dróttkvætt*, through the development of *hrynhent*, to the *rímur* and Faroese *kvæði*. It is no coincidence that this trajectory is also one toward collective, affectively colored, sung performance.

CHAPTER 6

A POETRY MACHINE

You face a large and complex mechanism (Plate 7). Twenty strings run horizontally across it; arranged in a row at the top are eleven round keys, of which "some get sound if you pull them towards yourself, some when you push them away from you."¹ These keys press wooden tangents against the strings and release them, altering their sonic characteristics. Somewhere in the guts of the machine, although you can't see it, is a rosin-smeared wooden wheel. Its role is to turn and rub against the strings, producing sound. You reach out and grasp the keys at the corners, tugging one toward you and pushing the other away; the wheel turns. What emerges is not the warbling drone of the *simphonie* or hurdy-gurdy—the medieval musical instrument that this diagram represents—but instead a string of syllables: *ab-bey-ad-dey-ag-gey-ak-key-al-ley-am-mey-an-ney-ap-pey-ar-rey-as-sey-at-tey-að-þey-az-vey-ac-hey-ax-qey*!

Rough music, for sure. How about something more harmonious?

> Now many things begin to happen, when words begin and a tune grows and voices ring out; that is also called song which has all those things; and now, that flock rushes forth on to the playing field, from all directions to the helm, which is called the tongue, and they call on her [i.e., the tongue] now for the language and the words and the song, [saying] that she should recite it all, and she does so, and bows to the helmsman and speaks thus: "Hosanna!" she says, which can be translated into our language as: "Save us!" [. . .] And when He has arranged His company on His right hand at Doomsday, then we shall lift up "Hallelujah," because that is no earthly song: ten companies of God's angels and men will sing that all together when almighty God travels with His retinue home to heaven's glory, and we shall then abide forever [. . .].²

These two passages conclude the two versions of the *Second Grammatical Treatise* (*SGT*), an anonymous text from medieval Iceland conventionally dated to the second half of the thirteenth century.³ The first passage, on the syllable-spewing hurdy-gurdy, or as I'll call it, the poetry machine, is how the treatise ends in Codex Upsaliensis (U). The second, on the tongue's helming of sacred song, closes the version of *SGT* in Codex Wormianus (W). These two fourteenth-century codices, already discussed in Chapter 4, combine redactions of the *Prose Edda* with other material pertaining to writing, grammar, and poetics.

When it registers the existence of multiple versions of *SGT* at all,[4] previous scholarship emphasizes the differences between them.[5] The Isidorean passages that frame *SGT* in Codex Wormianus have often been denigrated.[6] Finnur Jónsson's judgment that the Wormianus version is secondary is universally accepted, although his reasons for thinking this are not entirely convincing.[7] Such scholarly evaluations reveal a desire for "an original" in two senses of the word. *SGT*'s editors seek the lost original version of the treatise. Working from only two witnesses, they need a confident sense of where to draw the dividing line between "the proper sense of the treatise" and "extraneous elements [and] mere curiosit[ies]."[8] For many of the *SGT*'s commentators, Upsaliensis' two diagrams, the poetry machine and another one showing the letters of the Old Norse alphabet arranged in concentric rings (Plate 8), fall into the latter category. The search for the original version of the text is, therefore, also a search for its "aim and value," as Raschellà puts it. Two quite different hypotheses have been proposed in this connection, either that the *SGT* is a work of descriptive orthography (the position of the text's most recent editors, Finnur Jónsson and Fabrizio Raschellà) or that it is an exploration of poetics and, in particular, of rhyme (the position of Oskar Brenner, Eugen Mogk, Kurt Braunmüller, and Angela Beuerle).[9] In another sense of the word "original," the "general tendency to originality" of *SGT* has been noted and prized ever since the earliest scholarly commentary.[10] No close parallels for *SGT*'s comments on music or for Upsaliensis' diagrams have yet been found, so they are assumed to be indigenous inventions. Viewed as a medieval Icelandic innovation, the poetry machine regains its value, while the more obviously derivative Christian interpretive frame of Wormianus is deprecated. Mogk notes approvingly, of the Upsaliensis text, that "we find not a trace of a reference to God."[11]

From a medial perspective the two passages quoted above have much in common, and their commonalities offer a way into the text. The poetry machine is perhaps premodern Iceland's clearest example of what the media archaeologist Jussi Parikka calls an "imaginary medium."[12] It embodies "the dream life of technology [. . .] not what technology is or was, but what people desired it to be."[13] Imaginary media, so Parikka, facilitate heightened forms of mediation: communication with the afterlife and the divine. It isn't clear who the hurdy-gurdy player who elicits poetry's syllabic gurgle is, nor can we tell who is listening, but the second-person address in Upsaliensis is urgent, inviting "you" not just to assent to the master's claims, as is conventional in medieval didactic writing, but to interact physically with the text. "Your" imagined tugging and pushing of the hurdy-gurdy's tangents is the counterpart of the reader's manipulation of the diagrams on the page—running her finger along the poetry machine's "strings" (*regur*), perhaps, or rotating the codex to view the upside-down letters of the ring diagram. These interactional modes, characteristic of diagrammatic media, use the page as an "operational space."[14] Cultural techniques such as that of the grid convert the manuscript page from a surface for the passive archiving of an unfurling line of text to a virtual space in which cognitive operations can be carried out.[15] Abstracted (at least) twice, first by the conceit of the linguistic hurdy-gurdy and again by the visual conventions governing the representation of objects in two-dimensional space, the poetry machine makes sound operationally visible. I say "operationally" because the string of syllables I listed above as the machine's output is not strictly a quotation. These syllables appear nowhere on folio 46r of Codex Upsaliensis and are only generated in the course of the reader's interaction with the page. Upsaliensis' weird objects, then, invite reflection on the technological and bodily means for recording, producing, and reproducing sound. In the sense that a temporally and spatially distant audience is what every written text addresses, the poetry machine indeed proposes a communication with the afterlife.

Music as communication with and participation in the divine is at the heart of the celebration of sacred song that closes the Codex Wormianus version of *SGT*. Song enables humans to beg God for mercy, and it envelops the blessed in eternal concord at the end of time. In contrast to Upsaliensis' focus on the technological mediation of sound, Wormianus is interested in the physiology of voicing. The text gives its readers a close-up view of the hidden intellectual and physical processes within the body that give rise to the event of vocal sound. It varies the grammarians' metaphor of the tongue as plectrum with that of the tongue as a "helm" or "rudder" (*stýri*), whose helmsman is God.[16] The alphabet is depicted as writing that exists within the body of the singer. A selection, or "flock" (*flokkr*), chosen from among these letters gives material heft to the notional "word," "tune," and "voices" of the beginning of the passage, as they "rush forth" (*þyss framm*) to be governed by the tongue. An implicit analogy is drawn between the individual believer as a performing human body and the church as another kind of body, a community of believers singing *Hosanna*: "from Christ's name she [the church] is called Christian; we, who are Christians, call him our head, and ourselves his limbs and joints."[17]

As discussed above, premodern accounts of the mediation of meaning stress embodiment and sensory perception. Sound and the voice are virulent in the environment of *vocalité*, where the continued importance of live-ness constantly reaffirms what Paul Zumthor calls "the corporeal aspect of texts."[18] Wormianus' closing image of the singing mouth is more in the mainstream of premodern medial reflection than Upsaliensis' fantastical instrument. What the two passages share is their emphasis on *musical* sound. This is rather surprising, because the bulk of *SGT* is concerned with orthography, and its opening discussion of *vox* declares that *sǫngr*, or music (literally "song"), "is that sound that only lacks letters to be speech. This is made by the harps and even more so the larger musical instruments."[19]

Music is an unexpected choice of analogy if the *SGT* is, in fact, "a simple handbook of orthography, a sort of primer to be used in the schools for the teaching of the first elements of grammar to the students of the Trivium."[20] It is hard to see what point the musical analogies in both versions have in a project of orthographic description. References to music are not uncommon in grammatical literature, but they are usually confined to comparisons between letters and notes, the atomic particles of language and music respectively.[21] The *SGT* makes little attempt to attach itself to the genre of grammatical primer beyond its desultory use of the question-and-answer format in the opening of the Upsaliensis version, and its musical analogies go far beyond those of the grammatical tradition.[22] If instead, as I will argue, the *SGT* is primarily interested in exploring performance—in particular, the performance of poetry—as an intermedial practice linking bodies and texts, sound and writing, then its musical analogies make much more sense. Although structured and meaningful, music is, in Priscian's terms, neither *literatus* (literate) nor *articulatus* (writeable). By analogizing language to music, the *SGT* opens a space for the phenomenal, nonsemantic, but nonetheless rational noise of poetry, such as the rhymes (*hendingar*) ground out by the poetry machine. In Saussurean terms, the *SGT* is more interested in *parole* (articulatory phonetics) than in the *langue* (systematic rules of the signifying system) that fascinated contemporary speculative grammarians.²³

As well as being suggestive for a theorization of sound, music was an important element of the performance tradition that the compiler of *SGT* worked in. Recent studies confirm that vernacular poems based on Latin texts and original Latin poetry were composed in thirteenth- and fourteenth-century Iceland for performance on religious occasions.²⁴ In this regard, as in many others, Icelanders were joining the western European mainstream, where sung poetry in the rhymed, accentual style known as *rithmica* was enormously popular in both religious and secular settings. Poetry of this kind is probably what the tongue at the end of the Wormianus version is imagined to be singing. In an important article, Sverrir Tómasson sketched some possible connections between *SGT* and this new kind of poetry.²⁵ As I will show, much suggests that an analysis of parts of the skaldic tradition in terms of *rithmica* was underway in thirteenth-century Iceland. The two versions of the *SGT*, a project with both orthographic and poetological dimensions, offer strong support to this contention. The *SGT* is, to a significant degree, an "orthophony," a trait that can also be traced in *TGT* and *Háttatal*. The two textual supplements with which this chapter began, the diagrams of Upsaliensis and the prologue and epilogue of Wormianus, can be seen in this context as complementary twists of the volume knob, turning up the music in the *Second Grammatical Treatise*.

SOUND, SPEECH, AND MUSIC IN THE *SECOND GRAMMATICAL TREATISE*

An opening discussion of "voice" (*vox*) was virtually obligatory for antique and medieval grammarians, and the *SGT* is no exception.²⁶ In Upsaliensis, the text makes a brief nod to the didactic question-and-answer format ("What are the classes of sounds? Threefold. Which?")²⁷ before launching into a classification of sound (*hljóð*) as

1. "witless sounds" (*vitlaus hljóð*), mainly of inanimate objects, plus instrumental music;
2. animal "voice" (*rǫdd*), usually "senseless" (*skynlaus*), albeit potentially interpretable;
3. what humans have, namely "sound and voice and speech" (*hljóð ok rǫdd ok mál*).

A tripartite classification, especially one that sets out from sound, is unusual. Most Latin grammarians start with *vox* and divide it with either Donatus (mid 4th cent. CE), into two categories, articulate, or intelligible (*articulata*) and confused (*confusa*), or with Priscian (early 6th cent. CE), into four species: articulate, inarticulate (*inarticulata*), writeable (*literata*), and non-writeable (*illiterata*). Priscian's species are then combined to yield a four-position system.[28] Unlike the *Third Grammatical Treatise*, *SGT* shows no particular interest in Prisician's model. Nor do the passages cited by Raschellà from Roger Bacon's *Summulae dialectices* (first half of the 13th cent.) seem especially close.[29] Valeria Micillo suggests that *SGT*'s classification is actually twofold and based on an opposition between rational and irrational voice. Reason is undoubtedly important, but her claim neglects both the treatise's reference to music, whose relation to these two categories is complex, and the emphatic way that both redactions of *SGT* make a threefold, not a twofold, distinction of sound.[30]

The place of music in *vox* was a sticking point for late antique grammarians.[31] The observation that musical sound is measurable, ordered, and meaningful, but cannot be written, lies at the root of the problem. Some grammarians, such as Probus (4th cent.), place music in the "confused" category because it is not writeable; others, such as Marius Victorinus (4th cent.), are persuaded by the intelligibility of musical sounds that they belong in the "articulate" category; Diomedes (4th cent.) introduces a third category between speech and sound, "ringing" (*tinnitus*), for instrumental music.[32] None of these works are similar enough to *SGT* to suggest that they are its proximate source. Probus denies any articulate quality at all to music, Victorinus includes all instrumental music in the "articulate" category, and Diomedes' system, while tripartite like *SGT*'s, draws the lines in different places. Notwithstanding the difficulty of parsing the *SGT*'s statements on music, it is clear that they are more nuanced than this.

Medieval theorists of music, rather than antique grammarians, offer the closest parallels to *SGT*'s discussion of sound. Leach comments that

> relying predominantly on the definitions of Isidore of Seville's *Etymologies*, medieval music theorists typically define *vox* [...] as a subset of sound. All voice (*vox*) is sound (*sonus*), but not all sound is voice; the sound that is voice is specifically that produced by the voices of human beings or animals—that is, by the breath of something which is alive, has blood, and itself possesses a sense of hearing.[33]

Some combined this distinction with one allied to the grammarians' bipartite division, namely into "discrete" (*discreta*) and "continuous" (*continua*).[34] John Cotton (Johannes Afflighemensis) was the author of one of the most popular medieval texts of music theory. In his *De musica* (c. 1100), he

> divides natural sounds into 'discrete' sounds—i.e. musical intervals as produced on stringed instruments, bells and organs, and 'indiscrete' sounds, such as human laughter, groaning, barking and roaring, whistles and children's instruments.[35]

Similarly, *SGT*'s classification identifies two subclasses within the overarching phenomenon of sound. *Hljóð*, equivalent to Latin *sonus*, is both the name of the phenomenon as a whole and of its most general case, the inarticulate sounds of class 1 that are mainly produced by inanimate objects. The overarching phenomenon of *hljóð* also encompasses two further subclasses, *rǫdd* (animal voice) and *mál* (human language). Humans "have" (*hafa*) all three: sound, voice, and language. This claim is borne out by the descriptions of the preceding classes. Some of the sounds in the first class are made by humans, such as the noise of a crowd (*manna þysinn*), and humans obviously share voice with the animals of the second class, although no examples of human vocalization are given.[36]

This lack is rectified in the Wormianus text, which prefaces its discussion of *vox* with a passage on God-given *ratio* and the physiology of the human vocal tract:

> Now because man is adorned and ornamented with a rational spirit [*skynsamligum anda*], he understands and distinguishes all things precisely and more clearly than other creatures do: then let him use and enjoy this loan from God. The heart of man perceives [*kennir*] all, and both the windpipe and the gullet lie next to the heart, and spirit-sufflated [*andblásnar*] arteries run up from there and are rooted there, both [*sic*] those arteries which bear wind or breath, blood or song; and at the other end they meet at the roots of the tongue, because each is necessary; voice [*rǫdd*] also runs up for every word.[37]

Previous commentators are, again, certain that this passage bears no relation to the rest of the *SGT*.[38] But its argument that *vox* is the attribute of a rational, ensouled being, as it is rooted in the heart and co-present with breath and spirit, is in fact closely linked to the ensuing classification. If embodiment is (usually) what separates *vox* from *sonus*, rationality is what divides human from animal voice. The prefatory material in Wormianus ends with the statement that "these things have sound [*hljóð*], some voice [*rǫdd*] and some speech [*mál*], as was said."[39] Finnur Jónsson suggested inserting "some" (*sumir*) before "sound" to match the distinction made in Upsaliensis, but if the three categories work as I suggest, this emendation is superfluous.[40]

Both versions of the treatise agree that speech presupposes not only the possession of faultless vocal organs, but also cognitive capacities: "Memory is necessary in order to remember the pronunciation of the words, and [. . .] intelligence and [. . .] understanding in order that one may remember to speak the words that one wishes."[41] "Skill in speech" (*snilld málsins*), at the apex of the classification, also involves the command of rhetorical resources: intelligence (*vit*) again, as well as "knowledge of words" (*orðfrœði*; W has *orðfœri* "word-instruments") and "forethought" (*fyrirætlan*). Contrary to Micillo's assertion, rationality, expressed as "wit" (*vit*) and "sense" (*skyn*), crops up at several points. "Witless" (*vitlaus*) noises, a clattery lot, include both nouns denoting the natural sounds of inanimate objects—*gnýr, glymr, dynr, þrymr, hljómr* and so on, of rocks, water, and the weather—and non-semantic sounds potentially involving human agency, such as the clash (*brak*) of weapons, the noise of a crowd, or the splitting (*bresta*) of wood. The clash of weapons, mentioned twice in Upsaliensis, is the only item in this list that does not appear in the Latin sources. This may be due to its prominence in skaldic poetry, as explored in Chapter 5. The *SGT* grants significance of a limited kind to the voices of animals. It lists verbs for animal cries (*syngja, gjalla, klaka, blása*) and observes that these are "distinguished by various names,"[42] suggesting familiarity with the Latin genre of *voces animantium* ("voices of animate things"), lists of animal names paired with the verb for their proper vocalization.[43] It adds that "people understand the sense of what the animals seem to be indicating by many of their sounds,"[44] that is, that the noises and other actions of animals are not meaningless, but often significant and interpretable. Maurizio Bettini notes that

> For the ancient[s], the voices of animals represented ominous sounds, as happened precisely with birds singing (which was carefully scrutinized by specialist diviners) and asses braying. They were voices that forecast the weather or announced the season, and for this reason peasants or

seamen listened to them with much interest. The songs of birds, in particular [. . .] were a source of information on things to come.⁴⁵

This view is abundantly evident in the Old Norse corpus, for example in the talking birds of the *Poetic Edda*. Animals may themselves lack reason—"all these voices are very senseless," *skynlausar*, the *SGT* concludes, using the same word, *skyn*, as was used for humans' God-given *ratio*—but their behavior is not without meaning, in contrast to the natural sounds of class 1.

Music "made by the harps and even more so the larger musical instruments" is included not in the second class, with birdsong, nor in the third, with speech, but rather tacked on to the end of the first class, with the phrase *en hér um fram*, literally "but further on from here." Musical sound therefore takes up the same position in *SGT*—as a subset of natural sound, distinguished by its "discretion"—as it does in medieval theorists of music such as John Cotton. The claim that music lacks only letters to be speech (*mál*) implies that it is not irrational, as intelligence (*vit*) is associated with speech in the description of the third class. Specifying the harp focuses attention on the stringed instruments that were central to music's claim to rationality. Musical intervals were defined as numerical ratios of the length of a vibrating string, such as that of the instrument classically used in teaching, the monochord.⁴⁶ The complementary distribution between music and language that the *SGT* proposes is taken up again in Wormianus' conclusion, which compares the alphabet to the notes of the gamut (*gammi*):

> These letters [*stafir*] make all speech [*mál*], and speech catches various ones, just as, to draw a comparison, harp-strings make sound, or the keys are released in the *simphoníe*, or when an organ goes up and down, back and forth across the whole scale [*gammi*], that one which has nineteen keys and eight voices;⁴⁷ and now those five rings of letters which were discussed before come to meet them. They are called respectively the stave-row [i.e., alphabet] and the scale, and the 'sound-staves' [*hljóðstafir*] take there their sound, and the 'voice-staves' [*raddarstafir*] voice, 'speech-staves' [*málstafir*] the speech, and come together to form so many words that nothing is spoken [*mælt*] in this world unless these letters are made use of. And there is no such cry [*læti*] nor sound nor voice that it may not all be found in the scale.⁴⁸

Scale and alphabet are presented here as parallel technologies, imagined in concrete, tangible form: the scale in its realization in the strings and keys of musical instruments, and the alphabet in the five rings of the "word-instrument," or as it is called in the text, "playing-field" *(leikvǫllr)*. What the alphabet does for words, the Wormianus text argues, the scale does for nonverbal, humanly produced sound. In a grammatical commonplace, the smallest units of words, the letters, are equated with the smallest units of music, the notes. Both notes and letters have three species: sound, voice, and speech for letters; cry, sound, and voice (that is, everything except speech) for musical notes. Notes and letters are equivalent on one level, as both are the written media of sonic phenomena, and differentiated on another, as only letters mediate speech. This passage is linked back to the analyses in the rest of the treatise by the terms it uses for letters (*hljóðstafir, raddarstafir* and *málstafir*), which rather unexpectedly recapitulate *hljóð, rǫdd,* and *mál,* the three classes of sound from the introduction.[49] It is not clear what the significance of this repetition is, beyond the neatness with which it joins the end of the treatise to its beginning.[50] The overall message is clear, however. Speech "catches" (*hendir*) various letters (a reflection on the *hendingar* produced by the poetry machine may underlie the choice of this particular verb), combining them into words, just as notes are selected by plucking strings or releasing keys, yielding music. Rhymes, then, are harmonies. The conclusion sums up the twin preoccupations of the *SGT*, namely the superiority of speech over instrumental music due to the former's ability to embody rational, linguistically mediated meaning, and on the flipside, the enduring presence in it of extralinguistic sound—the noise of poetry.

THE NOISE OF POETRY

The *SGT* bears the imprint of speculative music theory both in its categorization of sound and in the pervasiveness of its musical metaphors. That the musical aspects of the treatise have attracted little attention so far is perhaps because previous scholarship has regarded it exclusively as a work of grammar. But crossings of the boundary between the arts of music and grammar had become common in the thirteenth century. Their placement in the *trivium* and the *quadrivium* respectively meant that grammar and music traditionally occupied distinct domains. While the language arts of the *trivium* (grammar, rhetoric, and dialectic) dealt with *thesei*, those things governed by human convention and varying over time and according to local custom, the mathematical arts of the *quadrivium* (arithmetic, geometry, music, and astronomy) were concerned with *physei*, the immutable things of nature, measurable as numbers, quantities, or magnitudes.[51] Although grammatical works often drew comparisons with music, and vice versa, the *thesei* of grammar were not susceptible to analysis in terms of number. Metrics—not one of the seven arts itself, but rather a subdivision of music—bridged this apparently unbridgeable gap. It offered a way to apply a science of measure to the ever-changing, contingent stuff of language, in its realization as poetry.[52]

In the twelfth and thirteenth centuries poetics thus began to be "emancipated from grammar."[53] It moved beyond rules for correct writing (*recte scribendi*) and eloquence (*bene loquendi*) to encompass the composition of new works drawing on the classical inheritance in accordance with up-to-date stylistic canons. The best-known of these new works on poetics are Matthew of Vendôme's *Ars versificatoria* (c. 1175), Geoffrey of Vinsauf's *Poetria nova* (1208–13), and John of Garland's *Parisiana poetria* (c. 1220).[54] The ambition to relaunch a tradition that had fallen into abeyance in the millennium since Horace composed his *Ars poetica* sounds forth in the name of Geoffrey's work. His treatise in particular quickly became immensely popular, and some two hundred manuscripts of it survive. John of Garland's *Parisiana poetria* was soon taken up in university instruction at Paris and remained in use for hundreds of years.[55] Icelanders were early adopters of the theological writings of the Paris schools, and it is likely that the new poetics soon found an audience in Iceland, too.[56] Many years ago Peter Foote showed that the anonymous author of the fourteenth-century skaldic poem *Lilja*, who polemicizes against "old words" (*fornyrði*, *Lil* 98), must have known the *Poetria nova* or an epitome or florilegium drawn from it, although neither remnant nor mention of this book has survived in Iceland.[57] The desire to preserve ancient verse and make it accessible to contemporary audiences and poets is powerfully apparent across the whole spectrum of Norse poetological writings, from the collections of eddic poetry, through the *Prose Edda* manuscripts, to the grammatical treatises. Most evident in *Gylfaginning* and *Skáldskaparmál*, where enormous effort is expended on codifying and explaining the referential world of ancient poems, I will argue that this interest also drives *Háttatal*'s and the *Second Grammatical Treatise*'s preoccupation with the acoustic experience of poetry.

The *Ars versificatoria*, *Poetria nova*, and *Parisiana poetria* were part of a relatively brief flowering of Latin *artes poeticae*. Their chief heirs were vernacular works on poetics of the later fourteenth century, such as those composed for the *Consistori del Gay Saber* ("Consistory of the Gay Science"), a society founded at Toulouse in 1323, which aimed to preserve the legacy of troubadour poetry, or the *Tabulatur* of the German *Meistersänger*.[58] The novelty of the thirteenth-century "arts" is itself only relative. The new poetics was more or less heavily indebted to a pre-existing discourse about meter elaborated in quadrivial speculations on the mathematical basis of music. An important point of intersection between Latin and vernacular poetics was in just these metrical discussions, in theories about the Latin poetic form known as *rithmica*. Born from the breakdown of quantity in medieval Latin, which led to the development of accentual, syllable-counting meters, *rithmica* is a site where vernacular and Latin poetics meet. In *De arte metrica* (c. 710 CE), Bede observes that

> It appears that rhythmus is similar to metric, for it is a composition with modulation of words, without metrical measure, but arranged by the number of syllables to please the ears, as are the songs of vernacular poets.[59]

In another early sign of this comparative enterprise, the Old High German *Ludwigslied* is rubricated as *rithmus teutonicus* in its ninth-century manuscript.[60] *Rithmica* was defined in the earlier Middle Ages entirely by its regular syllable count: "the constructive principle of *rhythmus* is the countability of syllables and thus a specific *numerositas* that is to be grasped functionally as the 'form' of the verse."[61] By the eleventh century the growing popularity of *rithmica*, which was typically sung, was apparent in both poetic and musical contexts. Technical terms describing *rithmica* were often borrowed from music, and it was mostly discussed in the context of the rhythms of vocal performance. Alberic of Monte Cassino (d. 1088), for example, includes in his letter-writing manual a section titled *De rithmis* ("On rhythms"), whose examples are taken from hymns.[62] Margot Fassler writes that

> The total penetration of the poetic and musical arts by the rhythmic style described by Alberic of Monte Cassino was the most significant single event of the twelfth century in either of these realms. Both poetry and music were completely transformed by this new poetics, and in a variety of ways. The new rhythmic poetry was always sung and its development insured a new period of interaction between the arts of poetry and music. As we might expect, at the close of the most intense period of creativity, a new theoretical tradition rose up to explain the art of rhythmic poetry to students—students, we may assume, of both poetry and music.[63]

Works of *ars rithmica*—still at this stage understood as part of music—proliferated in the twelfth century and formed the basis for the discussion of *rithmica* in John of Garland's *Parisiana poetria*, the most detailed of the *artes poeticae*.[64]

Latin verse in the *rithmica* style was certainly known in Iceland, and the art of composing *rithmica* seems to have been practiced there too. The fourteenth-century Latin office for St Þorlákr (*Sancti Thorlaci episcopi officia rythmica*), for example, uses a four-line stanza with end-rhyme and sporadic alliteration.[65] Fragments of original rhymed offices for Ambrosius and Jón also survive.[66] Cross-pollination occurred between stanzaic, syllable-counting *rithmica* and skaldic forms such as *hrynhent*, as evidenced by the Latin stanzas composed in *dróttkvætt* and *hrynhent* found in AM 732b 4to (c. 1300–25).[67] Schoolbooks teaching this art, or extracts from them, were possibly also available in Iceland, presumably alongside such bestsellers as the *Poetria nova*. The inventory of the monastery of Viðey from 1397 includes nine *versabækur* (books of Latin verse), and the skill of churchmen in *versagjörð* (verse-making) is mentioned several times in the bishops' sagas.[68]

There are also traces of the analytical discourse on *rithmica* in Norse poetological texts. Theorists of music such as Boethius (c. 475–526 CE) had adopted the arithmetical term *consonantia* to refer to the ratios embodied in musical intervals (diapason, diatessaron, diapente, etc.).[69] As time went on rhyme became an important feature of *rithmica*, and the term *consonantia* was used in treatises on *rithmica* in a transferred sense, to express the regular recurrence of units composed of a certain number of syllables and the repetition of sounds in rhyme. Thomas of Capua (c. 1185–1289), for example, writes that "rhythm, as in Hugh [Primas] [. . .] is constructed by the number of syllables and by the consonances of words [*sillabarum numero et vocum consonantiis*]" and refers to end-rhyme as *consonantia finalis*.[70] In Ólafr Þórðarson's discussion of the first *accidens* of the syllable (*samstafa*) in chapter 5 of the *Third Grammatical Treatise*, he claims that full rhyme of disyllabic words is common both in Norse and Latin poetry: "writings are composed with rhymes like this in Latin poetry."[71] He then quotes two lines of end-rhymed *rithmica* on Thomas à Becket and compares its style of rhyme to *runhent*, quoting a couplet from st. 83 of *Háttatal*. He concludes that

> Latin clerics also have this rhyme in verses which they call *consonantia*, and there should be the same vowel in the final syllable of each of two

words, as here: *estas terras*. Little use is made of this rhyme in Norse poetry when there are more syllables in a word than one.[72]

No Latin source has yet been identified for this passage.[73] Alongside the quotation of a passage of Latin verse in *rithmica*, the use of the word *consonantia* strongly suggests that Ólafr was acquainted with treatises about *rithmica* that used this word as a technical term. Evidently *runhent* was being compared to *rithmica* in thirteenth-century Iceland, and at least some elements of the type of analysis practiced in treatises on *rithmica* were known there.

The section on *runhent* in *Háttatal* offers further support for this hypothesis. With typical emphasis on *numerositas*, a late twelfth-century treatise on *rithmica* states that

> rhythm is a harmonious, consonant arrangement of utterances, uninterruptedly produced by uniformity of syllables. Rhythm comes from the Greek *rithmos*, meaning number, since it must be composed according to a fixed number of syllables. Number must be considered in rhythm first in the lines, and next in the syllables and consonances.[74]

The similarity of this analysis to *Háttatal*'s opening statement is remarkable:

> What kinds of number (*tala*) are there in the rule for verse-forms?
>
> Three.
>
> What are they?
>
> One kind of number is how many verse-forms are found in the poetry of major poets. The second is how many lines there are in one stanza in each verse-form. The third is how many syllables are put in each line in each verse-form.[75]

Háttatal's answer to the fundamental question of the role of *numerositas* in verse-forms begins, as do all the Norse poetological texts, with ancient verse. The works of the "chief skalds" (*hǫfuðskáld*) are at once the yardstick for contemporary achievements and an object of analysis in their own right. Although few of their stanzas are quoted, the verse of the chief skalds still provides *Háttatal* with its *raison d'être*, "acknowledging the aesthetic of the past, but remaking it according to contemporary notions of literary refinement."[76]

Playing off Horace's image of the forest of words that dies as the year advances (*Ars poetica*, ll. 60–62), Daniel Heller-Roazen writes that

> relics, ruins or monuments, the works of past poets have value as exemplars: instances of resistance or of commemoration, perhaps of resistance *and* commemoration, they testify to the passage of languages. Leaves scattered and dried out, the verses thus call to mind ancient forests. Yet, it happens also that the vestiges are effaced. In time, works become opaque, however crystalline they had once been. If one wants to pierce their obscurity and make out the brilliance of an initial beginning, a particular art is then necessary.[77]

What *Háttatal* thinks this "particular art" consists of has surprised many. Anthony Faulkes describes the exposition in the treatise's opening section, quoted above, as "illogical" and Judy Quinn as "curious."[78] Their surprise is understandable. After the number of traditional verse-forms, the next *tala* (number) is how many lines there are in a stanza. This is virtually invariant in *Háttatal*, which only moves away from the eight-line norm in two stanzas, close to the end of the poem, exemplifying *ljóðaháttr* and *galdralag*. In the analysis of *rithmica*, by contrast, this criterion is enormously important. Does *Háttatal*'s commentary borrow here from the analysis of *rithmica*, where stanza length played an important part? The third *tala* is that of syllable-count. Here again the commentary is oddly unsuited to skaldic metrics, but aligned with *rithmica*, which had syllable-count rather than quantity as its mensural basis. Variation in line length is certainly important in *Háttatal*, but *dróttkvætt* rhythm is no mere matter of counting syllables.[79] *Háttatal*'s commentary mentions elision (*bragarmál*), but it is not clear whether its author understands resolution, which is analyzed in terms of acoustic realization in performance by "quick" (*skjótar*) syllables.[80]

The next distinction drawn in the opening section of *Háttatal* is that between *málsgrein* (speech-element) and *hljóðsgrein* (sound-element). The commentary offers that

> The rule of letters structures all speech, but sound structures that quality of having long or short syllables, or hard or soft, and that is the rule of sound-elements, which we call rhymes, as here [. . .][81]

The meaning of this passage is not easy to grasp. In the commentary on the stanza that comes immediately after, *stafasetning* is aligned with alliteration and *setning hljóðsgreina* with rhyme; presumably, as Edith Marold suggests, because the author matches these two categories up with Latin *littera* (letter) and *syllaba* (syllable) respectively.[82] But the passage quoted above seems to be making a slightly different distinction, between the "rule of letters," which governs all speech (*mál*; or "language"), and syllabic patterning, which is poetry-specific: *er vér kǫllum hendingar*. This is reminiscent of *SGT*'s account of *hljóð* and *mál*. Speech/language (*mál*) selects the letters it needs (*stafir gjöra allt mál, ok hendir málit ýmsa*), while sound (*hljóð*) lacks letters, or is superordinate upon them, being rather the stuff of music, closely associated with rhyme (*hending*).

The opening of *Háttatal* establishes syllable-counting and -patterning as the distinguishing sonic features of the poetry that it will exemplify. The distribution of stanza-variants within the *centimetrum* reflects these priorities. Only eight of the poem's stanzas lack a consistent rhyme-scheme, and variation of rhyme is the distinguishing feature of almost one third of its stanzas.[83] The treatment of the fifteen variants of end-rhymed *runhent* (Ht sts. 80–94)—a quantity of examples in striking contrast to *runhent*'s lack of heft in the surviving skaldic tradition—is strongly shaped by *numerositas*.[84] Stephen Tranter suggests that the lack of a strong tradition of *runhent* composition gave Snorri *carte blanche* to organize these stanzas as he wished, observing that he does so with a "degree of abstractness [. . .] found nowhere else in *Háttatal*."[85] The stanza-names are not completely systematic, and some names have been added in the margin of the Codex Regius manuscript in a contemporary hand. The system of the *runhent* section is nonetheless clear. The fifteen stanzas make up five numbered sets (*bálkr*), and each set has three degrees (right/full, lesser, and least). *Háttatal*'s information about these stanzas is presented in Table 1.

Háttatal's prose commentary consistently specifies the number of syllables per line, whether by naming it directly, as in sts. 83, 85, and 86, referring to a meter whose syllable-count has been fixed earlier in the treatise (e.g., *tøglag*, st. 86, *dróttkvætt*, st. 88, or *hálfhnept*, st. 93), or by describing it as a catalectic (*hneptr, stýfðr*) version of a preceding stanza (e.g., sts. 82, 87, 89, 95). Rhyme is arranged in a hierarchy. Maintaining the same rhyme throughout the stanza (*rétt* or *full runhent*) is valued most highly, rhyme within the *helmingr* less (*minni*), and rhyme in couplets least (*minzt*). The rule that the penultimate syllable in the cadence should be long, strictly observed in the first two *kvæði* of *Háttatal* (sts. 1–67), is relaxed in the *smærir hættir* ("lesser meters") of sts.

TABLE 1.

Nr	Name in Háttatal	Rhyme-scheme	Cadence	Commentary in Háttatal
80	rétt runhenda (normal runhent)	AAAAAAAA	Feminine	Same rhyming syllable in each line.
81	hin minni runhenda (the lesser runhenda)	AAAABBBB	Feminine	Rhyming syllable differs in each helmingr.
82	in minzta runhenda (the least runhenda)	AABBCCDD	Masculine	Catalectic version of preceding st. Three syllables per line; rhymes in couplets; alliteration as in dróttkvætt.
83	enn runhendir (further runhent forms)	AAAAAAAA	Feminine	Full (full) runhent. Usually five syllables, six if fast.
84	annarr runhenda (second runhenda)	AAAABBBB	Masculine	Catalectic version of preceding stanza.
85	[un-named]	AABBCCDD	Feminine	Four syllables; alliteration on first stressed syllable as in dróttkvætt.
86	hinn þriði háttr runhendr (the third runhent form)	AAAAAAAA	Feminine	Normal (rétt) runhent. Usually four syllables, five if fast; based on tøglag.
87	hin minni runhenda (the lesser runhenda)	AAAABBBB	Masculine	Catalectic version of preceding st. Normal (rétt) runhent.
88	in minzta (the least)	AABBCCDD	Feminine	Based on dróttkvætt; same number and position of alliterating syllables as there.
89	inn fjórða bálkr runhendinga (the fourth group of runhendingar)	AAAAAAAA	Masculine	Catalectic version of preceding stanza.
90	minni runhenda (a lesser runhenda)	AAAABBBB	Feminine	Based on hrynhent.
91	[unnamed]	AABBCCDD	Masculine	Catalectic version of preceding stanza.
92	hinn fimti runhendr bálkr (the fifth runhent group)	AAAAAAAA	Feminine	Full (full) runhent.
93	hin minni runhenda (the lesser runhenda)	AAAABBBB	Masculine	Based on hálfhnept or náhent.
94	[unnamed]	AABBCCDD	Masculine	Catalectic version of preceding stanza.

68–102.⁸⁶ In the *runhent* section, many stanzas with feminine endings have short cadential syllables, which passes without explicit comment, while monosyllabic (masculine) rhymes in the cadence are explained as resulting from catalexis. The adequacy of the analysis in *Háttatal*'s commentary on *runhent* to what is actually going on in the stanzas has been investigated and found wanting on many points.⁸⁷ The syllable count frequently ignores resolution and elision; meters named as precursors often do not match the rhythm of the *runhent* stanza in question, while other stanzas in *Háttatal* that are a better match go unmentioned; the stanzas in a given *bálkr* do not always correspond to one another metrically; and stanzas with masculine cadences are not usually catalectic versions of the preceding stanza but rather rhythmically distinct.

Whether or not this suggests that *Háttatal*'s prose commentary and the stanzas themselves have different authors has been much debated.⁸⁸ One could also wonder in what reception context this commentary would have enjoyed descriptive adequacy. Here the treatises on *rithmica* offer parallels. I will take John of Garland's *Parisiana poetria* as an accessible example of their characteristic style of analysis.⁸⁹ John introduces his *divisio rithmi* (division of rhymed poetry) by saying that

> a simple rhymed poem may be dispondaic, trispondaic, or tetraspondaic; and this last kind is threefold: a tetraspondaic poem may have two, three or four lines to one rhyming sound.⁹⁰

He then gives poetic examples, stanza by stanza, with commentary. If the penultimate syllable is long, he calls the line "spondaic." The spondaic meters start with lines consisting of a single rhyming foot (two syllables), "as a kind of *tour de force*" (*egregie*), and proceed up through four-, six-, and eight-syllable lines, each of which can rhyme in couplets, tercets, or quatrains. He then does the same for "iambs" (lines with short penultimate syllables), which can have either eight or seven syllables, and rhyme in couplets, tercets, and quatrains. The bases of his classification are (1) the nature of the cadence; (2) the number of syllables in the line; and (3) the number of lines that share the same end-rhyme. These criteria are very similar to those used in the *runhent* section in *Háttatal*. John goes on to provide a number of extended compositions of his own as examples of *rithmica*, on subjects ranging from teaching, through praise of St Catherine and the Virgin Mary, to a secular poem (*exemplum domesticum*) on the licentiousness of boys.

It is clear from the *Third Grammatical Treatise* that thirteenth-century observers drew analogies between *rithmica* and *runhent*. The closeness of this analysis to *Háttatal*'s commentary on *runhent* suggests that its author was impressed enough by their similarity to structure his commentary after this model. Rather than exhibiting freedom in the treatment of a novel verse form, *Háttatal*'s account of *runhent* demonstrates that drawing-together of the worlds of Norse and Latin poetic analysis which is also discernable in the *SGT*.

DIAGRAMS AND THE NEW POETICS IN ICELAND

One way to locate *SGT* in this poetological landscape is the diagrams in Upsaliensis. Identifying their sources presents great challenges, however. Major parts of the vast and heterogeneous corpus of premodern diagrams remain unexplored.[91] Diagrams were often used in the schoolroom, presented on movable *tabulae* or in large-format manuscripts, and so were highly subject to loss.[92] And their visual schemata were both long-lived, often dating back to antiquity, and frequently repurposed.[93] The wheel and table layouts of Upsaliensis' two diagrams are among the most common schemata. Isidore's *Etymologies* included so many circular diagrams that it was known as the *Liber rotarum* (Book of Wheels). School texts such as the *Parisiana poetria* also made good use of figures and diagrams.[94] John's text includes both a table and a wheel.[95] He introduces his table as a memory-space, a device, he says, "essential for poets organizing their material."[96] It represents, John goes on, a well-lit area divided into three columns (*columpnas*). This grid-like space contains three estates of man (peasants, city-dwellers, and courtiers), "examples, sayings and facts from authors," and "all kinds of languages, sounds and voices of the various living creatures, explanations of words, distinctions between words, all in alphabetical order."[97] John's circular figure is the *rota Virgilii*, a set of three concentric rings around a central boss, which depict the high, middle, and low styles in Virgil's poetry.[98]

Upsaliensis' diagrams have some unusual features. The layout of the wheel diagram, with a central boss and a small number of segmented concentric rings, is not the most common type, nor are wheels often used to represent linguistic or poetic data.[99] The rectangular figure's use of a musical instrument as a schema for such data lacks any parallels, as far as is presently known.[100] Tabular diagrams are used in a vast range of settings in premodern manuscripts, from mathematical calculation, through the display of calendrical or astronomical data, to tables of contents and mnemonic material, and even depictions of board games.[101] Grids are sometimes used as operational spaces, for example, in tables used to calculate the date of Easter (Plate 9 shows a twelfth-century Icelandic example). Or they can be representative, standing in for a chessboard, perhaps, or for the castle carried by the elephant in the Old Norse *Physiologus* (Plate 10). Upsaliensis' diagrams straddle these possibilities. They are bound spaces, and as the name *leikvǫllr* reveals, their constructor drew an analogy between the rule-bound, demarcated space of the playing field and the space created by the diagram. They enable haptic manipulation of mental entities, what Sibylle Krämer calls the "handcraft of the intellect."[102] The tabular diagram, in particular, is a sophisticated object. It employs the "media-theoretical distinction between data and addresses," which Bernhard Siegert argues is key to the grid, "presuppos[ing] the ability to write absence."[103] Absences are made visible in the empty squares in the lowest eight rows of the table, addresses which do not correspond to any data (the Easter table and circular diagram, in this sense more primitive, lack this distinction). What is nonexistent in spoken language (a syllable beginning *ða*, for example) has a material presence on the page as an unfilled space in the grid.

The grid proposes "visibility, control and domination" over a surface with no depth, offering complete visibility of "a world of objects imagined by a subject.[104] It is unsurprising to find them in the context of encyclopedic learning about unfamiliar places, animals, and cultural practices. The *simphonie*, too, is usually encountered in Old Norse literature in romance descriptions of exotic luxury. Icelanders probably did have firsthand knowledge of hurdy-gurdies. These instruments were found all over the Continent in the Middle Ages.[105] They most likely made it to Iceland, although there is no direct evidence of them there.[106] If the grid in *Physiologus*'s elephant and castle image is examined closely, an optical illusion becomes apparent. The row of grid-squares at the bottom of the image is revealed above to be a rank of overlapping oblongs: a two-dimensional diagrammatic schema transforms into a representation of three-dimensional space. The *simphonie*'s relation to the real is almost as playful. Such openings to the invented and illusory are also among the potentials of the "free space of the flat surface."[107]

Upsaliensis' diagrams, then, represent a heightening of writing's fundamental claim to capture sound and make it independent of temporality.

Beuerle demonstrates in detail how the *SGT*'s exposition is primarily oriented to the issue of sound and its representation in writing.[108] This would be a relevant topic not just for those wishing to write down spoken language, but also for performers using a written text, like the singers at the end of the Wormianus text. The distinctions made in the ring diagram are mainly those of sound rather than orthography; long and short s, for instance, are treated together. The tabular diagram, for its part, represents the combinatorial possibilities of the syllable—which, as Beuerle points out, the *SGT* always refers to by the poetic term of art, *hending*, rather than the grammatical one, *samstafa*. It is therefore not surprising that *SGT*'s exposition, at times, recalls the metrical commentary of *Háttatal*. *SGT* observes of single-letter words (the prepositions *á* ["on"], *í* ["in"], and prefixes *ó* and *ú* [both meaning "un-"], as well as *ý* ["yew"], *æ* ["ah"], *ey* ["island"], and *ey/œ* ["ever"]) that "these letters, on their own, form many complete words, but they form short utterances."[109] This remark too has been written off as superfluous by commentators determined to see *SGT* solely in the context of *grammatica*.[110] It is paralleled in *Háttatal*, which remarks in the commentary on one of its *runhent* stanzas that

> Moreover it is considered not wrong if the vowel that constitutes the sound of poetry [i.e., the rhyme] stands on one occasion in place of a word.[111]

The word in question is *á* (on), which rhymes with *svá* in the first couplet of st. 82. These comments are traces of a contemporary *metrical*, rather than grammatical or orthographic, interest in the smallest possible rhyming units, such as John's "egregious" line consisting of a single rhyming foot.

"A symphony is a sweet singing together of different notes joined to one another," writes the anonymous author of the Carolingian *Musica enchiriadis*.[112] The instrument of *SGT* was surely imagined precisely because it evoked these pleasing and appropriate associations. More practical factors could also have made it a good choice. Writing the letter-names of the scale notes on the keys of hurdy-gurdies was a common practice, as it was for other medieval instruments used in the song-school. This made it possible to learn a new chant from a text, "without a master" (*sine magistro*).[113] An anonymous *Summa musicae*, written around 1300 in France or the Netherlands, observes that

> if [a singer] does not have a pliant voice—if he is a jarring singer—and if he lacks, perhaps, the good-will or the offered help of a teacher, he should

take pains to busy himself with musical instruments and in particular to employ types such as the monochord and the symphonia which is called organistrum; let him also work with an organ. On these instruments it is not easy to wander from the right note, nor need a false note linger; the notes may easily be observed by means of fixed, lettered keys and may be readily produced without the aid of a friend or a song-master.[114]

Diagrams in musical manuscripts occasionally illustrate scale relationships with images of annotated instruments.[115] Such a diagram could well have been one of the sources of inspiration for the *SGT*'s poetry machine. An instrument with lettered keys, whose name means "sweet singing together," makes an irresistible visual metaphor for the technological mediation of poetry by writing.

The poetry machine produces language (*mál*) and sound (*hljóð*) without voice (*rǫdd*): a "dream" technology, Parikka would say. In the context of *SGT*, the poetry machine is the result of interference between the pedagogy of chant and the theorizations of the new poetics. The practical and theoretical are in productive tension in *SGT*. Its observations on the notation of vowel length, for instance, could well have been useful to those whose job involved performing in church. The bishops' sagas stress the importance of expertise in performing from written texts and lament the trouble caused by inadequate reading aloud of sacred books.[116] Presumably its diagrams were not intended to be practically useful to the performing skald in the way that the *þulur* elsewhere in Upsaliensis were.[117] Rather, they are paradigmatic instances of the engagement of the Old Norse grammatical-poetological tradition with the page as sound recording technology and *leikvǫllr* of new medial potentialities. They flatten and make cognitively available the three-dimensional world of sense experience. For the scribe of Codex Upsaliensis, the *SGT* alone sufficed to represent this line of thinking in his compilation. Its rubric for *SGT* recognizes the intimate link between that text and *Háttatal*, which follows immediately after it in the manuscript: "Here it tells of the rule of the *clavis metrica*."[118]

* * * *

The twelfth-century vogue for accentual meters in religious poetry led to a new interest in the systematization of syllable length and rhyme, due to the need to notate such features for musical performances. Sverrir Tómasson writes:

I think these developments did not pass learned Icelanders of the twelfth and thirteenth centuries by, but this topic is regrettably unresearched, like so many other matters touching on the links between Latin and Icelandic verse-making.[119]

I agree that a Latinate analytical model drawn from music theory drives the concerns with sound, pronunciation, and rhyme evident in SGT and *Háttatal*. It has long been suspected that Latin hymn poetry in trochaic tetrameter inspired the first compositions in *hrynhent*, although this is difficult to prove.[120] As I have shown, the case for Latinate influences on how skaldic meter was *analyzed* is much stronger. It is buttressed by the importance given to music in SGT, the use of the technical term *consonantia* in TGT, and the foregrounding of the parameters of syllable count and rhyme scheme in *Háttatal*. The noise of poetry, meter rather than diction, seems to be the aspect of traditional Norse performance practice that first attracted analytical attention.[121] The *gai saber* of Latin texts on poetics, such as the *Poetria nova* and *Parisiana poetria* in early thirteenth-century France and England, finds an approximately contemporary parallel in Iceland. The Icelanders are typically precocious in their use of the vernacular (or deficient in Latin). The step of using these metrical analyses as a rulebook for new vernacular poetry seems not to have been taken by authors on the European mainland until a century later, by the imitators of troubadour lyric in France, or the Rhenish *Meistersänger*.[122] Continental authors and Icelanders alike drew on the rich vein of speculation about the sound of poetry at the interface of music and grammar.

Continental sources give a clear picture of the office of *cantor* or *precentor*, the person responsible in monastic communities for the liturgy and its music. Their tasks included managing liturgical materials and the monastery's library, assigning readings and chants to the singers, the use of *computus*, for example to establish the date of Easter, and composition of new devotional music and texts.[123] Such a person would be versed in musical and grammatical theory, interested in questions of performance, highly literate in Latin and the vernacular, and familiar with the technologies of codex and diagram. An Icelandic rule for priests from the fourteenth century prescribes that

> *prestr skal kunna tíða skipan ok látínu svá at hann viti hvárt hann kveðr karlkennt eða kvennkent. Hann skal kunna þýðing guðspjalla ok <h>omilíur Gregorii ok compotum svá at hann kunni at telja allt misseristal.*

(the priest shall understand the arranging of the service and Latin, so that he knows whether to use the masculine or feminine form [i.e. when performing the sacraments]. He shall know the translation of the Gospels and Gregory's *Homilies* and *computus*, so that he can calculate the calendar.)[124]

Clerical and monastic division of labor was less strict in Iceland than elsewhere. The bishops' sagas say that lower-ranked functionaries (of whom the cantor was one) also taught school, and the *kirkjuprestr* of the cathedral church often also acted as *rector chori*, although in one diploma from 1520 these offices are held by different people.[125] The cantor in twelfth-century Lund led the choir clad in a *cappa purpurea*; mentions of these garments also survive in Icelandic diplomas.[126] Such a person would have had a stake in the composition and correct performance of devotional verse, but also, perhaps, a curiosity about the aspects of vernacular poetics which overlapped with the fashionable *rithmica*. Within the larger frame of the Codex Upsaliensis, these pragmatic interests are subsumed into the orientation toward a "future poem" based on the best of past traditions, which so clearly resounds in the *causa scribendi* of *Skáldskaparmál*.

CONCLUSION

In the introduction to this book, I suggested that a medial perspective could unsettle the author-centrism of much classic work on skaldic poetry. Ears attuned to interferences from other speakers and media are less susceptible to the insistent voices of skaldic authors. Valuable though the study of skaldic authorships is, it leaves many paths unexplored.

In Part 1, I argued that *Ynglingatal* makes a claim of mediation. It gives poetic form to knowledge about the past borne by significant sites in the landscape and the shared memories that cohere around them. The *kviðuháttr* meter lends this claim its force, as its stanzaic form marks a decisive difference from traditional alliterative poetics. *Kviðuháttr*'s quatrains bind collective memories into a tightly linked, authored, and dedicated chain, useful for aspiring petty kings on the frontier to Francia. Parallels between *Ynglingatal*'s speaking voice and that of the Rök runestone suggest that a desire to emulate the memory places of neighboring Christian kingdoms was an important driver of such claims in southern Scandinavia. Inextricably associated with commemoration, the *kviðuháttr* form proved long-lived. In the pedantic accounting of the line of Norwegian kings in *Nóregs konungatal*, *kviðuháttr*'s metrically encoded tendency to catenulate organization figures forth a genealogy. *Nóregs konungatal*, in its turn, is emplaced in the fourteenth-century Flateyjarbók manuscript as part of a compilatory program demonstrating the working out of the divine plan in the fleshly kin(g)ship of the Norwegian royal house.

If my analysis of *Ynglingatal* and other *kviðuháttr* poems suggests that skaldic poetics has an intersubjective and intermedial potential, as the text re-mediates locational memory borne by anonymous, collective informants, my reading of the skaldic picture poems in Part 2 implies other roles for shared compositional labor and interferences between media. Ekphrastic composition has its roots in the sensual and intellectual grasping of visual puzzles—a valued practice of courtly sociability. Poets vied with one another to produce new interpretations of a singular visual stimulus. Cognitive and psychological aspects were important in medieval understandings of sense perception. Issues of the reliability of vision explored in homiletic, religious, and courtly texts crystallize in the *Prose Edda*'s figure of the *sjónhverfing* or "prestige." A courtly practice of visual trickery serves as a metaphor for the reader's imaginative experience of seeing the gods and mirrors the epiphanies of skaldic ekphrasis. In Christian skaldic poetry the ekphrastic resources of vivid description and emotional involvement are harnessed to unite poetic speaker, audience, and the saved in visionary experiences of compunction outside of historical time.

Use of the first-person plural to refer to the speaker of the poem is conventional in *dróttkvætt* encomium. The extradiegetic speakers of eddic poems, by contrast, tend to be singular, in what could be a trace of contrasting practices of performance and transmission.[1] In Part 3 I explored *dróttkvætt*'s phantasmatic voices. The clamor of war that fills Viking Age skaldic encomium reenacts battle's chaos and terror, glorifying the retinue's shared experience of sensory overload in the most resonant of the skaldic meters, *dróttkvætt*. Tongues and swords speak together in the "voice of red rims," insistently raising the question of the significance of sonic patterning. Regulated patterns combining both rhyme and alliteration offered skalds expanded possibilities for linking and contrasting lexemes across long runs of stanzas. The word *hending*, on the other hand, used of rhyme in the grammatical literature, embodies the listener's experience of being "caught up" by the skaldic stanza's intoxicating rush of sound—and perhaps also the poet's of being mastered by a divinely inspired gift. Repeated by many voices, *dróttkvætt*'s rhyming echoes approach the condition of music. By the thirteenth century, the author and scribes of the *Second Grammatical Treatise* are reflecting theoretically on crossovers between music and poetry that may originate in the song-school. Use of the grid, a preeminent cultural technique of medieval pedagogy, makes a manuscript page into a virtual machine grinding out the skalds' sonorous drone. In its interest in rhyme and number, *Háttatal*'s commentary applies up-to-the-minute ideas taken from the metrical analysis of Latin poetry to the task of renewing skaldic poetics.

As this summary suggests, transmission also looks different from a medial viewpoint. In a more processual, less author-centric account of skaldic poetics, the data of manuscript transmission can no longer be discounted as textual corruption. Rather they are the traces of a complex and ramifying practice of rewriting.

INTO THE FOREST OF REWRITINGS

Writing was in its origin the voice of an absent person. (Freud, *Civilization and Its Discontents*)[2]

Letters are tokens of things, the signs of words, and they have so much force that the utterances of those who are absent speak to us without a voice, for they present words through the eyes, not through the ears. (Isidore, *Etymologies*).[3]

There is nothing new under the sun—right? On a closer look, a difference between these formulations of writing as McLuhanesque "extension of man" is apparent. For Isidore writing is utterance "without a voice," while for Freud writing *is* voice. In Isidore "the voice" is tied up with ideas about the matter and significance of language and how it can be perceived by the senses, but for Freud it's all a matter of subjectivity. This polyvalence of "voice" stretches back to Latin discussions of *vox*, used to signify both sound and its meaning, and forward to the early Derrida of *La voix et le phénomène*, where hearing yourself talk makes for self-presence, with the inner voice an important metaphor for the subject.[4] Voice in writing raises the question of whether the meaning of a text is limited by an intention located in the mysterious depths of individual subjectivity. Derrida argues that this intention is a chimera. As text can always be cited, and so placed in a new context, its meaning cannot be fixed.

Paul Zumthor sets this discussion on its feet by exploring writing and voice in the context of a specific textual culture, that of the Middle Ages. He writes that medieval texts are "carriers of a discourse that we no longer hear [. . .] a whole entity that has been shattered."[5] No longer the trace of the singular presence of the author, voice is part of what Zumthor calls *vocalité*, the "whole entity" of cultural practices that interweave written and performed text. Despite the brilliance and usefulness of his concept of *vocalité*, Zumthor's nostalgia gives pause. What is left are mere fragments ("shattered") of a lost wholeness; the tradition loses material as time goes on but never gains it; this loss is inherently lamentable. And as "no longer *hear*" indicates, what gets lost is identified with the voice.

Shane Butler diagnoses the paradoxical quality of voice in this account: "While in one sense, we regularly assume that the voice is indeed what writing captures [. . .] we simultaneously suppose that the voice is precisely that quantity which, before Edison, eluded transcription. We seem to ourselves to resolve this paradox by asserting a distinction between the linguistic voice, which writing has long recorded, and the extralinguistic voice, which had to wait for the phonograph."[6] He argues instead that "literature, as a medium, is only incidentally concerned with the recording of language per se, and that literature may best be regarded [as] the use of language itself as a medium, for the recording of something not linguistic at all."[7] He identifies this "something" with the materiality or, with Barthes, "grain" of the voice and suggests it is free of the "hermeneutic imperative."[8] Butler seems to suggest here that intonation, for example, is nonlinguistic and writing an incomplete transcription of spoken language. The "phonographic claim" of his book, elaborated in a number of close studies of Greek and Latin poetry, is that these expressive and communicative but nonlinguistic features are, in fact, still traceable in writing. It turns out that the written medium is, again, valuable only insofar as an earlier state of plenitude can be reconstructed from it—another Zumthorean story of loss.

Linguists maintain, however, that writing and speech are separate language systems and that it is misguided to establish the characteristics of writing by contrasting it with speech. Geoffrey Nunberg sees punctuation as a specific medial affordance of writing that arose "as a response to the particular communicative requirements of written language texts [. . .] as an exploitation of the particular expressive resources that graphic representation makes available."[9] (The manuscript punctuation of skaldic poetry has never been studied, to my knowledge.) Eric Griffiths' *Printed Voice of Victorian Poetry* has a more optimistic perspective on voice in writing than Butler's.[10] For Griffiths, the uncertain relation of print to voice in Victorian poetry "gives an essential pleasure of reading, for as we meet the demand a text makes on us for our voices, we are engaged in an activity of imagination which is delicately and thoroughly reciprocal."[11] Qualities of vocal performance such as intonation, rhythm, and cadence are indeed linguistic, he argues, even if they resist writing. Griffiths concludes that the interpretive process by which the reader lends the printed text her voice is one of discerning and understanding the meaning of an author, but that this author is absent by design. The author's absence, he argues, is the condition of possibility of the medium of printed poetry in its pre-phonographic historical situation; "putting it sharply, intonation is the sound of intention."[12]

Such a focus on the medium nuances the "phonographic claim." Griffiths's close readings of printed Victorian poetry focus minutely on details of punctuation, line breaks, and wording, finding the keys to authorial intention in the combination of these indicators with the formative intellectual context of the individual authors. Neither the fixed, reproducible ductus of print, nor a deep knowledge of the intellectual background of the authors, are available to the student of premodern poetry. The lack of sources other than the poetry itself makes sketching out intellectual contexts for early skaldic verse extremely difficult and is a large part of why this poetry is so hard to interpret. If the manuscript medium makes a phonographic claim, it is a medially specific one, reflecting the alterity both of medieval manuscript culture and of the skaldic practices of composition and performance that are fleetingly glimpsed in the poems themselves.[13] The particular kind of reproducibility involved in writing skaldic poetry produces the figure of the performing skaldic author as its effect.

The pathos of the phonographic claim is an instance of what Walter Benjamin calls aura: an effect of authenticity derived from uniqueness, distance, and the trappings of ritual.[14] Jonathan Sterne points out that Benjamin's aura is necessarily retroactive, "a nostalgia that accompanies reproduction" and in fact depends on it, as "reproduction highlights the possibility of reality having an immediate self-presence in the first place."[15] Reproduction, he argues, is experienced as a "loss of fidelity or a *loss of being* between original and copy."[16] The distinction between live and reproduced performance is first brought into being by reproduction, and invariably accompanied by a strong positive valorization of the former. In the sagas, the "liveness" of skaldic performance is an effect of the data of author, audience, and occasion. These data are, in turn, produced by practices of textual reproduction that link a certain name to a piece of text, diagrammatically in *Skáldatal*, encyclopedically in *Skáldskaparmál*, or in a narrative, as in the many anecdotes in the kings' sagas and family sagas of skaldic performance. Old Icelandic textual culture insists on the occasionality of skaldic poetry, in striking contrast to how eddic poetry is presented in the two medieval manuscript collections. Why does it do this?

Skaldic performance seems to have been intersubjective and dialogical—in *dróttkvætt* the retinue talks *to* itself, *about* itself, and skaldic speakers compete with other voices and media—so its singularity and authoredness is at issue from the start. A number of anecdotes in the kings' sagas describe skaldic performers as revising their verses, and there is evidence in the manuscript transmission for discrepant oral versions of stanzas. The single originating instance presupposed by "liveness" is thus, at least to some degree, illusory. And if early skaldic verse is indeed a product of the ninth and tenth centuries, then a period of several hundred years of oral transmission separates the inaugural performance from its script. Features of meter, language, and diction with relevance for dating have been studied intensively for many years. Recent research tends to confirm the traditional dates, which in turn mostly match the internal chronology of the medieval sources (with some exceptions, mainly in the sagas of Icelanders).[17]

For traditional datings to be valid, rhapsodic re-performance of skaldic encomium must have been ubiquitous, but the sagas rarely mention it. One of the *articuli* of Styrmir Kárason to the *Legendary Saga of St Olaf* reports that Bersi Skáld-Torfuson was slandered (*rægðr*) by enemies who said he was "unable to compose or perform poetry that has not already been composed."[18] An anecdote added to *Sverris saga* has a more positive view. It reports that the poet Máni earned favor at the court of Magnús Erlingsson by performing a poem by Halldórr *skvaldri* (prattler) about the king's grandfather, *Útfarardrápa*.[19] The rarity of descriptions of nonauthorial performance could mean that this medial practice was transparent and taken for granted in the environment of *vocalité*. Its negative valence in the *Legendary saga* suggests, however, that it was also actively forgotten. It is not surprising that a historiographic tradition dependent on skaldic evidence would be uneasy about the fluidity of oral repetition.

The effect of this elision is to open a gulf—the distance that produces the aura of skaldic performance—between the reader of the written stanza, as it stands in the manuscript, and the performing skaldic author. Given such practices of reproduction, a "sound of intention," or "liveness," will only be faintly transmitted, if at all, to our listening ears. What the twenty-first-century reader can perhaps pick up is the *noise* of poetry, in Michel Serres's sense: the result of the interferences of multiple instances, from the performing skald, through rhapsodic oral re-performances, and on into *vocalité*.[20] Susan Stewart writes that with the passing of time, "as knowledge of reference necessarily withers, the poem does not lose fullness or complexity but rather acquires a residue of accrued meanings that expand the possibilities for poetry's significance. The particularity of the poem, its occasional quality, falls away as its form comes forward."[21] To trace this coming forward of the form has been one of my aims in this book. But in so doing, I have neglected a crucial medial feature of skaldic poetry: the fact that skaldic poetry is a particular, historically situated kind of writing. To address this issue properly would take another book. In closing I will very briefly sketch some of the changed contours that could result from such a study.

SKALDIC WRITING

Does *Arinbjarnarkviða* exist? The main text of *Egils saga* mentions a poem for Arinbjǫrn and leaves a space to quote its *upphaf* ("beginning": conventionally the first stanza), but this space was never filled. The sole medieval text of the poem known in modern scholarship as *Arinbjarnarkviða* was noted down on the back of a gathering of Möðruvallabók after the end of *Egils saga*, some time in the fourteenth century. The ink has been so rubbed and smeared over the centuries that it is now barely legible, and the poem's content and many of its readings are controversial. Some versions of *Grettis saga* mention a poem called *Grettisfærsla*, and it was appended to one manuscript of the saga in the late fifteenth century, but soon afterwards scraped off again with such thoroughness that only recent advances in imaging and data processing hold any promise of reading its text.[22] In a sense these poems are instances of the pathos of the nearly vanished, and the chancy survival of a single text separated from its narrative context might imply a lack of interest in these poems on the part of saga authors and scribes. From the perspective of *vocalité*, this preservation pattern could instead be taken as testimony to a vigorous oral transmission which meant that people saw no need to write these poems down.

A diametrically opposed situation holds for the single stanzas of skaldic verse quoted in various kinds of prosimetrum. These often occur in multiple manuscripts, enabling editors, at least in theory, to use the techniques of stemmatic recension to reconstruct an archetype: the earliest reconstructible ancestor of the surviving texts.[23] Behind the archetype lie lost manuscripts, as in almost all ancient and medieval text traditions, and then—less common—an unsecured leap over generations of oral transmission back to the original live performance. If we instead choose to take the new philological turn away from recension, the skaldic texts in the surviving manuscripts offer information on scribal authorship in the historically specific medial setting of *vocalité*.

If the preserved mass of skaldic poetry is regarded as a kind of writing rather than as the trace of a lost liveness, it is both very much larger and much later than is conventionally thought. According to the database of the Skaldic Editing Project, the total number of stanzas in the skaldic corpus is just under five thousand, with an average date (going by Finnur Jónsson's century-by-century groupings) lying somewhere in the early twelfth century.

If instead the corpus is taken to comprise the number of unique witnesses—the stanzas attested in the medieval manuscripts—it swells to almost three times as many stanza-instances, with an average date of 1380.[24] A proper exploration of manuscript variation in this material is, of course, a project in its own right.[25] It would involve the study not only of lexical variation, but also of layout, punctuation, and *mise en page*, across some 170 medieval vellums (although there is not really any principled reason to exclude post-medieval paper manuscripts, only the practical one that there are enormously many of them).

Keith Busby has recently undertaken a study of variance in approximately three thousand medieval manuscripts that preserve Old French verse narrative.[26] Some of the changes he tracks are very minor, for example the presence or absence of elisions and contractions, while others are more significant: changes in rhyming syllables, verb tenses, and word order, the substitution of near-synonyms, and of varying forms of fixed idioms. He concludes that while there is little evidence of thoroughgoing scribal revision (*remaniement*) in his corpus, the manuscript transmission contains a considerable amount of variation beyond the merely orthographic, which "bespeaks an attitude towards the text which, while implying a basic respect for [the author's] words, allows a certain freedom, a kind of variance or mouvance on a very limited scale."[27] A couple of provisional test holes drilled into the skaldic bedrock suggest that the amount of *mouvance* there is similar to, if not in fact greater than, that in Busby's corpus. It encompasses, for instance, variation of kenning components—something which goes to the heart of skaldic creativity.[28] Such studies could bring the seriality of text production into view, as one of the most significant features of skaldic writing.

NOTES

INTRODUCTION

1. *gerði sér títt við Arinbjǫrn ok var honum fylgjusamr*, ÍF 2, 105. Translation from Bernard Scudder, "Egil's saga," in *The Sagas of Icelanders: A Selection*, ed. Örnólfur Thorsson (London: Penguin, 2001), 65.
2. "'Hér mun vera,' segir Egill, 'sem opt er mælt, at segjanda er allt sínum vin,'" ÍF 2, 180–81; Scudder, "Egil's saga," 112.
3. "'Ef Egill hefir mælt illa til konungs, þá má hann þat bœta í lofsorðum þeim, er allan aldr megi uppi vera,'" ÍF 2, 180–81; Scudder, "Egil's saga," 112.
4. "'Nú vil ek þat ráð gefa, at þú vakir í nótt ok yrkir lofkvæði um Eirík konung; þœtti mér þá vel, ef þat yrði drápa tvítug ok mættir þú kveða á morgin, er vit komum fyrir konung,'" ÍF 2, 182; Scudder, "Egil's saga," 112.
5. Finnur Jónsson, ed., *Det norsk-islandske skjaldedigtning. A. Tekst efter håndskrifterne. B: Rettet tekst med tolkning*, 4 vols. (Copenhagen: Villadsen & Christiansen, 1912–15), 1:38–41. Translations are mine. The textual history of *Arinbjarnarkviða* is complex; I defer discussion of this subject to this book's conclusion.
6. Calvert Watkins, *How to Kill a Dragon: Aspects of Indo-European Poetics* (New York: Oxford University Press, 1995), 73–84, describes the Indo-European genre of "praise of the gift" (Sanskrit *dānastuti*). Poetic censure of niggardliness, as in sts. 1, 20–21, is also traditional; see Watkins, *How to Kill*, 186–87 for an Old Irish example, composed in the verse-form "slap on the arse *deibide*."
7. On the "head-ransom" as parodic gift, see Alison Finlay, "Risking One's Head: *Vafþrúðnismál* and the Mythic Power of Poetry," in *Myth, Legends and Heroes: Essays on Old Norse and Old English Literature in Honour of John McKinnell*, ed. Daniel Anlezark (Toronto: University of Toronto Press, 2011), 102.
8. On these rhetorical terms, see Jürg Glauser, "Zwischen Kohärenz und Fragment. Zur Poetik des 'Verschlungenen' in der altnordischen Skaldik," in *Lyrische Kohärenz im Mittelalter. Spielräume—Kriterien—Modellbildung*, ed. Susanne Köbele et al. (Heidelberg: Winter, 2019), 187–212.
9. See Judith Jesch, *The Viking Diaspora* (London: Routledge, 2015).
10. Hans Blumenberg, *Paradigms for a Metaphorology*, trans. Robert Savage (Ithaca: Cornell University Press, 2010), 4.
11. John D. H. Downing et al., eds., *The SAGE Handbook of Media Studies* (Thousand Oaks: Sage Publications, 2004).
12. Claude E. Shannon and Warren Weaver, *The Mathematical Theory of Communication* (Urbana: University of Illinois Press, 1949).
13. Raymond Williams, *Keywords: A Vocabulary of Culture and Society* (London: Fontana, 1983), 204, suggests that this is a nineteenth-century development,

but cf. Kevis Goodman, *Georgic Modernity and British Romanticism: Poetry and the Mediation of History* (Cambridge: Cambridge University Press, 2004), 148n29.

14. John Guillory, "Genesis of the Media Concept," *Critical Inquiry* 36 (2010): 321–62; Christian Kiening, "Mediologie-Christologie. Konturen einer Grundfigur mittelalterlicher Medialität," *Das Mittelalter* 15 (2010): 16–32.

15. Leo Spitzer, "Milieu and Ambiance: An Essay in Historical Semantics," *Philosophy and Phenomenological Research* 3 (1942): 1–42, 169–218.

16. Aristotle, *De anima* II.7, 419a, 15–21.

17. *De sensu* II.6, 446b, 25–26.

18. Bernhard Siegert, "Vögel, Engel und Gesandte: Alteuropas Übertragungsmedien," in *Gespräche—Boten—Briefe: Körpergedächtnis im Mittelalter*, ed. Horst Wenzel (Berlin: Schmidt, 1997), 45–62.

19. "*unus enim Deus unus et mediator Dei et hominum homo Christus Iesus*," 1 Timothy 2:5.

20. *medium debet habere aliquid de utroque extremorum.* Thomas of Aquinas, *Super I Epistolam B. Pauli ad Timotheum lectura*, cap. 2, lectio 1, cf. Christian Kiening, *Fülle und Mangel: Medialität im Mittelalter* (Zurich: Chronos, 2016).

21. See Hans Belting, *Likeness and Presence: A History of the Image before the Era of Art* (Chicago: University of Chicago Press, 1994); Alexander Nagel, *Medieval Modern: Art out of Time* (London: Thames & Hudson, 2012).

22. Marshal McLuhan, *Understanding Media: The Extensions of Man* (1964; repr., Cambridge: MIT Press, 1994); Friedrich A. Kittler, *Aufschreibesysteme 1800–1900* (1985; repr., Munich: Fink, 2003).

23. Dieter Mersch, *Medientheorien zur Einführung* (Hamburg: Junius, 2006).

24. Geoffrey Winthrop-Young, "Cultural Studies and German Media Theory," in *New Cultural Studies: Adventures in Theory*, ed. Gary Hall and Clare Birchall (Edinburgh: Edinburgh University Press, 2006); Bernard Dionysus Geoghegan, "Untimely Meditations: On Two Recent Contributions to 'German Media Theory,'" *Paragraph* 37, no. 3 (2014): 419–25.

25. Siegfried Zielinski, *Deep Time of the Media: Toward an Archaeology of Hearing and Seeing by Technical Means*, trans. Gloria Custance (Cambridge: MIT Press, 2006).

26. Ann Marie Rasmussen and Markus Stock, "Introduction: Medieval Media," *Seminar—A Journal of Germanic Studies* 52 (2016): 97–106; Christian Kiening, *Medieval Mediality: Abundance and Lack* (York: Arc Humanities Press, 2019).

27. *ein System von Kommunikationsmitteln, das wiederholte Kommunikation eines bestimmten Typs ermöglicht.* Roland Posner, quoted in Horst Wenzel, "Die 'fließende Rede' und der 'gefrorene Text': Metaphern der Medialität," in *Poststrukturalismus: Herausforderung an die Literaturwissenschaft*, ed. Gerhard Neumann (Stuttgart: Metzler, 1997), 481.

28. Hans Ulrich Gumbrecht and K. Ludwig Pfeiffer, *Materialities of Communication* (Stanford: Stanford University Press, 1994).

29. Franco Moretti, *Distant Reading* (London: Verso, 2013); Rita Felski, *Uses of Literature* (Malden, MA: Blackwell, 2008); Eve Kosofsky Sedgwick, "Paranoid Reading and Reparative Reading, or, You're So Paranoid, You Probably Think This Essay Is About You," in her *Touching Feeling: Affect, Pedagogy, Performativity* (Durham: Duke University Press, 2003), 123–51; Hans Ulrich Gumbrecht, *Production of Presence: What Meaning Cannot Convey* (Stanford: Stanford University Press, 2004). Michael Warner links the hegemonic status of critical reading in academia to the "material conditions for the objectification and segmentation of discourse" provided by the printed book. ("Uncritical Reading," in *Polemic: Critical or Uncritical*, ed. Jane Gallop [New York: Routledge, 2004], 21.)

30. See for example Christian Kiening, "Medialität in mediävistischer Perspektive," *Poetica* 39 (2008): 285–352; John Durham Peters, *The Marvelous Clouds: Toward a Philosophy of Elemental Media* (Chicago: University of Chicago Press, 2016).

31. See also Ursula Peters, "'Texte vor der Literatur?' Zur Problematik neuerer Alteritätsparadigmen der Mittelalter-Philologie," *Poetica* 39 (2007): 59–88; Bernhard Siegert, "Cultural Techniques: Or the End of the Intellectual Postwar Era in German Media Theory," *Theory, Culture & Society* 30 (2013): 48–65.

32. Eric A. Havelock, *The Literate Revolution in Greece and Its Cultural Consequences* (Princeton: Princeton University Press, 1982); Walter J. Ong, *Presence of the Word: Some Prolegomena for Cultural and Religious History* (New Haven: Yale University Press, 1967); Jack Goody and Ian Watt, "The Consequences of Literacy," *Comparative Studies in Society and History* 5 (1963): 304–45; Ruth Finnegan, *Literacy and Orality: Studies in the Technology of Communication* (Oxford: Blackwell, 1988); Michael T. Clanchy, *From Memory to Written Record: England 1066–1307*, 3rd ed. (Malden: Wiley-Blackwell, 2012).

33. Innis's major contribution to media theory is his *Empire and Communications* (Oxford: Clarendon, 1950).

34. Adam Parry, ed., *The Making of Homeric Verse: The Collected Papers of Milman Parry* (Oxford: Oxford University Press, 1971); Alan Bates Lord, *The Singer of Tales* (Cambridge: Harvard University Press, 1960). On the influence of studies of orality and literacy and the Oral Theory in Old Norse literary history, see Kate Heslop and Jürg Glauser, "Introduction," in our *RE:Writing: Medial Perspectives on Textual Culture in the Icelandic Middle Ages* (Zurich: Chronos, 2018).

35. For a concise account of *vocalité*, see Paul Zumthor, "The Text and the Voice," *New Literary History* 16 (1984): 67–92. Ursula Schaefer, *Vokalität: Altenglische Dichtung zwischen Mündlichkeit und Schriftlichkeit* (Tübingen: Gunter Narr, 1992), explores the implications of Zumthor's model for Old English literature.

36. Bernhard Siegert, *Cultural Techniques: Grids, Filters, Doors, and Other Articulations of the Real* (New York: Fordham University Press, 2015).

37. Vadstena's writings were studied in a Swedish project: *The Production of Texts and Manuscripts in the Vadstena Monastery: Production, Tradition and Reception*, accessed October 17, 2019, https://www.rj.se/anslag/2002/vadstenaklostret-som-text--och-handskriftsproducerande-miljo---produktion-tradition

-och-reception; *Njáls saga*, explored in *New Studies in the Manuscript Tradition of Njáls Saga: The Historia Mutila of Njála*, ed. Emily Lethbridge and Svanhildur Óskarsdóttir (Kalamazoo: Medieval Institute Publications, 2018); *Vǫluspá* in Judy Quinn, "Editing the Edda: the Case of *Völuspá*," *Scripta Islandica* 51 (2001): 69–92.

38. On *Skáldskaparmál*'s version of the star memorial, cf. my "Metaphors for Forgetting and Forgetting as Metaphor in Old Norse Poetics," in *Myth, Magic, and Memory in Early Scandinavian Narrative Culture. Studies in Honour of Stephen A. Mitchell*, ed. J. Glauser and P. Hermann (Turnhout: Brepols, 2021).

39. Jónas Kristjánsson and Vésteinn Ólason, eds., *Íslenzk Fornrit: Eddukvæði*, 2 vols. (Reykjavík: Hið íslenzka fornritafélag, 2014), I:392; translation from Carolyne Larrington, *The Poetic Edda*, 2nd rev. ed. (Oxford: Oxford University Press, 2014), 68.

40. Erich Auerbach, "Figura," in his *Scenes from the Drama of European Literature* (Minneapolis, University of Minnesota Press, 1984), 45; see also James Porter, "Disfigurations: Erich Auerbach's Theory of *Figura*," *Critical Inquiry* 44 (2017): 91–92.

41. Julia Zernack, "Vorläufer und Vollender: Olaf Tryggvason und Olaf der Heilige im Geschichtsdenken des Oddr Snorrason munkr," *Arkiv för nordisk filologi* 113 (1998): 77–95.

42. Anon, *Lil*, 98; Árni *Gd* 78.

43. On the Latin terms see D. W. Robertson Jr., "Some Medieval Terminology with Special Reference to Chrétien de Troyes," *Studies in Philology* 48 (1951): 669–92.

44. *Hann skrýddisk þá enn á nýja leik mǫrgum mannkostum ok allra mest þeim er Davíð kallaði kennimanninum í skyldasta lagi, at þeir skyldu skrýðask hjálpræðum ok réttlæti*, ÍF 16, 51. Ármann Jakobsson and David Clark, trans., *The Saga of Bishop Thorlak* (London: Viking Society, 2013), 3.

45. ÍF 16, 84. I am grateful to Jake Malone for discussing these passages with me.

46. ÍF 16, 257. See Heslop and Glauser, "Introduction," 16–17, for commentary on this passage.

47. "Scema ær kǫllvð agirzkv ænn skrvð a norenv [. . .]," Björn Magnússon Ólsen, ed., *Den tredje og fjærde grammatiske afhandling i Snorres Edda [. . .]* (Copenhagen: Møller, 1884), 91. Translation mine.

48. The final chapter of *Máríu saga*, containing the author's reflections on the saga, is rubricated as *Um kenning* (About the lesson) in Stock. Perg. 4to, no. 11, c. 1325–75 (fol. 26v); cf. C. R. Unger, ed., *Mariu saga. Legender om jomfru Maria og hendes jertegn*, 2 vols. (Christiania: Brøgger & Christie, 1871), 2:61.

49. Régis Debray, "Qu'est-ce que la médiologie?" trans. by Martin Irvine as "What Is Mediology?" *Le monde diplomatique* 8 (1999): 32.

50. Russell Poole, "Myth and Religion in the *Háleygjatal* of Eyvindr skáldaspillir," in *Learning and Understanding in the Old Norse World: Essays in Honour of Margaret Clunies Ross*, ed. Judy Quinn, Kate Heslop, and Tarrin Wills (Turnhout: Brepols, 2007), 153–76.

51. Régis Debray, *Transmitting Culture*, trans. Eric Rauth (New York: Columbia University Press, 2000), 47.

52. Susan Stewart, *Poetry and the Fate of the Senses* (Chicago: University of Chicago Press, 2002), 109.

RÖK AND *YNGLINGATAL*

1. Helmer Gustavson, "Rök. §2. Runologisches," in *RGA*, vol. 25, 62–72. Michael Barnes presents linguistic evidence that, in his view, "points to a relatively great age" (*"peker mot relativt høy alder"*). "Rök-steinen—noen runologiske og språklige overveielser," *Maal og minne*, 2007, 126. He does not commit himself to a concrete date but suggests that the ninth century may be too young.

2. E. Nyman, "Rök. §1. Namenkundliches," *RGA*, vol. 25, 62. The stone's present location, in the churchyard, is not original, but there is no reason to think it was moved far (cf. Ola Kyhlberg, "The Great Masterpiece: The Rök Stone and its Maker," *Current Swedish Archaeology* 18 [2010]: 177–201). Excavations have turned up little contextual information. Ploughing has also erased any trace of the memorial precinct surrounding the stone that has been postulated by some researchers largely due to their conviction that the inscription is incomplete. (Cf. Lydia Carstens, "Die dreizehn Geschichten auf dem Runenstein von Rök," in *Die Faszination des Verborgenen und seine Entschlüsselung—Rāði saR kunni*, ed. Jana Krüger et al. [Berlin: De Gruyter, 2017], 68–69).

3. On the form of the name, see Gun Widmark, "Vamod eller Vämod," in *Nordiska orter och ord: Festschrift till Bengt Pamp på 65-årsdagen*, ed. Göran Hallberg (Lund: Dialekt- och ortnamnsarkivet, 1993).

4. Barnes notes how few mistakes the carver makes ("Rök-steinen," 22).

5. On the sources, authorship, date, and transmission of *Heimskringla*, cf. Diana Whaley, *Heimskringla: An Introduction* (London: Viking Society, 1991).

6. Bjarni Aðalbjarnarson, ed., *Heimskringla* I (Reykjavik: Hið íslenzka fornritafélag, 1941); Marold et al., eds., "Þjóðólfr ór Hvini, *Ynglingatal*," in *Poetry from the Kings' Sagas, Vol. 1, From Mythical Times to c. 1035*, ed. Diana Whaley (Turnhout: Brepols, 2012), 3–58.

7. Lars Lönnroth, "Dómaldi's Death and the Myth of Sacral Kingship," in *Structure and Meaning in Old Norse Literature: New Approaches to Textual Analysis and Literary Criticism*, ed. John Lindow, Lars Lönnroth, and Gerd Wolfgang Weber (Odense: Odense University Press, 1986), 73–93.

8. Maurice Halbwachs, *On Collective Memory* (Chicago: University of Chicago Press, 1992); Pierre Nora, *Les lieux de mémoire*, 3 vols. (Paris: Gallimard, 1984–92).

9. Halbwachs, *Collective Memory*, 99, 116–18, 201–5.

10. Jan Assmann, *Das kulturelle Gedächtnis: Schrift, Erinnerung und politische Identität in frühen Hochkulturen* (Munich: Beck, 1992).

11. James Fentress and Chris Wickham, *Social Memory* (Oxford: Blackwell, 1992).

12. Andrew Jones, *Memory and Material Culture* (Cambridge: Cambridge University Press, 2007), 176, 224.

13. *Das was übrig bleibt von dem, was nicht mehr besteht und gilt.* Aleida Assmann, *Erinnerungsräume: Formen und Wandlungen des kulturellen Gedächtnisses* (Munich: Beck, 2006), 309.

14. She draws here on Pierre Nora's distinction between *milieux* and *lieux de mémoire* without, however, espousing his view that it is the experience of modernity that converts the former into the latter.

15. *Brücken über den Abgrund des Vergessens hinweg, den sie ebenfalls manifestieren.* Assmann, *Erinnerungsräume*, 311.

16. Anne Whitehead, *Memory* (London: Routledge, 2009), 133.

17. Nora Berend, *Christianization and the Rise of Christian Monarchy: Scandinavia, Central Europe and Rus' c. 900–1200* (Cambridge: Cambridge University Press, 2007), 4, 9.

18. Peter Brown, *The Cult of the Saints: Its Rise and Function in Latin Christianity* (Chicago: University of Chicago Press, 1981), 1.

19. Anders Andrén, "The Significance of Places: The Christianization of Scandinavia from a Spatial Point of View," *World Archaeology* 45 (2013): 41; see also Adolf Friðriksson and Orri Vésteinsson, "Landscapes of Burial: Contrasting the Pagan and Christian Paradigms of Burial in Viking Age and Medieval Scandinavia," *Archaeologia Islandica* 9 (2011): 50–64, for discussion of Icelandic archaeological material.

20. Geoffrey Koziol, *The Politics of Memory and Identity in Carolingian Royal Diplomas: The West Frankish Kingdom (840–987)* (Turnhout: Brepols, 2012), 536–37.

21. Michael S. Roth, Claire L. Lyons, and Charles Merewether, *Irresistible Decay: Ruins Reclaimed* (Los Angeles: Getty Research Institute, 1997), xi.

22. Kari Ellen Gade, *The Structure of Old Norse Dróttkvætt Poetry* (Ithaca: Cornell University Press, 1995), 226–38; "History of Old Norse Metrics," in *The Nordic Languages: An International Handbook of the History of the North Germanic Languages*, ed. Oskar Bandle et al. (Berlin: De Gruyter, 2002), 773–98; R. D. Fulk, "Eddic Metres," in *A Handbook to Eddic Poetry: Myths and Legends of Early Scandinavia*, ed. Carolyne Larrington, Judy Quinn, and Brittany Schorn (Cambridge: Cambridge University Press, 2016), 263–64.

23. Cf. Gade, *Structure*, 227–29.

24. In addition to the poems listed above, single stanzas in *kviðuháttr* appear in the *claves metricae*, the *fornaldarsögur* and some sagas of Icelanders, and the *Third Grammatical Treatise*. *Stjǫrnu-Odda draumr* and *Grettis saga* include long poems in *kviðuháttr*, titled *Geirviðarflokkr* and *Hallmundarkviða* respectively. This material bears witness to the exploration of minor meters in Icelandic poetological writings of the thirteenth century and later; cf. Konráð Gíslason, "Nogle bemærkninger angående Ynglingatal," *Aarbøger for nordisk oldkyndighed og historie* (1881): 247–51.

1. DEATH IN PLACE

1. Cf., e.g., Birger Nerman, *Studier över Svärges hedna litteratur* (Uppsala: Appelberg, 1913); Sune Lindqvist, *Uppsala högar och Ottarshögen* (Stockholm: Wahlström & Widstrand, 1936).

2. "to sider av samme sak." Bjørn Myhre, *Før Viken ble Norge: Borregravfeltet som religiøs og politisk arena* (Oslo: Kulturhistorisk Museum, 2015), 187–88; cf.

Dagfinn Skre, *Kaupang in Skiringssal: Excavation and Surveys at Kaupang and Huseby, 1998–2003* (Aarhus: Aarhus Universitetsforlag, 2007), 435.

3. Edward Casey, *Getting Back into Place: Toward a Renewed Understanding of the Place-World* (Bloomington: Indiana University Press, 2009), 131.

4. Casey, *Getting Back*, 112.

5. *Bjó*, past tense of *búa*, "to inhabit, lay to (in a ship), live as a married couple, raise livestock." A related verb, *byggva* (dwell), is used to describe Ymir's being at the beginning of time in the Codex Regius version of *Vǫluspá* (*ÍF Eddukvæði* I, 292).

6. Casey, *Getting Back*, 117.

7. Hans Ruin, "Speaking to the Dead—Historicity and the Ancestral," *Danish Yearbook of Philosophy* 48 (2013): 128.

8. Ann-Mari Hållans Stenholm, *Fornminnen: Det förflutnas roll i det kristna och förkristna Mälardalen* (Lund: Nordic Academic Press, 2012).

9. Stenholm, *Fornminnen*, 245.

10. Text and translation of *Ynglingatal* (*Yt*) from the edition of Marold et al., *SkP* I, 3–60. Subsequent citations are to this edition, by stanza number and abbreviated title.

11. *Ynglinga saga*'s prosimetrum may, of course, quote the stanzas out of order, but this is less likely to be the case when only one poem is incorporated, as here, than when saga authors combine stanzas from multiple poems in a single narrative. Internal evidence such as the alliterating names of the Swedish kings suggests that *Ynglinga saga* leaves the poem's ordering largely intact.

12. For Uppsala see below. Fýri (*Yt* 6) occurs several times in the compound Fýrisvellir/-vǫllr, while the skalds often mention Limafjǫrðr (*Yt* 12) and Nóregr (*Yt* 26). Fold (*Yt* 26) occurs in a *þula* of fjord-names in *Skáldskaparmál* (*SkP* III, 982).

13. Per Vikstrand, "Skúta and Vendil. Two Place Names in *Ynglingatal*," in *Namenwelten: Orts-und Personennamen in historischer Sicht*, ed. Astrid van Nahl, Lennart Elmevik, and Stefan Brink (Berlin: De Gruyter, 2004), 373–87.

14. Birgit Arrhenius, "Vendelzeit," in *RGA*, vol. 22, 132–33.

15. [. . .] *er þar síðan kǫlluð Agnafit á austanverðan Taurinum vestr frá Stokksundi*. ÍF 26, 38; translation from Anthony Faulkes and Alison Finlay, *Heimskringla I* (London: Viking Society, 2011), 22.

16. Elmevik suggests that *tǫr/tør* refers to Södertörn, ("Fornisl. *við taur, á austanverðum Taurinum* och det svenska ortnamnet Södertörn," in *Festschrift für Oskar Bandle zum 60. Geburtstag am 11. Januar 1986*, ed. Hans-Peter Naumann [Basel: Helbing & Lichtenhahn, 1986], 14–15). Evans ("King Agni: Myth, History or Legend?" in *Specvlvm Norroenvm: Norse Studies in Memory of Gabriel Turville-Petre*, ed. Ursula Dronke et al. [Odense: Odense University Press, 1981], 89–105) prefers *taur* ("necklace"). Marold et al., in their edition for *SkP*, obelize *taur*.

17. Sven B. F. Jansson, *Runinskrifter i Sverige* (Stockholm: Almqvist & Wiksell, 1963), 105–6. Olof Sundqvist reconstructs the Old Swedish form of the name as *Røning* ("Aspects of Rulership Ideology in Early Scandinavia—with Particular

Reference to the Skaldic Poem *Ynglingatal*," in *Das frühmittelalterliche Königtum: Ideelle und religiöse Grundlagen*, ed. Franz-Reiner Erkens [Berlin: de Gruyter, 2005], 92).

18. Hans-Peter Naumann, *Metrische Runeninschriften in Skandinavien: Einführung, Edition und Kommentare* (Tübingen: Narr, 2018), 188; cf. Alexandra Sanmark and Eva Bergström, *Tingsplatsen som arkeologiskt problem, etapp 1, Aspa: arkeologisk provundersökning, forskning: Raä 62, Aspa 2:11, Ludgo socken, Nyköpings kommun*, SAU Rapport 25 (Uppsala: Societas Archaeologica Upsaliensis, 2004).

19. Lydia Klos, *Runensteine in Schweden: Studien zu Aufstellungsort und Funktion* (Berlin: De Gruyter, 2009), 417, 240.

20. On runestone prestige markers, cf. Henrik Williams, "Runstenarnas sociala dimension," *Futhark* 4 (2013): 61–76. It is a strange coincidence that one of the Aspa stones, Sö 136 (now lost), calls its dedicatee *und hifni bæztr* (best under heaven; *SamRun*). Sö Fv 1948; 289 is dedicated to a "Ragnvaldr," a high-status name uncommon on Swedish runestones (S. B. F. Jansson, "Sörmlandska Runstensfynd," *Fornvännen* 43 [1948]: 293–97). According to Klos (*Runensteine*, 417) only Sö 137 and 138 still stand in their original places, but Sö Fv 1948; 289 is unlikely to have been moved far.

21. Stefan Brink, "Forntida vägar: Vägar och vägmiljöer," *Bebyggelsehistorisk tidskrift* 39 (2000): 53.

22. For the route of the *Eriksgata*, see the map in Måns Mannerfelt, "Där svenska riksvägar mötas," *Svenska turistförenings årsskrift*, (1930): 138; cf. also Gösta Hasselberg, "Eriksgata," *KLNM* 4 (1959), cols. 22–27; Adolf Schück, "Sveriges vägar och sjöleder under forntid och medeltid," in his *Handel och samfärdsel under medeltiden* (Stockholm: Bonnier, 1930), 241–46.

23. For a recent discussion of the challenges of identification and dating of premodern roads in Sweden, cf. John Bollaert, "Runstenar längs vägen: En undersökning av samband mellan runstenarnas placering och utformning" (master's thesis, Uppsala University, 2016); these problems have long been recognized, cf. Jöran Sahlgren, *Forntida vägar: Läbybron och Eriksgatan* (Uppsala: Berlings, 1909), 1–2.

24. Brink, "Forntida vägar," 53.

25. Gísli Sigurðsson, "Óláfr Þórdarson hvítaskáld and Oral Poetry in the West of Iceland c.1250: The Evidence of References to Poetry in *The Third Grammatical Treatise*," in *Old Icelandic Literature and Society*, ed. Margaret Clunies Ross (Cambridge: Cambridge University Press, 2009), 96–115; Alexandra Sanmark, *Viking Law and Order: Places and Rituals of Assembly in the Medieval North* (Edinburgh: Edinburgh University Press, 2017).

26. *En vinterväg, som gick mellan kungsgårdana längs norrlandskusten*. Brink, "Forntida vägar," 44.

27. Andrew Jones, *Memory and Material Culture* (Cambridge: Cambridge University Press, 2007), 195.

28. *ÍF Eddukvæði* I, 336; translation from Carolyne Larrington, *The Poetic Edda* (Oxford University Press, 2014), 22.

29. Several Swedish Viking Age inscriptions refer to the raising or setting of a *stafr* (sg.) as part of a memorial: U 226, U 332 (lost), Sö 196, Vs 1, possibly U 849. For archaeological evidence of such structures in contemporary burials in Iceland, see H. M. Roberts, "Journey to the Dead: The Litlu-Núpar Boat Burial," *Current World Archaeology* 32 (2008): 36–41; Elín Ósk Hreiðarsdóttir and Howell Roberts, "Þögnin rofin: Fyrstu niðurstöður fornleifarannsókna á eyðibyggð á Þegjandadal," in *Árbók Þingeyinga* (2008), 5–24.

30. Dagfinn Skre, "The Warrior Manor," in *Avaldsnes—A Sea-King's Manor in First-Millennium Western Scandinavia*, ed. Dagfinn Skre (Berlin: De Gruyter, 2018), 772–77.

31. ÞSjár *Frag* 1.

32. Cited in Catherine Cubitt, "Sites and Sanctity: Revisiting the Cult of Murdered and Martyred Anglo-Saxon Royal Saints," *Early Medieval Europe* 9 (2000): 68. Although the couplet is first attested as a marginal gloss in Latin manuscripts of the *vita* from the thirteenth century, the epithet *cynebearn* is already applied to Kenelm in the eleventh century, suggesting that this poetic tradition predates the *vita*; Eric Weiskott, "Saint Kenelm in an Imaginative Illustration," *Notes and Queries* 64 (2017): 217.

33. Cubitt, "Sites," 68–69.

34. František Graus, *Volk, Herrscher und Heiliger im Reich der Merowinger: Studien zur Hagiographie der Merowingerzeit* (Prague: NČSAV, 1965); Alan Thacker, "Membra Disjecta: The Division of the Body and the Diffusion of the Cult," in *Oswald: Northumbrian King to European Saint*, ed. Clare Stancliffe and Eric Cambridge (Stamford: Watkins, 1995), 97–127; Catherine Cubitt, "Memory and Narrative in the Cult of Early Anglo-Saxon Saints," in *The Uses of the Past in the Early Middle Ages*, ed. Yitzhak Hen and Matthew Innes (Cambridge: Cambridge University Press, 2000), 31–66; John Blair, *The Church in Anglo-Saxon Society* (Oxford: Oxford University Press, 2005), 144–49. Cf. Hilary Powell, "'Once Upon a Time There Was a Saint . . .': Re-evaluating Folklore in Anglo-Latin Hagiography," *Folklore* 121 (2010): 171–89.

35. Richard Firth Green, *Elf Queens and Holy Friars: Fairy Beliefs and the Medieval Church* (Philadelphia: University of Pennsylvania Press, 2016), 44.

36. John Blair, "A Saint for Every Minster? Local Cults in Anglo-Saxon England," in *Local Saints and Local Churches in the Early Medieval West*, ed. Alan Thacker and Richard Sharpe (Oxford: Oxford University Press, 2002), 478.

37. Blair, "A Saint?" 485.

38. See David Rollason, "The Cults of Murdered Royal Saints in Anglo-Saxon England," *Anglo-Saxon England* 11 (1983): 1–22.

39. André Vauchez, *Sainthood in the Later Middle Ages* (Cambridge: Cambridge University Press, 2005), 52, 152.

40. Sophus Bugge, *Bidrag til den ældste skaldedigtnings historie* (Christiania: Aschehoug, 1894), 108–57, 146–51, argued that the similarity between the *Fianna bátar* and *Ynglingatal* indicated that the latter was composed in Ireland in the late tenth century.

41. Amy C. Eichhorn-Mulligan, *A Landscape of Words: Ireland, Britain and the Poetics of Space, 700–1250* (Manchester: Manchester University Press, 2019), ch. 3.

42. Blair, "A Saint?" 486; for Brittany, see Julia M. H. Smith, "Oral and Written: Saints, Miracles, and Relics in Brittany, c. 850–1250," *Speculum* 65 (1990): 309–43.

43. Anne Pedersen, "Ancient Mounds for New Graves: An Aspect of Viking Age Burial Customs in Southern Scandinavia," in *Old Norse Religion in Long-Term Perspectives: Origins, Changes, and Interactions. An International Conference in Lund, Sweden, June 3–7, 2004*, ed. Anders Andrén (Lund: Nordic Academic Press, 2006), 346–53; Sarah Semple, *Perceptions of the Prehistoric in Anglo-Saxon England: Religion, Ritual, and Rulership in the Landscape* (London: Oxford University Press, 2013).

44. Andreas Heusler, *Die altergermanische Dichtung* (Berlin: Athenaion, 1923), 90; Walter Åkerlund, *Studier över Ynglingatal* (Lund: Gleerup, 1939), 77; Joan Turville-Petre, "On Ynglingatal," *Mediaeval Scandinavia* 11 (1978–79): 55–56; Vikstrand, "Skúta," 96.

45. John McKinnell, "Ynglingatal: A Minimalist Interpretation," *Scripta Islandica* 60 (2009): 29n24. For *Austrfararvísur*, see the discussion in *SkP* I, 578–82.

46. McKinnell, "Ynglingatal," 26.

47. Cf. Åkerlund, *Studier*; Lars Lönnroth, "Dómaldi's Death and the Myth of Sacral Kingship," in *Structure and Meaning in Old Norse Literature: New Analysis and Literary Criticism*, ed. John Lindow, Lars Lönnroth, and Gerd Wolfgang Weber (Odense: Odense University Press, 1986), 73–93; Kari Ellen Gade, "The Syntax of Old Norse Kviðuháttr Meter," *Journal of Germanic Linguistics* 17 (2005): 155–81.

48. [O]mstuvat [. . .] vantolkn[at], Lindqvist, *Uppsala högar*, 304.

49. David W. Rollason, "Lists of Saints' Resting-Places in Anglo-Saxon England," *Anglo-Saxon England* 7 (1978): 61–93. The manuscript of the *Secgan* dates from the eleventh century, but the text is most likely a cumulative composition. Rollason argues that the first part is older than the second.

50. Richard Bradley, *A Geography of Offerings: Deposits of Valuables in the Landscapes of Ancient Europe* (Philadelphia: Oxbow, 2017).

51. "In the Landscape and between Worlds: Bronze Age Deposition Sites around Lakes Mälaren and Hjälmaren in Sweden" (PhD diss., Umeå University, 2015), 52–53.

52. Bradley, *Geography*, 186.

53. Bradley, *Geography*, 168.

54. Rundkvist, "In the Landscape," 22.

55. The place-name Uppsala appears in three verses preserved in *fornaldarsögur* (StarkSt *Vík* 30, Hjálm *Lv* 8, Sigoa *Lv* 1). The Sjörup (DR 279) and Hällestad 1 (DR 295) stones commemorate different men who *flo ægi at Upsalum* ("did not flee at Uppsala"). This is often suggested to be a reference to the semi-legendary Battle of Fyrisvellir, c. 980 (cf. Judith Jesch, *Ships and Men in the Late Viking Age: The Vocabulary of Runic Inscriptions and Skaldic Verse* [Woodbridge: Boydell Press, 2001], 114, 222–25). The ninth-century Spärlosa stone (Vg 119) may also mention Uppsala (**ubsal**), but interpretation is very uncertain.

56. Reports on the main excavations are published in Władysław Duczko, *Arkeologi och miljögeologi i Gamla Uppsala*, 2 vols. (Uppsala: Societas Archaeologica Upsaliensis, 1993 & 1996). John Ljungkvist et al., "Gamla Uppsala—Structural Development of a Centre in Middle Sweden," *Archäologisches Korrespondenzblatt* 41 (2011): 571–85, offers a recent overview.

57. John Ljungkvist and Per Frölund, "Gamla Uppsala—The Emergence of a Centre and a Magnate Complex," *Journal of Archaeology and Ancient History* 16 (2015): 1–29.

58. Marianne Hem Eriksen surveys similar practices in "Commemorating Dwelling: The Death and Burial of Houses in Iron and Viking Age Scandinavia," *European Journal of Archaeology* 19 (2016): 477–96.

59. Ljungkvist and Frölund, "Gamla Uppsala—The Emergence," 19.

60. John Ljungkvist, "Monumentaliseringen av Gamla Uppsala," in *Gamla Uppsala i ny belysning*, ed. Olof Sundqvist and Per Vikstrand (Uppsala: Swedish Science Press, 2013), 33–67.

61. *Materiella vikingatida belägg för central kult, manifesta spår av kunglig/elitisk närvaro och judiciella sammankomster.* Ljungkvist, "Monumentaliseringen," 62.

62. Olof Sundqvist, "Religious Ruler Ideology in Pre-Christian Scandinavia: A Contextual Approach," in *More Than Mythology: Narratives, Ritual Practices and Regional Distribution in Pre-Christian Scandinavian Religions*, ed. Catharina Raudvere and Jens Peter Schjødt (Lund: Nordic Academic Press, 2012), 225–61. I discuss this concept further in Chapter 2.

63. *Nytolkning av det förgångna.* Svante Norr, "Gamla Uppsala, kungamakt och skriftliga källor," in *Arkeologi och miljögeologi i Gamla Uppsala*, vol. 2, ed. Władysław Duczko (Uppsala: Societas Archaeologica Upsaliensis, 1996), 34. Myhre, *Før Viken*, 121–22, 133, agrees. He sees the poem as composite, with layers including borrowings from a lost Swedish poem on the Ynglings and post-compositional changes taking place in oral and written transmission.

64. "Investeringarna i platsen under vendeltid har emellertid skapat en grund för en legendarisk och så småningom närmast självklar samlingsplats för såväl makthavare som ett bredare samhällsskikt. För vikingatidens makthavare var det antagligen inte nödvändigt att fortsätta manifestera platsen och sin egen närvaro med nya monument." Ljungkvist, "Monumentaliseringen," 59.

65. Myhre (*Før Viken*, ch. 15) argues that the mounds and equestrian graves containing objects ornamented in symmetrical style at Borre indicate emulation of an eastern Scandinavian style of funerary display. Whether at Borre or in *Ynglingatal*, such emulation need not be confined to Uppsala's glory days.

66. Åkerlund, *Studier*, 171–72.

67. Many of the place-names are monothematic. Fictional place-names in late eddic poems are, by contrast, dithematic and semantically transparent; cf., e.g., *Sólfjǫll, Logafjǫll, Hringstaðir, Frekasteinn, Gnipalundr*, in HH I (ÍF Eddukvæði II, 247–58).

68. Cf. Dagfinn Skre, *Kaupang in Skiringssal: Excavation and Surveys at Kaupang and Huseby, 1998–2003. Background and Results* (Aarhus: Aarhus Universitetsforlag,

2007), 407–29. Myhre, in *Før Viken*, addresses recent attempts to identify particular mounds at Borre with the kings mentioned in the poem. I share Myhre's skepticism about this endeavor.

69. If the first element is not, in fact, *søkk ("treasure"), cf. *SkP* I, 49.

70. The adverb *ofsa* could alternatively be interpreted as "with harsh rule/arrogance"; see Bergsveinn Birgisson, "Inn i skaldens sinn: kognitiv, estetiske og historiske skatter i den skaldediktingen" (PhD diss., University of Bergen, 2008), 394.

71. It is less likely to be a reference to the number of kings taken by Hel (as suggested in *SkP* I, 52). As this image is conventional and amounts merely to "died," there is no real reason to count the number of its occurrences.

72. Birgisson, "Inn i skaldens," 411–12.

73. The Kringla and J1 mss of *Yt* 27 have *heitumhǫr*, "promises-high," but this is probably the result of dittography of *of heitinn es* in the next line.

74. "High of rank" (*hög i rang*), proposed by Johan Palmér, relies on a gloss of "degree, rank" for *heiðr*, which is not otherwise attested in Old Norse, although it is for the Old High German and Old English cognates ("Betydelseutvecklingen i isl. heiðr," *Acta Philologica Scandinavica* 5 [1930–31], 297).

75. E.g., *með sœmðum ǫllum* ("with all honors"), Sturl, *Hryn*, 2; Bugge, *Bidrag*, 137–38.

76. De Vries suggests "flat area of common land on the spine of a mountain range, high plain" ("ebener auf dem gebirgsrücken gelegener teil der gemeinen mark, hochebene," *AEW* s.v. *heiðr* 2. f.). Jost Trier argues that *heiðr* has no particular topographical implications, but denotes common land on the edge of an inhabited area, including forest or stubblefields, with similar associations to *mǫrk*; compare Lat. *margo* ("Heide," *Archiv für Literatur und Volksdichtung* 1 [1949]: 63–103).

77. William Jervis Jones, *German Colour Terms: A Study in Their Historical Evolution from Earliest Times to the Present* (Amsterdam: Benjamins, 2013), 292, 307; C. P. Biggam, *Blue in Old English: An Interdisciplinary Semantic Study* (Amsterdam: Rodopi, 1997), 100. This phenomenon is not confined to Germanic languages. The non-blueness of the sea in Homeric Greek has given rise to many creative theories; see Kai Kupferschmidt, *Blau: Wie die Schönheit in die Welt kommt* (Hamburg: Hoffmann & Campe, 2019), 143–62.

78. "The Color Blue in Old Norse-Icelandic Literature," *Scripta Islandica*, 57 (2006): 63. Bbreiðv *Lv* 1 contrasts *blár* ("blue") with *gull viðr* ("golden woods"), but "blue" could just as well refer to sea as to sky, and the Modern Icelandic expression cited in *LP* as support for the latter is not dispositive.

79. *Blue: The History of a Color* (Princeton: Princeton University Press, 2001), 32. *Vsp* 9 uses *Bláinn* as an alternative name for Ymir, the most recent edition of the *Poetic Edda* suggests, because "the blue sky was made out of his skull" (*hinn blái himinn var gerður úr hausi hans*; *ÍF Eddukvæði* II, 293 n.). Dronke's suggestion that Bláinn "refers to [Ymir's] dark and deadly flesh" (*Poetic Edda, Vol. 2, Mythological Poems* [Oxford: Clarendon, 1997], 122) returns *blár* to a better-attested semantic

field. The only other blue skies appear in two sky names in *þulur*: *Víðbláinn* ("wide-blue one") and *Vindbláinn* ("wind-blue one") (Gurevich, ed., *SkP* III, 906, 916–17). These show influence from Christian teachings of three heavens and reflect the thirteenth-century rise in status of the color blue.

80. Aage Kabell, "Apokalypsen i Skarpåker," *Arkiv för nordisk filologi* 77 (1962): 53–55.

81. Lars Lönnroth, "Iǫrð fannz æva né upphiminn," in *Speculum Norroenum: Norse Studies in Memory of Gabriel Turville-Petre*, ed. Ursula Dronke et al. (Odense: Odense University Press, 1981), 310–27. For instances of the formula, cf., e.g., the Skarpåker runestone (Sö 154), *Vsp* 3, Arn *Hryn* 3, Hfr *ErfÓl* 27.

82. Pastoureau, *Blue*, 44–47, 51, 62; Florin Curta, "'Colour Perception, Dyestuffs, and Colour Terms in Twelfth-Century French Literature," *Medium Ævum* 73 (2004): 48–49.

83. Joyce Plesters, "Ultramarine Blue, Natural and Artificial," *Studies in Conservation* 11 (1966): 62–91.

84. Codices were frequently stolen on raids; cf. Simon Coupland, "Holy Ground? The Plundering and Burning of Churches by Vikings and Franks in the Ninth Century," *Viator* 45 (2014): 81–82. A contemporary annotation in the mid–eighth-century Stockholm Codex Aureus records the manuscript's ransoming from Vikings; cf. Michelle P. Brown, *The Book and the Transformation of Britain c. 550–1050* (London: British Library, 2011), Plate 9.

85. J. J. G. Alexander, *Medieval Illuminators and Their Methods of Work* (New Haven: Yale University Press, 1992), 40.

86. Pastoureau, *Blue*, 41.

87. Robert G. Calkins, *Illuminated Books of the Middle Ages* (Ithaca: Cornell University Press, 1983), 130.

88. Russell G. Poole, "Scholars and Skalds: The Northwards Diffusion of Carolingian Poetic Fashions," *Gripla* 24 (2013): 37.

89. Simon Coupland, "From Poachers to Gamekeepers: Scandinavian Warlords and Carolingian Kings," *Early Medieval Europe* 7 (1998): 85–114.

90. Daniel Melleno, "North Sea Networks: Trade and Communication from the Seventh to the Tenth Century," *Comitatus* 45 (2014): 65–89; "Between Borders: Franks, Danes, and Abodrites in the Trans-Elben World up to 827," *Early Medieval Europe* 25 (2017): 359–85.

91. Ildar H. Garipzanov, *The Symbolic Language of Royal Authority in the Carolingian World (c. 751–877)* (Leiden: Brill, 2008), 2.

92. Thomas F. X. Noble, *Images, Iconoclasm, and the Carolingians* (Philadelphia: University of Pennsylvania Press, 2009), 338–40.

93. Latin text in Ernst Dümmler, *Monumenta Germaniae Historica: Poetae Latini Aevi Carolini* (Berlin: Weidmann, 1894), 2:5–79; translation in Thomas F. X. Noble, *Charlemagne and Louis the Pious: The Lives by Einhard, Notker, Ermoldus, Thegan, and the Astronomer* (University Park: Pennsylvania State University Press, 2009), 119–86.

94. Noble, *Images*, 175–76.

95. Noble, *Images*, 176.

96. Walther Lammers, "Ein karolingisches Bildprogramm in der Aula regia von Ingelheim," in *Festschrift für Hermann Heimpel zum 70. Geburtstag am 19. September 1971* (Göttingen: Vandenhoeck & Ruprecht, 1972), 226–89; Noble, *Images*, 354–55. Finds at Ingelheim suggest it was decorated with geometric fields of color (Christoph Steigemann and Matthias Wemhoff, *799: Kunst und Kultur der Karolingerzeit. Karl der Große und Papst Leo III. in Paderborn*, 2 vols. [Mainz: von Zabern, 1999], 1:106–7, 139). The ninth-century decorative program of the church of the Abbey of St. John in Müstair involves multiple narrative sequences delineated by painted and architectural frames; see Jürg Goll, Matthias Exner, and Susanne Hirsch, *Müstair: Die mittelalterlichen Wandbilder in der Klosterkirche* (Zurich: NZZ Libro, 2009).

97. Lammers, "Bildprogramm," 282–86.

98. *SkP* I, 6; Skre, *Kaupang*, 407–29; Edith Marold, "Der 'mächtige Nachkomme'" in *Analecta Septentrionalia: Beiträge zur nordgermanischen Kultur-und Literaturgeschichte*, ed. Wilhelm Heizmann et al. (Berlin: De Gruyter, 2009), 745–77; Lars Pilø et al., *Things from the Town: Artefacts and Inhabitants in Viking-Age Kaupang* (Aarhus: Aarhus Universitetsforlag, 2011), 444.

99. Sophus Bugge, "Naar og hvor er Ynglingatal forfattet?" in *Bidrag til den ældste skaldedigtnings historie* (Christiania: Aschehoug, 1894).

100. Claus Krag, *Ynglingatal og ynglingesaga: En studie i historiske kilder* (Oslo: Rådet for humanistisk forskning, Universitetsforlaget, 1991); for a more recent statement from Krag, still advocating a twelfth-century date, see his "Rikssamlingshistorien og ynglingerekken," *Historisk tidsskrift* 91 (2012): 159–89.

101. Claus Krag, "8(c): The Early Unification of Norway," in *The Cambridge History of Scandinavia*, ed. Knut Helle, E. I. Kouri, and Jens E. Olesen (Cambridge: Cambridge University Press, 2003), 188.

102. Klaus Johan Myrvoll, "Kronologi i skaldekvæde: Distribusjon av metriske og språklege drag i høve til tradisjonell datering og attribuering" (PhD diss., University of Oslo, 2014); Christopher D. Sapp, "Dating *Ynglingatal*: Chronological Metrical Developments in *kviðuháttr*," *Skandinavistik* 30 (2000): 85–90. I am grateful to Klaus Johan for letting me see a copy of his unpublished dissertation.

103. Myhre, *Før Viken*, 125–26, discusses the archaeological evidence and research history.

104. *Skáldatal* also mentions Haraldr *hárfagri*, but the *Poem about Haraldr hárfagri* attributed to Þjóðólfr is probably not genuine, cf. *SkP* I, 60.

105. For Strút-Haraldr, see ÍF 26, 272–73 and n. 5.

106. Edith Marold, "Lebendige Skaldendichtung," in *Neue Ansätze in der Mittelalterphilologie/Nye Veier i middelalderfilologien. Akten der skandinavistischen Arbeitstagung in Münster vom 24.–26.10. 2002*, ed. Susanne Kramarz-Bein (Frankfurt: Lang, 2005), 247–71.

107. Ildar H. Garipzanov, "Frontier Identities: Carolingian Frontier and the *gens Danorum*," in *Franks, Northmen and Slavs: Identities and State Formation in Early*

Medieval Europe, ed. Patrick J. Geary, Ildar H. Garipzanov, and Przemysław Urbańcyzk (Turnhout: Brepols, 2008), 135.

108. Coupland, "From Poachers."

109. Paul Gazzoli, "*Denemearc, Tanmaurk ala*, and *Confinia nordmannorum*: The *Annales regni Francorum* and the Origins of Denmark," *Viking and Medieval Scandinavia* 7 (2011): 38–39.

110. Tom Schmidt, "Særtrekk ved stedsnavnmaterialet fra Østfold i jernalder og middelalder," in *Over grenser: Østfold og Viken i yngre jernalder og middelalder*, ed. Jón Viðar Sigurðsson and Per G. Norseng (Oslo: Senter for studier i vikingtid og nordisk middelalder, 2003), 71–100; Ellen Anne Pedersen, Frans-Arne Stygelar, and Per G. Norseng, *Øst for Folden* (Sarpsborg: Østfolds fylkeskommune, 2003), 389–90.

111. Birgit Maixner, "Die Begegnung mit dem Süden: Fränkische Rangzeichen und ihre Rezeption im wikingerzeitlichen Skandinavien," in *Die Wikinger und das Fränkische Reich: Identitäten zwischen Konfrontation und Annäherung*, ed. Kerstin P. Hofmann and Nicola Karthaus (Paderborn: Fink, 2014), 85–131.

112. Bjørn Myhre, "Borregravfeltet som historisk arena," *Viking* 66 (2003): 49–77.

113. Pedersen et al., *Øst for Folden*, 392. Another Østfold ship burial was discovered in 2018, using georadar, at Gjellestad near Halden. The excavators have dated the ship to the early Viking Age; the mound itself is older. "The Gjellestad Ship Excavation," Museum of Cultural History, accessed July 11, 2020, https://www.khm.uio.no/english/visit-us/viking-ship-museum/gjellestad-ship/index.html.

114. Pedersen et al., *Øst for Folden*, 294.

115. *Zur stabilisierenden Selbstdarstellung innerhalb der eigenen Gesellschaft [es] zu einer Entlehnung von Sachgütern und Gebräuchen des als überlegen empfundenen Partners käme*. Maixner, "Begegnung," 121.

116. *Produktive Aneignung des Fremden*. Hermann Kamp, "Einleitung," in *Die Wikinger und das Fränkische Reich: Identitäten zwischen Konfrontation und Annäherung*, ed. Kerstin P. Hofmann and Nicola Karthaus (Paderborn: Fink, 2014), 11.

117. *Mildgeðr markar dróttinn*, the closing lines of the poem in the Codex Frisianus manuscript. The word *mǫrk* (f.) usually means "forest" but is occasionally used to refer to borderlands, as when Haraldr *lúfa* swears not to cut his hair until he reigns *sva vitt sem Noregr er austr til marka oc norðr til hafs* ("as wide as Norway is east to the border and north to the sea"); Finnur Jónsson, ed., *Fagrskinna: Nóregs konunga tal* (Copenhagen: Møller, 1902–1903), 15.

118. I am grateful to Jonas Wellendorf for discussing this passage with me. Cf. Hilda Ellis Davidson, ed., *Saxo grammaticus: The History of the Danes*, 2 vols., trans. Peter Fisher (Cambridge: Brewer, 1979–80), 2:94. Davidson also compares the st. on the Karlevi stone; see below.

119. Davidson and Fisher translate this slightly differently, as "the general sense I have expressed in these four lines of translation" (Davidson, *Saxo grammaticus: The History of the Danes*, 1:162).

120. Text and translation from Karsten Friis-Jensen, ed., *Saxo grammaticus: Gesta Danorum*, 2 vols., trans. Peter Fisher (Oxford: Clarendon, 2015), 1:355–57.

121. *LP* suggests that *himinfjǫll*, which also occurs in the eddic Helgi poems, is a cloud-kenning. If this is the case, *und himinfjǫllum* here could mean "under the clouds," creating a close parallel to the last line of the *Gesta* stanza.

122. Saxo's use of *affigeret* could suggest that the poem was recorded on a material substrate. This is interesting in light of the runic evidence. The phrasing of the *dróttkvætt* stanza on the Karlevi runestone (Öl 1; ed. *Skj*, 177), erected on the island of Öland around 1000, shows close parallels to *Yt* 26: *ørgrandari ráða landi í Danmǫrku* ("more undamaging [man] rule over land in Denmark"); cf. "*ofsa réð víðri grund af Vestmari*" ("ruled powerfully over a wide area across Vestmarir") (*Yt*); "*folginn í þeimsi haugi*" ("buried in this mound"); cf. *haugi ausinn* ("surrounded by a mound") (*Yt*); *rógstarkr* ("battle-strong"); cf. *gunndjarfr* ("war-daring") (*Yt*). *Yt* 26 has also been compared to the stanza on the Rök stone: Are these traces of a genre of monumental commemorative poetry?

123. E. Sebo et al., "The Kalvestene: A Reevaluation of the Ship Settings on the Danish Island of Hjarnø," *Journal of Island and Coastal Archaeology* 16 (2021): 1–17.

124. Ed. Townend, *SkP* I, 863–76. See John Lindow, "St Olaf and the Skalds," in *Sanctity in the North: Saints, Lives, and Cults in Medieval Scandinavia*, ed. Thomas A. Dubois (Toronto: University of Toronto Press, 2008), 103–127.

125. Peter Brown, *The Cult of the Saints: Its Rise and Function in Latin Christianity* (Chicago: University of Chicago Press, 1981).

126. McKinnell, "Ynglingatal," and cf. *Sonatorrek*, 18.

127. Lindow, "St Olaf," 112; Matthew Townend, "Knútr and the Cult of St Óláfr: Poetry and Patronage in Eleventh Century Norway and England," *Viking and Medieval Scandinavia* 1 (2005): 257.

128. Ed. Jesch, *SkP* II, 617–19.

129. *Yt* 19; *Hallgarðr* "Slab-Garðr" (*ofljóst* play on the name *Grjótgarðr* ["Stones-Garðr"]), Eyv *Hál* 8; Anon *Nkt* 28, 40 (*grýtt fold*); 57 (*grundu ausinn*); 60 (*hauðri hulðr*); 62 (*hulðr vígðri moldu*); *fold, studd steini* ("earth studded with stones"), SnSt *Ht* 102; cf. also *tumulatum cespite* ("buried under turf") in Hjarni's stanza.

130. See my "Minni and the Rhetoric of Memory in Eddic, Skaldic and Runic Texts," in *Minni and Muninn: Memory in Medieval Nordic Culture*, ed. Pernille Hermann, Stephen A. Mitchell, and Agnes S. Arnórsdóttir (Turnhout: Brepols, 2014), 75–107.

2. FORGING THE CHAIN

1. Haraldr *hárfagri*'s mother, Ragnhildr, dreams of a tree in ch. 6 of *Hálfdanar saga svarta* in *Heimskringla*. On trees in medieval genealogical literature, see Christiane Klapisch-Zuber, "The Genesis of the Family Tree," *I Tatti Studies in the Italian Renaissance* 4 (1991): 105–29.

2. ÍF 29, 57–58. Much the same dream is reported in ch. 7 of *Hálfdanar saga svarta* (ÍF 26, 90–91).

3. Shakespeare is fond of puns linking *hair* and *heir* ("Had I as many sons as I have hairs, / I would not wish them to a fairer death," *Macbeth* V, viii, 48–49).

Perhaps there is a subterranean pun in the Norse text on *hár* (adj.) "high, noble; long-lasting"?

4. Cf. Claus Krag, "Norge som odel i Harald Hårfagres ætt: et møte med en gjenganger," *Historisk tidsskrift* 3 (1989): 288–302; Sverrir Jakobsson, "Erendringen om en mægtig Personlighed: Den norsk-islandske historiske tradisjon om Harald Hårfagre i et kildekritisk perspektiv," *Historisk tidsskrift* 81 (2007): 213–30; Sverrir Jakobsson, "The Early Kings of Norway, the Issue of Agnatic Succession, and the Settlement of Iceland," *Viator* 47 (2016): 171–88.

5. Sigrid Weigel, *Genea-Logik: Generation, Tradition, und Evolution zwischen Kultur- und Naturwissenschaften* (Munich: Fink, 2006).

6. Gabrielle M. Spiegel, *The Past as Text: The Theory and Practice of Medieval Historiography* (Baltimore: Johns Hopkins University Press, 1997), 108.

7. M. J. Carruthers, *The Book of Memory: A Study of Memory in Medieval Culture* (Cambridge: Cambridge University Press), 3.

8. *Edda*, trans. Faulkes, 177. "Þat málsorð er fyrst er í þessi vísu er síðars< t> *í hinni fyrri, ok er hin *síðari svá dregin af hinni fyrri." Snorri Sturluson, *Edda. Háttatal*, 2nd ed., ed. Anthony Faulkes (London: Viking Society, 2007), 11 (hereafter referred to as Faulkes, *Háttatál*). *Drǫgur* is equated with *anadiplosis* in the Third Grammatical Treatise (Björn Magnússon Ólsen, *Den tredje og fjærde grammatiske afhandling i Snorres Edda* [Copenhagen: Møller, 1884], 94). An end-rhymed *kviðuháttr*-like verse-form is called *belgdrǫgur* ("bellows-drawings") in *Háttalykill* (RvHbreiðm Hl, 13–14). Its name is unexplained.

9. The term is attested twice, once as a heading before st. 3 of *Háttalykill* and once in the *Third Grammatical Treatise*, in a discussion of a stanza from Egill's *Arinbjarnarkviða* (Magnússon Ólsen, *Den tredje*, 63). The *-kviða* element also occurs as the second part of many medievally attested poem names, a few in the *kviðuháttr* meter (*Glælognskviða*, *Hákonarkviða*, *Hallmundarkviða*), but a greater number in *fornyrðislag* and belonging to the eddic corpus (*Þrymskviða, Guðrúnarkviða*, etc.).

10. Elias Wessén, "Om kuida i namn på fornnordiska dikter," *Edda* 4 (1915): 127–41.

11. *Beowulf*, 2111–14, trans. R. M. Liuzza (Peterborough: Broadview, 2000), 117.

12. Cf. also *Beowulf* 3171–72, where the performance of a funeral dirge for the dead king Beowulf is called appositively *ceare cwīðan* ("lament sorrow"), and *Wanderer*, 51–55, where the speaker laments his lack of *maga gemynd* ("memory of kin") and *cuðra cwidegiedda* ("familiar speech").

13. Russell G. Poole, "Þulir as Tradition-Bearers and Prototype Saga-Tellers," in *Creating the Medieval Saga: Versions, Variability, and Editorial Interpretations of Old Norse Saga Literature*, ed. Judy Quinn and Emily Lethbridge (Odense: University Press of Southern Denmark, 2010), proposes a link between OE *þyle* and ON *þulr* similar to that proposed here for the OE verb *cwīðan* and ON *kviða*.

14. "Den övergick till minnesdikt, hjältens bragder utsmyckades och fortlevde i den heroiska sagan, det episka elementet blev allt starkare och slutligen framstod

den berättande dikten sådan vi känna den från Eddan och de tyska och fornengelska hjältesangerna." Wessén, "Om kuida," 141.

15. Finnur Jónsson, *Den oldnorske og oldislandske litteraturs historie* (Copenhagen: Gad, 1920), 2nd ed., 3 vols, 1:107n2. Finnur argues that *kviða* is the result of *Movierung* of *kviðr* (m. "decree, judgment, witness") to *kviða* (f. "poem"), under the influence of the feminine nouns *vísa* ("verse") and *drápa* ("long poem").

16. *Allmänna resonemang om goternas intelligens och kulturella betydelse*, E. Noreen, "Kuiða: En Hypotes," in *Festschrift Eugen Mogk. Zum 70. Geburtstag, 19 Juli 1924* (Halle an der Saale: Niemeyer, 1924), 63.

17. Edith Marold, "Kviðuháttr," in *RGA*, vol. 17, 515–18.

18. For an instance of this pattern in the skald sagas, see Margaret Clunies Ross, "Skald Sagas as a Genre," in *Skaldsagas: Text, Vocation, and Desire in the Icelandic Sagas of Poets*, ed. R. G. Poole (Berlin: De Gruyter, 2000), 25–49.

19. Lars Lönnroth, "Dómaldi's Death and the Myth of Sacral Kingship," in *Structure and Meaning in Old Norse Literature: New Approaches to Textual Analysis and Literary Criticism*, ed. John Lindow, Lars Lönnroth, and Gerd Wolfgang Weber (Odense: Odense University Press, 1986), 91.

20. Svanhildur Óskarsdóttir, "Dáið þér Ynglinga? Gróteskar hneigðir Þjóðólfs úr Hvini," in *Sagnaþing helgað Jónasi Kristjánssyni sjötugum*, 2 vols., ed. Sigurgeir Steingrímsson, Gísli Sigurðsson, and Guðrún Kvárán, (Reykjavík: Hið íslenska bókmenntafélag, 1994), 2:761–68; Rolf Stavnem, "Dødsmetaforik: Metaforisk sprog i Ynglingatal," *Opuscula* 12 (2005): 263–85; Bergsveinn Birgisson, "Inn i skaldens sinn. Kognitive, estetiske og historiske skatter i den norrøne skaldediktningen" (PhD diss., University of Bergen, 2008), 283–98; John McKinnell, "Ynglingatal—A Minimalist Interpretation," *Scripta Islandica* 60 (2009): 23–48; Richard North, "Kurzweilige Wahrheiten: Ari und das Ynglingatal in den Prologen der Heimskringla," in *Snorri Sturluson—Historiker, Dichter, Politiker*, ed. Heinrich Beck, Wilhelm Heizmann, and Jan van Nahl (Berlin: De Gruyter, 2013), 171–216; Erin Goeres, *The Poetics of Commemoration: Skaldic Verse and Social Memory* (Oxford: Oxford University Press, 2015).

21. Edith Marold, "Snorri und die Skaldik," in *Snorri Sturluson—Historiker, Dichter, Politiker*, ed. Heinrich Beck, Wilhelm Heizmann, and Jan van Nahl (Berlin: De Gruyter, 2013), 217–34.

22. Walter Baetke, *Yngvi und die Ynglinger: Eine quellenkritische Untersuchung über das nordische 'Sakralkönigtum'* (Berlin: Adakemie-Verlag, 1964); Klaus von See, *Kontinuitätstheorie und Sakraltheorie in der Germanenforschung: Antwort an Otto Höfler* (Berlin: Athenäum, 1972); Lönnroth, "Dómaldi's Death"; Eve Picard, *Germanisches Sakralkönigtum? Quellenkritische Studien zur Germania des Tacitus und zur altnordischen Überlieferung* (Heidelberg: Winter, 1991); Olof Sundqvist, *Freyr's Offspring: Rulers and Religion in Ancient Svea Society* (Uppsala: Uppsala Universitet, 2002); Roberta Frank, "The Lay of the Land in Skaldic Praise Poetry," in *Myth in Early Northwest Europe*, ed. Stephen O. Glosecki (Turnhout: Brepols, 2007), 175–96; Bernard Mees, "The Stentoften Dedication and Sacral Kingship,"

Zeitschrift für deutsches Altertum und deutsche Literatur 140 (2011): 281–305; Margaret Clunies Ross, "Royal Ideology in Early Scandinavia: A Theory Versus the Texts," *Journal of English and Germanic Philology* 113 (2014): 18–33.

23. See Olof Sundqvist, "Sakralkönigtum (Skandinavische Quellen)," in *RGA*, vol. 26, 279–93; Olof Sundqvist, "Religious Ruler Ideology in Pre-Christian Scandinavia: A Contextual Approach," in *More than Mythology: Narratives, Ritual Practices and Regional Distribution in Pre-Christian Scandinavian Religions*, ed. Catharina Raudvere and Jens Peter Schjødt (Lund: Nordic Academic Press, 2012), 225–61.

24. Cf., e.g., Charlotte Fabech, "Society and Landscape: From Collective Manifestations to Ceremonies of a New Ruling Class," in *Iconologia Sacra, Mythos, Bildkunst und Dichtung in der Religions- und Sozialgeschichte Alteuropas: Festschrift für Karl Hauck*, ed. Hagen Keller and Nikolaus Staubach (Berlin: De Gruyter, 1994), 132–143; Stefan Brink, "Political and Social Structures in Early Scandinavia: A Settlement-Historical Pre-Study of the Central Place," *Tor* 28 (1996): 235–82; Andres Siegfried Dobat, "The King and His Cult: The Axe-Hammer from Sutton Hoo and its Implications for the Concept of Sacral Leadership in Early Medieval Europe," *Antiquity* 80 (2006): 880–93.

25. Herwig Wolfram, "Frühes Königtum," in *Das frühmittelalterliche Königtum: ideelle und religiöse Grundlagen*, ed. Franz-Reiner Erkens (Berlin: De Gruyter, 2005), 42–64.

26. As Marold et al. note (*SkP* I, 30–31), *rjóðr* is nowhere else attested with a human object. While *Historia Norwegie* has no trace of *Heimskringla*'s kin-sacrifice story, similar folktales are widely attested; cf. S. Eitrem, "König Aun in Upsala und Kronos," in *Festschrift til Hj. Falk* (Oslo: Aschehoug, 1927), 245–61.

27. Sundqvist, *Freyr's Offspring*, 280; Lönnroth, "Dómaldi's Death," 91; Óskarsdóttir, "Dáið þér Ynglinga?" 768.

28. Stefan Helmreich, "The Genders of Waves," *Women's Studies Quarterly* 45 (2017): 29–51; Judy Quinn, "Mythologizing the Sea: The Nordic Sea-Deity Rán," in *Nordic Mythologies: Interpretations, Intersections and Institutions*, ed. Timothy R. Tangherlini (Berkeley: North Pinehurst Press, 2014), 85–87.

29. Goeres, *The Poetics of Commemoration*, 36–47.

30. *AEW*, s.v. 'hel.'

31. Christopher Abram, "Hel in Early Norse Poetry," *Viking and Medieval Scandinavia* 2 (2006): 1–29.

32. Anon *Nkt* 8, ed. Gade, *SkP* II, 761–806.

33. Hilda Ellis Davidson, *The Road to Hel: A Study of the Conception of the Dead in Old Norse Literature* (Cambridge: Cambridge University Press, 1943), 84; Abram, "Hel," 26.

34. For further instances of *ofljóst* in *kviðuháttr* poetry, see Eyv *Hál* 8, Egill *Arkv* 16, 17, Anon *Nkt* 8, 17, 23, 42, Sturl *Hákkv* 18.

35. On *troll*, see Ármann Jakobsson, "The Trollish Acts of Þorgrímr the Witch: The Meanings of *troll* and *ergi* in Medieval Iceland," *Saga-Book* 32 (2008): 55.

36. Ed. Poole, *SkP* I, 195–213.

37. The fact that the jarls of Lade are said to be the descendants of Týr and Freyr, just as the kings of *Ynglingatal* are, is itself a sign that the two poems do not trace two contrasting genealogies.

38. Judy Quinn, "The Gendering of Death in Eddic Cosmology," in *Old Norse Religion in Long-Term Perspectives: Origins, Changes and Interactions. An International Conference in Lund, Sweden, June 3–7*, ed. Anders Andrén, Kristina Jennbert, and Catharina Raudvere (Lund: Nordic Academic Press, 2004).

39. Sexual encounters between living men and women marked for death are described in Ahmad Ibn Faḍlān, "Mission to the Volga," in *Two Arabic Travel Books: Accounts of China and India and Mission to the Volga*, ed. and trans. James Montgomery (New York: NYU Press, 2015), 165–298; between the dead man in the grave and a living woman buried with him in Ibn Rustah, "Rustah's Book of Precious Things: A Reexamination and Translation of an Early Source on the Rūs," ed. and trans. William Watson, *Canadian-American Slavic Studies* 38 (2004): 292. For the archaeological material, cf. Neil Price, *The Viking Way: Religion and War in Late Iron Age Scandinavia* (Uppsala: Department of Archaeology and Ancient History, 2002), 46.

40. *HHII* 49. ÍF *Eddukvæði* II:282; Larrington, *Poetic Edda*, 140.

41. "Pantheon? What Pantheon? Concepts of a Family of Gods in Pre-Christian Scandinavian Religions," *Scripta Islandica* 66 (2015): 59.

42. M. J. Carruthers, *The Book of Memory: A Study of Memory in Medieval Culture*, 2nd ed. (Cambridge: Cambridge University Press, 2008), 62; Judy Quinn, "From Orality to Literacy in Medieval Iceland," in *Old Icelandic Literature and Society*, ed. Margaret Clunies Ross (Cambridge: Cambridge University Press, 2000), 30–60.

43. The Old Swedish laws refer to a privileged class of witnesses called *talumæn*, one of whose tasks was to recite lists of boundary markers (Stefan Brink, "I.12: Law," in *Handbook of Pre-Modern Nordic Memory Studies, Interdisciplinary Approaches*, 2 vols., ed. Jürg Glauser, Pernille Hermann, and Stephen A. Mitchell, (Berlin: De Gruyter, 2018), 1:190.

44. *tvén ok þrén*. Egill *St* 15, *Skj* BI, 40.

45. *Nú hefk mart [. . .] greipat. SkP* III, 489.

46. Marold et al., *SkP* I, 7.

47. "Ursprung und Kontinuität ergeben sich [. . .] als die beiden zentralen Problemkonstellationen jeder genealogischen Ordnung." *Ursprung und Kontinuität: Studien zum genealogischen Wissen im Mittelalter* (Munich: Fink, 2004), 108.

48. Konráð Gíslason, *Nogle bemærkninger angående Ynglingatal: Bemærking til en 'vísuhelmingr' af Snorri Sturluson* (Copenhagen: Thiele, 1881); skeptical discussion in Baetke, *Yngvi*, 96–103; cf. Walter Åkerlund, *Studier över Ynglingatal* (Lund: Gleerup, 1939), 127.

49. *Skilfingr* is widely attested; see *SkP* I, 34, n. to l.14, for discussion and references.

50. Cf. Edith Marold, "Der 'mächtige Nachkomme'," in *Analecta Septentrionalia: Beiträge zur nordgermanischen Kultur-und Literaturgeschichte*, ed. Wilhelm Heizmann, Klaus Böldl, and Heinrich Beck (Berlin: De Gruyter, 2009), 745–77.

51. For supporting data, see my "Fathers and Sons: Carnal and Spiritual Kinship in Viking Age Encomium," in *An Icelandic Literary Florilegium. A Festschrift in Honor of Úlfar Bragason*, ed. Marianne Kalinke and Kirsten Wolf (Ithaca, NY: Cornell University Library, 2021).

52. Jan M. Vansina, *Oral Tradition as History* (Madison: University of Wisconsin Press, 1985), 23–24.

53. *Samnordisk runtextdatabas* has six Viking Age inscriptions that mention a father's father (Ög 152, Sö 195, U 241, U 350, U 992, and U Fv1986; 84), one that mentions a mother's father (U 472), and one that may mention a grandfather (*afi*), although the context is unclear (U 1181). Two older futhark inscriptions, DR IK 58 (C-type bracteate from Fyn, late fifth and early sixth century) and N KJ 17 (early sixth-century silver-gilt brooch from Fonnås in Norway), may refer further back, to a great-grandfather and a grandmother. I am grateful to Judith Jesch for help with these inscriptions.

54. S. B. F. Jansson, *Runinskrifter i Sverige* (Stockholm: Almqvist & Wiksell, 1963), 100. Stefan Brink agrees, connecting it with the stipulations on *óðal* land in the *Gulaþingslǫg* ("Law and Legal Customs in Viking Age Scandinavia," in *The Scandinavians from the Vendel Period to the Tenth Century: An Ethnographic Perspective*, ed. Judith Jesch [Woodbridge: Boydell Press, 2002], 103–5).

55. Klaus Düwel, *Runenkunde* (Stuttgart: Metzler, 2008), 129–30. See also Brink, "Law and Legal Customs," 103–5. Zachrisson argues that the land rights of the raiser had been questioned ("Ärinvards minne: Om runstenen i Norra Sandsjö," in *Om runstenar i Jönköpings län*, ed. Jan Agertz and Linnéa Varenius [Jönköping: Jönköpings läns museum, 2002], 35–54). The suspiciously generic names Þegn and Karl early in the sequence on Sm 71 prompt Jesch to suggest that the pedigree is invented ("Discussion" following Brink, "Law and Legal Customs," 125).

56. *SkP* I, 196.

57. Cf. Klaus von See, "Polemische Zitate in der Skaldendichtung: Hallfrøðr vandræðaskáld and Haldórr ókristni," in his *Edda, Saga, Skaldendichtung* (Heidelberg: Winter, 1981), 384–88.

58. David McDougall, ed., *An Account of the Ancient History of the Norwegian Kings = Historia de Antiquitate Regum Norwagiensium* (London: Viking Society, 1998), 1.

59. *Ynglinga saga*'s prose does not show any interest in the itinerary structure I traced for *Ynglingatal* in Chapter 1—another sign that the saga preserves something close to the poem's original stanza-ordering.

60. Robert Nisbet, quoted in Spiegel, *Past as Text*, 108.

61. The capsule plot summaries of *Ynglinga saga* are taken from Marold et al.'s edition of *Ynglingatal* in *SkP* I.

62. David Murray Schneider, *A Critique of the Study of Kinship* (Ann Arbor: University of Michigan Press, 1984), 174.

63. Schneider, *Critique*, 175.

64. Christopher H. Johnson et al., eds., *Blood and Kinship: Matter for Metaphor from Ancient Rome to the Present* (New York: Berghahn, 2013), 3.

65. Spiegel, *Past as Text*, 109.

66. Hans Hummer, *Visions of Kinship in Medieval Europe* (Oxford: Oxford University Press, 2018), 28.

67. Hummer, *Visions*, 11.

68. Sverrir Jakobsson, "Early Kings," 178.

69. David Dumville points out the lack of evidence for the cultivation of genealogy by early medieval Germanic kings ("Kingship, Genealogies and Regnal Lists," in *Early Medieval Kingship*, ed. P. H. Sawyer and I. N. Wood [Leeds: School of History, University of Leeds, 1977], 96). He thinks any oral element in the Anglo-Saxon royal lineages extends back only a couple of generations, "the limit of normal human memory at the time of the English conversion to Christianity in the first half of the seventh century" (91). Donnchadh Ó Córrain is more categorical about the Irish material: "The genealogies are historical sources based on a written transmission, there is no convincing evidence that the texts preserved in the great medieval codices are oral materials later committed to writing, and they and related documents were produced and preserved by clerical scholars, often masters of monastic schools" ("Creating the Past: The Early Irish Genealogical Tradition," *Peritia* 12 [1998]: 188).

70. Peter Smith, "Early Irish Historical Verse: The Development of a Genre," in *Ireland and Europe in the Early Middle Ages: Text and Transmission*, ed. Próinséas Ni Chatháin and Michael Richter (Dublin: Four Courts Press, 2002), 328–29, 332.

71. Robert Fulk notes a similar dynamic with respect to Eyvindr's *Hákonarmál*, which "responds to [*Eiríksmál*] and surpasses it in its praise for the fallen king" (*SkP* I, 172).

72. The reading *goðum glíkr* is found in the version of the stanza in *Óláfs þáttr Geirstaðaálfs* in *Flateyjarbók*; cf. the variant apparatus to this stanza in *SkP* I, 55.

73. Cf. Helmut de Boor, "Die religiöse Sprache der Vǫluspá und verwandter Denkmäler," *Deutsche Islandforschung* 1 (1930): 68–142; Edith Marold, "Das Walhallbild den *Eiríksmál* und *Hákonarmál*," *Mediaeval Scandinavia* 5 (1972): 19–33; Folke Ström, "Poetry as an Instrument of Propaganda: Jarl Hakon and his Poets," in *Specvlvm Norroenvm: Norse Studies in Memory of Gabriel Turville-Petre*, ed. by Ursula Dronke et al. (Odense: Odense University Press, 1981), 440–58; Christopher Abram, *Myths of the Pagan North: The Gods of the Norsemen* (London: Continuum, 2011), 131.

74. *Writing and the Ancient State: Early China in Comparative Perspective* (Cambridge: Cambridge University Press, 2014), 225.

75. The judgment of Guðbrandur Vigfússon and F. York Powell, *Corpus Poeticum Boreale*, 2 vols. (Oxford: Clarendon Press, 1883), 260.

76. In the introduction to her edition (*SkP* II, 699–727). Gade's edition is cited in my text by stanza number.

77. On the *ævikviða*, see Margaret Clunies Ross, "The Autographical Turn in Late Medieval Icelandic Poetry," in *Skandinavische Schriftlandschaften: Vänbok till Jürg Glauser*, ed. Klaus Müller-Wille et al. (Tübingen: Narr, 2017), 150–54.

78. Roberta Frank has recently argued that these Hel-kennings are also *ofljóst* and refer to battle-axes, as Hel was the name of St. Óláfr's axe ("The Storied Verse of Sturla Þórðarson," in *Sturla Þórðarson: Skald, Chieftain, and Lawman*, ed. Jón Viðar Sigurðsson and Sverrir Jakobsson [Leiden: Brill, 2017], 140). Given the prevalence of *ofljóst* elsewhere in the *kviðuháttr* corpus, this is not unlikely.

79. *SkP* II, 717.

80. Gúðrun Nordal, "Sturla: The Poet and Creator of Prosimetrum," in *Sturla Þórðarson: Skald, Chieftain, and Lawman*, ed. Jón Viðar Sigurðsson and Sverrir Jakobsson (Leiden: Brill, 2017), 131.

81. Sverre Bagge, *From Gang Leader to the Lord's Anointed: Kingship in Sverris saga and Hákonar saga Hákonarsonar* (Odense: Odense University, 1996), 115.

82. Sturla Þórðarson, *The Saga of Hakon and a Fragment of the Saga of Magnus with Appendices*, trans. G. W. Dasent (London: Rerum Britannicarum Medii Ævi Scriptores, 1894), 245–56.

83. Adam Oberlin, "Vita Sancti, Vita Regis: The Saintly King in *Hákonar saga Hákonarsonar*," *Neophilologus* 95 (2011): 313–28.

84. See David Brégaint, *Vox Regis: Royal Communication in High Medieval Norway* (Leiden: Brill, 2016), 45–52, for a summary of the law's stipulations.

85. Hummer, *Visions*, 28.

86. Kolbrún Haraldsdóttir, "Für welchen Empfänger wurde die Flateyjarbók ursprünglich konzipiert?," *Opuscula* 13 (2010): 1–53; Guðvarður Már Gunnlaugsson, "The Speed of the Scribes: How Fast Could Flateyjarbók Have Been Written?" in *RE: Writing: Medial Perspectives on Textual Culture in the Icelandic Middle Ages*, ed. Kate Heslop and Jürg Glauser (Zurich: Chronos, 2018), 195–224.

87. Guðvarður Már Gunnlaugsson gives a useful tabular overview of Flateyjarbók's content, and a detailed account of the division of labor between the scribes ("Speed of the Scribes," 205–6, 198–201). The evidence for the dates and extent of the writing campaigns is detailed in Kolbrún Haraldsdóttir, "Für welchen Empfänger."

88. This suggestion seems originally to have been made by Ólafur Halldórsson. See Julia Zernack, "Hyndluljoð, Flateyjarbók und die Vorgeschichte der Kalmarer Union," *Skandinavistik* 29 (1999): 89–114; Elizabeth Ashman Rowe, *The Development of Flateyjarbók: Iceland and the Norwegian Dynastic Crisis of 1389* (Odense: University Press of Southern Denmark, 2005).

89. Jonna Louis-Jensen, *Kongesagastudier: Kompilationen Hulda-Hrokkinskinna* (Copenhagen: Reitzel, 1977), 7–9, 14.

90. Sverrir Tómasson, "Konungs lof. Nóregs konunga tal í Flateyjarbók," *Skírnir* 176 (2002): 265.

91. The refrain appears in *Hynd* 16, 17, 20, 23, 24, 26, 27, 28, and 29 (ÍF *Eddukvæði* I, 460–69).

92. Anita Guerreau-Jalabert, "Flesh and Blood in Medieval Language about Kinship," in Johnson et al., *Blood and Kinship*, 61–82.

93. Gustav Indrebo, ed., *Gamal Norsk Homiliebok: Cod. AM 619 4 to* (Oslo: Dybwad, 1931), 39. The phrase appears in the Bible at Isaiah 40:6 and 1 Peter 1:24.

94. *En þat at auk at mest er at þa er þeir hafa fram geingit vm almenniligar dyr daudans, sem ekki holld ma forðazst hafa þeir tekit sitt verdkaup þat er at skilia eilijft ríki med allzualdanda gude vtan enda sem þesse Æirekr sem nu var fra sagt.* Gudbrand Vigfusson and C. R. Unger, eds., *Flateyjarbók. En samling af norske konge-sagaer med indskudte mindre fortællinger om begivenheder i og udenfor Norge samt annaler*, 3 vols. (Christiania: Malling, 1860–8), 1:36. Translation from Alison Finlay, *Flateyjarbók* (forthcoming).

STONE—STANZA—MEMORY

1. Helmer Gustavson, "Rök. §2. Runologisches," in *RGA*, vol. 25, 62–72.

2. Elias Wessén, *Runstenen vid Röks kyrka* (Stockholm: Almqvist & Wiksell, 1958). The *Samnordisk runtextdatabas* essentially reproduces Wessén's reading, albeit with differences in the details of the interpretation, so in that sense it remains canonical.

3. The idea that the inscription is a sequence of riddles was introduced by Lars Lönnroth ("The Riddles of the Rök Stone: A Structural Approach," *Arkiv för nordisk filologi* 92 [1977]: 1–57). For a recent overview of the debate over the reading and interpretation of the inscription, see Mats Malm, "I.15. Runology," in *Handbook of Pre-Modern Nordic Memory Studies, Interdisciplinary Approaches*, 2 vols., ed. Jürg Glauser, Pernille Hermann, and Stephen A. Mitchell, (Berlin: De Gruyter, 2018), 1:190–92.

4. Bo Ralph, "Gåtan som lösning. Ett bidrag till förståelsen av Rökstenens runinskrift," *Maal og minne* (2007): 133–57; Per Holmberg, "Svaren på Rökstenens gåtor: En socialsemiotisk analys av meningsskapande och rumslighet," *Futhark* 6 (2015): 65–106.

5. Ralph, "Gåtan," 150. Although no analysis of their methodology as a whole has yet appeared, commentators have objected to the disappearance of Theoderic. Cf., e.g., Lars Lönnroth, "Theodoric Rides On," in *Skandinavische Schriftlandschaften: Vänbok til Jürg Glauser*, ed. Klaus Müller-Wille et al. (Tübingen: Narr, 2017), 5–10. Lydia Carstens finds Holmberg's count of eighteen "speech acts" (*språkhandlingar*) to be inconsistent ("Die dreizehn Geschichten auf dem Runenstein von Rök," in *Die Faszination des Verborgenen und seine Entschlüsselung—Rāði saR kunni*, ed. Jana Krüger et al. [Berlin: De Gruyter, 2017], 75).

6. As Holmberg admits. ("Svaren," 66.)

7. Henrik Schück, *Bidrag till tolkning af Rök-Inskriften* (Uppsala: Almqvist & Wiksell, 1908), 27–28; Sophus Bugge, *Der Runenstein von Rök in Östergötland, Schweden* (Stockholm: Hæggströms, 1910), 242–44; Walter Åkerlund, *Studier över Ynglingatal* (Lund: Gleerup, 1939), 121–22.

8. *En sorts robot.* "Tolkningen som social konstruktion," in *Runor och ABC: Elva föreläsningar från ett symposium i Stockholm våren 1995*, ed. Staffan Nyström (Stockholm: Stockholms Medeltidsmuseum, 1997), 173; cf. Mats Malm, "Rökstenens tilltal," in *'Vi ska alla vara välkomna!' Nordiska studier tillägnade Kristinn Jóhannesson*, ed. Auður Magnúsdottir, Henrik Janson, and Karl G. Johansson (Gothenburg: Meijerbergs arkiv för svensk ordforskning, 2008), 342–57; Mats Malm, "Skalds, Runes, and Voice," *Viking and Medieval Scandinavia* 6 (2010): 135–46.

9. Alfred Gell's "technology of enchantment" suggests something of the stone's effect. "The Technology of Enchantment and the Enchantment of Technology," in *Anthropology, Art, and Aesthetics*, ed. Jeremy Coote and Anthony Shelton (Oxford: Clarendon, 1992), 40–63.

10. Cf. Joseph Harris, "Philology, Elegy, and Cultural Change," *Gripla* 24 (2009): 257–80. Harris's argument for Frankish influence rests on echoes of pre-Christian mythology in *Sonatorrek* and the Rök inscription and common traces of a West Germanic tradition of elegy. Elias Wessén and, following him, Widmark emphasize the presence of a Frankish mission at Birka in the ninth century (Wessén, *Runstenen*, 77). Widmark further suggests that the Rök monument attempts to preserve traditional knowledge threatened by the new religion ("Tolkningen," 172).

11. John Blair, *The Church in Anglo-Saxon Society* (Oxford: Oxford University Press, 2005), 53.

12. Wessén, *Runstenen*, 52, suggests that the inscription's "Ingoldings" (**igold[i]ga**) are the eponyms of the village of Ingvaldstorp, about two kilometers away from Rök, while Hermann Reichert connects them with the Ingeld of *Beowulf* ("Runeninschriften als Quellen der Heldensagenforschung," in *Runeninschriften als Quellen interdisziplinärer Forschung*, ed. Klaus Düwel [Berlin: De Gruyter, 1998], 75).

13. Michael Barnes views this as an archaic trait ("Rök-steinen—noen runologiske og språklige overveielser," *Maal og minne* [2007]: 128).

14. The move is reported in cap. 94 of the *Liber pontificalis* of the Ravennan priest Agnellus (for a translation, see Deborah Mauskopf Deliyannis, *The Book of Pontiffs of the Church of Ravenna* [Washington, DC: Catholic University of America Press, 2004], 205–6). Agnellus was born c. 800 so presumably never saw the statue himself, and the details of his description will not bear the weight Kees Samplonius puts on them ("Rex non reditvrvs," *Amsterdamer Beiträge zur älteren Germanistik* 37 [1993]: 21–31). Charlemagne's removal of spolia from Ravenna is well documented in contemporary sources, and there are good reasons to believe Agnellus's account (Andreas Goltz, *Barbar—König—Tyrann: Das Bild Theoderichs des Großen in der Überlieferung des 5. bis 9. Jahrhunderts* [Berlin: De Gruyter, 2008], 600).

15. Transliteration and normalized text from *Samnordisk runtextdatabas*. Translation from Lars Lönnroth, "Theodoric." Most commentators concur on the reading of the stanza, although some interpret its first word as *Reið* ("rode") rather than *Réð* ("ruled").

16. For a discussion of the conflicting ideological currents that surged around the Theoderic statue in Charlemagne's court, see Horst Bredekamp, *Der*

schwimmende Souverän. Karl der Grosse und die Bildpolitik des Körpers: Eine Studie zum schematischen Bildakt (Berlin: Wagenbach, 2014), 68–87.

17. Deliyannis, *Book of Pontiffs*, 75.

18. Otto von Friesen read the last four staves as *menni* "man" (dat.) rather than *minni* "memory" and construed *sagum ungmenni* as "I say to the young man." (*Rökstenen: Runstenen vid Röks kyrka, Lysings härad Östergötland* [Stockholm: J. Bragges Söner, 1920]). Aslak Liestøl's analysis of the orthography of this phrase in the part of the inscription written in the older *fuþark* suggests that *menni* is more likely. ("The Viking Runes: The Transition from the Older to the Younger *Fuþark*," *Saga-Book* 20 [1981]: 255–56.) It may be a collective: "young men, youth." (Harris, "Philology," 258).

19. Klaus von See, *Germanische Verskunst* (Stuttgart: Metzler, 1967), 47–48; Kari Ellen Gade, "History of Old Nordic Metrics," in *The Nordic Languages: An International Handbook of the History of the North Germanic Languages*, ed. Oskar Bandle et al. (Berlin: De Gruyter, 2002), 858–59.

20. For the sound changes, see Bo Ralph, "Phonological and Graphematic Developments from Ancient Nordic to Old Nordic," in *The Nordic Languages: An International Handbook of the History of the North Germanic Languages*, ed. Oskar Bandle et al. (Berlin: De Gruyter, 2002), 703–19; for a survey of their effects on poetic meter, see Winfred Lehmann, *The Development of Germanic Verse Form* (Austin: University of Texas Press, 1956), 77–84.

21. The Rök stanza has *skialdi*, the result of breaking, alongside unsyncopated *sitiʀ, garuʀ,* and *strandu*. For a discussion of the dating of the first and second syncopes, see Tomas Riad, *Structures in Germanic Prosody: A Diachronic Study with Special Reference to the Nordic Languages* (Stockholm: Stockholm University Press, 1992), ch. 3. He dates the second syncope (of bisyllabic light stems in *i* and *u*, e.g., garuʀ > gǫrr), to c. 830. Rök would, on this account, be one of the latest instances showing unsyncopated forms, but as Riad observes, there is "a poor understanding of what is regional variation and what is chronological or indeed orthographic variation amongst the runic forms attested" (115).

22. Kari Ellen Gade, *The Structure of Old Norse Dróttkvætt Poetry* (Ithaca: Cornell University Press, 1995), 234–36.

23. *Jede Form gleichsam mit ihrer eigenen Vergangenheit kommuniziert.* "Metrik, eine Wissenschaft zwischen Zählen und Schwärmen? Überlegungen zu einer Semantik der Formen mittelhochdeutscher gebundener Rede," in *Mittelalter: neue Wege durch einen alten Kontinent*, ed. Jan-Dirk Müller and Horst Wenzel (Stuttgart: Hirzel, 1999), 326.

24. Kristján Árnason, "The Rise of the Quatrain in Germanic: Musicality and Word Based Rhythm in Eddic Meters," in *Formal Approaches to Poetry: Recent Developments in Metrics*, ed. Bezalel E. Dresher and Nila Friedberg (Berlin: De Gruyter, 2006). For a statistically informed account of the stanza in *fornyrðislag*, see Seiichi Suzuki, *The Meters of Old Norse Eddic Poetry: Common Germanic Inheritance and North Germanic Innovation* (Berlin: De Gruyter, 2014), 389–421.

Eight-line stanzas dominate Suzuki's corpus (69 percent). The distribution of metrical types across the eight-line *fornyrðislag* stanza suggests that the most strongly marked lines are 1 and 4, i.e., that the stanza is made up of two quatrains.

25. See, e.g., Lehman, *Development*, 31; von See, *Verskunst*, 39; Árnason, "Rise." The importance of the self-contained stanza in *dróttkvætt* composition is reflected in the rarity of syntactic links between stanzas (Hans Kuhn, "Die Dróttkvættstrophe als Kunstwerk," in *Festschrift für Konstantin Reichardt*, ed. Christian Gellinek [Bern: Francke, 1969], 63); for a list of instances of this phenomenon, see Faulkes, *Hát*, 77.

26. Kari Ellen Gade, "The Syntax of Old Norse *Kviðuháttr* Meter," *Journal of Germanic Linguistics* 17 (2005): 155–81.

3. THE VIKING EYE

1. Hans Belting, "Image, Medium, Body: A New Approach," *Critical Inquiry* 31 (2005): 306.

2. "Framing the Hero: Medium and Metalepsis in Old Norse Heroic Narrative," in *Old Norse Mythology—Comparative Perspectives*, ed. Pernille Hermann, Stephen A. Mitchell, and Jens Peter Schjødt (Cambridge: Harvard University Press, 2017), 53–88.

3. For the distinction between narrative and descriptive imagery in premodern art, see Luca Giuliani, *Image and Myth: A History of Pictorial Narration in Greek Art* (Chicago: University of Chicago Press, 2013). For a study of this distinction in the Scandinavian context, see Nancy L. Wicker, "The Scandinavian Animal Styles in Response to Mediterranean and Christian Narrative Art," in *The Cross Goes North: Processes of Conversion in Northern Europe, AD 300–1300*, ed. M. O. H. Carver (Woodbridge: Boydell & Brewer, 2003), 531–50.

4. Belting, "Image," 305.

5. Robert S. Nelson, "Descarte's Cow and Other Domestications of the Visual," in *Visuality Before and Beyond the Renaissance: Seeing as Others Saw*, ed. Robert S. Nelson (Cambridge: Cambridge University Press, 2000), 2.

6. For a classic instance, see Martin Jay, *Downcast Eyes: The Denigration of Vision in Twentieth-Century French Thought* (Berkeley: University of California Press, 1993).

7. Hal Foster, ed., *Vision and Visuality* (Seattle: Bay Press, 1988), ix.

8. For the concept of a "period eye," see Michael Baxandall, *Painting and Experience in Fifteenth-Century Italy: A Primer in the Social History of Pictorial Style* (Oxford: Oxford University Press, 1988).

9. Early contrasting opinions on the date of *Ragnarsdrápa* are found in Sophus Bugge, *Bidrag til den ældste skaldedigtnings historie* (Christiania: Aschehoug, 1894), 54; Finnur Jónsson, "De ældste skjalde og deres kvad," *Arkiv för nordisk filologi* (1897) 13:363–69. Hans Kuhn points out archaic features, such as sporadic absence of internal rhyme and etymological use of the expletive particle *of* (*Das Dróttkvætt* [Heidelberg: Winter, 1983]); Klaus Johan Myrvoll concurs ("The

Constitutive Features of the *Dróttkvætt* Metre," in *Approaches to Nordic and Germanic Poetics*, ed. Kristján Árnason et al. [Reykjavík: University of Iceland Press, 2016], 229–56); cf. however Edith Marold, "Ragnarsdrápa und Ragnarssage," in *Germanic Dialects: Linguistic and Philological Investigations*, ed. Bela Brogyanyi and Thomas Krömmelbein (Amsterdam: Benjamins, 1986), 427–55.

10. Bragi *Rdr*. Ed. Clunies Ross, *SkP* III, 27–47.

11. Bragi *Þórr*.

12. Þjóð *Haustl*.

13. ÚlfrU *Húsdr*.

14. Translation from Keneva Kunz, Örnólfur Thorsson, ed., *The Sagas of Icelanders: A Selection* (New York: Penguin, 2001), 323–24, slightly modified. *Þat sumar lét Óláfr gera eldhús í Hjarðarholti, meira ok betra en menn hefði fyrir sét. Váru þar markaðar ágætliga sǫgur á þilviðinum ok svá á ræfrinu; var þat svá vel smíðat, at þá þótti miklu skrautligra, er eigi váru tjǫldin uppi [. . .] eptir þat fastnar Geirmundr sér Þuríði, ok skal boð vera at áliðnum vetri í Hjarðarholti; þat boð var allfjǫlmennt, því at þá var algǫrt eldhúsit. Þar var at boði Úlfr Uggason ok hafði ort kvæði um Óláf Hǫskuldsson ok um sǫgur þær, er skrifaðar váru á eldhúsinu, ok færði hann þar at boðinu. Þetta kvæði er kallat Húsdrápa ok er vel ort.* ÍF 5, 79–80. The English translation renders both *markaðar* and *skrifaðar* as "carved."

15. *Skáldskaparmál*, ed. Faulkes, 18–19.

16. Hallvard Lie, "Billedbeskrivende dikt," *KLNM* vol. 1, cols. 542–45.

17. Hallvard Lie, 'Natur' og 'unatur' i skaldekunsten (1957; repr. in his *Om sagakunst og skaldskap* [Øvre Ervik: Alvheim & Eide, 1982], 202.

18. Alois Riegl, *Die spätrömische Kunst-Industrie nach den Funden in Österreich-Ungarn [. . .]* (Vienna: Staatsdruckerei, 1901), 215.

19. Cf., e.g., Gert Kreutzer, "'Eine der unverfrorensten Verirrungen der Literaturgeschichte'?: Zur Ästhetik und literarischen Wertung der Skaldendichtung," *Skandinavistik* 19 (1989): 36–52; Rolf Stavnem, "The Kennings in *Ragnarsdrápa*," *Mediaeval Scandinavia* 14 (2004): 161–84; Jürg Glauser, "Zwischen Kohärenz und Fragment. Zur Poetik des 'Verschlungenen' in der altnordischen Skaldik," in *Lyrische Kohärenz im Mittelalter. Spielräume—Kriterien—Modellbildung*, ed. Susanne Köbele et al. (Heidelberg: Winter, 2019), 187–212.

20. Ruth Webb, "Ekphrasis Ancient and Modern: The Invention of a Genre," *Word & Image* 15 (1999): 10.

21. Signe Horn Fuglesang, "Billedbeskrivende dikt," in *Ting og Tekst*, ed. Else Mundal and Anne Ågnotes (Bergen: Bryggens Museum, 2002), 119–42; Margaret Clunies Ross, "The Cultural Poetics of the Skaldic Ekphrasis Poem in Medieval Norway and Iceland," in *Medieval Cultural Studies*, ed. H. Fulton, R. Evans, and D. Matthews (Cardiff: University of Wales Press, 2006), 227–40; *Viking and Medieval Scandinavia* 3 (2007), a special issue based on a roundtable held at the 13th International Saga Conference in Durham, England, in 2006; Russell Poole, "Scholars and Skalds. The Northwards Diffusion of Carolingian Poetic Fashions," *Gripla* 24 (2013): 7–44.

22. J. A. W. Heffernan, "Ekphrasis and Representation," *New Literary History* 22 (1991): 299; see, e.g., Margaret Clunies Ross, "Stylistic and Generic Identifiers of the Old Norse Skaldic Ekphrasis," *Viking and Medieval Scandinavia* 3 (2007): 162; cf. Fuglesang's reservations in her contribution to the special issue ("Ekphrasis and Surviving Imagery in Viking Scandinavia," 193).

23. Michael Squire, *Image and Text in Graeco-Roman Antiquity* (New York: Cambridge, 2009), 122.

24. Squire, *Image and Text*, 121.

25. O. Taplin, "The Shield of Achilles within the 'Iliad,'" *Greece & Rome* 27 (1980): 3, and references cited there; Haiko Wandhoff, *Ekphrasis: Kunstbeschreibungen und virtuelle Räume in der Literatur des Mittelalters* (Berlin: De Gruyter, 2003), 199ff.

26. Gísli Brynjúlfsson, *Brage den Gamles Kvad om Ragnar Lodbrogs Skjold* (Copenhagen: Det kongelige nordiske Oldskrift-selskab, 1860); W. H. Vogt, "Bragis Schild," *Acta Philologica Scandinavia* 5 (1930): 1–28.

27. Kurt Schier, "Die Húsdrápa von Úlfr Uggason und die bildliche Überlieferung altnordischer Mythen," in *Minjar og menntir: Afmælsrit helgað Kristjáni Eldjárn*, ed. Guðni Kolbeinsson (Reykjavík: Bókaútgáfa Menningarsjóðs, 1976), 425–43; Richard North, *The Haustlǫng of Þjóðólfr of Hvinir* (Middlesex: Hisarlik, 1997); Richard North, "Image and Ascendancy in Úlfr's *Húsdrápa*," in *Text, Image, and Interpretation: Studies in Anglo-Saxon Literature and its Insular Context in Honour of Éamonn Ó Carragáin*, ed. Alastair Minnis and Jane Roberts (Turnhout: Brepols, 2007), 369–404; Clunies Ross, "Stylistic and Generic"; John Hines, "Ekphrasis as Speech-Act: *Ragnarsdrápa* 1–7," *Viking and Medieval Scandinavia* 3 (2007): 233–35.

28. Tooled designs on sheaths for knives and axes range from patterns of parallel lines or hatching inside panels to simple interlace; there is little sign of figurative ornamentation; cf. Quita Mould, Ian Carlisle, and Esther Cameron, *Leather and Leatherworking in Anglo-Scandinavian and Medieval York* (York: Council for British Archaeology, 2003), 3262–63, 3354–91, 3431. A rare exception is the leather sword-sheath from Valsgärde Grave 7 (sixth and seventh centuries) depicting a single standing figure (Greta Arwidsson, *Valsgärde 7: Die Gräberfunde von Välsgarde III* [(Uppsala: Uppsala University Museum, 1977], Plate 15). Rare fragments of painted leather Roman cavalry shields survive, e.g., one from the third century CE decorated with a map of the Black Sea region. M. Franz Cumont, "Fragment de bouclier portant une liste d'étapes," *Syria* 6 (1925): 1–15.

29. G. Bersu and D. M. Wilson, *Three Viking Graves in the Isle of Man* (London: Society for Medieval Archaeology, 1966), 60–61.

30. For images of the ship and grave mound, see Gokstad, Kulturhistorisk Museum, https://www.khm.uio.no/besok-oss/vikingskipshuset/utstillinger/gokstad.

31. Kirsten Christensen, Andres S. Dobat, and Per Mandrup, "Trelleborgskjoldet," *Skalk* 5 (2009): 3–7.

32. Ingrid Stoumann, *Ryttergraven fra Grimstrup og andre vikingetidsgrave ved Esbjerg* (Esbjerg: Sydvestjyske Museer, 2009), 33–39.

33. Concentric circles, central bosses, perpendicular lines of dots, and whorls are common and may reflect shield construction. Concentric circles correspond to the riveting of the rim and boss, and whorls to the piecing and stitching of the leather cover (Lori Elaine Eshleman, "Monumental Stones of Gotland" [PhD diss., University of Minnesota, 1983], 255).

34. Valg *Har* 7, c. 1040s, refers to the king splitting a *ríkula ristin rít* ("richly engraved shield") on campaign in Denmark. Gísl *Magnkv* 12, c. 1103 or shortly after, says Hugh of Shrewsbury's shield is *kapps vel skrifuð* ("powerfully well painted") (so Frískbok; Morkinskinna has *skipuð* ["equipped"]). If *skrifuð* is original, this is the earliest datable instance (cf. *EK* VI, 669).

35. For a recent discussion from a narratological perspective, see Torfi H. Tulinius, "Milli skriptanna, spengr af gulli: On the Conversion of Gold and Other Valuables in Sagas and Skaldic Poetry," in *Gold in der europäischen Heldensage*, ed. Heike Sahm, Wilhelm Heizmann, and Victor Millet (Berlin: De Gruyter 2019), 264–74.

36. *Hans skjǫld var margfaldr [according to Finch corrected from markaðr] ok laugaðr í rauðu gulli ok skrifaðr á einn dreki [. . .] Ok því var dreki markaðr á hans vápnum ǫllum at, er hann er sénn, má vita hverr þar ferr af ǫllum þeim er frétt hafa at hann drap þann mikla dreka er Væringjar kalla Fáfni.* R. G. Finch, ed. and trans., *The Saga of the Volsungs [Vǫlsunga saga]* (London: Nelson, 1965), ch. 23.

37. Karsten Friis-Jensen, ed., *Saxo grammaticus: Gesta Danorum*, 2 vols., trans. Peter Fisher (Oxford: Clarendon, 2015), 1:508–9.

38. *Textinterne Projektionsflächen*. Wandhoff, *Ekphrasis*, 42.

39. The closest is the *Fourth Grammatical Treatise*'s list of four figures of description, *topographia, bethgraphia, cosmographia,* and *chronographia,* Björn Magnússon Ólsen, ed., *Den tredje og fjærde grammatiske afhandling i Snorres Edda* [. . .] (Copenhagen: Møller, 1884), 122–23. No source has yet been found for the word *bethgraphia*, a unique compound of Hebrew *beth* ("house") and Greek *graphia* ("writing").

40. Descriptions of animals are frequent in Arabic hunt poetry, cf., e.g., Jaroslav Stetkevych, *The Hunt in Arabic Poetry: From Heroic to Lyric to Metapoetic* (Notre Dame: University of Notre Dame Press, 2016), and such material has been analyzed in terms of ekphrasis, cf., e.g., A. M. Sumi, *Description in Classical Arabic Poetry: Waṣf, Ekphrasis, and Interarts Theory* (Leiden: Brill, 2004).

41. Franz Graf, "Ekphrasis: Die Entstehung der Gattung in der Antike," in *Beschreibungskunst-Kunstbeschreibung. Ekphrasis von der Antike bis zur Gegenwart,* ed. Gottfried Boehm and Helmut Pfotenhauer (Munich: Fink, 1995), 143.

42. Quintilian, *Institutio oratoria*, ed. Michael Winterbottom (Oxford: Clarendon, 1970), vi, 2.

43. John Sardianos, from a commentary on the Aphthonian *Progymnasmata* quoted in Ruth Webb, *Ekphrasis, Imagination and Persuasion in Ancient Rhetorical Theory and Practice* (Surrey: Ashgate, 2009), 203.

44. Quintilian, *Institutio oratoria*, viii, 3.

45. Webb, *Ekphrasis, Imagination*, 122.
46. Webb, *Ekphrasis, Imagination*, 128.
47. Simon Goldhill, "What is Ekphrasis For?" *Classical Philology* 1 (2007): 2.
48. Webb, "Ekphrasis Ancient and Modern," 14.
49. Squire, *Image and Text*, 351.
50. Verity J. Platt, *Facing the Gods: Epiphany and Representation in Graeco-Roman Art, Literature and Religion* (Cambridge: Cambridge University Press, 2011).
51. *Et bezta blóðkerti, glæst með gulli*. Ed. Jesch, SkP II, 620–21.
52. *Gerðu vísu um athǫfn þess manns, er þar er á tjaldinu, ok haf eigi síðarr lokit þinni vísu en ek minni. Haf ok engi þau orð í þinni vísu, er ek hefi í minni vísu*. ÍF 34, 202; my translation. The verses are edited by Jesch in SkP II, 590–91, 614–16.
53. Russell Poole, "Some Southern Perspectives on Starcatherus," *Viking and Medieval Scandinavia* 2 (2006): 141–166, and "Ekphrasis: Its 'Prolonged Echoes' in Scandinavia," *Viking and Medieval Scandinavia* 3 (2007): 245–67. Jesch (SkP II, 614) disagrees with Poole's reading, but her double *ofljóst* is more forced than his assumption of a context-dependent kenning in *bandalfr* ("elf of bandages"). (The line in which this kenning occurs is repeated almost exactly in another verse on a legendary Danish hero, KormQ *Lv* 4.) The identification of the figure on the tapestry as the aged hero Starkaðr motivates the strange information that he is *beinrangr* ("bandy-legged") (Rv *Lv* 13) and *herðilútr* "bent-shouldered" (Oddi *Lv* 1).
54. ÍF 23, 270–84; my translation.
55. Snegl *Lvv* 1, 5.
56. ÞjóðA *Lvv* 5, 6.
57. "*Eigi em ek jafn gott skáld sem Þjóðólfr, en þá mun mér first of fara ef ek emk eigi við staddr*." Text and translation from SkP II, 169–72.
58. *þu er lyðskaðr sem riddarar. þo at <þu> ser klerkr*. Ólafur Halldórsson, ed., *Saga Óláfs Tryggvasonar en mesta*, 3 vols. (Copenhagen: Munksgaard, 1958–2000), 1:149. My translation.
59. *En er Olafr konungr sa skiolldinn hugði hann at vandliga huat þar var aa markat. ok fannz mikit vm. hann mælti þa til Þangbrandz. huern dyrðkit þer kristnir menn aa krossi pindan. Þangbrandr svar(aði). drottinn varn Iesum Krist dyrðkum ver. konungr sp(urði). huat misgiorði hann er hann var sva pindr. Þangbrandr sagði honum þa inniliga fra pisl drottins ok taknum krossins. þa faladi Olafr konungr skiolldinn. en Þangbrandr gaf honum*. Ólafur Halldórsson, *Saga Óláfs Tryggvasonar*, 1:149–50. My translation.
60. ÞjóðA *Har*. Ed. Whaley, as *Stanzas about Haraldr Sigurðarson's leiðangr*, SkP II, 147–58.
61. Cf. Judith Jesch, "Women and Ships in the Viking World," *Northern Studies* 36 (2001): 49–68.
62. Judith Jesch, *Ships and Men in the Late Viking Age: The Vocabulary of Runic Inscriptions and Skaldic Verse* (Woodbridge: Boydell Press, 2001), 123–24, 127–28.

She notes that other serpent words are used as synonyms for *dreki* and the metaphor is often extended; both are true of Þjóðólfr's verses.

63. E.g., shield mounts from Åker, Norway, sixth and seventh centuries (images in Perry Rolfsen, "Det rette pipet: Metalldetektorbruk i Norge," in *Pløyejord som kontekst: Nye utfordringer for forskning, forvaltning og formidling*, ed. Jens Martens and Mads Ravn [Oslo: Kulturhistorisk Museum, 2016], 111–26); Valsgärde graves 7 and 8, Vendel grave 12, Sweden, sixth and seventh centuries (images in Michaela Helmbrecht, "Wirkmächtige Kommunikationsmedien: Menschenbilder der Vendel- und Wikingerzeit und ihre Kontexte" [PhD diss., Lund University, 2011], 189, figs. 48i, 50g–j); Gammel Skørping, Denmark, (image in Lotte Hedeager, *Iron Age Myth and Materiality* [New York: Routledge, 2011], 72). Forty-four percent of the shield-related finds in English burials of this period are animal-shaped mounts; cf. Tania M. Dickinson, "Symbols of Protection: The Significance of Animal-Ornamented Shields in Early Anglo-Saxon England," *Medieval Archaeology* 49 (2005): 109–63.

64. Claus von Carnap-Bornheim, "Der 'Helmbeschlag' aus Domagnano—Überlegungen zur Herkunft des 'Vogel-Fisch' Motivs," in '... *Trans Albim Fluvium': Forschungen zur vorromischen, kaiserzeitlichen und mittelalterlichen Archäologie: Festschrift für Achim Leube zum 65. Geburtstag*, ed. Michael Meyer (Rahden: Leidorf, 2001), 223–38.

65. Michael Neiß, "Fixeringsbilder från Vestervang: Försök till en metodisk motividentifiering för vikingatida djurornamentik," in *ROMU 2011: Årsskrift fra Roskilde Museum*, ed. Jens Molter Ulriksen (Roskilde: Roskilde Museums Forlag, 2012), 35–69; "Viking Age Animal Art," in *The Head Motif in Past Societies in a Comparative Perspective*, ed. Leszek Gardeła and Kamil Kajkowski (Bytów: Muzeum Zachodniokaszubskie w Bytowie, 2013).

66. Neiß, "Viking Age Animal Art," 75.

67. "The Sense of Being Seen: Ocular Effects at Sutton Hoo," *Journal of Social Archaeology* 11 (2011): 104.

68. Roberta Frank, *Old Norse Court Poetry: The Dróttkvætt Stanza* (Ithaca: Cornell University Press, 1978), 109.

69. *CVC*, s.v. *kenna*.

70. For discussion see, e.g., Margaret Clunies Ross, *Skáldskaparmál: Snorri Sturluson's 'Ars poetica' and Medieval Theories of Language* (Odense: Odense University Press, 1987), 50–55; Frederic Amory, "Second Thoughts on *Skáldskaparmál*," *Scandinavian Studies* 62 (1990): 331–39; Klaus von See, "Snorri Sturluson and the Creation of a Norse Cultural Ideology," *Saga-Book* 25 (2001): 374–75; Faulkes, *Skáldskaparmál*, xxxii–iv. Mats Malm has recently emphasized the role of the senses, especially vision, and memory in the kenning: "Varför heter det kenning?" in *Snorres Edda i europeisk og islandsk kultur*, ed. Jon Gunnar Jørgensen (Reykholt: Snorrastofa, 2009), 73–90; Mats Malm, "Two Cultures of Visual(ized) Cognition," in *Intellectual Culture in Medieval Scandinavia, c. 1100–1350*, ed. Stefka Eriksen (Turnhout: Brepols, 2016), 309–34.

71. Cf. Fritzner, *Ordbog*, s.v. kenna 10.

72. *Gylfaginning*'s stress on deception is probably influenced by the patristic image of Satan as Leviathan, snapping at Christ's human form but fooled by the hook of his divinity.

73. *Hamð* 24. ÍF *Eddukvæði* II, 412; Larrington, *Poetic Edda*, 233.

74. For counts of anthropomorphic imagery on Viking Age image-bearers, see Helmbrecht, "Wirkmächtige Kommunikationsmedien."

75. *Die Intimität der Berührung mit den Fingern*. Horst Bredekamp, *Der schwimmende Souverän: Karl der Grosse und die Bildpolitik des Körpers: eine Studie zum schematischen Bildakt* (Berlin: Wagenbach, 2014), 6, 8.

76. Margaret Clunies Ross, "Hildr's Ring: A Problem in *Ragnarsdrápa*," *Mediaeval Scandinavia* 6 (1973): 74–92.

77. Battleaxes are elsewhere said to gape at warriors "with iron mouths" (*járnmunnum*, Hfr *ErfÓl* 6, Hókr *Eirfl* 7).

78. As argued by Aðalheiður Guðmundsdóttir, "Saga Motifs on Gotland Picture Stones: The Case of Hildr Högnadóttir," in *Gotland's Picture Stones: Bearers of an Enigmatic Legacy*, ed. Maria Herlin Karnell (Visby: Gotlands Museum, 2012), 59–72.

79. Fuglesang, "Ekphrasis and Surviving Imagery," 197.

80. Aðalheiður Guðmundsdóttir, "Saga motifs," 70, 67.

81. *HHII*, 23. ÍF *Eddukvæði* II, 276; Larrington, *Poetic Edda*, 133 (translation slightly modified).

82. *HHII*, 43. ÍF *Eddukvæði* II, 280; Larrington, *Poetic Edda*, 136.

83. [. . .] *das immer erneute Anheimfallen an die Dämonen und Ungeheuer der Unterwelt*. Edith Marold, *Kenningkunst: Ein Beitrag zu einer Poetik der Skaldendichtung* (Berlin: De Gruyter, 1983), 105.

84. For images and discussion see Torsten Capelle, *Anthromorphe Holzidolen in Mittel und Nordeuropa* (Stockholm: Almquist and Wiksell, 1995); Wijnand van der Sanden and Torsten Capelle, *Götter—Götzen—Holzmenschen* (Oldenburg: Isensee, 2002).

85. Tom Christensen, "A Silver Figurine from Lejre," *Danish Journal of Archaeology* 2 (2013): 65–78.

86. Ruth Blankenfeldt, "Fünfzig Jahre nach Joachim Werner: Überlegungen zur kaiserzeitlichen Kunst," in *Bilddenkmäler zur germanischen Götter- und Heldensage*, ed. Sigmund Oehrl and Wilhelm Heizmann (Berlin: De Gruyter, 2015), 47.

87. See, e.g., Styrmir Kárason's *articulus* 23, Oddr Snorrason's *Óláfs saga Tryggvasonar*, ch. 47, and *Þáttr Sveins ok Finns* in *Flateyjarbók*.

88. One of Þórólfr *Mostrarskegg*'s high-seat pillars has Þórr carved on it (*Eyrbyggja saga*, ch. 4), and Hallfreðr is accused of carrying an ivory image of Þórr in his purse (*Hallfreðar saga*, ch. 6). Sculptures of Þórr stand in Járnskeggi's temple near Hlaðir (*Óláfs saga Tryggvasonar*, ch. 69), in Þorgrímr *goði*'s on Kjalarnes (*Kjalnesinga saga*, ch. 2), and in Dala-Guðbrandr's in central Norway (*Óláfs saga helga*, ch. 112–14).

89. Axel Olrik, "Irminsul og Gudestøtter," *Maal og minne* (1910), 1–9; Franz Rolf Schröder, "Thor und der Wetzstein," *Beiträge zur Geschichte der deutschen Sprache und Literatur* 51 (1927): 33–35; Mats Bertell, *Tor och den nordiska åskan: föreställningar kring världsaxeln* (Edsbruk: Akademitryck, 2003), 218–41.

90. *I afgudabelætens hufvud slao the en staolnagel eller spiic och itt styke flintsten, ther med Tor skall slao eld*. Quoted in Helge Ljungberg, *Tor: Undersökningar i indoeuropeisk och nordisk religionshistoria* (Uppsala: Lundequist, 1947), 156.

91. Ljungberg, *Tor*, 156.

92. Andreas Oldeberg, "Några träidoler från förhistorisk och senare tid," *Fornvännen* 52 (1957): 247–58.

93. Greger Bennström, "Ett samisk offerfynd i Falun?" *Dalarnas hembygdsbok* 76 (2006): 57–66.

94. Jonas Wellendorf, "The Æsir and their Idols," in *Old Norse Mythology in its Comparative Contexts*, ed. Stephen Mitchell, Pernille Hermann, and Jens Peter Schjødt (Cambridge: Harvard University Press, 2018), 89–110.

95. The first *helmingr* of st. 14 is difficult to interpret, cf. *SkP* III, 453. All that can be said with any certainty is that the audience sees Þórr on his way to Grjótún.

96. Steinunn *Lv* 1–2. Fulk, in his edition of these verses (*SkP* V), suggests that they represent an early attempt on the part of a Christian poet to ventriloquize the attitudes of a Þórr worshipper.

97. Faulkes, *Gylfaginning*, 44.

98. E.g., Þrymr, Herkir, Hrungnir, Aurgelmir (Anon *Þul Jǫtna I*, ed. Gurevich, *SkP* III, 707–22).

99. *Hafrar* ("goats") is an emendation; the manuscripts have "hafrir," an otherwise unattested form, *hafði* ("had" 3rd pers. sg.), or *hǫfðu* ("had" 3rd pers. pl.).

100. There is no reason to emend "hofregin," the reading of all the manuscripts, to *hafregin* ("lifted deity") as *Skj* does (BI, 17). *Hofgylðir* ("temple-wolf" [i.e., fire]) occurs in Þjóð *Yt* 21.

101. *SkP* III, 456. On *hof* place-names, see Per Vikstrand, "Ortnamnet Hov—sakralt, terrängbetecknande eller bägge delarna?," in *Sakrale navne: Rapport fra NORNAs sekstende symposium i Gilleleje 30.11–2.12 1990*, ed. Gillian Fellows-Jensen and Bente Holmberg (Uppsala: Norna-Förlaget, 1992), 123–39; Orri Vésteinsson, "*Hann reisti hof mikið hundrað fóta langt* . . . : Um uppruna *hof*-örnefna og stjórnmál á Íslandi í lok 10. aldar," *Saga* 45 (2007): 53–91.

102. Vetrl *Lv*, Þdís *Þórr*, Bragi *Frag* 3; John Lindow, "Addressing Thor," *Scandinavian Studies* 60 (1988): 119–36.

103. As in the description of Þórólfr Mostrarskegg's *ǫndvegissúlur* washing up on the beach in *Eyrbyggja saga*, ch. 4, *Þórr var á land kominn með súlurnar*. (Þórr had come to land with the posts.)

104. This magical view of the power of images was widespread in premodernity. Belting argues that when images were reinstated in Byzantine churches after iconoclasm, such views needed to be actively combated: "In order to control their effect and to distract attention from magical expectations, images had to be explained

rationally, emphasizing the immaterial presence of the archetype and devaluing any material presence of the image as object" (*Likeness and Presence: A History of the Image before the Era of Art* [Chicago: University of Chicago Press, 1994], 172).

105. See E. R. Truitt, *Medieval Robots: Mechanism, Magic, Nature, and Art* (Philadelphia: University of Pennsylvania Press, 2015).

106. The most common alternative suggestion is that the word is a nominal compound whose first element is ǫnd (f. "soul, breath") (*AEW*, s.v. ǫndóttr, ǫnd 3.) or ǫnn (f. "trouble, trial, sorrow") (Ásgeir Blöndal Magnússon, *Íslensk orðsifjabók*, s.v. öndóttur, ǫndóttr). Cf. *EK* II, 565–66.

107. ÍF *Eddukvæði* I, 426. Larrington, *Poetic Edda*, 96. The words *eldr of* are not in Codex Regius and have been supplied from a later paper manuscript.

108. Otto Holzapfel, "Stabilität und Variabilität einer Formel. Zur Interpretation der Bildformel 'Figur zwischen wilden Tieren' mit besonderer Berücksichtigung skandinavischer Beispiele," *Mediaeval Scandinavia* 6 (1973): 7–38.

109. Egon Wamers, "Von Bären und Männern: Berserker, Bärenkämpfer und Bärenführer im frühen Mittelalter," *Zeitschrift für Archäologie des Mittelalters* 37 (2009): 28–30. Klaus Düwel and Sigmund Oehrl list a number of *Tierbezwinger* images where the animals are serpentlike ("Überlegungen zur Bild- und Runenritzung von Aspö in Södermanland (Sö 175)," in *Die Faszination des Verborgenen und seine Entschlüsselung—Rāði saR kunni*, ed. Jana Krüger et al. [Berlin: De Gruyter, 2017], 95–107).

110. Ships, e.g., ÞjóðA *Har*, Þloft *Tøgdr* 2, Mark *Lv* 1; women, e.g., Hfr *Lv* 24, where a woman is compared to a ship with gilded tackle; nuts, e.g., Ótt *Lv* 1, Sigv *Lv* 9. For recent lists of skaldic ekphraseis, see Clunies Ross, "Stylistic and Generic," 167, and *SkP* III, 27. An earlier list, with some differences, is to be found in Lie, "Billedbeskrivender dikt."

111. Þjazi, in eagle form, tears "horribly" (*slíðrliga*) at the roasted meat; even *Húsdrápa*'s nameless giant, the "heavy-set fat one" (*þjokkvaxinn þiklingr*, *Húsdr* 5), has been gorging himself on something. Þórr's prowess at eating is interesting in this context.

112. Marold, "Ragnarsdrápa und Ragnarssage," 445–46.

113. Egill *Berdr*. Ed. Clunies Ross, *SkP* V.

114. Egill *Skjalddr*. Ed. Clunies Ross, *SkP* V.

115. A formulaic phrase often used metaphorically, cf. Anon *Pl* 44.

4. SEEING, KNOWING, AND BELIEVING IN THE *PROSE EDDA*

1. *Efþu girndesc at vesa petrrus. þa verer þu etke. þuiat þu girndesc annat at vesa an þu ert. Enn þar vill enge meire dvrþ hafa enn hann es verþ[r] sua sem her vill eige fotr vesa hond ne aýra at vesa auga.* Evelyn Scherabon Firchow, ed., *The Old Norse Elucidarius* (Columbia, SC: Camden House, 1992), 104–5. The Latin text reads: "*Nam, si cuperes Petrus esse, cuperes non subsistere. Si enim tuam essentiam exueres, nihil esses. Quamvis nullus ibi plus cupiat quam promeruit, sicut nec pes cupit oculus esse aut manus auris vel vir esse mulier.*"

2. This hierarchy is not inevitable; for example, the Word and hearing are foremost in biblical accounts of creation and salvation (cf. Hans Blumenberg, "Light as a Metaphor for the Truth," in *Modernity and the Hegemony of Vision*, ed. David Michael Kleinberg-Levin [Berkeley: University of California Press, 1993], 46–47); see further below on its resonances in the *Prologue* to the *Prose Edda*.

3. *Timaeus and Critias*, trans. Desmond Lee (New York: Penguin, 1977), 65.

4. *Basic Works of Aristotle*, trans. Richard McKeon (New York: Random House, 1941), 689.

5. David Summers, *The Judgment of Sense: Renaissance Naturalism and the Rise of Aesthetics* (Cambridge: Cambridge University Press, 1987), 32–33.

6. Eve Sweetser, *From Etymology to Pragmatics: Metaphorical and Cultural Aspects of Semantic Structure* (Cambridge: Cambridge University Press, 1990), 32–39.

7. Isidore, *The Etymologies of Isidore of Seville*, trans. Stephen A. Barney et al. (Cambridge: Cambridge University Press, 2006), x1.i.18.

8. Mark S. R. Jenner draws the logical conclusion: "One could argue that, rather than producing histories of smell, taste, hearing, touch, and sight, we should be investigating how and when the five-sense model has been established and how it has been maintained." "Follow Your Nose? Smell, Smelling, and Their Histories," *The American Historical Review* 116 (2011): 349.

9. *De anima* ii.5, 418a–423b.

10. Margaret Clunies Ross, "*Fimm líkamsins vit*: The Development of a New Lexical Set in Early Norse Christian Literature," *Arkiv för nordisk filologi* 102 (1987): 197–206.

11. Katherine O'Brien O'Keeffe, "Hands and Eyes, Sight and Touch: Appraising the Senses in Anglo-Saxon England," *Anglo-Saxon England* 45 (2016): 119–20. The commonest "alternate" ordering inverts the order of smell and taste and is also found in Old Norse.

12. There are some thirty-three Old Norse manuscripts containing homilies and sermons, mostly from Iceland (see Thomas N. Hall, "Old Norse-Icelandic Sermons," in *The Sermon*, ed. Beverly Mayne Kienzle [Turnhout: Brepols, 2000], 661–709). While good editions of the Old Norwegian (AM 619 4to) and Old Icelandic (Holm. perg. 15 4to) homily books exist (Gustav Indrebø, ed., *Gamal norsk homiliebok, Cod. AM 619, 4°* [Oslo: Universitetsforlaget, 1966] and Andrea van Arkel-de Leeuw van Weenen, ed., *The Icelandic Homily Book: Perg. 15 4° in the Royal Library, Stockholm* [Reykjavík: Stofnun Árna Magnússonar á Íslandi, 1993] respectively), many sermon manuscripts are unedited. The discussion that follows draws only on the Old Norwegian and Old Icelandic homily books. The two books are treated collectively; where significant differences between them exist, these are signaled in the notes. In the interests of readability, the homilies are cited where possible in normalized form, from the edition in modern Icelandic orthography of Sigurbjörn Einarsson, Guðrún Kvaran, and Gunnlaugur Ingólfsson (*Íslensk hómilíubók* [Reykjavík: Hið íslenska bókmenntafélag, 1993]). Translations are my own.

13. A Lenten homily, for example, offers six items ordered in three pairs: "[The body's] increase and touch, taste and smell, sight and hearing" (*Hans gróði ok kennisemi, berging ok ilming, sýn og heyrn* [. . .], *Íslensk hómilíubók*, 174).

14. *Íslensk hómilíubók*, 80.

15. C. M. Woolgar, *The Senses in Late Medieval England* (New Haven: Yale University Press, 2006), 10.

16. Cynthia Hahn, "*Visio Dei*: Changes in Medieval Visuality," in *Visuality before and beyond the Renaissance: Seeing as Others Saw*, ed. Robert S. Nelson (Cambridge: Cambridge University Press, 2000), 181.

17. *En er Jesús var borinn í musteri, þá tók Símeon höndum við honum. Mikils er virðandi miskunn Guðs, er hann veitir oss framar en vér kynnim biðja. Þess bað Símeon, að hann næði að sjá Christum. En honum var því framar veitt, að hann náði að hafa hann með höndum. Símeon tók í hendur sér manndóms óstyrkt, en hann kenndi guðdóms afl í manndómi. Íslensk hómilíubók*, 122.

18. Anatoly Liberman notes that Old Norse has many words for optical illusions (e.g., *glámsýni, missýni, sjónhverfing, þversýning*) and suggests that medieval Icelanders "deliberated seriously on the lack of correspondence between the products of human vision and reality." "Mistaken Identity and Optical Illusion in Old Icelandic Literature," in *ÜberBrücken: Festschrift für Ulrich Groenke zum 65. Geburtstag*, ed. Knut Brynhildsvoll (Hamburg: Buske, 1989), 109.

19. Sweetser, *From Etymology*, 28.

20. Origen quoted in Mark J. McInroy, "Origen of Alexandria," in *The Spiritual Senses: Perceiving God in Western Christianity*, ed. Paul L. Gavrilyuk and Sarah Coakley ([Cambridge: Cambridge University Press, 2011), 21–22.

21. On premodern optical theory, see A. Mark Smith, *From Sight to Light: The Passage from Ancient to Modern Optics* (Chicago: University of Chicago Press, 2015); David C. Lindberg and Katherine H. Tachau, "The Science of Light and Color, Seeing and Knowing," in *The Cambridge History of Science*, ed. Michael H. Shank (Cambridge: Cambridge University Press, 2013).

22. Aristotle analyzes the rainbow in his *Meteorology*, and Euclid's *Optics* explores paradoxes of vision. Smith, *From Sight*, 25–28, 47–55.

23. Smith, *From Sight*, ix–x.

24. The thirteenth-century Icelandic treatises on *computus* known as *Algorismus* and *Rím II* allude to the Arab mathematicians al-Farghani and al-Kindi, and they show some familiarity with the works of Ptolemy and Euclid, which became known in the West in translations from Arabic carried out in twelfth-century Spain. Christian Etheridge dates the earliest influence of Arabic science in Iceland to the late eleventh century ("The Evidence for Islamic Scientific Works in Medieval Iceland," in *Fear and Loathing in the North: Jews and Muslims in Medieval Scandinavia and the Baltic Region*, ed. Cordelia Heß and Jonathan Adams (Berlin: De Gruyter, 2015), 49–74).

25. ÍF 5, 109.

26. *Brunnu beggja kinna bjort ljós á mik drósar*, KormQ Lv 2. On the "aggressive eye" in medieval love poetry, see M. A. Jacobs, "*Hon stóð ok starði*: Vision,

Love, and Gender in *Gunnlaugs saga ormstungu*," *Scandinavian Studies* 86 (2014): 148–68.

27. Lance K. Donaldson-Evans suggests that extramissive imagery in love poetry originates in early Greek literature and was taken up in Arabic love lyric from the sixth century and passed from there to the troubadours (*Love's Fatal Glance: A Study of Eye Imagery in the Poets of the École Lyonnaise* [University, MS: Romance Monographs, 1980], 9, 26–30). It is also possible, especially given this difference between the Arabic and Provençal poetry, on one hand, and skaldic love poetry, on the other, that the intuitive attractiveness of extramission led to similar ideas being developed independently.

28. *Hefka opt ennileiptr af unnar eldspǫng*, Anon *Morg*.

29. Lindberg and Tachau, "Science of Light," 7.

30. Indrebø, *Gamal norsk homiliebok*, 96–98.

31. Hahn, "*Visio Dei*"; Thomas F. X. Noble, "The Vocabulary of Vision and Worship in the Early Carolingian Period," in *The Invisible in Late Antiquity and the Early Middle Ages*, ed. Giselle de Nie, Karl F. Morrison, and Marco Mostert (Turnhout: Brepols, 2005), 215–39.

32. *lux, una est et unum omnes qui vident et amant eam [. . .] corporalis [. . .] incelebrosa ac periculosa dulcedine condit vitam saeculi caecis amatoribus [. . .] curiosa cupiditas nomine cognitionis et scientiae palliata*. Augustine, *Confessions*, 2 vols., ed. Carolyn J. B. Hammond (Cambridge, MA: Harvard University Press, 2014), 156–57, 160–61.

33. The "heart's eye" is the usual biblical image for this idea, see Eric Jager, *The Book of the Heart* (Chicago: University of Chicago Press, 2000), 9–10; on the mind's eye in Old Norse, see Pernille Hermann, "The Mind's Eye: The Triad of Memory, Space and the Senses in Old Norse Literature," *European Journal of Scandinavian Studies* 47 (2017): 203–17.

34. Smith, *From Sight*, 252.

35. A. Mark Smith, "What is the History of Medieval Optics Really About?" *Proceedings of the American Philosophical Society* 148 (2004): 180–94.

36. The common sense is an elusive entity with a complex history that cannot be fully unfolded here. For a recent book-length treatment, see Daniel Heller-Roazen, *The Inner Touch: Archaeology of a Sensation* (New York: Zone Books, 2007).

37. Eugene Vance, "Seeing God: Augustine, Sensation and the Mind's Eye," in *Rethinking the Medieval Senses: Heritage, Fascinations, Frames*, ed. Stephen G. Nichols, Andreas Kablitz, and Alison Calhoun (Baltimore: Johns Hopkins University Press, 2008), 19.

38. My account of Augustine's theory of vision is dependent on Smith, *From Sight*, 150–54. Vance, "Seeing God," provides additional detail.

39. Suzanne Conklin Akbari, *Seeing through the Veil: Optical Theory and Medieval Allegory* (Toronto: University of Toronto Press, 2004), 44.

40. *En það er eigi fjallamannvit, að maðurinn viti það, hvað hann er eða hverjar greinir hans vesningar eru. Líkami heitir einn, inn óæðsti hlutur mannsins og inn*

ysti. En sá heitir önd, er bæði er innri og æðri. En sá heitir andi, er miklu er æðstur og göfgastur og innstur. Líkaminn er sýnilegur hlutur, en öndin er ósýnileg. Hans gróði og kennisemi, berging og ilming, sýn og heyrn, þeir hlutir allir eru af öndinni honum gefnir. Og allt líf hans er af hennar dugnuðum og afl og hræringar. En þau bæði eru eitt kykvendi og eru kölluð inn ytri maður. Því að þótt hún sé ósýnileg og í þeirra hluta tölu, er andlegir eru, þá er þó hún þess eins ávíta, er líkamlegt er og munúðsamlegt, en einskis þess, er guðdómlegt er. Inn þriðji hlutur heitir andi, sá er miklu göfgastur og innstur og æðstur er í manninum. Sá gefur hugkvæmi og skilning, dómspekt og minni, mál og skynsemi, næmleik guðstrúar og sjálfræði manninum. Hann er kallaður inn innri maður og engill. Honum er á hendi fólgið forráð alls mannsins. Íslensk hómilíubók, 174.

41. *CVC,* s.v. *hugkvæmr.* On the role of memory in imagination, cf. Mary Carruthers, *The Craft of Thought: Meditation, Rhetoric, and the Making of Images* (Cambridge: Cambridge University Press, 2000), 70.

42. The classic account is Harry Austryn Wolfson, "The Internal Senses in Latin, Arabic, and Hebrew Philosophic Texts," *Harvard Theological Review* 28 (1935): 69-133.

43. See Margaret Clunies Ross, *Skáldskaparmál: Snorri Sturluson's 'ars poetica' and Medieval Theories of Language* (Odense: Odense University Press, 1987); *Prolonged Echoes: Old Norse Myths in Medieval Northern Society, Vol. 1, The Myths* (Odense: Odense University Press, 1994); Guðrún Nordal, *Tools of Literacy: The Role of Skaldic Verse in Icelandic Textual Culture of the Twelfth and Thirteenth Centuries* (Toronto: University of Toronto Press, 2001).

44. Snorri Sturluson, *Edda: Skáldskaparmál,* ed. Anthony Faulkes (London: Viking Society, 1998), 5. Subsequent citations of this edition as Faulkes, *Skm.* Translation from Anthony Faulkes, *Snorri Sturluson: Edda* (London: Everyman, 1987), 64. Subsequent citations to this translation as Faulkes, *Edda.*

45. *SkP* III, cxxxix.

46. Margaret Clunies Ross, "Snorri's *Edda* as Narrative," in *Snorri Sturluson: Beiträge zu Werk und Rezeption,* ed. Hans Fix (Berlin: De Gruyter, 1998), 9-21.

47. Clunies Ross, *Skáldskaparmál,* 21; cf. Jonas Wellendorf, *Gods and Humans in Medieval Scandinavia: Retying the Bonds* (Cambridge: Cambridge University Press, 2018); Heinrich Beck, *Snorri Sturlusons Sicht der paganen Vorzeit: Gylfaginning* (Göttingen: Vandenhoeck & Ruprecht, 1994); Heinrich Beck, "Snorri Sturlusons Mythologie: Euhemerismus oder Analogie?," in *Snorri Sturluson: Historiker, Dichter, Politiker,* ed. Heinrich Beck, Wilhelm Heizmann, and Jan Alexander van Nahl (Berlin: De Gruyter, 2014); 1-21, followed by Jan Alexander van Nahl, "The Skilled Narrator: Myth and Scholarship in the Prose Edda," *Scripta Islandica* 66 (2015): 123-41; Anne Holtsmark, *Studier i Snorres mytologi* (Oslo: Universitetsforlag, 1964); Gerd Wolfgang Weber, "Intellegere historiam: Typological Perspectives of Nordic Prehistory (in Snorri, Saxo, Widukind and others)," in *Tradition og historieskrivning: Kilderne til Nordens ældste historie,* ed. Kirsten Hastrup and Preben Meulengracht Sørensen (Aarhus: Aarhus University Press, 1987), 95-141; *Ein*

sprach- und dichtungsskeptischer Zug [. . .] Verunsicherung [. . .] narrativ inszeniert, einerseits auf der thematischen, andererseits auf der diskursiven Ebene, Jürg Glauser, *Skandinavische Literaturgeschichte* (Stuttgart: Metzler, 2006), 10–11.

48. The texts quoted here, from Faulkes's editions, are largely based on Codex Regius (R). Both passages are present in all manuscripts that transmit complete versions of the *Prose Edda* (i.e., R, T, W, and U), and their texts are very similar, although U's version of Ægir's visit is somewhat abbreviated. None of the manuscripts that preserve only *Skáldskaparmál* (A, B, C) include Ægir's visit. For a semi-diplomatic text of the R version with variants, see Finnur Jónssson, ed., *Edda Snorra Sturlusonar* (Copenhagen: Gyldendal, 1931), 8–9, 78–79.

49. Translation from Faulkes, *Edda*, 7–8. *En er hann [Gylfi] kom inn í borgina þá sá hann þar háva hǫll, svá at varla mátti hann sjá yfir hana [. . .] Gylfi sá mann í hallar durunum ok lék at handsǫxum ok hafði sjau senn á lopti [. . .] þar sá hann mǫrg gólf ok mart fólk [. . .] Þá litaðisk hann umb ok þótti margir hlutir ótrúligir þeir er hann sá. [. . .] Hann sá þrjú hásæti ok hvert upp frá ǫðru, ok sátu þrír menn, sinn í hverju.* Snorri Sturluson. *Edda: Prologue and Gylfaginning*, ed. Anthony Faulkes (Oxford: Clarendon, 1982), 7–8. Subsequent citations of this edition as Faulkes, *Gylf*.

50. Translation from Faulkes, *Edda*, 59. *Hann [Ægir] gerði ferð sína til Ásgarðs [. . .] Ok um kveldit er drekka skyldi, þá lét Óðinn bera inn í hǫllina sverð, ok váru svá bjǫrt at þar af lýsti, ok var ekki haft ljós annat meðan við drykkju var setit. [. . .] Ægi þótti gǫfugligt þar um at sjásk. Veggþili ǫll váru þar tjǫlduð með fǫgrum skjǫldum.* Faulkes, *Skm*, 1.

51. *Eptir Nóa flóð lifðu átta menn þeir er heiminn bygðu ok kómu frá þeim ættir, ok varð enn sem fyrr at þá er fjǫlmentisk ok bygðisk verǫldin þá var þat allr fjǫlði mannfólksins er elskaði ágirni fjár ok metnaðar en afrœktusk guðs hlýðni, ok svá mikit gerðisk af því at þeir vildu eigi nefna guð. En hverr mundi þá segja sonum þeira frá guðs stórmerkjum? Svá kom at þeir týndu guðs nafni . . .* Faulkes, *Gylf*, 1.

52. Blumenberg, "Light as a Metaphor," 47.

53. The *Prologue* is transmitted in all manuscripts that transmit complete versions of the *Prose Edda* (i.e., R, T, W, and U), although the beginning is missing in R and the U version is abbreviated. The passage quoted above shows only minor variation among the redactions.

54. Faulkes, trans., *Edda*, 1. *En eigi at síðr veitti guð þeim jarðligar giptir, fé ok sælu, er þeir skyldu við vera í heiminum. Miðlaði hann ok spekina svá at þeir skildu alla jarðliga hluti ok allar greinir þær er sjá mátti loptsins ok jarðarinnar. Þat hugsuðu þeir ok undruðusk [. . .].* Faulkes, *Gylf*, 3. It is interesting to note that *miðla*, literally "mediate," is the verb used to describe God's apportioning of his wisdom to humans. (R and T are defective and U has *veitti* ["gave"], but W has *miðla*, as do the post-medieval copies of R.)

55. Aristotle, *Metaphysics*, 982b–983a; translation from McKeon, *Basic Works*, 692.

56. *Speculum naturale*, xxix, ch. xi.

57. With the exception of Jürg Glauser's suggestion that the *sjónhverfingar* of the frame narrative function as "tutorial[s] in deconstructive reading" ("Sensory Deceptions: Concepts of Mediality in the Prose Edda," in *Á austrvega: Saga and East Scandinavia: Preprint Papers of the 14th International Saga Conference*, ed. Agneta Ney, Henrik Williams, and Fredrik Charpentier [Gävle: Gävle University Press, 2009], 301), the *sjónhverfingar* have so far been examined from a theological standpoint. See, e.g., Walter Baetke, *Die Götterlehre der Snorra-Edda* (Berlin: Akademie, 1950), although he also sees it as a literary device (36); Beck, "Snorri Sturlusons Mythologie," 11, who sees it as an *Entrückung* intended to parallel the opening of the heavens at the baptism of Jesus; van Nahl, "Skilled Narrator," who follows Beck.

58. *Etymologies* viii.9.23.

59. See, e.g., Stephan K. Maksymiuk, *The Court Magician in Medieval German Literature* (Frankfurt: Lang, 1996); Corinne Saunders, *Magic and the Supernatural in Medieval English Romance* (Cambridge: Boydell & Brewer, 2010).

60. Edited in Bjarni Vilhjálmsson, *Riddarasögur*, 6 vols. (Reykjavik: Íslendingasagnaútgáfan, 1982), 5:1–61.

61. Jonson, *Masque of Blackness*, quoted in Felix E. Schelling, "The English Masque," in *Elizabethan Drama, 1558–1642* (New York: Houghton Mifflin & Company, 1904), 105.

62. Stuart Clark, *Vanities of the Eye: Vision in Early Modern European Culture* (Oxford: Oxford University Press, 2007), 81.

63. *Galldramenninir gordu dárasamliga ginning ok seonhverfing þeirra manna augum sem þar saa upp aa*. C. R. Unger, ed., *Stjórn* (Christiania: Feilberg & Landmark, 1862), 267. My translation.

64. In *Óláfs saga helga* (Oscar Johnsen and Jón Helgason, eds., *Saga Óláfs konungs hins helga*, 2 vols. [Oslo: Dybwad, 1941], 1:749–50) an illusion of St Olaf is described as a *sjónhverfing*.

65. "J þorpi nǫkkorv Vormacensi sá menn mikinn fiǫlða vápnaðra riddera riða ór fealli einv til samtals. *ok* at nóni aptr i feallit. Þá tréystiz einn at heraðsmonnvm vel signaðr með r[æ]ddzlv at fara n[æ]r þeim. *ok* sǿra einn af fólki þeira til sin. at segia hvat monnvm þeir v[æ]ri. Hann sagði honom. *ok* þetta með. Vér ervm *eigi* séonhverfingar sem þér hyggit. *ok eigi* riddera lið sem yðr sýniz. helldr sálvr þeira riddera er skǫmmv fellv. Vápn *ok* búnaðr er oss var i lifi tól til misgǫrða. Þat er oss nú efni til pisla. *ok* allt er þat elldligt er þér sét oss hafa. Þó at þér megit þat eigi likhamligvm ávgvm greina." Gustav Storm, ed., *Islandske Annaler indtil 1578* (Christiania: Norske historiske kildeskriftfond, 1888), 112. My translation.

66. Blumenberg, "Light as a Metaphor," 47.

67. Nordal, *Tools of Literacy*, 232.

68. Nordal, *Tools of Literacy*, 248–49.

69. Faulkes, *Edda*, 153. *Augu heita sjón ok lit eða viðrlit, ørmjǫt. Þau má svá kenna at kalla sól eða tungl, skjǫldu ok gler eða gimsteina eða stein brá eða brúna, hvarma eða ennis.* Faulkes, *Skm*, 108.

70. Cf. Ture Johnannisson, "Ordet *ärende* och dess släktskapsförhållanden," *Meijerbergs arkiv för svensk ordforskning* 4 (1941): 33; Karl Ó. Ólafsson, "Örmjöt: Athugun á stakyrði," *Mímir* 40 (2001): 62–69.

71. *Skript eða skjǫld, ljós eða lopt [. . .], stein eða stjǫrnur, gull eða geisla, ok alla birti.* W (AM 242 fol), 85r. My normalization and translation.

72. Nordal, *Tools of Literacy*, 245, translates as "writing," but "picture, image" is a more common gloss for *skript* and more plausible in the context of vision.

73. On luminosity, cf. Camille, "Before the Gaze," 203–4.

74. Early skalds seem to have thought the moon and/or sky emitted light: "Then the divinely gentle bedmate of Glenr <mythical being> [Sól, the personified sun] strides with her beams into the goddess's sanctuary; the good light of the grey-shirt of Máni ('Moon') [SKY] comes down." (*Síðan veðr goðblíð beðja Glens með geislum í vé gyðju; gótt ljós gránserks Mána kemr ofan*, Skúli *Lv* 1). "Sun" first occurs as a base word for eye-kennings in EGils *Guðkv* 32–34, which describe Guðmundr's miraculous healing of a child afflicted with an eye disease.

75. *De anima* ii.5, 418a; *De sensu* iii, 439a–440b.

76. Some argue that the extended poetic quotations are interpolations (most recently in Snorri Sturluson, *The Uppsala Edda: DG 11 4to*, ed. Heimir Pálsson, trans. Anthony Faulkes [London: Viking Society, 2012], lxxv n.). As Faulkes points out (*Skm*, xlii–xliii), the fact that the names of the skalds and poems are mentioned at the corresponding places in U speaks against this, as does the convincing evidence that U, like A and B, is a revised version of an exemplar with a similar text to RT presented in Daniel Sävborg, "Blockbildningen i Codex Upsaliensis: En ny metod att lösa frågan om Snorra Edda ursprungsversion," *Maal og minne* (2012): 12–53.

77. Finnur Jónsson, "Indledning," in *Edda Snorra Sturlusonar*, xxxvi–xxxix.

78. Finnur Jónsson, "Indledning," in *Edda Snorra Sturlusonar*, xiv.

79. W was treated with urine in the seventeenth century, obliterating all its rubrics, but the space corresponds to a two-line initial.

80. Faulkes, *Edda*, 81. *Þá mælir Ægir: "Mikill þótti mér Hrungnir fyrir sér."* Faulkes, *Skm*, 24.

81. The coincidence of the names of the frame's narrator and the text's second-most often cited poet has ironic potential (Faulkes, *Skm*, xx), to similarly dizzying effect as the doublings of "the Æsir" at the end of *Gylfaginning*.

82. Faulkes, *Edda*, 106. *Eptir þessum sǫgum hafa flest skáld ort ok tekit ymsa þáttu.* Faulkes, *Skm*, 50.

83. Faulkes, *Edda*, 123. *Svá er sagt í kvæðum at Hjaðningar skulu svá bíða ragnarøkrs.* Faulkes, *Skm*, 72.

84. Cf. Ill *Har*, ÞjóðA *Lv* 6, Þorf *Lv* 1. According to the interpolated version of the *Separate saga of St Olaf*, Sigvatr's *Erfidrápa* for Óláfr Haraldsson originally had

a *stef* based on the Sigurðr story (*efter Sigurðr sǫgu*), although the most recent editor of the poem doubts this (*SkP* I, 663).

85. Aleida Assmann, "Was sind kulturelle Texte?" in *Literaturkanon—Medienereignis—kultureller Text: Formen interkultureller Kommunikation und Übersetzung*, ed. Andreas Poltermann (Berlin: Erich Schmidt, 1995), 232–44.

86. The "classic" is a kind of canonical text with potential for "imitation, variation, quotation, recycling," cf. Jan Assmann, "Form as a Mnemonic Device: Cultural Texts and Cultural Memory," in *Performing the Gospel: Orality, Memory, and Mark*, ed. Richard A. Horsely et al. (Minneapolis: Fortress, 2006), 82.

87. On "hot" and "cold" remembering, see J. Assmann, *Das kulturelle Gedächtnis*, 66–78.

88. In R: *Jómsvíkingadrápa* (Bjbp *Jóms*), which conjoins the legendary battle of the Jómsvíkingar with the amatory troubles of its author, Bjarni Kolbeinsson; in A: *Íslendingadrápa* (HaukrV *Ísldr*), a catalog of *Íslendingasaga* fights.

89. See, e.g., Barbara Nolan, *The Gothic Visionary Perspective* (Princeton: Princeton University Press, 1977); Akbari, *Seeing through the Veil*; Dallas G. Denery, *Seeing and Being Seen in the Later Medieval World: Optics, Theology and Religious Life* (Cambridge: Cambridge University Press, 2005); Shannon Gayk, *Image, Text, and Religious Reform in Fifteenth-Century England* (Cambridge: Cambridge University Press, 2010).

90. ESk *Geisl* ed. Chase, *SkP* VII, 5–65; Anon *Líkn* ed. Tate, *SkP* VII, 228–86.

91. Selma Jónsdóttir argues that carved wooden panels found at the farm Bjarnastaðarhlíð in 1924 are the remains of a Byzantine-style Last Judgment, the central element of which is a Pantocrator (*An Eleventh-Century Byzantine Last Judgement in Iceland* [Reykjavík: Almenna Bókafélagið, 1959]). The *arma Christi* are depicted, with Latin captions, as the frame of a crucifixion on fol. 14v of Icelandic modelbook *Teiknibókin*; cf. Guðbjörg Kristjánsdóttir, *Íslenska teiknibókin* (Reykjavik: Crymogea, 2013).

5. THE NOISE OF POETRY

1. Roberta Frank, *Old Norse Court Poetry: The Dróttkvætt Stanza* (Ithaca: Cornell University Press, 1978), 142.

2. Diana Whaley, "The Fury of the Northmen and the Poetics of Violence," in *Narration and Hero: Recounting the Deeds of Heroes in Literature and Art of the Early Medieval Period*, ed. Victor Millet and Heike Sahm (Berlin: De Gruyter, 2014), 75.

3. Sophie Grace Chappell, *Knowing What to Do: Imagination, Virtue, and Platonism in Ethics* (Oxford University Press, 2014), ch. 7.

4. Chappell, *Knowing*, 160.

5. ÍF *Eddukvæði* II, 332, 333, 279; translations from Carolyne Larrington, *The Poetic Edda*, 2nd ed. (Oxford: Oxford University Press, 2014), 174, 175, 135.

6. Alasdair MacIntyre, quoted in Chappell, *Knowing*, 162.

7. Cf. Þhorn *Gldr* 2; Arn *Hardr* 13, *Hryn* 12, 17; Sigv *ErfÓl* 5, *Víkv* 5, *Berv* 5; Sturl *Hákfl* 5.

8. Poems about strife between blood kin such as *Fafnismál,* the Atli poems, and *Hamðismál* explore the self-destructiveness of violence; *Hávamál* advocates for measure in its use.

9. Whaley concludes that there is little discernible difference in early post-Conversion poetry and suggests that the subject needs more research ("Fury," 89–90).

10. Chappell, *Knowing,* 173–74.

11. That the skald's praise must be deserved is the point of the often-quoted passage in the *Prologue* to *Heimskringla* asserting that skalds would only praise rulers in the presence of their sons and retainers for battles and journeys they had actually undertaken, as anything else would be *háð en eigi lof* ("scorn and not praise." ÍF 26, 5).

12. Faulkes, *Skm,* 83; translation from Faulkes, *Edda,* 132.

13. Roberta Frank, "Why Skalds Address Women," in *Poetry in the Scandinavian Middle Ages: The Seventh International Saga Conference (12° Congresso Internazionale di Studi sull'Alto Medioevo), Spoleto,* ed. Teresa Paroli (Spoleto: Presso la Sede del Centro Studi, 1988), 67–83; Bjarne Fidjestøl, "'Out They Will Look, The Lovely Ladies:' Views of Women in Norse Literature," in his *Selected Papers* (Odense: Odense University Press, 1997), 333–42.

14. Frank Heidermanns, *Etymologisches Wörterbuch der germanischen Primäradjektive* (Berlin: De Gruyter, 1993), 349.

15. Cf. John Lindow, *Comitatus, Individual and Honor: Studies in North Germanic Institutional Vocabulary* (Berkeley: University of California Press, 1976).

16. *ONP* offers an interpretive gloss, "fit for recital at court"—but the *drótt* is a group of people, not a place. Fritzner, *Ordbog,* opts for mere description, as "det sædvanlige Versemaal i de egentlige Æredigte til fornemme Mænd," while *CVC* is bolder, defining it as "the metre used in the drápas (q. v.) or poems which were recited before a king and the king's men (drótt), whence the name probably comes."

17. Chappell, *Knowing,* 174n17.

18. Cf. however *Liðsmannaflokkr* (Verses of the household troops), said in *Knýtlinga saga* to be the composition of the *liðsmenn* "household troops" of Knútr inn ríki. Poole observes that these stanzas are "composed from the viewpoint of the rank-and-file participant" (*SkP* I, 1016).

19. Bjarne Fidjestøl finds that the kings with the most poets were those with the greatest financial resources ("'Have You Heard a Poem Worth More?': A Note on the Economic Background of Early Skaldic Praise-Poetry," in his *Selected Papers,* 117–32).

20. *höfische Erziehung.* Horst Wenzel, "Imaginatio und Memoria: Medien der Erinnerung im höfischen Mittelalter," in *Mnemosyne: Formen und Funktionen der kulturellen Erinnerung,* ed. Aleida Assmann and Dietrich Harth (Frankfurt: Fischer, 1991), 57.

21. Judith Jesch, *Ships and Men in the Late Viking Age: The Vocabulary of Runic Inscriptions and Skaldic Verse* (Woodbridge: Boydell, 2001), 243–47.

22. There seems to be only one reference in the encomiastic poetry of the kings' sagas to the groans of the dying: *Stunðu seggir [. . .] benjar svíddu*, "men moaned [. . .] wounds smarted" (Ív *Sig* 38).

23. Described in horrifying detail in Hillel Schwartz's *Making Noise: From Babel to the Big Bang and Beyond* (New York: Zone, 2011), 559–82, from where the quotations in this paragraph are taken.

24. Michel Serres, "Noise," *SubStance* 12 (1983): 50–51.

25. Schwartz, *Making Noise*, 566.

26. Marie Thompson, *Beyond Unwanted Sound: Noise, Affect and Aesthetic Moralism* (New York: Bloomsbury, 2017), 5.

27. With the notable exception of *HHI* (e.g., sts. 16, 17, 20, 25, 27, 54), violence in the *Poetic Edda* tends not to be associated with sound.

28. Jacques Attali, *Noise: The Political Economy of Music*, trans. Brian Massumi (Minneapolis: University of Minnesota Press, 1985), 3.

29. M. S. Griffith, "Convention and Originality in the Old English 'Beasts of Battle' Typescene," *Anglo-Saxon England* 22 (1993): 189.

30. Alice Jorgensen, "The Trumpet and the Wolf: Noises of Battle in Old English Poetry," *Oral Tradition* 24 (2009): 323.

31. From the nineteenth-century Black American spiritual *Joshua Fought the Battle of Jericho*, first published in *Jubilee Songs* by M. G. Slayton, 1882. The song is full of expressive effects, from the long, drawn-out vowel of *sound*, imitating the trumpets, to the descending notes that accompany the final line and suggest the collapse of the walls.

32. *Gehyre se ðe wille! Exodus* l. 7, quoted in Jorgensen, "Trumpet," 330.

33. Brigitte Cazelles, *Soundscape in Early French Literature* (Tempe, AZ: ACMRS Press, 2005), 71.

34. Cf. Judith Jesch, "'Eagles, Ravens and Wolves': Beasts of Battle, Symbols of Victory and Death,'" in *The Scandinavians from the Vendel Period to the Tenth Century* (Woodbridge: Boydell Press, 2003), 251–71. A group of *lausavísur* preserved in *Landnámabók* and *Hrómundar þáttr halta* (Hróm *Lv* 1, Þþyn *Lv* 1, Hást *Lv* 7) exceptionally take the doom-filled cry of the raven as their theme.

35. ÞSjár *Róðdr*, Bǫlv *Hardr* 1, ÞGísl *Búdr* 7, HSt *Rst* 18; Arn *Þorfdr* 8 (st. 18 adds horns), Sigv *Lv* 21.

36. Eyv *Hák* 5. Ms. K has *glymringar* "ringers" for *gylfringar* "swords"; the latter is argued in *LP*, followed by Fulk in his edition for *SkP*, to be connected to *gjálfr* "["noise of"] the sea."

37. GunnLeif *Merl* II 34.

38. Sigv *Nesv* 8.

39. A search in the Skaldic Project database's list of battle-kennings yields around 150 kennings containing a noise-word (excluding words for articulate

sound, which are discussed separately below). The database is incomplete at the time of writing, covering only vols. 1–3, 7 and 8.

40. Rudolf Meissner, *Die Kenningar der Skalden: Ein Beitrag zur skaldischen Poetik* (Bonn and Leipzig: Schroeder, 1921), 189.

41. Leanne Hinton, Johanna Nichols, and John J. Ohala, *Sound Symbolism* (Cambridge: Cambridge University Press, 2006), 5.

42. Hinton et al., *Sound Symbolism*, 5. A classic study is Dwight L. Bolinger, "Rime, Assonance, and Morpheme Analysis," *Word* 6 (1950): 117–36.

43. Hinton et al., *Sound Symbolism*, 3–4.

44. *Klang wird dabei einerseits im Lied auf der Objektebene thematisch, anderseits und vor allem als Klang (euphonisch, euphorisch) hörbar.* Susanne Köbele, "Rhetorik und Erotik: Minnesang als 'süßer Klang,'" *Poetica* 45 (2013): 306.

45. *SkP* I, 73–75.

46. Þhorn *Gldr*, ed. Marold et al., *SkP* I, 73–91.

47. Instead of *sand-*, the version of this stanza in *Óláfs saga Tryggvasonar en mesta* reads *land-* ("land") in ll. 3 and 4, which is semantically equivalent but changes the alliterating letter in these lines to *l*.

48. Ms. F reads *-seið* ("fish") rather than *-skíð* ("plank"). The construal of st. 1 is controversial; see *SkP* I, 76–77 and especially Bjarne Fidjestøl, *Det norrøne fyrstediktet* (Bergen: University of Bergen, 1982), 73–80, for surveys of previous attempts.

49. Faulkes, *Hát*, 21. Only ms. K has *bryn-* in l. 4. All other manuscripts have *ben-* ("wound"), which makes an equally good kenning. If we read *ben-*, the *alhent* pattern vanishes, but a *dunhent*-like pattern is formed with *ben* in the previous line.

50. Hfr *Lv* 11, ed. Whaley, *SkP* V.

51. The shimmering signifiers are Barthes's, quoted in Shane Butler, *The Ancient Phonograph* (New York: Zone, 2015), 81.

52. The title *Oddmjór* ("Narrow-point") may refer to sound, although its poor preservation makes it hard to be certain. Arnórr's *Hrynhenda* is named after its meter, and in some manuscripts is called *Hrynjandi* ("Rushing one"); see further below. These are the only other medievally attested titles that could refer to sound.

53. *Eine wirkliche Funktion, ein tatsächliches Verhältnis.* Meissner, *Kenningar*, 25.

54. Glúm *Gráf* 4, ed. Finlay, *SkP* I, 245–65.

55. E.g., Hharð *Lv* 14, where the adjective *haldorðr* (otherwise unattested, but cf. *haldinorðr*, "one who stays silent, keeps their own counsel") indicates that the woman mentioned is no ordinary human, but a personification of battle (a valkyrie) or even, as the saga prose suggests, Haraldr's mailcoat, Emma.

56. *CVC*, s.v. *enda* vb II.

57. A similar point is already made by Meissner, *Kenningar*, 197.

58. On eddic poem titles, cf. Judy Quinn, "The Naming of Eddic Mythological Poems in Medieval Manuscripts," *Parergon* 8 (1990): 97–115.

59. Þmáhl *Máv* 7.

60. Quoted in Schwartz, *Making Noise*, 573.

61. Susan A. Stewart, *Poetry and the Fate of the Senses* (Chicago: University of Chicago Press, 2002), 109.

62. Alliteration is known in German as *Stabreim* ("stave-rhyme"). The word appears to have been coined by Karl Lachmann in a lecture of 1834/5, drawing on the ON *technical term stafr*, as it appears in *Háttatal* (cf., e.g., *hǫfuðstafr*); Bernhard Asmuth, "Reim," in *Historisches Wörterbuch der Rhetorik*, ed. Gert Ueding (Tübingen: Niemeyer, 2005), vol. 7, cols. 1115–1144.

63. T. V. F. Brogan, S. Cushman, and K. Chang, "Rhyme," in *The Princeton Encyclopedia of Poetry and Poetics: Fourth Edition*, ed. by Roland Greene et al. (Princeton,: Princeton University Press, 2012), 1182.

64. See, e.g., Bridget Gordon Mackenzie, "On the Relation of Norse Skaldic Verse to Irish Syllabic Poetry," in *Specvlvm Norrœnvm: Norse Studies in Memory of Gabriel Turville-Petre*, ed. Ursula Dronke et al. (Odense: University Press of Southern Denmark, 1981), 337–56; Kristján Árnason, "Um hendingar í dróttkvæðum hætti," *Íslenskt mál og almenn málfræði* 9 (1987): 65–66.

65. Kristján Árnason, "On the Principles of Nordic Rhyme and Alliteration," *Arkiv för nordisk filologi* 122 (2007): 79–114.

66. The *skot-* element ("shot?" i.e., "inserted") has attracted most commentary, cf. Stephen Tranter, "Divided and Scattered, Trussed and Supported: Stanzaic Form in Irish and Old Norse Tracts," in *Metrik und Medienwechsel/Metrics and Media*, ed. Hildegard L. C. Tristram (Tübingen: Narr, 1991), 258, and references there.

67. Kari Ellen Gade argues that her interpretation of the terms *fang* (lit. "catch") and *fall* (lit. "fall") in SnH Lv 7 as "metrically marked" (and so "catching" the ear) and "metrically unmarked" (failing to do so), is supported by the use of *henda* to refer to internal rhyme ("*Fang* and *fall*: Two Skaldic *termini technici*," *Journal of English and Germanic Philology* 90 [1991]: 361–74). It is not known what errors these words referred to.

68. Cf., e.g., *CVC* s.v. *hending* II: "the ancient double rhymes were both placed in the same line, so as to 'catch' one another."

69. *vísur þessar námu menn þegar.* Oscar Albert Johnsen and Jón Helgason, eds., *Den store saga om Olav den Hellige* (Oslo: Dybwad, 1941), 545.

70. Asmuth, "Reim," 4. On kennings as memory-images, see, e.g., Bergsveinn Birgisson, "The Old Norse Kenning as a Mnemonic Figure," in *The Making of Memory in the Middle Ages*, ed. Lucie Doležalová (Leiden: Brill, 2009), 199–214.

71. *Mælti [. . .] alt hendingum, svá sem nú er þat kveðit, er skáldskapr heitir.* ÍF 26, 16; translation from Anthony Faulkes and Alison Finlay, *Snorri Sturluson: Heimskringla*, 3 vols. (London: Viking Society, 2011–15), 1:10, slightly altered. *Talaði allt hendingum, svá skjótt sem hann læsi af bók.* C. R. Unger, ed., *Mariu saga. Legender om jomfru Maria og hendes jertegn*, 2 vols. (Christiania: Brögger & Christie, 1871), 2: 680. *Maríu saga* draws here on a mid-twelfth-century miracle collection composed by Hugh Farsit, a canon of Saint-Jean de Vignes in Soissons.

72. *í þat form, er þeir kalla rithmos, en vér köllum hendingum.* Gustav Cederschiöld, ed., *Fornsögur Suðrlanda* (Lund: Berling, 1884), 1.

73. Cf. *OED* s.v. *rhyme* n. No Old French forms with the medial consonant of *rhythmus* are attested. The alternative explanation is derivation from Gmc. *rīm* ("sequence, series, number"), cf. ON *rím* "calendar"; *AEW* s.v. *rím* 1.

74. On the relative importance of quantitative and accentual features in *dróttkvætt*, see Kristján Árnason, *The Rhythms of Dróttkvætt and Other Old Icelandic Metres* (Reykjavík: University of Iceland, 1991), esp. ch. 6. I explore the links between the thirteenth-century treatises and *rithmica* further in Chapter 6.

75. *TGT*, 95–96. My translation.

76. Margaret Clunies Ross, *A History of Old Norse Poetry and Poetics* (Cambridge: Brewer, 2005), 200.

77. Jonathan Culler, *On Puns: The Foundation of Letters* (Oxford: Blackwell, 1988), 3.

78. *der ältere Bruder des Reims oder dessen Auftakt*. Quoted in Asmuth, "Reim," 4.

79. Culler, *On Puns*, 4.

80. Margarete de Grazia, "Homonyms before and after Lexical Standardization," *Jahrbuch/Deutsche Shakespeare-Gesellschaft West* (1990): 153; Cazelles, *Soundscape*, 97–98.

81. *Skáldskaparmál*'s instances include pairs such as *lið* ("limb") and *líð* ("ale"). These would often be identical in writing, as vowel length is marked only sporadically in medieval manuscripts, but were presumably not strict homonyms in speech.

82. Grazia, "Homonyms," 153.

83. Jurij Lotmann, quoted in Brogan et al., "Rhyme," 1188; Stewart, *Poetry and the Fate*, 43.

84. *Spielwelt des Klangs [. . .] auf eine analytisch schwer fassbare Weise von Semantik entlastet, ohne asemantisch, athematisch oder gar Unsinn zu sein*. Köbele, "Rhetorik," 318–19.

85. Brogan et al., "Rhyme," 1187.

86. Cf. though *Frá Vǫlundi* in the *Poetic Edda*, which suggests an equivalence between valkyries and migratory water birds in the form of swan maidens.

87. Definitions of *figura etymologica* vary in their strictness. Some require that the repeated etymologically related words belong to different parts of speech rather than merely being distinct inflections. According to this definition only the third *hlymja* would be *figura etymologica*, as the first two are (presumably) nouns.

88. ÍF *Eddukvæði* I, 383; Larrington, *Poetic Edda*, 59.

89. Hfr *Erfól*, ed. Heslop, *SkP* I, 400–41.

90. Stanza-ordering in encomiastic *drápur* is rarely certain, but the ordering of the citations in *Óláfs saga Tryggvasonar* and the fact that the king is still alive in st. 15 suggest that it precedes st. 18.

91. Cf. Maria Elena Ruggerini, "Alliterative Lexical Collocations in Eddic Poetry," in *A Handbook to Eddic Poetry: Myths and Legends of Early Scandinavia*, ed.

Carolyne Larrington, Judy Quinn, and Brittany Schorn (Cambridge: Cambridge University Press, 2016), 310–30.

92. Finnur Jónsson, ed., *Óláfs saga Tryggvasonar* (Copenhagen: Gad, 1932), 233–34, 256.

93. *Morð* is a common battle-*heiti*. Occasionally the context suggests that *morð* means "murder," e.g., Sigv *Erlfl* 8, Anon *Mv I* 11 (*vígi er morð ordið*, "manslaughter has turned into murder"). Its use here for the death of an individual makes the case for interpreting it as "murder" stronger. Possibly Hallfreðr is casting Óláfr as a royal martyr, especially in light of the treachery and desertion mentioned earlier in the poem.

94. Butler, *Ancient Phonograph*, 86.

95. Text and translation from Marold's edition for *SkP* VI.

96. Hans Ulrich Gumbrecht, "Rhythmus und Sinn," in *Materialität der Kommunikation*, ed. Hans Ulrich Gumbrecht and Karl Ludwig Pfeiffer (Frankfurt: Suhrkamp, 1988), 720.

97. Max-Planck-Gesellschaft, "Singing after Stroke? Why Rhythm and Formulaic Phrases May Be More Important than Melody." Science Daily, accessed September 28, 2019, www.sciencedaily.com/releases/2011/09/110922093728.htm.

98. For audio samples, see "Speech-to-Song Illusion," Diana Deutsch, accessed September 28, 2019, deutsch.ucsd.edu/psychology/pages.php?i=212. Samples 1 and 2 demonstrate the effect.

99. Diana Deutsch, *Musical Illusions and Phantom Words: How Music and Speech Unlock Mysteries of the Brain* (Oxford: Oxford University Press, 2019), ch. 11.

6. A POETRY MACHINE

1. *sumir taka hljóð er þú kippir at þér, sumir, er þú hrindir frá þér*. Heimir Pálsson, ed., *The Uppsala Edda: DG 11 4to* (London: Viking Society, 2012), 256–57. The Upsaliensis version of the *Second Grammatical Treatise* and its translation are quoted here and elsewhere from this edition. Codex Upsaliensis' prose refers to the vertical lines as *regur* and the spaces between them, where the consonants are written, as *spacione*. Raschellà thinks the latter is the same word as *spázía* (f. "margin,") while *rega* (f.) is a *hapax legomenon*; he compares MLG *rêge, rige* (Fabrizio D. Raschellà, ed., *The So-Called Second Grammatical Treatise: An Orthographic Pattern of Late Thirteenth-Century Icelandic* [Florence: Le Monnier, 1982], 72n71b, hereafter cited as Raschellà, *SGT*). Lat. *spacium* and *regula* are used to refer to the spaces between the lines and the lines themselves in the stave notation introduced by Guido of Arezzo (fl. 992–1033), cf. *Lexicon musicum Latinum medii aevi*, s.v. *regula* 7; J. Smits van Waesberghe, "The Musical Notation of Guido of Arezzo," *Musica Disciplina* 5 (1951): 15–53.

2. *Nú tekr svá fremi mikit um gjörast, er orðin hefjast upp ok hljómrinn vex ok raddirnar glymja á, nefnist ok svá fremi söngr, er þetta hefir allt til, ok nú þýss sjá flokkr framm á leikvöllinn, ok öllummegin at stýrinu, því er túngan heitir, ok heita*

nú á hana til málsins ok orðanna ok söngsins, at hon kveði þat allt upp, ok hon gjörir svá ok hneigir sik til stýrimannsins ok mælir [ms. maler] svá: Ósanna! segir hon, þat þýðist á vára túngu svá: græð þú oss! [. . .] ok þá er hann hefir skipt sínu liði sér til hægri handar eptir dómsdag, þá skulum vér hefja upp Allelúja, fyrir því at þat er eigi jarðneskr söngr, syngja þetta þá allir smana tíu fylki guðs engla ok manna, þá er almáttigr guð ferr meðr sína ferð heim í himnríkis dýrð, ok skulum þá una í sífellu [. . .]. Jón Sigurðsson et al., eds., *Edda Snorra Sturlusonar: Edda Snorronis Sturlaei*, 3 vols. (Copenhagen: Legatum Arnamagnaeanum, 1848–87), 2:58. The text of the Wormianus version of *SGT* is quoted here and elsewhere in the normalized form of the Arnamagnæan edition for the sake of ease of reading. (Raschellà gives only semi-diplomatic transcriptions of W.) The editors' emendations are marked in the text. Translations are my own.

3. The *terminus ante quem* is the date of Codex Upsaliensis, c. 1300. Raschellà argues for a dating late in the thirteenth century, possibly due to the parallels he sees with the *modistae*. The coalescence of *æ* and *œ* that he adduces in support is too imprecisely dated to be of help (cf. Sverrir Tómasson, "'Nikulám skulu vér heiðra hér . . .': Spjall um annan málfræðinginn, kveðskap og musik," in *Til heiðurs og hugbótar: Greinar um trúarkveðskap fyrri alda*, ed. Svanhildur Óskarsdóttir and Anna Guðmundsdóttir [Reykholt: Snorrastofa, 2003], 78).

4. Raschellà includes the opening and closing sections of the Wormianus text in his useful parallel transcription of the two versions, but he silently omits them from the "Restored Text and Translation" and refers the reader to the nineteenth-century Arnamagnæan edition of the *Prose Edda,* where the Wormianus version is translated into Latin. Mikael Males recently translated parts of the closing section into Swedish ("Wormianusredaktören: Språk, tro och sanning vid 1300-talets mitt," *Arkiv för nordisk filologi* 128 [2013]: 41–78), but the opening section seems not to have been translated into any modern language.

5. Raschellà (*SGT*), Kurt Braunmüller ("Der sog. zweite grammatische Traktat: Eine verkanntes Zeugnis altisländischer Sprachanalyse," in his *Beiträge zur skandinavistischen Linguistik* [Oslo: Novus, 1995], 210–26) and Angela Beuerle (*Sprachdenken im Mittelalter: Ein Vergleich mit der Moderne* [Berlin: De Gruyter, 2010]) exclude the W version from consideration as unoriginal. Thomas Krömmelbein ("Creative Compilers: Observations on the Manuscript Tradition of Snorri's *Edda*," in *Snorrastefna, 25-27. Júlí 1990*, edited by Úlfar Bragason [Reykjavik: Stofnun Sigurðar Nordals, 1992], 113–29), Sandra Schneeberger ("Der *Zweite Grammatische Traktat*—Spielfeld für Schrift und Klang," in *Skandinavische Schriftlandschaften: Vänbok til Jürg Glauser*, ed. Klaus Müller-Wille et al. [Tübingen: Narr, 2017], 73–77), Stefanie Gropper ("Der sogenannte *Zweite Grammatische Traktat*: Sprache und Musik," in *Skandinavische Schriftlandschaften*, ed. Müller-Wille et al., 78–83), and Guðrún Nordal ("Metrical Learning and the First Grammatical Treatise," in *Versatility in Versification*, ed. Tonya Kim Dewey and Frog [New York: Peter Lang, 2009], 23–38) do not express an opinion on which version has priority but nonetheless focus exclusively on the U version. Karl Johansson (*Studier i Codex*

Wormianus: skrifttradition och avskriftsverksamhet vid ett isländskt skriptorium under 1300-talet [Göteborg: Acta Universitatis Gothoburgensis, 1997]) argues that the contents and ordering of W are original and are due to a compiler, who collected and copied a number of texts on language and grammar and gave his copies, as exemplars, to the scribe. Males, "Wormianusredaktören," argues that the frame of the W version of *SGT* is by the compiler.

6. The passage quoted above draws on Isidore's discussion of *Osanna* and *Alleluia* in *Etymologies* vi.19.21–2; Males also detects echoes of Gregory's *Homiliae in Ezechielem* ("Wormianusredaktören," 51). The account of the physiology of the speech organs at the beginning of the W version of *SGT* has parallels in Isidore's etymology of "heart" (*Etymologies* xi.1.118), as well as in discussions of the "natural instruments" of *vox* in speculative music theory.

7. W's additions are called "banal monkish observations" (*banale munkebetragtninger*, Verner Dahlerup and Finnur Jónsson. *Islands grammatiske litteratur i middelalderen, Vol. 1, I. Den første og anden grammatiske afhandling i Snorres Edda* [Copenhagen: Møller, 1884], xxvi); a "sorry effort" (*machwerk*, Eugen Mogk, *Der sogenannte zweite grammatische Traktat des Snorra-Edda* [Halle: Buchdruckerei des Waisenhauses, 1889], 12); and "alien to the original of *SGT*" (Raschellà, *SGT*, 49). The prejudice against Christian learning, which is common in older studies of Norse material, is bolstered by a claim that the words of U are "concise, simple, energetic and undoubtedly original" ("korte, simple, energiske, og uden tvivl oprindelig"), Dahlerup and Finnur Jónsson, *Islands grammatiske litteratur*, xxvi); Raschellà quotes V. A. Dearing to the same effect (Raschellà, *SGT*, 20). Normative binary assumptions lie not far beneath the surface of these judgments. W's text is, in fact, often more concise than U's (for instance, U lists the noise of weapons twice in its account of irrational sounds).

8. Raschellà, *SGT*, 3.

9. Dahlerup and Finnur Jónsson, *Islands grammatiske litteratur*; Raschellà, *SGT*; Oscar Brenner, "Der traktat der Upsala-Edda '*af setningu hattalykils*'," *Zeitschrift für deutsche Philologie* 21 (1889): 272–80; Mogk, *Der sogenannte*; Braunmüller, "Der sog. Zweite"; Beuerle, *Sprachdenken*.

10. Raschellà, *SGT*, 121; see also Braunmüller, "Der sog. zweite"; Valeria Micillo, "Die grammatische Tradition des insularen Mittelalters in Island: Spuren insularer Einflüsse im *Dritten Grammatischen Traktat*," in *Übersetzung, Adaptation und Akkulturation im insularen Mittelalter*, ed. Erich Poppe and Hildegard L. C. Tristram (Munster: Nodus, 1999), 215n1.

11. *Von einem hinweis auf gott finden wir keine spur.* Mogk, *Der sogenannte*, 12.

12. Jussi Parikka, *What is Media Archaeology?* (Cambridge: Polity, 2012), 41.

13. Zoe Beloff, quoted in Parikka, *What is Media Archaeology?* 52.

14. Cf. Sybille Krämer, "'Operationsraum Schrift': Über einen Perspektivenwechsel in der Betrachtung der Schrift," in *Schrift: Kulturtechnik zwischen Auge, Hand und Maschine*, ed. Gernot Grube, Werner Kogge, and Sybille Krämer (Munich: Fink, 2005), 23–57.

15. This is, of course, a simplification of the complex layout of a medieval manuscript page (or of the one you are presently reading). But it is closer to being true of most Icelandic codices, with their unadorned *en bloc* texts, than it is of many other medieval manuscript traditions.

16. The *Glosule* to Priscian's *Institutiones grammaticae* says that voice is air formed *plectro linguae* ("by the plectrum of the tongue"), quoted in Charles Burnett, "Sound and Its Perception in the Middle Ages," in *The Second Sense: Studies in Hearing and Musical Judgement from Antiquity to the Seventeenth Century* (London: Warburg Institute, 1991), 47n42. The tongue is compared to a rudder in James 3:4–5. In *Skáldskaparmál*'s section on body-kennings, the rudder (*stýrit*) is suggested as a *nýgerving* for the tongue (Faulkes, *Skm*, 108), and this image appears several times in Christian poetry (e.g., *Leið* 37, Arn *Guðdr* 2). It does not seem to occur in early poetry. Cf. Guðrún Nordal, *Tools of Literacy: The Role of Skaldic Verse in Icelandic Textual Culture of the Twelfth and Thirteenth Centuries* (Toronto: University of Toronto Press, 2001), 250–53.

17. *hann skapaði hana, ok af Krists nafni er kristnin kölluð; vér, er kristnir erum, köllum hann höfuð várt, en vér hans limir ok liðir*. Jón Sigurðsson et al., *Edda Snorronis Sturlæi*, 2:58.

18. Paul Zumthor, *La Poésie et la voix dans la civilisation médiévale*. (Paris: Presses Universitaires de France, 1984), 11–12.

19. *er þat hljóð er stafina eina skortir til málsins. Þat gera horpunar ok enn heldr hin meiri songförin*. Heimir Pálsson, *Uppsala Edda*, 250–51. Raschellà's translation of the first sentence is slightly different ("that sound for which letters alone are not sufficient to (make) a discourse," *SGT*, 51); cf. the Latin translation in the Arnamagnæan edition, which has *cui literae solae ad sermonem desunt* (Jón Sigurðsson et al., *Edda Snorronis Sturlæi*, 2:47). The differences between W and U are not significant here.

20. Raschellà, *SGT*, 9–10.

21. Cf. Blair Sullivan, *The Classical Analogy between Speech and Music and Its Transmission in Carolingian Music Theory* (Tempe, AZ: ACMRS, 2011), viii–ix. Margaret Bent points out that musical treatises adduce a wider range of grounds for comparing music to grammar ("Grammar and Rhetoric in Late-Medieval Polyphony: Modern Metaphor or Old Simile?" in *Rhetoric Beyond Words: Delight and Persuasion in the Arts of the Middle Ages*, ed. Mary Carruthers [Cambridge: Cambridge University Press, 2010], 52–53).

22. I am grateful to Celine Vezina for discussions of these points.

23. Beuerle, *Sprachdenken*, 423–33, explores this comparison extensively.

24. Cf., e.g., *SkP* VII, xlii–xlviii; Katrina Attwood, "Christian Poetry," in *A Companion to Old Norse-Icelandic Literature and Culture*, ed. Rory McTurk (Malden: Blackwell, 2005), 56–63.

25. Sverrir Tómasson, "'Nikulám skulu vér heiðra hér ...'"

26. Martin Irvine, *The Making of Textual Culture: "Grammatica" and Literary Theory* (Cambridge: Cambridge University Press, 1994), 91.

27. *Hvat er hljóðs grein? Þrenn. Hver?* Heimir Pálsson, *Uppsala Edda*, 250–51.

28. For a brief account of Priscian's system, see Valerie J. Allen, "Broken Air," *Exemplaria* 16 (2004): 305–22. Elizabeth Eva Leach, *Sung Birds: Music, Nature, and Poetry in the Later Middle Ages* (Ithaca: Cornell University Press, 2018), Appendix 1, offers a series of useful tables summarizing the divisions and examples used by late antique and medieval explicators of *vox*.

29. As he admits: "the affinity between the two text[s] does not go far beyond their overall structure" (Raschellà, *SGT*, 110). Lucio Melazzo compares *SGT*'s discussion of sound with the grammarians listed above (Probus, Donatus, Victorinus, Diomedes, Priscian, and their commentators). He finds that none are very close and suggests that the writer of the *SGT* used a "collection of either glosses or excerpts concerned with both *vox* and *litterae*" ("The Opening of the So-Called Second Grammatical Treatise," in *Cultura Classica e Cultura Germanica Settentrionale: Atti del Convegno Internazionale di Studi, Università di Macerata, Facoltà di Lettere e Filosofia, Macerata—S. Severino Marche, 2–4 maggio 1985* [Rome: Bulzoni, 1988], 424).

30. Valeria Micillo, "Classical Tradition and Norse Tradition in the Third Grammatical Treatise," *Arkiv för nordisk filologi* 108 (1993): 74–75. W speaks of *ein grein / önnur grein / þridja grein* (the first branch / the second branch / the third branch).

31. Elizabeth Eva Leach, "Grammar and Music in the Medieval Song-School," *New Medieval Literature* 11 (2009): 198.

32. Diomedes's account is not otherwise reminiscent of the *SGT*. See Blair Sullivan, "The Unwritable Sound of Music: The Origins and Implications of Isidore's Memorial Metaphor," *Viator* 30 (1999): 1–14, for citations from the primary sources and commentary.

33. Leach, "Grammar and Music," 197.

34. Calvin Bower writes that "the parallel between *vox articulata* and *confusa* in grammatical treatises and *vox discreta* and *continua* in musical treatises is obvious, and the analogous nature associated with *vox articulata* and *discreta* is even more striking." ("*Sonus, vox, chorda, nota*: Thing, Name, and Sign in Early Medieval Theory," *Quellen und Studien zur Musiktheorie des Mittelalters* 3 [2001]: 52.)

35. Burnett, "Sound in the Middle Ages," 48. The body of medieval musical theory (much in the form of glosses on earlier works) is enormous; John Cotton is cited here as a representative, widely disseminated example. Philipp Jeserich, *Musica naturalis: Tradition und Kontinuität spekulativ-metaphysischer Musiktheorie in der Poetik des französischen Spätmittelalters* (Stuttgart: Steiner, 2008) offers a systematic account of speculative music theory as it relates to poetics; for his discussion of John Cotton, see 192–93.

36. The noise of a crowd (Gk. *thorubos*) as an instance of disordered sound goes back to antiquity; cf. Burnett, "Sound in the Middle Ages," 46–47.

37. *Nú fyrir því at maðrinn sé skynsamligum anda skrýddr ok prýddr, þá skilr hann ok greinir alla [ms. allra] luti gjörr ok glöggra en önnur kykvendi: þá neyti ok*

njóti þess láns með guði. Hjarta manns kennir alls, ok við hjartað liggr bæði barki ok vélendi, ok andblásnar æðar renna þar upp ok rætast, bæði þær æðar, er bera vind eða blástr, blóð eða ljóð; ok á annan veg horfa þær svá, at þær mætast við túnguraetr, með því hver [ms. hverr] er þarf; renn ok rödd upp fyrir hverju orði. Jón Sigurðsson et al., *Edda Snorronis Sturlæi*, 2:44–46. Possibly *bæði* qualifies the first occurrence of *æðar* rather than the second (there is no punctuation here in the manuscript).

38. Finnur Jónsson and Verner Dahlerup write that "it is impossible for it to have belonged to the actual treatise, because nothing is to be found in it [the treatise] that these words either prepare for or are logically connected to" (*Islands grammatiske litteratur*, xxv). In fact, its relationship to the Wormianus version's closing account of the role of the body in sacred song is quite clear, and discussions of the "natural instrument" are common in medieval musical theory.

39. *Nú hafa þessir lutir hljóð, sumir rödd ok sumir mál, sem sagt var.* Jón Sigurðsson et al., *Edda Snorronis Sturlæi*, 46. "As was said" is difficult to explain. Mogk suggests that the scribe was thinking of a line a little later in the treatise that introduces the third class of sounds (those made by humans).

40. Dahlerup and Finnur Jónsson, *Islands grammatiske litteratur*, 83.

41. *Minnit þarf til þess at muna atkvæði orðanna, en vitit ok skilninga til þess at hann muni at mæla þau orðin er hann vill.* Pálsson, *Uppsala Edda*, 250–51.

42. *greind með mörgum nöfnum.* Jón Sigurðsson et al., *Edda Snorronis Sturlæi*, 46. Upsaliensis has *með ymsum háttum ok nǫfnum ok kunnǫstum eru greind ymsa vega dýra nǫfnin* ("moreover by means of various methods and names and techniques the names of animal[s' voices] are distinguished"), Pálsson, *Uppsala Edda*, 250–51. So much for "concise, simple, energetic" (see n. 7 above)!

43. On the *voces animantium*, see Maurizio Bettini, *Voci: Antropologia sonora del mondo antico* (Turin: Einaudi, 2008). *SGT*'s inclusion of sea creatures (*sækykvendi*) in its list is unusual. Sea-dwelling creatures appear neither in the *voces animantium* nor in grammatical discussions of *vox*. Classical commentary taught that as fish do not breathe air, they also lack *vox*, although dolphins enjoy music, Isidore notes (*Etymologies* iii.17.3).

44. *kunnu menn skyn hvat kykvendin þikkjast benda með mǫrgum sínum látum.* Pálsson, *Uppsala Edda*, 250–51.

45. Maurizio Bettini, "Sound," in *The Encyclopedia of Ancient History*, ed. Roger S. Bagnall (Malden: Wiley-Blackwell, 2013), 6338–39.

46. "Number" (*numerositas*) is an important quality of music according to antique and medieval theorists, both in terms of consonance (harmony) and proportion (rhythm). See Jeserich, *Musica naturalis*, ch. 7, for a survey.

47. These numbers are close, but not identical, to the numbers of keys (11) and strings (20), i.e., vowels and consonants, in Upsaliensis' rectangular diagram.

48. *Þessir stafir gjöra allt mál, ok hendir málit ýmsa, svá til at jafna sem hörpustrengir gjöra hljóð, eða eru leystir luklar í simphonie, eða þá er organ gengr upp ok niðr, aptr ok framm um allan gamma, þann er með sér hefir nítján lukla ok átta*

raddir, ok nú koma til móts þessir fimm hringar stafanna, er áðr var um rætt: kallast nú hvárir við aðra stafróf ok gammi, ok taka nú hljóðstafir þar sín hljóð, ok raddarstafir rödd, málstafir málit, ok samnast til orðanna svá margra, at ekki er þess mælt í heiminum, at eigi sé þessir stafir til hafðir. Nú eru eingi þau læti eða hljóð eða raddir, at eigi muni þat allt finnast í gammanum. Jón Sigurðsson et al., *Edda Snorronis Sturlæi*, 2:56–58. Faulkes translates the phrase *hendir málit ýmsa*, which also occurs in Upsaliensis at an earlier point in the text, as "the speech reaches many" (Pálsson, *Uppsala Edda*, 250–51). This is a possible interpretation (although *ýmiss* usually means "various, by turns" rather than "many"), but it does not seem to be how the author of the Wormianus passage understood the phrase.

49. Males, "Wormianusredaktören," takes this passage as evidence that the compiler of W is also the author of the additions to *SGT* in that manuscript. He suggests that terms taken from all the grammatical treatises are used here (*hljóðstafr*, *raddarstafr*, and *málstafr*) because the compiler had recently read the whole manuscript. As the first elements of all three compounds appear in the opening of *SGT*, this assumption is unwarranted.

50. Both *hljóðstafr* and *raddarstafr* occur elsewhere in the grammatical literature, where they mean "vowel," whereas the rest of *SGT* always uses *hljóðstafr* for "vowel." *Málstafr* is used only in *SGT*, where it means "consonant." See the table in Raschellà, *SGT*, 116. *Málstafr* also appears in one of the example sentences in the *First Grammatical Treatise*, where it means "runic letter."

51. Daniel Heller-Roazen, "Le gai savoir des vers vieillis," *Comptes rendus des séances de l'Académie des Inscriptions et Belles-Lettres* 2 (2009): 575–83.

52. This position is argued in Heller-Roazen, "Le gai savoir," and exemplified in Jeserich, *Musica naturalis*. For the interrelationships of grammar and music in medieval theorizations of the two disciplines, cf. Sullivan, *Classical Analogy*; Bent, "Grammar and Rhetoric."

53. Jeserich, *Musica naturalis*, 253.

54. See James J. Murphy, *Rhetoric in the Middle Ages: A History of Rhetorical Theory from St. Augustine to the Renaissance* (Berkeley: University of California Press, 1974), 135–93, for an introduction to these works.

55. William G. Waite, "Johannes de Garlandia, Poet and Musician," *Speculum* 35 (1960): 180.

56. A copy of John of Cornwall's *Eulogium ad Alexandrum papam tertium*, written in Paris c. 1178, was already in Iceland by around 1200. So many Icelandic clerics traveled to France to study at this time that it was feared parish churches would lack personnel. See Dario Bullitta, *Niðrstigningar saga: Sources, Transmission, and Theology of the Old Norse "Descent into Hell"* (Toronto: University of Toronto Press, 2018), 87, 95.

57. Peter G. Foote, "Latin Rhetoric and Icelandic Poetry: Some Contacts," in *Aurvandilstá: Norse Studies*, ed. Michael Barnes, Hans Bekker-Nielsen, and Gerd Wolfgang Weber (Odense: Odense University Press, 1984), 249–70; see also Sverrir

Tómasson, "Nýsköpun eða endurtekning? Íslensk skaldmennt og Snorra Edda fram til 1609," in *Guðamjöður og arnarleir: Safn ritgerða um eddulist*, ed. Sverrir Tómasson (Reykjavík: Háskólaútgáfan, 1996), 18–20. Fredrik Paasche (*Norges og Islands literatur inntil utgangen av middelalderen* [Oslo: Aschehoug, 1947], 412) thinks that *Háttatal* shows echoes of the *Poetria nova*, and Frederic Amory ("Second Thoughts on *Skáldskaparmál*," *Scandinavian Studies* 62 [1990]: 331–39) suggests that the term *ofljóst* in the *Prose Edda* is a reaction to that work's notion of *clair-obscure*. Edith Marold is also convinced that the new Latin poetics exerted an influence on the *Prose Edda*, and she proposes a number of possible routes on which these influences could have traveled, from Anglo-Norman England via Bergen, from France, or through Orkney ("Zur Poetik von Háttatal und Skáldskaparmál," in *Quantitätsproblematik und Metrik: Greifswalder Symposion zur germanischen Grammatik* [Amsterdam: Rodopi, 1995], 103–24).

58. See, on these later works, ch. 15–16 of *The Cambridge History of Literary Criticism*, vol. 2: *The Middle Ages*, ed. Alastair Minnis and Ian Johnson (Cambridge: Cambridge University Press, 2008).

59. *Videtur autem rhythmus metris esse consimilis, quae est verborum modulata compositio, non metrica ratione, sed numero syllabarum ad iudicium aurium examinata, ut sunt carmina vulgarum poetarum.* Murphy, *Rhetoric*, 78.

60. Walter Haug and Benedikt Konrad Vollmann, *Frühere deutsche Literatur und lateinische Literatur in Deutschland 800–1150* (Frankfurt: Deutscher Klassiker Verlag, 1991), 1:146, 1135.

61. Jeserich, *Musica naturalis*, 259.

62. Murphy, *Rhetoric*, 209–10. Murphy concludes that "Latin *rithmus* was being discussed and probably taught at the Benedictine monastery of Monte Cassino in the 1070s and 1080s" (210).

63. Margot E. Fassler, "Accent, Meter, and Rhythm in Medieval Treatises 'De rithmis,'" *Journal of Musicology* 5 (1987): 174.

64. Treatises on *rithmica* are collected in Giovanni Mari, *I trattati medievali di ritmica latina* (Milan: Hoepli, 1899). For a discussion of the metrical characteristics of *rithmica*, see Dag Norberg, *An Introduction to the Study of Medieval Latin Versification* (Washington: Catholic University of America Press, 2012), ch. 6.

65. Jón Þorkelsson, ed., *Íslenzkar ártíðarskrár*, 2 vols. (Copenhagen: Hið íslenzka bókmenntafjelag, 1893–96), 1:146–53. There must have been an earlier office for the saint, who died in 1193, but it is completely lost.

66. Gottskálk Jensson, "The Latin Fragments of *Þorláks saga helga* and their Classical Context," in *Scandinavia and Christian Europe in the Middle Ages: Papers of the 12th International Saga Conference, Bonn/Germany, 28th July–2nd August 2003*, ed. Rudolf Simek and Judith Meurer (Bonn: Hausdruckerei der Universität Bonn, 2003), 258n5.

67. For an edition of these stanzas see *SkP* VII, 472–74.

68. Jón Sigurðsson, Jón Þorkelsson et al., eds., *Diplomatarium Islandicum. Íslenzkt fornbréfasafn*, 16 vols. (Copenhagen: Möller, 1857–1972), 4:111. The French priest

Ríkinni taught *versagjörð* at Hólar in the early twelfth century, according to *Jóns saga biskups*; Bishop Páll Jónsson at Skálholt learned the same art in England. The fourteenth-century bishop of Hólar, Lárentíus Kálfsson, was known for his ability to compose Latin prose and verse (*dikta ok versa*) as fast as other men could speak Latin (ÍF 17, 229). He taught this skill to Egill Eyjólfsson, later schoolmaster and eventually bishop at Hólar: *kunni hann sér vel í nyt at færa, varð hann framr til lærdóms ok versificator sæmiligr* (ÍF 17, 318); "the man knew well how to turn it into profit, and became a ripe scholar and a fine versifier" (Oliver Elton, trans., *The Life of Laurence, Bishop of Hólar in Iceland* [London: Rivingtons, 1890], 60).

69. Jeserich, *Musica naturalis*, 133.

70. Jeserich, *Musica naturalis*, 260.

71. "erv hendingv*m* diktvð ritin ilatinv skalldskap sem þe*t*ta." Björn Magnússon Ólsen, ed., *Den tredje og fjærde grammatiske afhandling i Snorres Edda* [. . .] (Copenhagen: Møller, 1884), 8. My translation. The editor adds *vers* ("verses") after *diktuð* ("composed"). This is the Wormianus text; ms. A (AM 748 II 4to) instead has *eru þessar hendingar víða settar í latínuskáldskap* ("these rhymes are widely found in Latin poetry").

72. "Latinv klerkar hafa *ok* þessa hending i v*er*sv*m* er þeir kalla *con*sonancía *ok* skal hin*n* sami raddar stafr v*er*a i effstv samstǫfv hvarrar tveggiv sagn*ar* sem h*er*. estas t*er*ras þessar heding*ar* er litt gæymt í norrænv*m* skalldskap, þegar er fleiri sa*m*stofv*r* erv i æin*n*i sǫgn en æín." Ólsen, *Den tredje*, 9. My translation.

73. Micillo, "Die grammatische Tradition," 226, suggests that Boethius's *De institutione musica* (c. 500 CE) influenced Óláfr's discussion of sound in the first part of the *TGT*, but the earliest instance of the distinction *TGT* draws between *musica naturalis* and *artificialis* (under the names *nattúrligt* and *listuligt*, cf. Ólsen, *Den tredje*, 2-3) seems to be Regino of Prüm's *Epistola de armonica institutione* (c. 899-915), where the term *cœlestis harmonia* ("harmony of the heavens"), used by Óláfr, and a reference to Plato shared by Óláfr also occur; cf. Jeserich, *Musica naturalis*, 176-79. The *naturalis/artificialis* distinction has a long career in musical and metrical theory, so it is possible that Óláfr took it from a source deriving from Regino. The use of the word *consonantia* to describe rhyme is found in neither Boethius nor Regino, by contrast, and is rather characteristic of treatises on *rithmica*. Finnur Jónsson takes *TGT*'s mention of *cœlestis harmonia* to be an interpolation, claiming it has nothing to do with *vox*, but discussions of *musica mundana* and *humana* are ubiquitous in speculative music theory; cf. Jeserich, *Musica naturalis*, 192.

74. *Rithmus enim est congrua diccionum ordinatio, consona, continenter sillabarum aequalitate prolata. Dicitur autem rithmus a graeco rithmos, idest numero, quoniam certa lege numerorum constituendus est. Numerus ergo in ipso notandus est, primo quidem in distinccionibus, postmodum vero in sillabis et consonanciis.* Mari, *I trattati*, 28. Translation from Jeserich, *Musica naturalis*, 260-61.

75. *Hvat er tala setningar háttanna? Þrenn. Hver? Sú er ein tala, hversu margir hættir hafa fundizk í kveðskap hǫfuðskálda. Ǫnnur tala er þat, hversu mǫrg vísuorð*

standa í einu eyrindi í hverjum hætti. In þriðia tala er sú, hversu margar samstǫfur eru settar í hvert vísuorð í hverjum hætti, Faulkes, *Hát,* 4; Faulkes, *Edda,* 165).

76. Judy Quinn, "*Eddu list*: The Emergence of Skaldic Pedagogy in Medieval Iceland," *Alvíssmál* 4 (1994): 77.

77. *Reliques, ruines ou monuments, les œuvres de ces poètes passés prennent alors valeur d'exemple: instances de résistance ou de commémoration, peut-être de résistance et de commémoration, elles témoignent du passage des langues. Feuilles éparses et desséchées, les vers rappellent ainsi d'anciennes forêts. Pourtant, il arrive aussi que les vestiges s'effacent. Avec le temps, les œuvres deviennent opaques, pour cristallines qu'elles aient été. Si l'on veut percer leur obscurité et y entrevoir l'éclat d'un premier commencement, un art particulier est alors requis.* Heller-Roazen, "Le gai savoir," 575.

78. Faulkes, *Hát,* 47; Quinn, "*Eddu list*," 29.

79. Kristján Árnason compares the *Prose Edda*'s analysis with skaldic practice and concludes that "the definition of the dróttkvætt as a syllable counting meter is a simplification, since the number of syllables in a regular dróttkvætt line can vary" (*The Rhythms of Dróttkvætt and Other Old Icelandic Metres* [Reykjavík: University of Iceland, 1991], 93).

80. On elision, see Faulkes, *Hát,* 8; on resolution, Faulkes, *Hát,* 7. Faulkes suggests in his commentary that the author of *Háttatal*'s prose does not understand the latter phenomenon (Faulkes, *Hát,* 51).

81. *Stafasetning greinir mál allt, en hljóð greinir þat at hafa samstǫfur langar eða skammar, harðar eða linar, ok þat er setning hljóðsgreina er vér kǫllum hendingar, sem hér [. . .].* Faulkes, *Hát,* 3. My translation. Faulkes translates as: "All meaning is distinguished by spelling, but sound is distinguished by having syllables long or short, hard or soft, and there is a rule of distinctions of sound that we call rhymes, as in this verse [...]" (Faulkes, *Edda,* 165). My translation is closer to that of Möbius: *Buchstaben sind es, die jedwede Rede bilden oder aus denen jedwede Rede besteht; aber der Laut unterscheidet lange od. kurze, harte od. weiche Silben und die Anwendung dieser Lautunterschiede, bez. Silben nennen wir hendingar* (Theodor H. Möbius, ed., *Háttatal,* 2 vols. [Halle an der Saale: Verlag der Buchhandlung des Waisenhauses, 1881], 2:41). For further discussion of the nuances of *málsgrein,* see Margaret Clunies Ross, *A History of Old Norse Poetry and Poetics* (Cambridge: Brewer, 2005), 154n16, and references there.

82. Marold, "Zur Poetik," 108.

83. Quinn, "*Eddu list*," 33.

84. Faulkes, *Hát,* 86–88, surveys the occurrence of *Háttatal*'s *runhent* variants elsewhere in the poetic corpus. He notes that there are no examples of *full runhenda* (the same rhyme in all eight lines) before Snorri.

85. Stephen Tranter, *Clavis Metrica: Háttatal, Háttalykill and the Irish Metrical Tracts* (Basel: Helbing & Lichtenhahn, 1997), 118.

86. Tranter, *Clavis Metrica,* 170n39.

87. See the introduction to Möbius, ed., *Háttatal*; R. C. Boer, "Om kommentaren til Háttatal," *Arkiv för nordisk filologi* 43 (1927): 262–309; Faulkes, *Hát,* x–xi;

Stephen Tranter, "Medieval Icelandic artes poeticae," in *Old Icelandic Literature and Society*, ed. Margaret Clunies Ross (Cambridge: Cambridge University Press, 2000), 154–55.

88. Cf., e.g., Boer, "Om kommentaren"; Faulkes, *Hát*, xi; Clunies Ross, *A History*, 164.

89. *Háttatal* is conventionally dated to the 1220s, after Snorri's visit to Norway in 1218–20. If the commentary is also by Snorri (an economical and generally accepted assumption, although there is no evidence for it), this would rule out the influence of the roughly contemporary *artes*. John of Garland's text is taken here simply as an instance of the style of metrical analysis practiced in treatises on *rithmica*, many of which are of considerably earlier dates, as discussed above.

90. *Item rithmus simplex alius dispondeius siue dispondaycus, alius trispondeus, alius tetraspondeus, et iste triplex: quia tetraspondeus alius bimembris, alius trimembris, alius quadrimembris.* Traugott Lawler, ed., *The Parisiana Poetria of John of Garland* (New Haven: Yale University Press, 1974), 160–61.

91. John E. Murdoch, *Album of Science: Antiquity and the Middle Ages* (New York: Scribner's Sons, 1984), is exclusively concerned with scientific diagrams, narrowly conceived ("technological" images are excluded), while John Bender and Michael Marrinan, *The Culture of Diagram* (Stanford: Stanford University Press, 2010), and Sybille Krämer, *Figuration, Anschauung, Erkenntnis: Grundlinien einer Diagrammatologie* (Berlin: Suhrkamp, 2016), focus on post-medieval material. E. C. Lutz, *Diagramm und Text: Diagrammatische Strukturen und die Dynamisierung von Wissen und Erfahrung: Überstorfer Colloquium 2012* (Wiesbaden: Reichert, 2014), presents a rare collection of nonscientific medieval diagrams. Christel Meier warns that "the state of research into diagrams is generally still unsatisfactory—also for the Middle Ages" (*die Erforschung der Diagrammatik ist—auch für das Mittelalter—insgesamt immer noch unbefriedigend*, "Die Quadratur des Kreises: Die Diagrammatik des 12. Jahrhunderts als symbolische Denk- und Darstellungsform," in *Die Bildwelt der Diagramme Joachims von Fiore*, ed. Alexander Patschovsky [Ostfildern: Thorbecke, 2003], 23).

92. Karl August Wirth, "Von mittelalterlichen Bildern und Lehrfiguren im Dienste der Schule und des Unterrichts," in *Studien zum städtischen Bildungswesen des späten Mittelalters und der frühen Neuzeit*, ed. Bernd Möller et al. (Göttingen: Vandenhoeck & Ruprecht, 1983), 256–370.

93. Olga Weijers, *Le maniement du savoir: Pratiques intellectuelles à l'époque des premières universités (XIIIe–XIVe siècles)* (Turnhout: Brepols, 1996), 224.

94. Four manuscripts with complete texts of the *Parisiana poetria* survive, plus one with only the *ars rhythmica*, and a number with only the *ars dictaminis*; see Lawler, *Parisiana poetria*, xix–xxi. For further details see Elsa Marguin-Harmon, "Tradition manuscrite de l'œuvre de Jean de Garlande," *Revue d'Histoire des Textes* 1 (2006): 189–257.

95. James Murphy comments that the *Parisiana poetria* is "so clearly a school-related text that John may have expected its users to make their own oral

252 NOTES TO PAGES 178–80

connections and summaries for their young students" ("The Arts of Poetry and Prose," in *The Cambridge History of Literary Criticism*. Volume 2, *The Middle Ages*, ed. Alastair Minnis and Ian Johnson [Cambridge: Cambridge University Press, 2008], 58).

96. *que poetis materiam ordinantibus est necessaria.* Lawler, *Parisiana poetria,* 36–37.

97. *exempla et dicta et facta autentica [. . .] omnia genera linguarum, sonorum et uocum diuersorum animancium, et ethimologias, interpretationes, differentias, secundum ordinem alphabeti.* Lawler, ed., *Parisiana poetria* (1974), 36–37.

98. For a drawing see Lawler, ed., *Parisiana poetria*, pages following 38–39.

99. See the plates in Murdoch, *Album*, 52–61, and Lutz, *Diagramm*.

100. Diagrams in music-theoretical texts concentrate on the visual representation of intervals, by means of circular arcs or winglike shapes (cf. Matteo Nanni, "Musikalische Diagramme: Spätantike und Karolingerzeit," *Das Mittelalter* 22 [2017]: 273–293). I have not found any parallel for the use of a musical instrument in a diagram depicting linguistic relationships.

101. Murdoch, *Album*, 52, 32–37, 88–97; Lutz, *Diagramm*, Pl. 142–8.

102. *Handwerk des Geistes*. Krämer, *Figuration*, 12.

103. Bernhard Siegert, *Cultural Techniques: Grids, Filters, Doors, and Other Articulations of the Real* (New York: Fordham University Press, 2015), 98–99.

104. Krämer, *Figuration*, 15–16; Siegert, *Cultural Techniques*, 98.

105. Christopher Page, "Medieval Organistrum and Symphonia: 1: A Legacy from the East?" *The Galpin Society Journal* 35 (1982): 37–44.

106. Jón Þórarinsson, *Íslensk tónlistarsaga 1000–1800* (Reykjavík: Tónlistarsafn Íslands, 2012), 155. According to *Flateyjarannáll*, Arngrímr Brandsson brought an *organum* (probably a portative organ) out to Iceland in 1329; *Lárentíus saga* claims that Arngrímr was taught on the *organum* by a master in Trondheim (ÍF 17, 414). Neither portative organ nor hurdy-gurdy survives, in Iceland, from the Middle Ages.

107. *Freiraum der Fläche*. Krämer, *Figuration*, 17.

108. Beuerle, *Sprachdenken*, 387–89.

109. *þessir stafir einir saman gera mǫrg full orð, en skamt mál gera þeir.* Heimir Pálsson, *Uppsala Edda*, 254–55. W has only the first five letters and their corresponding words.

110. "interesting at the level of linguistic curiosity [. . .] of course, quite irrelevant as far as phonology and orthography are concerned," Raschellà, *SGT*, 94.

111. *en finnsk þat svá at eigi er rangt ef stendr einu sinni fyrir málsorð hljóðstafr sá er kveðandi rœðr.* Faulkes, *Hát*, 34. Faulkes offers the translation given above as an alternative (Faulkes, *Hát*, 70). His translation of the *Edda* has "Moreover it is considered not wrong if the sound that determines the alliteration comes only once at the beginning of a word" (Faulkes, *Edda*, 213). He notes, however, that *hljóðstafr* does not otherwise refer to alliteration (elsewhere in *Hát* and *SGT* it is associated with rhyme, in fact). Although the word *kveðandi* ("poetical effect,

sound of poetry") is usually used to describe the effect of alliteration, it clearly refers to rhyme on one other occasion in *Háttatal* (*Qnnur stafasetning er sú er fylgir setning hljóðs þess er hátt gerir ok kveðandi*, Faulkes, *Hát*, 4; "There is a second aspect of the spelling that is involved in the rule of the sound which constitutes the verse-form and poetical effect," Faulkes, *Edda*, 166).

112. "*symphonia vocum disparium inter se iunctarum dulcis concentus.*" Sullivan, *Classical analogy*, ix.

113. Page, "Medieval Organistrum and Symphonia: 1."

114. *Et si flexibilem uocem non habeat, sed dissonus fuierit, et si favorem forte, etiam adiutorium doctoris obiectum amiserit, curam impendat, instrum mnusica exerceat, et sepius eis vtatur qualia sunt monocordium [et] sympho que dicitur organistrum; in organis etiam cantare laboret. In his etiam ins mentis nota a facili errare non potest, et a sono suo longius distorqueri, eo quod note per claues certas et signatas facile possunt considerari, et prompte proferri absque socio uel magistro cantore*. Christopher Page, "Medieval Organistrum and Symphonia: 2: Terminology," *Galpin Society Journal* 36 (1983): 75–76.

115. See, e.g., Christopher Page, "The Earliest English Keyboard," *Early Music* 7 (1979): fig. 2.

116. Bishop Lárentíus is noted for his loud, clear reading in church (ÍF 17, 248), as is Bishop Auðunn: *rödd hafði hann svá fagra, háfa ok skæra at öllum þótti yndi at heyra á hans song* (ÍF 17, 328); "a voice so beautiful, loud and clear that everyone was ravished to hear his chanting" (Elton, *Life of Laurence*, 65). The priest Eilífr of Gufudalr is stripped of his office for his inability to read the liturgy (ÍF 17, 273–75), and Lárentíus remonstrates with his deacons after services for their careless reading (ÍF 17, 375).

117. Cf. Beuerle, *Sprachdenken*, 389, who sees the rectangular figure as an *Arbeitstabelle* for poets.

118. *Hér segir af setningu háttalykilsins*, DG 11 fol, 44r.

119. *Ég hygg að íslenskir fræðimenn á 12. og 13. öld hafi ekki farið varhluta af þessum breytingum, en þetta efni er því miður enn órannsakað eins og margt annað sem varðar tengsl latneskrar versagerðar við íslenska*. Sverrir Tómasson, "'Nikulám skulu vér heiðra hér. . . '."

120. Cf., e.g., Andreas Heusler, *Deutsche Versgeschichte* (Berlin: De Gruyter, 1925), 1:305–6; Kristján Árnason, *Rhythms*, 85–86.

121. The *First Grammatical Treatise* (conventionally dated to the mid-twelfth century) is mainly interested in the phonology of Old Norse and its orthographic representation, as are the *SGT* and the first part of *TGT* ("*Málfræðinnar grundvǫllr*"). *Háttalykill* has no less interest in rhyme and syllable count than *Háttatal*. Forty of its eighty-two stanzas exemplify variations of one or both of these parameters.

122. The *Meistersänger* used syllable-counting to align their new works with those of the *Minnesänger*; cf. Christoph März, *Der silben zall, der chunsten grunt: Die gezählte Silbe in Sangspruch und Meistergesang*, *Zeitschrift für deutsche Philologie* 119 (2000): 73–84.

123. Katie Ann-Marie Bugyis, A. B. Kraebel, and Margot E. Fassler, eds., *Medieval Cantors and Their Craft: Music Liturgy and the Shaping of History, 800–1500* (Woodbridge: Boydell and Brewer, 2017), 2–3.

124. *Diplomatarium Islandicum*, vol. 3, 151. My translation.

125. *KLNM*, "Liturgiska funktionärer: Island" (X, cols. 616–17). Bishop Lárentíus' chaplain, Valþjófr, was *rector chori* (ÍF 17, 373) at Hólar and taught song (*kenndi [. . .] söngnám*); (ÍF 17, 381).

126. A *cantoriskápa* (cantor's robe) is mentioned in the inventory of Staður church in Kinn from 1394 (*Diplomatarium Islandicum*, III, 575).

CONCLUSION

1. Cf. *Hljóðs biðk allar* "I ask for silence from all," *Vsp* 1 (here the *vǫlva* may be speaking); *Heyrði ek segja* ("I heard said"), *Oddrgr* 1; *Þá frá ek sennu;* "Then I heard quarrelling," *Ghv* 1; the challenge to a more skillful poet in *Hym* 38 also refers to him in the singular (*hverr*).

2. The text of the *Standard Edition*. The German original has *die Schrift ist ursprünglich die Sprache des Abwesenden* ("writing is originally the speech of the absent one," *Das Unbehagen in der Kultur* [1930], 49).

3. Isidore, *Etymologies*, trans. Stephen A. Barney, et al. (Cambridge: Cambridge University Press, 2006), i.3.

4. Jacques Derrida, *La voix et le phénomène: Introduction au problème du signe dans la phénomenologie de Husserl* (Paris: Presses Universitaire de France, 1967).

5. "The Text and the Voice," *New Literary History* 16 (1984): 69; see also his *La poésie et la voix dans la civilisation médiévale* (Paris: Presses Universitaires de France, 1984).

6. Shane Butler, *The Ancient Phonograph* (New York: Zone, 2015), 13.

7. Butler, *Ancient Phonograph*, 24.

8. Butler, *Ancient Phonograph*, 83.

9. *The Linguistics of Punctuation* (Stanford, CA: Center for the Study of Language and Information, 1990), 7.

10. Eric Griffiths, *The Printed Voice of Victorian Poetry*, 2nd ed. (1989; repr., Oxford: Oxford University Press, 2018).

11. Griffiths, *Printed Voice*, 12.

12. Griffiths, *Printed Voice*, 40.

13. Ursula Peters, "'Texte vor der Literatur'? Zur Problematik neuerer Alteritätsparadigmen der Mittelalter-Philologie," *Poetica* 39 (2007): 59–88.

14. Walter Benjamin, "L'œuvre d'art à l'époque de sa reproduction méchanisée," trans. Pierre Klossowski, *Zeitschrift für Sozialforschung* 5 (1936): 40–68.

15. Jonathan Sterne, *The Audible Past: Cultural Origins of Sound Reproduction* (Durham: Duke University Press, 2003), 220–21.

16. Sterne, *Audible Past*, 218.

17. A significant caveat is that dating studies have thus far worked with edited texts. Even if students of skaldic metrics scrutinize emendations and exclude

corrupt lines from consideration, the fact that the editors used many of the same formal criteria to select readings from the pool of manuscript variants introduces an element of circularity.

18. *Bersi var rægðr við konunginn ok sagt at hann kynni ekki at yrkja né kveða þat er ei var áðr kveðit.* Oscar Johnsen and Jón Helgason, eds., *Saga Óláfs konungs hins helga*, 2 vols. (Oslo: Dybwad, 1941), 1:690.

19. ÍF 30, 130.

20. Michel Serres, *Le parasite* (Paris: Bernard Grasset, 1980). Specifically on noise, cf. Michel Serres, "Noise," *SubStance* 12 (1983): 48–60.

21. Susan A. Stewart, *Poetry and the Fate of the Senses* (Chicago: University of Chicago Press, 2002), 39.

22. Cf. my "Grettir in Ísafjörður: *Grettisfærsla* and *Grettis saga*," in *Creating the Medieval Saga: Versions, Variability and Editorial Interpretations of Old Norse Literature*, ed. J. Quinn and E. Lethbridge (Odense: University Press of Southern Denmark, 2010), 213–36. Beeke Stegmann, Tim Tangherlini, and I are currently using multispectral imaging in an attempt to reveal the illegible text on these leaves of AM 556a 4to.

23. Margaret Clunies Ross, "Conjectural Emendation in Skaldic Editing Practice, with Reference to *Egils Saga*," *Journal of English and Germanic Philology* 104 (2005): 12–30, outlines the practical difficulties, not least the ubiquity of horizontal "contamination," although she thinks that Icelandic scribes were less interventionist than their Continental colleagues.

24. I am grateful to Tarrin Wills for supplying me with these figures.

25. Case studies to date include Russell Poole, "Variants and Variability in the Text of Egill's *Hǫfuðlausn*," in *The Politics of Editing Medieval Texts: Papers Given at the Twenty-Seventh Annual Conference on Editorial Problems, University of Toronto, 1–2 November 1991*, ed. Roberta Frank (New York: AMS, 1993), 65–105; Edith Marold, "Lebendige Skaldendichtung," in *Neue Ansätze in der Mittelalterphilologie/Nye veier i middelalderfilologien. Akten der skandinavistischen Arbeitstagung in Münster vom 24.–26.10. 2002*, ed. Susanne Kramarz-Bein (Frankfurt am Main: Lang, 2005), 247–71; Christopher Abram, "Scribal Authority in Skaldic Verse: Þórbjǫrn hornklofi's *Glymdrápa*," *Arkiv för nordisk filologi* 116 (2001): 5–19. Jonna Louis-Jensen (*Kongesagastudier: Kompilationen Hulda-Hrokkinskinna* [Copenhagen: Reitzel, 1977]) takes a dimmer view of scribal variation, though her discussion of manuscript variation in the verses of the Hulda-Hrokkinskinna compilation is thought-provoking.

26. Keith Busby, *Codex and Context. Vol. 1, Reading Old French Verse Narrative in Manuscript* (Amsterdam: Rodopi, 2002).

27. Busby, *Codex and Context*, 79.

28. I presented these preliminary results at the 2020 meeting of the Modern Languages Association in Seattle.

REFERENCES

EDITIONS AND TRANSLATIONS OF PRIMARY TEXTS

Agnellus, Andreas. *The Book of Pontiffs of the Church of Ravenna*. Translated by Deborah Mauskopf Deliyannis. Washington, DC: Catholic University of America Press, 2004.

Ármann Jakobsson, ed. *Morkinskinna*. *Íslenzk fornrit*, Vol. 23. Reykjavík: Hið íslenzka fornritafélag, 2011.

Ármann Jakobsson and David Clark, trans. *The Saga of Bishop Thorlak* (London: Viking Society, 2013).

Ásdís Egilsdóttir, ed. *Biskupa sögur* II. Íslenzk fornrit 16. Reykjavik: Hið íslenzka fornritafélag, 2002.

Augustine. *Confessions*. Edited by Carolyn J. B. Hammond. Vols. 26–27, Loeb Classical Library. Cambridge, MA: Harvard University Press, 2014.

Bjarni Aðalbjarnarson, ed. *Heimskringla*, Vol. 1. Íslenzk fornrit 26. Reykjavik: Hið íslenzka fornritafélag, 1979.

Bjarni Einarsson, ed. *Ágrip af Nóregskonunga sögum—Fagrskinna*. Íslenzk fornrit 29. Reykjavík: Hið íslenzka fornritafélag, 1985.

Bjarni Vilhjálmsson, ed. *Riddarasögur*. 6 vols. Reykjavik: Íslendingasagnaútgáfan, 1982.

Cederschiöld, Gustaf, ed. *Fornsögur Suðrlanda: Magus saga jarls, Konraðs saga, Baerings saga, Flovents saga, Bevers saga*. Lund: Berling, 1884.

Clunies Ross, Margaret, ed. *Skaldic Poetry of the Scandinavian Middle Ages*. Vol. 7, *Poetry on Christian Subjects*. Turnhout: Brepols, 2007.

Clunies Ross, Margaret, ed. *Skaldic Poetry of the Scandinavian Middle Ages*. Vol. 8, *Poetry in fornaldarsögur*. Turnhout: Brepols, 2017.

Dahlerup, Verner, and Finnur Jónsson, eds. *Islands grammatiske litteratur i middelalderen. I. Den første og anden grammatiske afhandling i Snorres Edda*. Samfund til udgivelse af gammel nordisk litteratur, Volume 16. Copenhagen: Møller, 1884.

Dasent, George Webbe, trans. *The Saga of Hakon and a Fragment of the Saga of Magnus with Appendices*. London: Rerum Britannicarum Medii Ævi Scriptores, 1894.

Dronke, Ursula, ed. and trans. *The Poetic Edda*. Vol. 2, *Mythological Poems*. Oxford: Clarendon, 1997.

Dümmler, Ernst. *Monumenta Germaniae Historica*. Vol 2, *Poetae Latini Aevi Carolini* II. Berlin: Weidmann, 1894.

Einar Ól. Sveinsson, ed. *Laxdæla saga*. Íslenzk fornrit 5. Reykjavík: Hið íslenzka fornritafélag, 1934.

Elton, Oliver, trans. *The Life of Laurence, Bishop of Hólar in Iceland*. London: Rivingtons, 1890.

Faulkes, Anthony, trans. *Snorri Sturluson: Edda*. London: Everyman, 1987.
Finch, R. G., ed. and trans. *The Saga of the Volsungs [Völsunga saga]*. London: Nelson, 1965.
Finlay, Alison, trans. *Flateyjarbók*, forthcoming.
Finnbogi Guðmundsson, ed. *Orkneyinga saga*. Íslenzk fornrit 34. Reykjavík: Hið íslenzka fornritafélag, 1965.
Finnur Jónsson, ed. *Fagrskinna: Nóregs kononga tal*. Copenhagen: Møller, 1902–3.
Finnur Jónsson, ed. *Edda Snorra Sturlusonar*. Copenhagen: Gyldendal, 1931.
Finnur Jónsson, ed. *Det norsk-islandske skjaldedigtning. A. Tekst efter håndskrifterne. B: Rettet tekst med tolkning*. 4 vols., Copenhagen: Villadsen & Christiansen, 1912–15.
Firchow, Evelyn Scherabon, ed. *The Old Norse Elucidarius*. Columbia, SC: Camden House, 1992.
Gade, Kari Ellen, ed. *Skaldic Poetry of the Scandinavian Middle Ages. Vol 2, Poetry from the Kings' Sagas 2: From c. 1035 to c. 1300*. Turnhout: Brepols, 2009.
Gade, Kari Ellen, and Edith Marold, eds. *Skaldic Poetry of the Scandinavian Middle Ages. Vol. 3, Poetry from Treatises on Poetics*. Turnhout: Brepols, 2017.
Guðbjörg Kristjánsdóttir, ed. *Íslenska teiknibókin*. Reykjavik: Crymogea, 2013.
Guðbrandur Vigfússon and C. R. Unger, eds. *Flateyjarbók. En samling af norske konge-sagaer med indskudte mindre fortællinger om begivenheder i og udenfor Norge samt annaler*. 3 vols. Christiania: Malling, 1860–68.
Guðrún Ása Grímsdóttir, ed. *Biskupa sögur* III. Íslenzk fornrit 17. Reykjavik: Hið íslenzka fornritafélag, 1998.
Ibn Faḍlān, Aḥmad. "Mission to the Volga." In *Two Arabic Travel Books: Accounts of China and India and Mission to the Volga*, edited and translated by James Montgomery, 165–298. New York: NYU Press, 2015.
Ibn Rustah. "Ibn Rustah's Book of Precious Things: A Reexamination and Translation of An Early Source on The Rūs," edited and translated by William Watson. *Canadian-American Slavic Studies* 38 (2004): 289–99.
Indrebø, Gustav, ed. *Gamal Norsk Homiliebok: Cod. AM 619 4*. Norsk Historisk Kildeskriftfond, Skrifter 54. Oslo: Dybwad, 1931.
Isidore. *The Etymologies of Isidore of Seville*. Translated by Stephen A. Barney, W. J. Lewis, J. A. Beach, and Oliver Berghof. Cambridge: Cambridge University Press, 2006.
Johnsen, Oscar, and Jón Helgason, eds. *Saga Óláfs konungs hins helga*. 2 vols. Oslo: Dybwad, 1941.
Jón Sigurðsson et al., eds. *Diplomatarium Islandicum—Íslenzkt Fornbréfasafn*. 16 vols. Copenhagen: Möller, 1897.
Jón Sigurðsson and Jón Þorkelsson, eds. *Edda Snorra Sturlusonar: Edda Snorronis Sturlaei*. 3 vols. Copenhagen: Legatum Arnamagnaeanum, 1848–87.
Jón Þorkelsson, ed. *Íslenzkar ártíðarskrár*. 2 vols. Copenhagen: Hið íslenzka bókmenntafjelag, 1893–96.

Jónas Kristjánsson and Vésteinn Ólason, eds. *Eddukvæði*. 2 vols. Reykjavík: Hið íslenzka fornritafélag, 2014.

Larrington, Carolyne, trans. *The Poetic Edda*. 2nd edition. Oxford: Oxford University Press, 2014.

Liuzza, R. M., trans. *Beowulf*. Peterborough: Broadview, 2000.

Mari, Giovanni. *I trattati medievali di ritmica latina*, Memorie del Reale Istituto lombardo di scienze e lettere; Classe di lettere, scienze morali e storiche, vol. 20, fasc. 8. Milan: Hoepli, 1899.

McDougall, David, ed. *An Account of the Ancient History of the Norwegian Kings = Historia de Antiquitate Regum Norwagiensium*. London: Viking Society, 1998.

McKeon, Richard, trans., *The Basic Works of Aristotle*. New York: Random House, 1941.

Möbius, Theodor H., ed. *Háttatal*. 2 vols. Halle an der Saale: Buchhandlung des Waisenhauses, 1881.

Mogk, Eugen, ed. *Der sogenannte zweite grammatische Traktat des Snorra-Edda*. Halle: Buchdruckerei des Waisenhauses, 1889.

Noble, Thomas F. X., ed. *Charlemagne and Louis the Pious: The Lives by Einhard, Notker, Ermoldus, Thegan, and the Astronomer*. University Park: Pennsylvania State University Press, 2009.

Nordal, Sigurður, ed. *Egils saga Skallagrímssonar*. Íslenzk fornrit 2. Reykjavík: Hið íslenzka fornritafélag, 1933.

Oddr Snorrason. *Óláfs saga Tryggvasonar*. Edited by Finnur Jónsson. Copenhagen: Gad, 1932.

Ólafur Halldórsson, ed. *Saga Óláfs Tryggvasonar en mesta*. 3 vols. Copenhagen: Munksgaard, 1958–2000.

Ólsen, Björn Magnússon, ed. *Den tredje og fjærde grammatiske afhandling i Snorres Edda tilligemed de grammatisk afhandlingers prolog og to andre tillæg*. Copenhagen: Møller, 1884.

Örnólfur Thorsson, ed. *The Sagas of Icelanders: A Selection*. New York: Penguin, 2001.

Phelpstead, Carl, ed. *Historia Norwegie—A History of Norway and The Passion and Miracles of the Blessed Óláfr*. Translated by Devra Kunin. London: Viking Society, 2001.

Plato. *Timaeus and Critias*. Translated by Desmond Lee. New York: Penguin, 1977.

Quintilian. *Institutio oratoria*. Edited by Michael Winterbottom. Oxford: Clarendon, 1970.

Raschellà, Fabrizio D., ed. *The So-Called Second Grammatical Treatise: An Orthographic Pattern of Late Thirteenth-Century Icelandic*. Florence: Le Monnier, 1982.

Saxo grammaticus. *Gesta Danorum*. Edited by Karsten Friis-Jensen. Translated by Peter Fisher. 2 vols. Oxford: Clarendon, 2015.

Saxo grammaticus. *The History of the Danes*. Edited by Hilda Ellis Davidson. Translated by Peter Fisher. 2 vols. Cambridge: Brewer, 1979–80.

Sigurbjörn Einarsson, Guðrún Kvaran, and Gunnlaugur Ingólfsson, eds. *Íslensk hómilíubók*. Reykjavík: Hið íslenska bókmenntafélag, 1993.
Snorri Sturluson. *Edda. Háttatal*. 2nd edition. Edited by Anthony Faulkes. London: Viking Society, 2007.
Snorri Sturluson. *Edda: Prologue and Gylfaginning*. Edited by Anthony Faulkes. Oxford: Clarendon, 1982.
Snorri Sturluson. *Edda: Skáldskaparmál*. Edited by Anthony Faulkes. London: Viking Society, 1998.
Snorri Sturluson. *Heimskringla*. 3 vols. Translated by Anthony Faulkes and Alison Finlay. London: Viking Society, 2011.
Snorri Sturluson. *The Uppsala Edda: DG 11 4to*. Edited by Heimir Pálsson. Translated by Anthony Faulkes. London: Viking Society, 2012.
Storm, Gustav, ed. *Islandske Annaler indtil 1578*. Christiania: Norske historiske kildeskriftfond, 1888.
Turville-Petre, Gabriel, ed. and trans. *Scaldic Poetry*. Oxford: Clarendon, 1976.
Unger, C. R., ed. *Stjórn*. Christiania: Feilberg & Landmark, 1862.
———. *Mariu saga. Legender om jomfru Maria og hendes jertegn*. 2 vols. Christiania: Brögger & Christie, 1871.
Uppsala Universitet. "Samnordisk runtextdatabas." Accessed September 25, 2020. http://www.nordiska.uu.se/forskn/samnord.htm.
Van Arkel-de Leeuw van Weenen, Andrea, ed. *The Icelandic Homily Book: Perg. 15 4° in the Royal Library, Stockholm*. Reykjavík: Stofnun Árna Magnússonar, 1993.
Whaley, Diana, ed. *Skaldic Poetry of the Scandinavian Middle Ages. Volume 1, Poetry from the Kings' Sagas 1: From Mythical Times to c. 1035*. Turnhout: Brepols, 2012.
Wills, Tarrin, Kari Ellen Gade, and Margaret Clunies Ross, eds. *Skaldic Poetry of the Scandinavian Middle Ages. Vol. 5, Poetry in Sagas of Icelanders*. Turnhout: Brepols, forthcoming.
Þorleifur Hauksson, ed. *Sverris saga*. Íslenzk fornrit 30. Reykjavik: Hið íslenzka fornritafélag, 2007.

SECONDARY SOURCES

Abram, Christopher. "Scribal Authority in Skaldic Verse: Þórbjǫrn hornklofi's *Glymdrápa*." *Arkiv för nordisk filologi* 116 (2001): 5–19.
———. "Hel in Early Norse Poetry." *Viking and Medieval Scandinavia* 2 (2006): 1–29.
———. *Myths of the Pagan North: The Gods of the Norsemen*. London: Continuum, 2011.
Aðalheiður Guðmundsdóttir. "Saga Motifs on Gotland Picture Stones: The Case of Hildr Högnadóttir." In *Gotland's Picture Stones: Bearers of an Enigmatic Legacy*, edited by Maria Herlin Karnell, 59–72. Visby: Gotlands Museum, 2012.
Adolf Friðriksson and Orri Vésteinsson. "Landscapes of Burial: Contrasting the Pagan and Christian Paradigms of Burial in Viking Age and Medieval Scandinavia." *Archaeologia Islandica* 9 (2011): 50–64.

Akbari, Suzanne Conklin. *Seeing through the Veil: Optical Theory and Medieval Allegory*. Toronto: University of Toronto Press, 2004.
Åkerlund, Walter. *Studier över Ynglingatal*. Lund: Gleerup, 1939.
Alexander, Jonathan J. G. *Medieval Illuminators and Their Methods of Work*. New Haven: Yale University Press, 1992.
Allen, J. "Broken Air." *Exemplaria* 16 (2004): 305–22.
Amory, Frederic. "Second Thoughts on *Skáldskaparmál*." *Scandinavian Studies* 62 (1990): 331–339.
Andrén, Anders. "The Significance of Places: The Christianization of Scandinavia from a Spatial Point of View." *World Archaeology* 45 (2013): 27–45.
Ármann Jakobsson. "The Trollish Acts of Þorgrímr the Witch: The Meanings of *troll* and *ergi* in Medieval Iceland." *Saga-Book* 32 (2008): 39–68.
Arrhenius, Birgit. "Vendelzeit." In *Reallexikon der germanischen Altertumskunde*, Vol. 32, edited by Heinrich Beck, Dieter Geuenich and Heiko Steuer, 132–33. Berlin: De Gruyter, 1973–2008.
Arwidsson, Greta. *Valsgärde 7: Die Gräberfunde von Välsgarde III*. Uppsala: Uppsala University Museum, 1977.
Ásgeir Blöndal Magnússon. *Íslensk orðsifjabók*. Reykjavík: Orðabók Háskólans, 1989.
Asmuth, Bernhard. "Reim." In *Historisches Wörterbuch der Rhetorik*, edited by Gert Ueding, cols. 115–1144. Tübingen: Niemeyer, 2005.
Assmann, Aleida. "Was sind kulturelle Texte?" In *Literaturkanon—Medienereignis—kultureller Text: Formen interkultureller Kommunikation und Übersetzung*, edited by Andreas Poltermann, 232–44. Berlin: Schmidt, 1995.
———. *Erinnerungsräume: Formen und Wandlungen des kulturellen Gedächtnisses*. Munich: Beck, 2006.
Assmann, Jan. *Das kulturelle Gedächtnis: Schrift, Erinnerung und politische Identität in frühen Hochkulturen*. Munich: Beck, 1992.
———. "Form as a Mnemonic Device: Cultural Texts and Cultural Memory." In *Performing the Gospel: Orality, Memory, and Mark*, edited by Richard A. Horsely, Jonathan A. Draper, and John Miles Foley, 67–82. Minneapolis: Fortress, 2006.
Attali, Jacques. *Noise: The Political Economy of Music*, translated by Brian Massumi. Minneapolis: University of Minnesota Press, 1985.
Attwood, Katrina. "Christian Poetry." In *A Companion to Old Norse-Icelandic Literature and Culture*, edited by Rory McTurk, 56–63. Malden: Blackwell, 2005.
Auerbach, Erich. *Scenes from the Drama of European Literature*. Minneapolis: University of Minnesota Press, 1984.
Baetke, Walter. *Die Götterlehre der Snorra-Edda*. Berlin: Akademie, 1950.
———. *Yngvi und die Ynglinger: Eine quellenkritische Untersuchung über das nordische 'Sakralkönigtum.'* Berlin: Akademie, 1964.
Bagge, Sverre. *From Gang Leader to the Lord's Anointed: Kingship in Sverris saga and Hákonar saga Hákonarsonar*. Odense: Odense University Press, 1996.

Barnes, Michael P. "Rök-steinen—noen runologiske og språklige overveielser." *Maal og minne* 99 (2007): 120–32.
Baxandall, Michael. *Painting and Experience in Fifteenth-Century Italy: A Primer in the Social History of Pictorial Style.* Oxford: Oxford University Press, 1988.
Beck, Heinrich. *Snorri Sturlusons Sicht der paganen Vorzeit: (Gylfaginning).* Göttingen: Vandenhoeck & Ruprecht, 1994.
———. "Snorri Sturlusons Mythologie: Euhemerismus oder Analogie?" In *Snorri Sturluson: Historiker, Dichter, Politiker,* edited by Heinrich Beck, Wilhelm Heizmann, and Jan Alexander van Nahl, 1–21. Berlin: De Gruyter, 2014.
Belting, Hans. *Likeness and Presence: A History of the Image before the Era of Art.* Chicago: University of Chicago Press, 1994.
———. "Image, Medium, Body: A New Approach." *Critical Inquiry* 31 (2005): 302–319.
Bender, John, and Michael Marrinan. *The Culture of Diagram.* Stanford: Stanford University Press, 2010.
Benjamin, Walter. "L'œuvre d'art à l'époque de sa reproduction méchanisée." Translated by Pierre Klossowski. *Zeitschrift für Sozialforschung* 5 (1936): 40–68.
Bennström, Greger. "Ett samisk offerfynd i Falun?" *Dalarnas hembygdsbok* 76 (2006): 57–66.
Bent, Margaret. "Grammar and Rhetoric in Late-Medieval Polyphony: Modern Metaphor or Old Simile?" In *Rhetoric Beyond Words: Delight and Persuasion in the Arts of the Middle Ages,* edited by Mary Carruthers, 52–71. Cambridge: Cambridge University Press, 2010.
Berend, Nora. *Christianization and the Rise of Christian Monarchy: Scandinavia, Central Europe and Rus' c. 900–1200.* Cambridge: Cambridge University Press, 2007.
Bergsveinn Birgisson. "Inn i skaldens sinn: Kognitiv, estetiske og historiske skatter i den skaldediktingen." PhD diss., University of Bergen, 2008.
———. "The Old Norse Kenning as a Mnemonic Figure." In *The Making of Memory in the Middle Ages.* Edited by Lucie Doležalová, 199–214. Leiden: Brill, 2009.
Bersu, Gerhard, and David M. Wilson. *Three Viking Graves in the Isle of Man.* London: Society for Medieval Archaeology, 1966.
Bertell, Mats. *Tor och den nordiska åskan: föreställningar kring världsaxeln.* Edsbruk: Akademitryck, 2003.
Bettini, Maurizio. *Voci: Antropologia sonora del mondo antico.* Turin: Einaudi, 2008.
———. "Sound." In *The Encyclopedia of Ancient History,* edited by Roger S. Bagnall, 6338–39. Malden: Wiley-Blackwell, 2013.
Beuerle, Angela. *Sprachdenken im Mittelalter: Ein Vergleich mit der Moderne.* Berlin: De Gruyter, 2010.
Biggam, Carole Patricia. *Blue in Old English: An Interdisciplinary Semantic Study.* Amsterdam: Rodopi, 1997.
Blair, John. "A Saint for Every Minster? Local Cults in Anglo-Saxon England." In *Local Saints and Local Churches in the Early Medieval West,* edited by Alan Thacker and Richard Sharpe, 455–94. Oxford: Oxford University Press, 2002.

———. *The Church in Anglo-Saxon Society*. Oxford: Oxford University Press, 2005.
Blankenfeldt, Ruth. "Fünfzig Jahre nach Joachim Werner: Überlegungen zur kaiserzeitlichen Kunst." In *Bilddenkmäler zur germanischen Götter-und Heldensage*, edited by Sigmund Oehrl and Wilhelm Heizmann, 9–82. Berlin: De Gruyter, 2015.
Blumenberg, Hans. "Light as a Metaphor for the Truth." In *Modernity and the Hegemony of Vision*, edited by David Michael Kleinberg-Levin, 46–47. Berkeley: University of California Press, 1993.
———. *Paradigms for a Metaphorology*. Translated by Robert Savage. Ithaca, N.Y: Cornell University Press, 2010.
Boer, R. C. "Om kommentaren til Háttatal." *Arkiv för nordisk filologi* 43 (1927): 262–309.
Bolinger, Dwight L. "Rime, Assonance, and Morpheme Analysis." *Word* 6 (1950): 117–36.
Bollaert, John. "Runstenar längs vägen: En undersökning av samband mellan runstenarnas placering och utformning." Master's thesis, Uppsala University, 2016.
Bower, Calvin M. "*Sonus, vox, chorda, nota*: Thing, Name, and Sign in Early Medieval Theory." *Quellen und Studien zur Musiktheorie des Mittelalters* 3 (2001): 47–61.
Bradley, Richard. *A Geography of Offerings: Deposits of Valuables in the Landscapes of Ancient Europe*. Philadelphia: Oxbow, 2017.
Braunmüller, Kurt. "Der sog. zweite grammatische Traktat: Ein verkanntes Zeugnis altisländischer Sprachanalyse." In *Beiträge zur skandinavistischen Linguistik*, 210–26. Oslo: Novus, 1995.
Bredekamp, Horst. *Der schwimmende Souverän. Karl der Grosse und die Bildpolitik des Körpers: eine Studie zum schematischen Bildakt*. Berlin: Wagenbach, 2014.
Brégaint, David. *Vox Regis: Royal Communication in High Medieval Norway*. Leiden: Brill, 2016.
Brenner, Oscar. "Der traktat der Upsala-Edda '*af setningu hattalykils*.'" *Zeitschrift für deutsche Philologie* 21 (1889): 272–80.
Brink, Stefan. "Political and Social Structures in Early Scandinavia: A Settlement-Historical Pre-Study of the Central Place." *Tor* 28 (1996): 235–82.
———. "Forntida vägar: Vägar ock vägmiljöer." *Bebyggelsehistorisk tidskrift* 39 (2000): 23–64.
———. "Law and Legal Customs in Viking Age Scandinavia." In *The Scandinavians from the Vendel Period to the Tenth Century: An Ethnographic Perspective*, edited by Judith Jesch, 87–117. Woodbridge: Boydell, 2002.
———. "I.12: Law." In *Handbook of Pre-Modern Nordic Memory Studies: Interdisciplinary Approaches*. Edited by Jürg Glauser, Pernille Hermann, and Stephen A. Mitchell, 185–97. Berlin: De Gruyter, 2018.
Brogan, T. V. F., S. Cushman, and K. Chang. "Rhyme." In *The Princeton Encyclopedia of Poetry and Poetics*, 4th ed., edited by Roland Greene, Stephen Cushman, Clare Cavanagh, Jahan Ramazani, and Raul Rouzer, 182–92. Princeton: Princeton University Press, 2012.

Brown, Michelle P. *The Book and the Transformation of Britain c. 550–1050*. London: British Library, 2011.
Brown, Peter. *The Cult of the Saints: Its Rise and Function in Latin Christianity*. Chicago: University of Chicago Press, 1981.
Bugge, Sophus. "Naar og hvor er Ynglingatal forfattet?" In *Bidrag til den ældste skaldedigtnings historie*. Christiania: Aschehoug, 1894.
———. *Der Runenstein von Rök in Östergötland, Schweden*. Stockholm: Ivar Hæggströms Boktryckeri, 1910.
Bugyis, Katie Ann-Marie, A. B. Kraebel, and Margot E. Fassler, eds. *Medieval Cantors and Their Craft: Music Liturgy and the Shaping of History, 800–1500*. Woodbridge: Boydell and Brewer, 2017.
Bullitta, Dario. *Niðrstigningar saga: Sources, Transmission, and Theology of the Old Norse "Descent into Hell."* Toronto: University of Toronto Press, 2018.
Burnett, Charles. "Sound and Its Perception in the Middle Ages." In *The Second Sense: Studies in Hearing and Musical Judgement from Antiquity to the Seventeenth Century*, edited by Charles Burnett, Michael Fend, and Penelope Gouk, 43–69. London: Warburg Institute, 1991.
Busby, Keith. *Codex and Context*. Vol. 1, *Reading Old French Verse Narrative in Manuscript*. Amsterdam: Rodopi, 2002.
Butler, Shane. *The Ancient Phonograph*. New York: Zone, 2015.
Calkins, Robert G. *Illuminated Books of the Middle Ages*. Ithaca: Cornell University Press, 1983.
Camille, Michael. "Before the Gaze: The Internal Senses and Late Medieval Practices of Seeing." In *Visuality before and beyond the Renaissance*, edited by Robert S. Nelson, 197–223. Cambridge: Cambridge University Press, 2000.
Capelle, Torsten. *Anthromorphe Holzidolen in Mittel- und Nordeuropa*. Stockholm: Almquist & Wiksell, 1995.
Carruthers, Mary. *The Craft of Thought: Meditation, Rhetoric, and the Making of Images*. Cambridge: Cambridge University Press, 2000.
———. *The Book of Memory: A Study of Memory in Medieval Culture*. 2nd ed. Cambridge: Cambridge University Press, 2008.
Carstens, Lydia. "Die dreizehn Geschichten auf dem Runenstein von Rök." In *Die Faszination des Verborgenen und seine Entschlüsselung—Rāði saR kunni*, edited by Jana Krüger, Vivian Busch, Katharina Seidel, Christiane Zimmermann, and Ute Zimmermann, 65–84. Berlin: De Gruyter, 2017.
Casey, Edward. *Getting Back into Place: Toward a Renewed Understanding of the Place-World*. Bloomington: Indiana University Press, 2009.
Cazelles, Brigitte. *Soundscape in Early French Literature*. Tempe, AZ: ACMRS Press, 2005.
Chappell, Sophie Grace. *Knowing What to Do: Imagination, Virtue, and Platonism in Ethics*. Oxford: Oxford University Press, 2014.
Christensen, Kirsten, Andres S. Dobat, and Per Mandrup. "Trelleborgskjoldet." *Skalk* 5 (2009): 3–7.

Christensen, Tom. "A Silver Figurine from Lejre." *Danish Journal of Archaeology* 2 (2013): 65–78.
Clanchy, Michael T. *From Memory to Written Record: England 1066–1307*. 3rd ed. Malden: Wiley-Blackwell, 2012.
Clark, Stuart. *Vanities of the Eye: Vision in Early Modern European Culture*. Oxford: Oxford University Press, 2007.
Cleasby, Richard, Gudbrand Vigfusson, and W. A. Craigie. *Icelandic-English Dictionary*. 2nd ed. Oxford: Clarendon Press, 1957.
Clunies Ross, Margaret. "Hildr's Ring: A Problem in *Ragnarsdrápa*." *Mediaeval Scandinavia* 6 (1973): 74–92.
———. "*Fimm líkamsins vit*: The Development of a New Lexical Set in Early Norse Christian Literature." *Arkiv för nordisk filologi* 102 (1987): 197–206.
———. *Skáldskaparmál: Snorri Sturluson's 'ars poetica' and Medieval Theories of Language*. Odense: Odense University Press, 1987.
———. *Prolonged Echoes: Old Norse Myths in Medieval Northern Society*, vol. 1, *The Myths*. Odense: Odense University Press, 1994.
———. "Snorri's *Edda* as Narrative." In *Snorri Sturluson: Beiträge zu Werk und Rezeption*, edited by Hans Fix, 9–21. Berlin: De Gruyter, 1998.
———. "Skald Sagas as a Genre." In *Skaldsagas: Text, Vocation, and Desire in the Icelandic Sagas of Poets*, edited by Russell G. Poole, 25–49. Berlin: De Gruyter, 2000.
———. *A History of Old Norse Poetry and Poetics*. Cambridge: D. S. Brewer, 2005.
———. "Conjectural Emendation in Skaldic Editing Practice, with Reference to *Egils Saga*." *JEGP* 104 (2005): 12–30.
———. "The Cultural Poetics of the Skaldic Ekphrasis Poem in Medieval Norway and Iceland." In *Medieval Cultural Studies*, edited by H. Fulton, R. Evans, and D. Matthews, 227–40. Cardiff: University of Wales Press, 2006.
———. "Stylistic and Generic Identifiers of the Old Norse Skaldic Ekphrasis." *Viking and Medieval Scandinavia* 3 (2007): 159–92.
———. "Royal Ideology in Early Scandinavia: A Theory Versus the Texts." *Journal of English and Germanic Philology* 113 (2014): 18–33.
———. "The Autographical Turn in Late Medieval Icelandic Poetry." In *Skandinavische Schriftlandschaften: Vänbok till Jürg Glauser*, edited by Klaus Müller-Wille, Kate Heslop, Anna Katharina Richter, and Lukas Rösli, 150–154. Tübingen: Narr, 2017.
Coupland, Simon. "From Poachers to Gamekeepers: Scandinavian Warlords and Carolingian Kings." *Early Medieval Europe* 7 (1998): 85–114.
———. "Holy Ground? The Plundering and Burning of Churches by Vikings and Franks in the Ninth Century." *Viator* 45 (2014): 73–98.
Cubitt, Catherine. "Memory and Narrative in the Cult of Early Anglo-Saxon Saints." In *The Uses of the Past in the Early Middle Ages*, edited by Yitzhak Hen and Matthew Innes, 29–66. Cambridge: Cambridge University Press, 2000.

———. "Sites and Sanctity: Revisiting the Cult of Murdered and Martyred Anglo-Saxon Royal Saints." *Early Medieval Europe* 9 (2000): 53–83.
Culler, Jonathan. *On Puns: The Foundation of Letters*. Oxford: Blackwell, 1988.
Cumont, M. Franz. "Fragment de bouclier portant une liste d'étapes." *Syria* 6 (1925): 1–15.
Curta, Florin. "Colour Perception, Dyestuffs, and Colour Terms in Twelfth-Century French Literature," *Medium Ævum* 73 (2004): 43–65.
Davidson, Hilda Ellis. *The Road to Hel: A Study of the Conception of the Dead in Old Norse Literature*. Cambridge: Cambridge University Press, 1943.
De Boor, Helmut. "Die religiöse Sprache der Vǫluspá und verwandter Denkmäler." *Deutsche Islandforschung* 1 (1930): 68–142.
Debray, Régis. "What Is Mediology?" Translated by Martin Irvine. *Le monde diplomatique* 8 (1999): 32.
———. *Transmitting Culture*. Translated by Eric Rauth. New York: Columbia University Press, 2000.
De Grazia, Margarete. "Homonyms before and after Lexical Standardization." *Jahrbuch/Deutsche Shakespeare-Gesellschaft West* (1990): 143–56.
Denery, Dallas G. *Seeing and Being Seen in the Later Medieval World: Optics, Theology and Religious Life*. Cambridge: Cambridge University Press, 2005.
Derrida, Jacques. *La voix et le phénomène: Introduction au problème du signe dans la phénomenologie de Husserl*. Paris: Presses Universitaire de France, 1967.
Deutsch, Diana. *Musical Illusions and Phantom Words: How Music and Speech Unlock Mysteries of the Brain*. Oxford: Oxford University Press, 2019.
———. "Speech to Song Illusion." Accessed September 28, 2019. http://deutsch.ucsd.edu/psychology/pages.php?i=212.
De Vries, Jan. *Altnordisches etymologisches Wörterbuch*. 2nd ed. Leiden: Brill, 1977.
Dickinson, Tania M. "Symbols of Protection: The Significance of Animal-Ornamented Shields in Early Anglo-Saxon England." *Medieval Archaeology* 49 (2005): 109–63.
Dobat, Andres Siegfried. "The King and His Cult: The Axe-Hammer from Sutton Hoo and its Implications for the Concept of Sacral Leadership in Early Medieval Europe." *Antiquity* 80 (2006): 880–93.
Donaldson-Evans, Lance K. *Love's Fatal Glance: A Study of Eye Imagery in the Poets of the École Lyonnaise*. University, MS: Romance Monographs, 1980.
Downing, John D. H., Denis McQuail, Philip Schlesinger, and Ellen Wartella, eds., *The SAGE Handbook of Media Studies*. Thousand Oaks: Sage Publications, 2004.
Duczko, Władysław. *Arkeologi och miljögeologi i Gamla Uppsala*. 2 vols. Uppsala: Societas Archaeologica Upsaliensis, 1993 & 1996.
Dumville, David. "Kingship, Genealogies and Regnal Lists." In *Early Medieval Kingship*, edited by Peter H. Sawyer and Ian N. Wood, 72–104. Leeds: School of History, University of Leeds, 1977.
Düwel, Klaus. *Runenkunde*. Stuttgart: Metzler, 2008.

Düwel, Klaus and Sigmund Oehrl. "Überlegungen zur Bild- und Runenritzung von Aspö in Södermanland (Sö 175)." In *Die Faszination des Verborgenen und seine Entschlüsselung—Rāđi saR kunni*, edited by Jana Krüger et al., 95–107. Berlin: De Gruyter, 2017.

Eichhorn-Mulligan, Amy C. *A Landscape of Words: Ireland, Britain and the Poetics of Space, 700–1250*. Manchester: Manchester University Press, 2019.

Eitrem, S. "König Aun in Upsala und Kronos." In *Festschrift til Hjalmar Falk*, 245–61. Oslo: Aschehoug, 1927.

Elín Ósk Hreiðarsdóttir and Howell Roberts. "Þögnin rofin: Fyrstu niðurstöður fornleifarannsókna á eyðibyggð á Þegjandadal." *Árbók Þingeyinga* (2008): 5–24.

Elmevik, L. "Fornisl. *við taur, á austanverðum Taurinum* och det svenska ortnamnet Södertörn." In *Festschrift für Oskar Bandle zum 60. Geburtstag am 11. Januar 1986*, edited by Hans-Peter Naumann, 11–17. Basel: Helbing & Lichtenhahn, 1986.

Eriksen, Marianne Hem. "Commemorating Dwelling: The Death and Burial of Houses in Iron and Viking Age Scandinavia." *European Journal of Archaeology* 19 (2016): 477–96.

Eshleman, Lori Elaine. "Monumental Stones of Gotland." PhD diss., University of Minnesota, 1983.

Etheridge, Christian. "The Evidence for Islamic Scientific Works in Medieval Iceland." In *Fear and Loathing in the North: Jews and Muslims in Medieval Scandinavia and the Baltic Region*, edited by Cordelia Heß and Jonathan Adams, 49–74. Berlin: De Gruyter, 2015.

Evans, David A. H. "King Agni: Myth, History or Legend?" In *Specvlvm Norroenvm: Norse Studies in Memory of Gabriel Turville-Petre*, edited by Ursula Dronke, Guðrún P. Helgadóttir, Gerd Wolfgang Weber, and Hans Bekker-Nielsen, 89–105. Odense: Odense University Press, 1981.

Fabech, Charlotte. "Society and Landscape: From Collective Manifestations to Ceremonies of a New Ruling Class." In *Iconologia Sacra, Mythos, Bildkunst und Dichtung in der Religions- und Sozialgeschichte Alteuropas: Festschrift für Karl Hauck*, edited by Hagen Keller and Nikolaus Staubach, 132–143. Berlin: De Gruyter, 1994.

Fassler, Margot E. "Accent, Meter, and Rhythm in Medieval Treatises 'De rithmis.'" *Journal of Musicology* 5 (1987): 164–190.

Felski, Rita. *Uses of Literature*. Malden, MA: Blackwell, 2008.

Fentress, James, and Chris Wickham. *Social Memory*. Oxford: Blackwell, 1992.

Fidjestøl, Bjarne. *Det norrøne fyrstediktet*. Øvre Ervik: Alvheim & Eide, 1982.

———. "Arnórr Þórðarson: Skald of the Orkney Jarls." In *The Northern and Western Isles in the Viking World: Survival, Continuity and Change*, edited by Alexander Fenton and Hermann Pálsson, 239–257. Edinburgh: Donald, 1984.

———. "'Have You Heard a Poem Worth More?' A Note on the Economic Background of Early Skaldic Praise-Poetry." In *Selected Papers*, translated by Peter

Foote, edited by Odd Einar Haugen and Else Mundal, 117–32. Odense: Odense University Press, 1997.

———. "'Out They Will Look, The Lovely Ladies': Views of Women in Norse Literature." In *Selected Papers*, translated by Peter Foote, edited by Odd Einar Haugen and Else Mundal, 333–342. Odense: Odense University Press, 1997.

Finnegan, Ruth. *Literacy and Orality: Studies in the Technology of Communication*. Oxford: Blackwell, 1988.

Finlay, Alison. "Risking One's Head: *Vafþrúðnismál* and the Mythic Power of Poetry." In *Myth, Legends and Heroes: Essays on Old Norse and Old English Literature in Honour of John McKinnell*, edited by Daniel Anlezark, 91–108. Toronto: University of Toronto Press, 2011.

Finnur Jónsson. "De ældste skjalde og deres kvad." *Arkiv för nordisk filologi* 13 (1897): 363–69.

———. *Den oldnorske og oldislandske litteraturs historie*. 3 vols. Copenhagen: Gad, 1920.

———. *Lexicon Poeticum Antiquæ Linguæ Septentrionalis. Ordbog over det norsk-islandske skjaldesprog*. Copenhagen: Møller, 1931.

Foote, Peter G. "Latin Rhetoric and Icelandic Poetry: Some Contacts." In *Aurvandilstá: Norse Studies*, edited by Michael Barnes, Hans Bekker-Nielsen, and Gerd Wolfgang Weber, 249–70. Odense: Odense University Press, 1984.

Foster, Hal, ed. *Vision and Visuality*. Seattle: Bay Press, 1988.

Frank, Roberta. *Old Norse Court Poetry: The Dróttkvætt Stanza*. Ithaca: Cornell University Press, 1978.

———. "Why Skalds Address Women." In *Poetry in the Scandinavian Middle Ages: The Seventh International Saga Conference (12° Congresso Internazionale di Studi sull'Alto Medioevo), Spoleto*, edited by Teresa Paroli, 67–83. Spoleto: Presso la Sede del Centro Studi, 1988.

———. "The Lay of the Land in Skaldic Praise Poetry." In *Myth in Early Northwest Europe*, edited by Stephen O. Glosecki, 175–96. Turnhout: Brepols, 2007.

———. "The Storied Verse of Sturla Þórðarson." In *Sturla Þórðarson: Skald, Chieftain, and Lawman*, edited by Jón Viðar Sigurðsson and Sverrir Jakobsson, 133–47. Leiden: Brill, 2017.

Freud, Sigmund. *Das Unbehagen in der Kultur*. Vienna: Internationaler Psychoanalytischer Verlag, 1930.

Fuglesang, Signe Horn. "Billedbeskrivende dikt." In *Ting og Tekst*, edited by Else Mundal and Anne Ågotnes, 119–142. Bergen: Bryggens Museum, 2002.

———. "Ekphrasis and Surviving Imagery in Viking Scandinavia." *Viking and Medieval Scandinavia* 3 (2007): 193–224.

Fulk, Robert D. "Eddic Metres." In *A Handbook to Eddic Poetry: Myths and Legends of Early Scandinavia*, edited by Carolyne Larrington, Judy Quinn, and Brittany Schorn, 252–270. Cambridge: Cambridge University Press, 2016.

Gade, Kari Ellen. "*Fang* and *fall*: Two Skaldic *termini technici*." *Journal of English and Germanic Philology* 90 (1991): 361–74.

———. *The Structure of Old Norse Dróttkvætt Poetry*. Ithaca: Cornell University Press, 1995.

———. "History of Old Nordic Metrics." In *The Nordic Languages: An International Handbook of the History of the North Germanic Languages*. 2 vols, edited by Oskar Bandle, Kurt Braunmüller, Lennart Elmevik, Ernst Hakon Jahr, Gun Widmark, Hans-Peter Naumann, Allan Karker, and Ulf Telemann, 1: 856–870. Berlin: De Gruyter, 2002.

———. "The Syntax of Old Norse *kviðuháttr* Meter." *Journal of Germanic Linguistics* 17 (2005): 155–81.

———. "The term *rekit* in *Háttalykill* and *Háttatal*." In *Die Faszination des Verborgenen und seine Entschlüsselung—Rāði saR kunni*, edited by Jana Krüger et al., 109–120. Berlin: De Gruyter, 2017.

Garipzanov, Ildar H. "Frontier Identities: The Carolingian Frontier and the *gens Danorum*." In *Franks, Northmen and Slavs: Identities and State Formation in Early Medieval Europe*, edited by Patrick J. Geary, Ildar H. Garipzanov, and Przemysław Urbańcyzk, 113–43. Turnhout: Brepols, 2008.

———. *The Symbolic Language of Royal Authority in the Carolingian World (c. 751–877)*. Leiden: Brill, 2008.

Gayk, Shannon. *Image, Text, and Religious Reform in Fifteenth-Century England*. Cambridge: Cambridge University Press, 2010.

Gazzoli, Paul. "*Denemearc, Tanmaurk ala*, and *Confinia nordmannorum*: The *Annales regni Francorum* and the Origins of Denmark." *Viking and Medieval Scandinavia* 7 (2011): 29–44.

Gell, Alfred. "The Technology of Enchantment and the Enchantment of Technology." In *Anthropology, Art, and Aesthetics*, edited by Jeremy Coote and Anthony Shelton, 40–63. Oxford: Clarendon, 1992.

Geoghegan, Bernard Dionysus. "Untimely Meditations: On Two Recent Contributions to 'German Media Theory.'" *Paragraph* 37 (2014): 419–25.

Gísli Brynjúlfsson. *Brage den Gamles Kvad om Ragnar Lodbrogs Skjold*. Copenhagen: Det kongelige nordiske Oldskrift-selskab, 1860.

Gísli Sigurðsson. "Óláfr Þórdarson hvítaskáld and Oral Poetry in the West of Iceland c.1250: The Evidence of References to Poetry in *The Third Grammatical Treatise*." In *Old Icelandic Literature and Society*, edited by Margaret Clunies Ross, 96–115. Cambridge: Cambridge University Press, 2009.

Glauser, Jürg. *Skandinavische Literaturgeschichte*. Stuttgart: Metzler, 2006.

———. "Sensory Deceptions: Concepts of Mediality in the Prose Edda." In *Á austrvega: Saga and East Scandinavia: Preprint Papers of the 14th International Saga Conference*, edited by Agneta Ney, Henrik Williams, and Fredrik Charpentier, 296–302. Gävle: Gävle University Press, 2009.

———. "Zwischen Kohärenz und Fragment. Zur Poetik des 'Verschlungenen' in der altnordischen Skaldik." In *Lyrische Kohärenz im Mittelalter. Spielräume—Kriterien—Modellbildung*, edited by Susanne Köbele, Andrea Möckli, Eva Locher, and Lena Oetjens, 187–212. Heidelberg: Winter, 2019.

Glauser, Jürg, Pernille Hermann, and Stephen A. Mitchell, eds. *Handbook of Pre-Modern Nordic Memory Studies, Interdisciplinary Approaches*. Berlin: De Gruyter, 2018.

Goeres, Erin. *The Poetics of Commemoration: Skaldic Verse and Social Memory, c. 890–1070*. Oxford: Oxford University Press, 2015.

Goldhill, Simon. "What Is Ekphrasis For?" *Classical Philology* 1 (2007): 1–19.

Goll, Jürg, Matthias Exner, and Susanne Hirsch. *Müstair: Die mittelalterlichen Wandbilder in der Klosterkirche*. Zurich: NZZ Libro, 2009.

Goltz, Andreas. *Barbar—König—Tyrann: Das Bild Theoderichs des Großen in der Überlieferung des 5. bis 9. Jahrhunderts*. Berlin: De Gruyter, 2008.

Goodman, Kevis. *Georgic Modernity and British Romanticism: Poetry and the Mediation of History*. Cambridge: Cambridge University Press, 2004.

Goody, Jack, and Ian Watt. "The Consequences of Literacy." *Comparative Studies in Society and History* 5 (1963): 304–45.

Gottskálk Jensson. "The Latin Fragments of *Þorláks saga helga* and Their Classical Context." In *Scandinavia and Christian Europe in the Middle Ages: Papers of the 12th International Saga Conference, Bonn/Germany, 28th July—2nd August 2003*, edited by Rudolf Simek and Judith Meurer, 257–267. Bonn: Hausdruckerei der Universität Bonn, 2003.

Graf, Fritz. "Ekphrasis: Die Entstehung der Gattung in der Antike." In *Beschreibungskunst-Kunstbeschreibung. Ekphrasis von der Antike bis zur Gegenwart*, edited by Gottfried Boehm and Helmut Pfotenhauer, 143–155. Munich: Fink, 1995.

Graus, František. *Volk, Herrscher und Heiliger im Reich der Merowinger: Studien zur Hagiographie der Merowingerzeit*. Prague: NČSAV, 1965.

Green, Richard Firth. *Elf Queens and Holy Friars: Fairy Beliefs and the Medieval Church*. Philadelphia: University of Pennsylvania Press, 2016.

Griffith, M. S. "Convention and Originality in the Old English 'Beasts of Battle' Typescene." *Anglo-Saxon England* 22 (1993): 179–99.

Griffiths, Eric. *The Printed Voice of Victorian Poetry*. 2nd ed. Oxford: Oxford University Press, 2018.

Gropper, Stefanie. "Der sogenannte *Zweite Grammatische Traktat*: Sprache und Musik." In *Skandinavische Schriftlandschaften*, edited by Müller-Wille, et al., 78–83. Tübingen: Francke, 2017.

Guðbrandur Vigfússon and F. York Powell. *Corpus Poeticum Boreale*. 2 vols. Oxford: Clarendon, 1883.

Guðrún Nordal. *Tools of Literacy: The Role of Skaldic Verse in Icelandic Textual Culture of the Twelfth and Thirteenth Centuries*. Toronto: University of Toronto Press, 2001.

———. "Metrical Learning and the First Grammatical Treatise." In *Versatility in Versification*, edited by Tonya Kim Dewey and Frog, 23–38. New York: Peter Lang, 2009.

———. "Sturla: The Poet and Creator of Prosimetrum." In *Sturla Þórðarson: Skald, Chieftain, and Lawman*, edited by Jón Viðar Sigurðsson and Sverrir Jakobsson, 120–32. Leiden: Brill, 2017.

Guðvarður Már Gunnlaugsson. "The Speed of the Scribes: How Fast Could *Flateyjarbók* Have Been Written?" In *RE:writing: Medial Perspectives on Textual Culture in the Icelandic Middle Ages*, edited by Kate Heslop and Jürg Glauser, 195–224. Zurich: Chronos, 2018.

Guerreau-Jalabert, Anita. "Flesh and Blood in Medieval Language about Kinship." *Blood and Kinship: Matter for Metaphor from Ancient Rome to the Present*, edited by Christopher H. Johnson, Bernhard Jussen, David Warren Sabean, and Simon Teuscher, 61–82. New York: Berghahn, 2013.

Guillory, John. "Genesis of the Media Concept." *Critical Inquiry* 36 (2010): 321–62.

Gumbrecht, Hans Ulrich. "Rhythmus und Sinn." In *Materialität der Kommunikation*, edited by Hans Ulrich Gumbrecht and Karl Ludwig Pfeiffer, 714–729. Frankfurt: Suhrkamp, 1988.

———. *Production of Presence: What Meaning Cannot Convey*. Stanford: Stanford University Press, 2004.

Gumbrecht, Hans Ulrich, and K. Ludwig Pfeiffer, eds. *Materialities of Communication*. Stanford: Stanford University Press, 1994.

Gunnell, Terry. "Pantheon? What Pantheon? Concepts of a Family of Gods in Pre-Christian Scandinavian Religions." *Scripta Islandica* 66 (2015): 55–76.

Gustavson, Helmer. "Rök. §2. Runologisches." In *Reallexikon der germanischen Altertumskunde*. Vol. 25, edited by Heinrich Beck et al., 62–72. Berlin: De Gruyter, 1973–2008.

Hahn, Cynthia. "*Visio Dei*: Changes in Medieval Visuality." In *Visuality before and beyond the Renaissance: Seeing as Others Saw*, edited by Robert S. Nelson, 176–183. Cambridge: Cambridge University Press, 2000.

Halbwachs, Maurice. *On Collective Memory*. Chicago: University of Chicago Press, 1992.

Hall, Thomas N. "Old Norse-Icelandic Sermons." In *The Sermon*, edited by Beverly Mayne Kienzle, 661–709. Turnhout: Brepols, 2000.

Harris, Joseph. "Philology, Elegy, and Cultural Change." *Gripla* 24 (2009): 257–80.

Hasselberg, Gösta. "Eriksgata." In *Kulturhistorisk leksikon for nordisk middelalder fra vikingetid til reformationstid*. Vol. 4. Edited by Johannes Brøndsted, Bernt Hjejle, Peter Skautrup, Lis Jacobsen, and John Danstrup., cols. 22–27. Copenhagen: Rosenkilde & Bagger, 1956–78.

Haug, Walter, and Benedikt Konrad Vollmann. *Frühere deutsche Literatur und lateinische Literatur in Deutschland 800–1150*. Frankfurt: Deutscher Klassiker Verlag, 1991.

Havelock, Eric A. *The Literate Revolution in Greece and Its Cultural Consequences*. Princeton: Princeton University Press, 1982.

Hedeager, Lotte. *Iron Age Myth and Materiality*. New York: Routledge, 2011.

Heffernan, J. A. W. "Ekphrasis and Representation." *New Literary History* 22 (1991): 297–316.
Heidermanns, Frank. *Etymologisches Wörterbuch der germanischen Primäradjektive*. Berlin: De Gruyter, 1993.
Heller-Roazen, Daniel. *The Inner Touch: Archaeology of a Sensation*. New York: Zone, 2007.
———. "Le gai savoir des vers vieillis." *Comptes rendus des séances de l'Académie des Inscriptions et Belles-Lettres* 2 (2009): 575–83.
Helmbrecht, Michaela. "Wirkmächtige Kommunikationsmedien: Menschenbilder der Vendel- und Wikingerzeit und ihre Kontexte." PhD diss., Lund University, 2011.
Helmreich, Stefan. "The Genders of Waves." *Women's Studies Quarterly* 45 (2017): 29–51.
Hermann, Pernille. "The Mind's Eye: The Triad of Memory, Space and the Senses in Old Norse Literature." *European Journal of Scandinavian Studies* 47 (2017): 203–17.
Heslop, Kate. "Grettir in Ísafjörður: *Grettisfærsla* and *Grettis saga*." In *Creating the Medieval Saga: Versions, Variability and Editorial Interpretations of Old Norse Literature*, Vol. 18, Viking Collection, edited by J. Quinn and E. Lethbridge, 213–36. Odense: University Press of Southern Denmark, 2010.
———. "Minni and the Rhetoric of Memory in Eddic, Skaldic and Runic Texts." In *Minni and Muninn: Memory in Medieval Nordic Culture*, edited by Pernille Hermann, Stephen A. Mitchell, and Agnes S. Arnórsdóttir, 75–107. Turnhout: Brepols, 2014.
———. "Framing the Hero: Medium and Metalepsis in Old Norse Heroic Narrative." In *Old Norse Mythology—Comparative Perspectives*, edited by Pernille Hermann, Stephen A. Mitchell, and Jens Peter Schjødt, 53–88. Cambridge: Harvard University Press, 2017.
———. "Metaphors for Forgetting and Forgetting as Metaphor in Old Norse Poetics." In *Myth, Magic, and Memory in Early Scandinavian Narrative Culture. Studies in Honour of Stephen A. Mitchell*, edited by J. Glauser and P. Hermann, 237–54. Turnhout: Brepols, 2021.
———. "Fathers and Sons: Carnal and Spiritual Kinship in Viking Age Encomium." In *An Icelandic Literary Florilegium. A Festschrift in Honor of Úlfar Bragason*, edited by Marianne Kalinke and Kirsten Wolf, 35–73. Ithaca, NY: Cornell University Library, 2021.
Heslop, Kate, and Jürg Glauser, eds. *RE:Writing: Medial Perspectives on Textual Culture in the Icelandic Middle Ages*. Zurich: Chronos, 2018.
Heusler, Andreas. *Die altergermanische Dichtung*. Berlin: Athenaion, 1923.
———. *Deutsche Versgeschichte*. Berlin: De Gruyter, 1925.
Hines, John. "Ekphrasis as Speech-Act: *Ragnarsdrápa* 1–7." *Viking and Medieval Scandinavia* 3 (2007): 225–44.
Hinton, Leanne, Johanna Nichols, and John J. Ohala. *Sound Symbolism*. Cambridge: Cambridge University Press, 2006.

Holmberg, Per. "Svaren på Rökstenens gåtor: En socialsemiotisk analys av meningsskapande och rumslighet." *Futhark* 6 (2015): 65–106.
Holtsmark, Anne. *Studier i Snorres mytologi*. Oslo: Universitetsforlag, 1964.
Holzapfel, Otto. "Stabilität und Variabilitat einer Formel. Zur Interpretation der Bildformel 'Figur zwischen wilden Tieren' mit besonderer Berücksichtigung skandinavischer Beispiele." *Mediaeval Scandinavia* 6 (1973): 7–38.
Hummer, Hans. *Visions of Kinship in Medieval Europe*. Oxford: Oxford University Press, 2018.
Innis, Harold. *Empire and Communications*. Oxford: Clarendon, 1950.
Irvine, Martin. *The Making of Textual Culture: 'Grammatica' and Literary Theory*. Cambridge: Cambridge University Press, 1994.
Jacobs, M. A. "*Hon stóð ok starði*: Vision, Love, and Gender in *Gunnlaugs saga ormstungu*." *Scandinavian Studies* 86 (2014): 148–68.
Jager, Eric. *The Book of the Heart*. Chicago: University of Chicago Press, 2000.
Jansson, Sven B. F. "Sörmländska Runstensfynd." *Fornvännen* 43 (1948): 282–314.
———. *Runinskrifter i Sverige*. Stockholm: Almqvist & Wiksell, 1963.
Jay, Martin. *Downcast Eyes: The Denigration of Vision in Twentieth-Century French Thought*. Berkeley: University of California Press, 1993.
Jenner, Mark S. R. "Follow Your Nose? Smell, Smelling, and Their Histories." *The American Historical Review* 116 (2011): 335–51.
Jesch, Judith. *Ships and Men in the Late Viking Age: The Vocabulary of Runic Inscriptions and Skaldic Verse*. Woodbridge: Boydell Press, 2001.
———. "Women and Ships in the Viking World." *Northern Studies* 36 (2001): 49–68.
———. "Eagles, Ravens and Wolves: Beasts of Battle, Symbols of Victory and Death." In *The Scandinavians from the Vendel Period to the Tenth Century*, edited by Judith Jesch, 251–71. Woodbridge: Boydell, 2003.
———. *The Viking Diaspora*. London: Routledge, 2015.
Jeserich, Philipp. *Musica naturalis: Tradition und Kontinuität spekulativ-metaphysischer Musiktheorie in der Poetik des französischen Spätmittelalters*. Stuttgart: Steiner, 2008.
Johnannisson, Ture. "Ordet *ärende* och dess släktskapsförhållanden." *Meijerbergs Arkiv för Svensk Ordforskning* 4 (1941): 1–54.
Johansson, Karl. *Studier i Codex Wormianus: skrifttradition och avskriftsverksamhet vid ett isländskt skriptorium under 1300-talet*. Göteborg: Acta Universitatis Gothoburgensis, 1997.
Johnson, Christopher H., Bernhard Jussen, David Warren Sabean, and Simon Teuscher, eds. *Blood and Kinship: Matter for Metaphor from Ancient Rome to the Present*. New York: Berghahn, 2013.
Jón Þórarinsson. *Íslensk tónlistarsaga 1000–1800*. Reykjavík: Tónlistarsafn Íslands, 2012.
Jones, Andrew. *Memory and Material Culture*. Cambridge: Cambridge University Press, 2007.
Jones, William Jervis. *German Colour Terms: A Study in Their Historical Evolution from Earliest Times to the Present*. Amsterdam: Benjamins, 2013.

Jorgensen, Alice. "The Trumpet and the Wolf: Noises of Battle in Old English Poetry." *Oral Tradition* 24 (2009): 319–36.
Kabell, Aage. "Apokalypsen i Skarpåker." *Arkiv för nordisk filologi* 77 (1962): 53–55.
Karl Ó. Ólafsson. "Örmjöt: Athugun á stakyrði." *Mímir* 40 (2001): 62–69.
Kamp, Hermann. "Einleitung." In *Die Wikinger und das fränkische Reich: Identitäten zwischen Konfrontation und Annäherung*, edited by Kerstin P. Hofmann and Nicola Karthaus, 9–20. Paderborn: Fink, 2014.
Kellner, Beate. *Ursprung und Kontinuität: Studien zum genealogischen Wissen im Mittelalter*. Munich: Fink, 2004.
Kiening, Christian. "Medialität in mediävistischer Perspektive." *Poetica* 39 (2008): 285–352.
———. "Mediologie-Christologie. Konturen einer Grundfigur mittelalterlicher Medialität." *Das Mittelalter* 15 (2010): 16–32.
———. *Fülle und Mangel: Medialität im Mittelalter*. Zurich: Chronos, 2016.
———. *Medieval Mediality: Abundance and Lack*. York: Arc Humanities Press, 2019.
Kittler, Friedrich A. *Aufschreibesysteme 1800–1900*. Munich: Fink, 2003. First published 1985.
Klapisch-Zuber, Christiane. "The Genesis of the Family Tree." *I Tatti Studies in the Italian Renaissance* 4 (1991): 105–29.
Klos, Lydia. *Runensteine in Schweden: Studien zu Aufstellungsort und Funktion*. Berlin: De Gruyter, 2009.
Köbele, Susanne. "Rhetorik und Erotik: Minnesang als 'süßer Klang.'" *Poetica* 45 (2013): 299–331.
Kolbrún Haraldsdóttir. "Für welchen Empfänger wurde die Flateyjarbók ursprünglich konzipiert?" *Opuscula* 13 (2010): 1–53.
Konráð Gíslason. "Nogle bemærkninger angående Ynglingatal." *Aarbøger for nordisk oldkyndighed og historie* (1881): 185–251.
Koziol, Geoffrey. *The Politics of Memory and Identity in Carolingian Royal Diplomas: The West Frankish Kingdom (840–987)*. Turnhout: Brepols, 2012.
Krag, Claus. "Norge som odel i Harald Hårfagres ætt: et møte med en gjenganger." *Historisk tidsskrift* 3 (1989): 288–302.
———. *Ynglingatal og ynglingesaga: En studie i historiske kilder*. Oslo: Rådet for humanistisk forskning, Universitetsforlaget, 1991.
———. "8(c): The Early Unification of Norway." In *The Cambridge History of Scandinavia*, edited by Knut Helle, E. I. Kouri, and Jens E. Olesen, 184–201. Cambridge: Cambridge University Press, 2003.
———. "Rikssamlingshistorien og ynglingerekken." *Historisk tidsskrift* 91 (2012): 159–89.
Krämer, Sybille. "'Operationsraum Schrift:' Über einen Perspektivenwechsel in der Betrachtung der Schrift." In *Schrift: Kulturtechnik zwischen Auge, Hand und Maschine*, edited by Gernot Grube, Werner Kogge, and Sybille Krämer, 23–57. Munich: Fink, 2005.

———. *Figuration, Anschauung, Erkenntnis: Grundlinien einer Diagrammatologie*. Berlin: Suhrkamp, 2016.
Kreutzer, Gert. "'Eine der unverfrorensten Verirrungen der Literaturgeschichte'?": Zur Ästhetik und literarischen Wertung der Skaldendichtung." *Skandinavistik* 19 (1989): 36–52.
Kristján Árnason. "Um hendingar í dróttkvæðum hætti." *Íslenskt mál og almenn málfræði* 9 (1987): 41–69.
———. *The Rhythms of Dróttkvætt and Other Old Icelandic Metres*. Reykjavík: University of Iceland, 1991.
———. "The Rise of the Quatrain in Germanic: Musicality and Word Based Rhythm in Eddic Meters." In *Formal Approaches to Poetry: Recent Developments in Metrics*, edited by Bezalel E. Dresher and Nila Friedberg, 151–172. Berlin: De Gruyter, 2006.
———. "On the Principles of Nordic Rhyme and Alliteration." *ANF* 122 (2007): 79–114.
Krömmelbein, Thomas. "Creative Compilers: Observations on the Manuscript Tradition of Snorri's *Edda*." In *Snorrastefna, 25.-27. Júlí 1990*, edited by Úlfar Bragason, 113–129. Reykjavik: Stofnun Sigurðar Nordals, 1992.
Kuhn, Hans. "Die Dróttkvættstrophe als Kunstwerk." In *Festschrift für Konstantin Reichardt*, edited by Christian Gellinek, 63–72. Bern: Francke, 1969.
———. *Das Dróttkvætt*. Heidelberg: Winter, 1983.
Kupferschmidt, Kai. *Blau: Wie die Schönheit in die Welt kommt*. Hamburg: Hoffmann & Campe, 2019.
Kyhlberg, Ola. "The Great Masterpiece: The Rök Stone and its Maker." *Current Swedish Archaeology* 18 (2010): 177–201.
Lammers, Walther. "Ein karolingisches Bildprogramm in der Aula regia von Ingelheim." In *Festschrift für Hermann Heimpel: zum 70. Geburtstag am 19. September 1971*, 226–289. Göttingen: Vandenhoeck & Ruprecht, 1972.
Leach, Elizabeth Eva. "Grammar and Music in the Medieval Song-School." *New Medieval Literature* 11 (2009): 195–211.
———. *Sung Birds: Music, Nature, and Poetry in the Later Middle Ages*. Ithaca: Cornell University Press, 2018.
Lehmann, Winfred. *The Development of Germanic Verse Form*. Austin: University of Texas Press, 1956.
Lethbridge, Emily, and Svanhildur Óskarsdóttir, eds., *New Studies in the Manuscript Tradition of Njáls saga: The historia mutila of Njála*. Kalamazoo: Medieval Institute Publications, 2018.
Liberman, Anatoly. "Mistaken Identity and Optical Illusion in Old Icelandic Literature." In *ÜberBrücken: Festschrift für Ulrich Groenke zum 65. Geburtstag*, edited by Knut Brynhildsvoll, 99–110. Hamburg: Buske, 1989.
Lie, Hallvard. "Billedbeskrivende dikt." In *Kulturhistorisk leksikon for nordisk middelalder fra vikingetid til reformationstid*, Vol. 1, edited by Johannes Brøndsted et al., cols. 542–45. Copenhagen: Rosenkilde & Bagger, 1956–78.

———. "'Natur' og 'unatur' i skaldekunsten." First published 1957. Reprinted in his *Om sagakunst og skaldskap*, 201–315. Øvre Ervik: Alvheim & Eide, 1982.
Liestøl, Aslak. "The Viking Runes: the Transition from the Older to the Younger fuþark." *Saga-Book* 20 (1981): 247–66.
Lindberg, David C., and Katherine H. Tachau. "The Science of Light and Color, Seeing and Knowing." In *The Cambridge History of Science*, edited by Michael H. Shank, 485–511. Cambridge: Cambridge University Press, 2013.
Lindow, John. *Comitatus, Individual and Honor: Studies in North Germanic Institutional Vocabulary*. Berkeley: University of California Press, 1976.
———. "Addressing Thor." *Scandinavian Studies* 60 (1988): 119–36.
———. "St Olaf and the Skalds." In *Sanctity in the North: Saints, Lives, and Cults in Medieval Scandinavia*, edited by Thomas A. Dubois, 103–127. Toronto: University of Toronto Press, 2008.
Lindqvist, Sune. *Uppsala högar och Ottarshögen*. Stockholm: Wahlström & Widstrand, 1936.
Ljungberg, Helge. *Tor: Undersökningar i indoeuropeisk och nordisk religionshistoria*. Uppsala: Lundequist, 1947.
Ljungkvist, John. "Monumentaliseringen av Gamla Uppsala." In *Gamla Uppsala i ny belysning*, edited by Olof Sundqvist and Per Vikstrand, 33–67. Uppsala: Swedish Science Press, 2013.
Ljungkvist, John, Per Frölund, Hans Göthberg, and Daniel Löwenborg, "Gamla Uppsala—Structural Development of a Centre in Middle Sweden." *Archäologisches Korrespondenzblatt* 41 (2011): 571–85.
Ljungkvist, John and Per Frölund. "Gamla Uppsala—The Emergence of a Centre and a Magnate Complex." *Journal of Archaeology and Ancient History* 16 (2015): 1–29.
Lönnroth, Lars. "The Riddles of the Rök-Stone: A Structural Approach." *ANF* 92 (1977): 1–57.
———. "Iǫrð fannz æva né upphiminn." In *Speculum Norroenum: Norse Studies in Memory of Gabriel Turville-Petre*, edited by Ursula Dronke, Guðrún P. Helgadóttir, Gerd Wolfgang Weber, and Hans Bekker-Nielsen, 310–327. Odense: Odense University Press, 1981.
———. "Dómaldi's Death and the Myth of Sacral Kingship." In *Structure and Meaning in Old Norse Literature: New Approaches to Textual Analysis and Literary Criticism*, edited by John Lindow, Lars Lönnroth, and Gerd Wolfgang Weber, 73–93. Odense: Odense University Press, 1986.
———. "Theodoric Rides On." In *Skandinavische Schriftlandschaften: Vänbok til Jürg Glauser*, edited by Klaus Müller-Wille et al., 5–10. Tübingen: Narr, 2017.
Louis-Jensen, Jonna. *Kongesagastudier: Kompilationen Hulda-Hrokkinskinna*. Copenhagen: Reitzel, 1977.
Lord, Alan Bates. *The Singer of Tales*. Cambridge: Harvard University Press, 1960.
Lutz, E. C. *Diagramm und Text: Diagrammatische Strukturen und die Dynamisierung von Wissen und Erfahrung: Überstorfer Colloquium 2012*. Wiesbaden: Reichert, 2014.

Mackenzie, Bridget Gordon. "On the Relation of Norse Skaldic Verse to Irish Syllabic Poetry." In *Specvlvm Norrœnvm: Norse Studies in Memory of Gabriel Turville-Petre*, edited by Ursula Dronke, Guðrún P. Helgadóttir, Gerd W. Weber, and Hans Bekker-Nielsen, 337–356. Odense: University Press of Southern Denmark, 1981.

Maixner, Birgit. "Die Begegnung mit dem Süden: Fränkische Rangzeichen und ihre Rezeption im wikingerzeitlichen Skandinavien." In *Die Wikinger und das Fränkische Reich: Identitäten zwischen Konfrontation und Annäherung*, edited by Kerstin P. Hofmann and Nicola Karthaus, 85–131. Paderborn: Fink, 2014.

Maksymiuk, Stephan K. *The Court Magician in Medieval German Literature*. Frankfurt: Lang, 1996.

Males, Mikael. "Wormianusredaktören: Språk, tro och sanning vid 1300-talets mitt." *Arkiv för nordisk filologi* 128 (2013): 41–78.

Malm, Mats. "Rökstenens tilltal." In *"Vi ska alla vara välkomna!" Nordiska studier tillägnade Kristinn Jóhannesson*, edited by Auður Magnúsdottir, Henrik Janson, and Karl G. Johansson, 342–357. Gothenburg: Meijerbergs arkiv för svensk ordforskning, 2008.

———. "Varför heter det kenning?" In *Snorres Edda i europeisk og islandsk kultur*, edited by Jon Gunnar Jørgensen, 73–90. Reykholt: Snorrastofa, 2009.

———. "Skalds, Runes, and Voice." *Viking and Medieval Scandinavia* 6 (2010): 135–46.

———. "Two Cultures of Visual(ized) Cognition." In *Intellectual Culture in Medieval Scandinavia, c. 1100–1350*, edited by Stefka Eriksen, 309–334. Turnhout: Brepols, 2016.

———. "I.15. Runology." In *Handbook of Pre-Modern Nordic Memory Studies, Interdisciplinary Approaches*, edited by Jürg Glauser, Pernille Hermann, and Stephen A. Mitchell, 190–92. Berlin: De Gruyter, 2018.

Mannerfelt, Måns. "Där svenska riksvägar mötas." *Svenska turistförenings årsskrift* (1930): 134–44.

Marguin-Harmon, Elsa. "Tradition manuscrite de l'œuvre de Jean de Garlande." *Revue d'Histoire des Textes* 1 (2006): 189–257.

Marold, Edith. "Das Walhallbild den *Eiríksmál* und *Hákonarmál*." *Mediaeval Scandinavia* 5 (1972): 19–33.

———. *Kenningkunst: Ein Beitrag zu einer Poetik der Skaldendichtung*. Berlin: De Gruyter, 1983.

———. "Ragnarsdrápa und Ragnarssage." In *Germanic Dialects: Linguistic and Philological Investigations*, edited by Bela Brogyanyi and Thomas Krömmelbein, 427–55. Amsterdam: Benjamins, 1986.

———. "Zur Poetik von Háttatal und Skáldskaparmál." In *Quantitätsproblematik und Metrik: Greifswalder Symposion zur germanischen Grammatik*, edited by Hans Fix, 103–24. Amsterdam: Rodopi, 1995.

———. "Kviðuháttr." In *Reallexikon der germanischen Altertumskunde*, vol. 17, edited by Heinrich Beck et al., 515–518. Berlin: De Gruyter, 1973–2008.

———. "Lebendige Skaldendichtung." In *Neue Ansätze in der Mittelalterphilologie/ Nye Veier i middelalderfilologien. Akten der skandinavistischen Arbeitstagung in*

Münster vom 24.–26.10. 2002, edited by Susanne Kramarz-Bein, 247–71. Frankfurt: Lang, 2005.

———. "Der 'mächtige Nachkomme.'" In *Analecta Septentrionalia: Beiträge zur nordgermanischen Kultur-und Literaturgeschichte*, edited by Wilhelm Heizmann, Klaus Böldl, and Heinrich Beck, 745–77. Berlin: De Gruyter, 2009.

———. "Snorri und die Skaldik." In *Snorri Sturluson—Historiker, Dichter, Politiker*, edited by Heinrich Beck, Wilhelm Heizmann, and Jan van Nahl, 217–234. Berlin: De Gruyter, 2013.

März, Christoph. "Metrik, eine Wissenschaft zwischen Zählen und Schwärmen? Überlegungen zu einer Semantik der Formen mittelhochdeutscher gebundener Rede." In *Mittelalter: neue Wege durch einen alten Kontinent*, edited by Jan-Dirk Müller and Horst Wenzel, 317–32. Stuttgart: Hirzel, 1999.

———. "*Der silben zall, der chunsten grunt*: Die gezählte Silbe in Sangspruch und Meistergesang." *Zeitschrift für deutsche Philologie* 119 (2000): 73–84.

Max-Planck-Gesellschaft. "Singing after Stroke? Why Rhythm and Formulaic Phrases May Be More Important than Melody." Science Daily. Accessed September 28, 2019. http://www.sciencedaily.com/releases/2011/09/110922093728.htm.

McInroy, Mark J. "Origen of Alexandria." In *The Spiritual Senses: Perceiving God in Western Christianity*, edited by Paul L. Gavrilyuk and Sarah Coakley, 20–35. Cambridge: Cambridge University Press, 2011.

McKinnell, John. "*Ynglingatal*: A Minimalist Interpretation." *Scripta Islandica* 60 (2009): 23–48.

McLuhan, Marshal. *Understanding Media: The Extensions of Man*. Cambridge: MIT Press, 1994. First published 1964 by McGraw-Hill (New York).

Mees, Bernard. "The Stentoften Dedication and Sacral Kingship." *Zeitschrift für deutsches Altertum und deutsche Literatur* 140 (2011): 281–305.

Meier, Christel. "Die Quadratur des Kreises: Die Diagrammatik des 12. Jahrhunderts als symbolische Denk- und Darstellungsform." In *Die Bildwelt der Diagramme Joachims von Fiore*, edited by Alexander Patschovsky, 23–53. Ostfildern: Thorbecke, 2003.

Meissner, Rudolf. *Die Kenningar der Skalden: Ein Beitrag zur skaldischen Poetik*. Bonn: Schroeder, 1921.

Melazzo, Lucio. "The Opening of the So-Called Second Grammatical Treatise." In *Cultura Classica e Cultura Germanica Settentrionale: Atti del Convegno Internazionale di Studi, Università di Macerata, Facoltà di Lettere e Filosofia, Macerata—S. Severino Marche, 2-4 maggio 1985*, edited by Pietro Janni, Diego Poli, and Carlo Santini, 399–424. Rome: Bulzoni, 1988.

Melleno, Daniel. "North Sea Networks: Trade and Communication from the Seventh to the Tenth Century." *Comitatus* 45 (2014): 65–89.

———. "Between Borders: Franks, Danes, and Abodrites in the Trans-Elben World up to 827." *Early Medieval Europe* 25 (2017): 359–85.

Mersch, Dieter. *Medientheorien zur Einführung*. Hamburg: Junius, 2006.

Micillo, Valeria. "Classical Tradition and Norse Tradition in the Third Grammatical Treatise." *Arkiv för nordisk filologi* 108 (1993): 68–79.

———. "Die grammatische Tradition des insularen Mittelalters in Island: Spuren insularer Einflüsse im *Dritten Grammatischen Traktat*." In *Übersetzung, Adaptation und Akkulturation im insularen Mittelalter*, edited by Erich Poppe and Hildegard L. C. Tristram, 215–29. Munster: Nodus, 1999.

Minnis, Alastair, and Ian Johnson, eds. *The Cambridge History of Literary Criticism*. Vol. 2, *The Middle Ages*. Cambridge: Cambridge University Press, 2008.

Moretti, Franco. *Distant Reading*. London: Verso, 2013.

Mould, Quita, Ian Carlisle, and Esther Cameron. *Leather and Leatherworking in Anglo-Scandinavian and Medieval York*. York: Council for British Archaeology, 2003.

Murdoch, John E. *Album of Science: Antiquity and the Middle Ages*. New York: Scribner's Sons, 1984.

Murphy, James J. *Rhetoric in the Middle Ages: A History of Rhetorical Theory from St. Augustine to the Renaissance*. Berkeley: University of California Press, 1974.

———. "The Arts of Poetry and Prose." In *The Cambridge History of Literary Criticism*. Vol. 2, *The Middle Ages*, edited by Alastair Minnis and Ian Johnson, 42–67. Cambridge: Cambridge University Press, 2008.

Myhre, Bjørn. "Borregravfeltet som historisk arena." *Viking* 66 (2003): 49–77.

———. *Før Viken ble Norge: Borregravfeltet som religiøs og politisk arena*. Oslo: Kulturhistorisk Museum, Universitet i Oslo, 2015.

Myrvoll, Klaus Johan. "Kronologi i skaldekvæde: Distribusjon av metriske og språklege drag i høve til tradisjonell datering og attribuering." PhD diss., University of Oslo, 2014.

———. "The Constitutive Features of the Dróttkvætt Metre." In *Approaches to Nordic and Germanic Poetics*, edited by Kristján Árnason, Stephen M. Carey, Tonya Kim Dewey, Haukur Þorgeirsson, Ragnar Ingi Aðalsteinsson frá Vaðbrekku, and Þórhallur Eyþórsson, 229–256. Reykjavík: University of Iceland Press, 2016.

Nagel, Alexander. *Medieval Modern: Art out of Time*. London: Thames & Hudson, 2012.

Nanni, Matteo. "Musikalische Diagramme: Spätantike und Karolingerzeit." *Das Mittelalter* 22 (2017): 273–293.

Naumann, Hans-Peter. *Metrische Runeninschriften in Skandinavien: Einführung, Edition und Kommentare*. Tübingen: Narr, 2018.

Neiß, Michael. "Fixeringsbilder från Vestervang: Försök till en metodisk motividentifiering för vikingatida djurornamentik." In *ROMU 2011: Årsskrift fra Roskilde Museum*, edited by Jens Molter Ulriksen, 35–69. Roskilde: Roskilde Museums Forlag, 2012.

———. "Viking Age Animal Art." In *The Head Motif in Past Societies in a Comparative Perspective*, edited by Leszek Gardela and Kamil Kajkowski, 74–87. Bytów: Muzeum Zachodniokaszubskie w Bytowie, 2013.

Nelson, Robert S. "Descartes' Cow and Other Domestications of the Visual." In *Visuality before and beyond the Renaissance: Seeing as Others Saw*, edited by Robert S. Nelson, 1–21. Cambridge: Cambridge University Press, 2000.

Nerman, Birger. *Studier över Svärges hedna litteratur*. Uppsala: Appelberg, 1913.

Noble, Thomas F. X. "The Vocabulary of Vision and Worship in the Early Carolingian Period." In *The Invisible in Late Antiquity and the Early Middle Ages*, edited by Giselle de Nie, Karl F. Morrison, and Marco Mostert, 215–239. Turnhout: Brepols, 2005.

———. *Images, Iconoclasm, and the Carolingians*. Philadelphia: University of Pennsylvania Press, 2009.

Nolan, Barbara. *The Gothic Visionary Perspective*. Princeton: Princeton University Press, 1977.

Nora, Pierre. *Les lieux de mémoire*. 3 vols. Paris: Gallimard, 1984–92.

Norberg, Dag. *An Introduction to the Study of Medieval Latin Versification*. Washington: Catholic University of America Press, 2012.

Noreen, E. "Kuiða: En Hypotes." In *Festschrift Eugen Mogk. Zum 70. Geburtstag, 19. Juli 1924*, 61–65. Halle an der Saale: M. Niemeyer, 1924.

Norr, Svante. "Gamla Uppsala, kungamakt och skriftliga källor." In *Arkeologi och miljögeologi i Gamla Uppsala*, Vol. 2, edited by Władysław Duczko, 21–36. Uppsala: Societas Archaeologica Upsaliensis, 1996.

North, Richard. *The* Haustlǫng *of Þjóðólfr of Hvinir*. Middlesex: Hisarlik, 1997.

———. "Image and Ascendancy in Úlfr's *Húsdrápa*." In *Text, Image, and Interpretation: Studies in Anglo-Saxon Literature and its Insular Context in Honour of Éamonn Ó Carragáin*, edited by Alastair Minnis and Jane Roberts, 369–404. Turnhout: Brepols, 2007.

———. "Kurzweilige Wahrheiten: Ari und das Ynglingatal in den Prologen der Heimskringla." In *Snorri Sturluson—Historiker, Dichter, Politiker*, edited by Heinrich Beck, Wilhelm Heizmann, and Jan van Nahl, 171–213. Berlin: De Gruyter, 2013.

Nunberg, Geoffrey. *The Linguistics of Punctuation*. Stanford, CA: Center for the Study of Language and Information, 1990.

Nyman, Eva. "Rök. §1. Namenkundliches." In *Reallexikon der germanischen Altertumskunde*, Vol. 25, edited by Heinrich Beck et al., 62. Berlin: De Gruyter, 1973–2008.

Oberlin, Adam. "Vita Sancti, Vita Regis: The Saintly King in *Hákonar saga Hákonarsonar*." *Neophilologus* 95 (2011): 313–28.

Ó Córrain, Donnchadh. "Creating the Past: The Early Irish Genealogical Tradition." *Peritia* 12 (1998): 177–208.

O'Keeffe, Katherine O'Brien. "Hands and Eyes, Sight and Touch: Appraising the Senses in Anglo-Saxon England." *Anglo-Saxon England* 45 (2016): 105–40.

Oldeberg, Andreas. "Några träidoler från förhistorisk och senare tid." *Fornvännen* 52 (1957): 247–58.

Olrik, Axel. "Irminsul og Gudestøtter." *Maal og Minne* (1910): 1–9.

Ong, Walter J. *Presence of the Word: Some Prolegomena for Cultural and Religious History*. New Haven: Yale University Press, 1967.

Orri Vésteinsson. "Hann reisti hof mikið hundrað fóta langt . . . : Um uppruna hof-örnefna og stjórnmál á Íslandi í lok 10. aldar." *Saga* 45 (2007): 53–91.

Paasche, Fredrik. *Norges og Islands literatur inntil utgangen av middelalderen*. Oslo: Aschehoug, 1947.

Page, Christopher. "The Earliest English Keyboard." *Early Music* 7 (1979): 309–314.

———. "Medieval Organistrum and Symphonia." Vol. 1, "A Legacy from the East?" *The Galpin Society Journal* 35 (1982): 37–44.

———. "Medieval Organistrum and Symphonia." Vol. 2, "Terminology." *The Galpin Society Journal* 36 (1983): 71–87.

Palmér, Johan. "Betydelseutvecklingen i isl. *heiðr*." *Acta Philologica Scandinavica* 5 (1930–31): 289–304.

Parikka, Jussi. *What Is Media Archaeology?* Cambridge: Polity, 2012.

Parry, Adam, ed., *The Making of Homeric Verse: The Collected Papers of Milman Parry*. Oxford: Oxford University Press, 1971.

Pastoureau, Michel. *Blue: The History of a Color*. Princeton: Princeton University Press, 2001.

Pedersen, Anne. "Ancient Mounds for New Graves: An Aspect of Viking Age Burial Customs in Southern Scandinavia." In *Old Norse Religion in Long-Term Perspectives: Origins, Changes, and Interactions. An International Conference in Lund, Sweden, June 3–7, 2004*, edited by Anders Andrén, 346–53. Lund: Nordic Academic Press, 2006.

Pedersen, Anne, Frans-Arne Stygelar, and Per G. Norseng, *Øst for Folden*. Sarpsborg: Østfolds fylkeskommune, 2003.

Peters, John Durham. *The Marvelous Clouds: Toward a Philosophy of Elemental Media*. Chicago: University of Chicago Press, 2016.

Peters, Ursula. "'Texte vor der Literatur'? Zur Problematik neuerer Alteritätsparadigmen der Mittelalter-Philologie." *Poetica* 39 (2007): 59–88.

Picard, Eve. *Germanisches Sakralkönigtum? Quellenkritische Studien zur Germania des Tacitus und zur altnordischen Überlieferung*. Heidelberg: Winter, 1991.

Pilø, Lars, Dagfinn Skre, Birgitta Hårdh, Egon Wamers, James Graham-Campbell, Heid Gjøstein Resi, Unn Plahter, Bjarne Gaut, Alan Vince, Irene Baug, and Ingvild Øye. *Things from the Town: Artefacts and Inhabitants in Viking-Age Kaupang*. Aarhus: Aarhus Universitetsforlag, 2011.

Platt, Verity J. *Facing the Gods: Epiphany and Representation in Graeco-Roman Art, Literature and Religion*. Cambridge: Cambridge University Press, 2011.

Plesters, Joyce. "Ultramarine Blue, Natural and Artificial." *Studies in Conservation* 11 (1966): 62–91.

Poole, Russell. "Variants and Variability in the Text of Egill's *Hǫfuðlausn*." In *The Politics of Editing Medieval Texts: Papers Given at the Twenty-Seventh Annual Conference on Editorial Problems, University of Toronto, 1–2 November 1991*, edited by Roberta Frank, 65–105. New York: AMS, 1993.

———. "Some Southern Perspectives on Starcatherus." *Viking and Medieval Scandinavia* 2 (2006): 141–66.

———. "Ekphrasis: Its 'Prolonged Echoes' in Scandinavia." *Viking and Medieval Scandinavia* 3 (2007): 245–67.

———. "Myth and Religion in the *Háleygjatal* of Eyvindr skáldaspillir." In *Learning and Understanding in the Old Norse World: Essays in Honour of Margaret Clunies Ross*, ed. Judy Quinn, Kate Heslop, and Tarrin Wills, 153–76. Turnhout: Brepols, 2007.

———. "*Þulir* as Tradition-Bearers and Prototype Saga-Tellers." In *Creating the Medieval Saga: Versions, Variability, and Editorial Interpretations of Old Norse Saga Literature*, edited by Judy Quinn and Emily Lethbridge, 237–60. Odense: University Press of Southern Denmark, 2010.

———. "Scholars and Skalds: The Northwards Diffusion of Carolingian Poetic Fashions." *Gripla* 24 (2013): 7–44.

Porter, James. "Disfigurations: Erich Auerbach's Theory of *Figura*." *Critical Inquiry* 44 (2017): 80–113.

Powell, Hilary. "'Once Upon a Time There Was a Saint . . .': Re-evaluating Folklore in Anglo-Latin Hagiography." *Folklore* 121 (2010): 171–89.

Price, Neil. "The Viking Way: Religion and War in Late Iron Age Scandinavia." PhD diss., Uppsala University, 2002.

Quinn, Judy. "The Naming of Eddic Mythological Poems in Medieval Manuscripts." *Parergon* 8 (1990): 97–115.

———. "*Eddu list*: The Emergence of Skaldic Pedagogy in Medieval Iceland." *Alvíssmál* 4 (1994): 69–92.

———. "From Orality to Literacy in Medieval Iceland." In *Old Icelandic Literature and Society*, edited by Margaret Clunies Ross, 30–60. Cambridge: Cambridge University Press, 2000.

———. "Editing the Edda: The Case of *Vǫluspá*." *Scripta Islandica* 51 (2001): 69–92.

———. "The Gendering of Death in Eddic Cosmology." In *Old Norse Religion in Long-Term Perspectives: Origins, Changes and Interactions. An International Conference in Lund, Sweden, June 3–7*, edited by Anders Andrén, Kristina Jennbert, and Catharina Raudvere, 54–57. Lund: Nordic Academic Press, 2004.

———. "Mythologizing the Sea: The Nordic Sea-Deity Rán." In *Nordic Mythologies: Interpretations, Intersections and Institutions*, edited by Timothy R. Tangherlini, 71–99. Berkeley: North Pinehurst Press, 2014.

———. "The Principles of Textual Criticism and the Interpretation of Old Norse Texts Derived from Oral Tradition." In *Studies in the Transmission and Reception of Old Norse Literature: The Hyperborean Muse*, edited by Judy Quinn and Adele Cipolla, 47–78. Turnhout: Brepols, 2016.

Ralph, Bo. "Phonological and Graphematic Developments from Ancient Nordic to Old Nordic." In *The Nordic Languages: An International Handbook of the History of the North Germanic Languages*, Vol. 1, edited by Oskar Bandle, Kurt Braunmuller, Ernst Hakon Jahr, et al., 703–19. Berlin: De Gruyter, 2002.

———. "Gåtan som lösning. Ett bidrag till förståelsen av Rökstenens runinskrift." *Maal og minne* (2007): 133–57.
Rasmussen, Ann Marie, and Markus Stock. "Introduction: Medieval Media." *Seminar—A Journal of Germanic Studies* 52 (2016): 97–106.
Reichert, Hermann. "Runeninschriften als Quellen der Heldensagenforschung." In *Runeninschriften als Quellen interdisziplinärer Forschung*, edited by Klaus Düwel, 66–102. Berlin: De Gruyter, 1998.
Riad, Tomas. *Structures in Germanic Prosody: A Diachronic Study with Special Reference to the Nordic languages*. Stockholm: Stockholm University Press, 1992.
Riegl, Alois. *Die spätrömische Kunst-Industrie nach den Funden in Österreich-Ungarn [. . .]*. Vienna: Staatsdruckerei, 1901.
Roberts, H. M. "Journey to the Dead: The Litlu-Núpar Boat Burial." *Current World Archaeology* 32 (2008): 36–41.
Robertson, D. W. Jr. "Some Medieval Terminology with Special Reference to Chrétien de Troyes." *Studies in Philology* 48 (1951): 669–92.
Rolfsen, Perry. "Det rette pipet: Metalldetektorbruk i Norge." In *Pløyejord som kontekst: Nye utfordringer for forskning, forvaltning og formidling*, edited by Jens Martens and Mads Ravn, 111–26. Oslo: Kulturhistorisk Museum, 2016.
Rollason, David W. "Lists of Saints' Resting-Places in Anglo-Saxon England." *Anglo-Saxon England* 7 (1978): 61–93.
———. "The Cults of Murdered Royal Saints in Anglo-Saxon England." *Anglo-Saxon England* 11 (1983): 1–22.
Roth, Michael S., Claire L. Lyons, and Charles Merewether. *Irresistible Decay: Ruins Reclaimed*. Los Angeles: Getty Research Institute, 1997.
Rowe, Elizabeth Ashman. *The Development of Flateyjarbók: Iceland and the Norwegian Dynastic Crisis of 1389*. Odense: University Press of Southern Denmark, 2005.
Ruggerini, Maria Elena. "Alliterative Lexical Collocations in Eddic Poetry." In *A Handbook to Eddic Poetry: Myths and Legends of Early Scandinavia*, edited by Carolyne Larrington, Judy Quinn, and Brittany Schorn, 310–330. Cambridge: Cambridge University Press, 2016.
Ruin, Hans. "Speaking to the Dead—Historicity and the Ancestral." *Danish Yearbook of Philosophy* 48 (2013): 115–37.
Rundkvist, Martin. "In the Landscape and between Worlds: Bronze Age Deposition Sites around Lakes Mälaren and Hjälmaren in Sweden." PhD diss., Umeå University, 2015.
Sahlgren, Jöran. *Forntida vägar: Läbybron och Eriksgatan*. Uppsala: Berlings, 1909.
Samplonius, Kees. "Rex non reditvrvs." *Amsterdamer Beiträge zur älteren Germanistik* 37 (1993): 21–31.
Sanmark, Alexandra. *Viking Law and Order: Places and Rituals of Assembly in the Medieval North*. Edinburgh: Edinburgh University Press, 2017.
Sanmark, Alexandra, and Eva Bergström. *Tingsplatsen som arkeologiskt problem, etapp 1, Aspa: arkeologisk provundersökning, forskning: Raä 62, Aspa 2:11, Ludgo*

socken, Nyköpings kommun, SAU Rapport 25. Uppsala: Societas Archaeologica Upsaliensis, 2004.

Sapp, Christopher D. "Dating *Ynglingatal*: Chronological Metrical Developments in *kviðuháttr*." *Skandinavistik* 30 (2000): 85–90.

Saunders, Corinne. *Magic and the Supernatural in Medieval English Romance*. Cambridge: Boydell & Brewer, 2010.

Sävborg, Daniel. "Blockbildningen i Codex Upsaliensis: En ny metod att lösa frågan om Snorra Edda ursprungsversion." *Maal og Minne* (2012): 12–53.

Schaefer, Ursula. *Vokalität: Altenglische Dichtung zwischen Mündlichkeit und Schriftlichkeit*. Tübingen: Gunter Narr, 1992.

Schelling, Felix E. "The English Masque." In *Elizabethan Drama, 1558–1642*. New York: Houghton Mifflin, 1904.

Schier, Kurt. "Die Húsdrápa von Úlfr Uggason und die bildliche Überlieferung altnordischer Mythen." In *Minjar og menntir: Afmælsrit helgað Kristjáni Eldjárn*, edited by Guðni Kolbeinsson, 425–43. Reykjavík: Bókaútgáfa Menningarsjóðs, 1976.

Schmidt, Tom. "Særtrekk ved stedsnavnmaterialet fra Østfold i jernalder og middelalder." In *Over grenser: Østfold og Viken i yngre jernalder og middelalder*, edited by Jón Viðar Sigurðsson and Per G. Norseng, 71–100. Oslo: Senter for studier i vikingtid og nordisk middelalder, 2003.

Schneeberger, Sandra. "Der *Zweite Grammatische Traktat*—Spielfeld für Schrift und Klang." In *Skandinavische Schriftlandschaften: Vänbok til Jürg Glauser*, edited by Klaus Müller-Wille et al., 73–77. Tübingen: Narr, 2017.

Schneider, David Murray. *A Critique of the Study of Kinship*. Ann Arbor: University of Michigan Press, 1984.

Schröder, Franz Rolf. "Thor und der Wetzstein." *Beiträge zur Geschichte der deutschen Sprache und Literatur* 51 (1927): 33–35.

Schück, Adolf. "Sveriges vägar och sjöleder under forntid och medeltid." In *Handel och samfärdsel under medeltiden*, Nordisk kultur 16B, 229–255. Stockholm: Bonnier, 1930.

Schück, Henrik. *Bidrag till tolkning af Rök-Inskriften*. Uppsala: Almqvist & Wiksell, 1908.

Schwartz, Hillel. *Making Noise: From Babel to the Big Bang and Beyond*. New York: Zone, 2011.

Sebo, E., C. Wiseman, J. McCarthy, P. Baggaley, K. Jerbic, and J. Benjamin. "The Kalvestene: A Reevaluation of the Ship Settings on the Danish Island of Hjarnø." *Journal of Island and Coastal Archaeology* 16 (2021): 1–17.

Sedgwick, Eve Kosofsky. *Touching Feeling: Affect, Pedagogy, Performativity*. Durham: Duke University Press, 2003.

Selma Jónsdóttir. *An 11th-Century Byzantine Last Judgement in Iceland*. Reykjavík: Almenna Bókafélagið, 1959.

Semple, Sarah. *Perceptions of the Prehistoric in Anglo-Saxon England: Religion, Ritual, and Rulership in the Landscape*. London: Oxford University Press, 2013.

Serres, Michel. *Le parasite*. Paris: Bernard Grasset, 1980.
———. "Noise." *SubStance* 12 (1983): 48–60.
Shannon, Claude E., and Warren Weaver. *The Mathematical Theory of Communication*. Urbana: University of Illinois Press, 1949.
Siegert, Bernhard. "Vögel, Engel und Gesandte: Alteuropas Übertragungsmedien." In *Gespräche—Boten—Briefe: Körpergedächtnis im Mittelalter*, edited by Horst Wenzel, 45–62. Berlin: Schmidt, 1997.
———. "Cultural Techniques: Or the End of the Intellectual Postwar Era in German Media Theory." *Theory, Culture & Society* 30 (2013): 48–65.
———. *Cultural Techniques: Grids, Filters, Doors, and Other Articulations of the Real*. New York: Fordham University Press, 2015.
Skomedal, Trygve, and Klaus Johan Myrvoll. "Tonelagsskilnad i islendsk i Tridje grammatiske avhandling." *Maal og minne* (2010): 68–97.
Skre, Dagfinn. *Kaupang in Skiringssal: Excavation and Surveys at Kaupang and Huseby, 1998–2003*. Aarhus: Aarhus Universitetsforlag, 2007.
———. "The Warrior Manor." In *Avaldsnes—A Sea-King's Manor in First-Millennium Western Scandinavia*, edited by Dagfinn Skre, 767–782. Berlin: De Gruyter, 2018.
Smith, A. Mark. "What Is the History of Medieval Optics Really About?" *Proceedings of the American Philosophical Society* 148 (2004): 180–94.
———. *From Sight to Light: The Passage from Ancient to Modern Optics*. Chicago: University of Chicago Press, 2015.
Smith, Julia M. H. "Oral and Written: Saints, Miracles, and Relics in Brittany, c. 850–1250." *Speculum* 65 (1990): 309–43.
Smith, Peter. "Early Irish Historical Verse: The Development of a Genre." In *Ireland and Europe in the Early Middle Ages: Text and Transmission*, edited by Próinséas Ni Chatháin and Michael Richter, 326–341. Dublin: Four Courts Press, 2002.
Spiegel, Gabrielle M. *The Past as Text: The Theory and Practice of Medieval Historiography*. Baltimore: Johns Hopkins University Press, 1997.
Spitzer, Leo. "Milieu and Ambiance: An Essay in Historical Semantics." *Philosophy and Phenomenological Research* 3 (1942): 1–42.
Squire, Michael. *Image and Text in Graeco-Roman Antiquity*. New York: Cambridge, 2009.
Stavnem, Rolf. "The Kennings in *Ragnarsdrápa*." *Mediaeval Scandinavia* 14 (2004): 161–84.
———. "Dødsmetaforik: Metaforisk sprog i Ynglingatal." *Opuscula: Bibliotheca Arnamagnæana* 12 (2005): 263–85.
Steigemann, Christoph, and Matthias Wemhoff. *799: Kunst und Kultur der Karolingerzeit. Karl der Große und Papst Leo III. in Paderborn*. Mainz: Zabern, 1999.
Stenholm, Ann-Mari Hållans. *Fornminnen: Det förflutnas roll i det kristna och förkristna Mälardalen*. Lund: Nordic Academic Press, 2012.

Sterne, Jonathan. *The Audible Past: Cultural Origins of Sound Reproduction.* Durham: Duke University Press, 2003.
Stetkevych, Jaroslav. *The Hunt in Arabic Poetry: From Heroic to Lyric to Metapoetic.* Notre Dame: University of Notre Dame Press, 2016.
Stewart, Susan A. *Poetry and the Fate of the Senses.* Chicago: University of Chicago Press, 2002.
Stoumann, Ingrid. *Ryttergraven fra Grimstrup og andre vikingetidsgrave ved Esbjerg.* Esbjerg: Sydvestjyske Museer, 2009.
Strachey, J., ed. *The Standard Edition of the Complete Psychological Works of Sigmund Freud.* London: Hogarth, 1963.
Ström, Folke. "Poetry as an Instrument of Propaganda: Jarl Hakon and His Poets." In *Specvlvm Norroenvm: Norse Studies in Memory of Gabriel Turville-Petre*, edited by Ursula Dronke et al., 440–458. Odense: Odense University Press, 1981.
Sullivan, Blair. "The Unwritable Sound of Music: The Origins and Implications of Isidore's Memorial Metaphor." *Viator* 30 (1999): 1–14.
———. *The Classical Analogy between Speech and Music and Its Transmission in Carolingian Music Theory.* Tempe, AZ: ACMRS, 2011.
Sumi, A. M. *Description in Classical Arabic Poetry: Waṣf, Ekphrasis, and Interarts Theory.* Leiden: Brill, 2004.
Summers, David. *The Judgment of Sense: Renaissance Naturalism and the Rise of Aesthetics.* Cambridge: Cambridge University Press, 1987.
Sundqvist, Olof. *Freyr's Offspring: Rulers and Religion in Ancient Svea Society.* Uppsala: Uppsala Universitet, 2002.
———. "Sakralkönigtum (Skandinavische Quellen)." In *Reallexikon der germanischen Altertumskunde*, vol. 26, edited by Heinrich Beck et al., 279–93. Berlin: De Gruyter, 1973–2008.
———. "Aspects of Rulership Ideology in Early Scandinavia—with Particular Reference to the Skaldic Poem *Ynglingatal*." In *Das frühmittelalterliche Königtum: Ideelle und religiöse Grundlagen*, edited by Franz-Reiner Erkens. Berlin: de Gruyter, 2005.
———. "'Religious Ruler Ideology' in Pre-Christian Scandinavia: A Contextual Approach." In *More Than Mythology: Narratives, Ritual Practices and Regional Distribution in Pre-Christian Scandinavian Religions*, edited by Catharina Raudvere and Jens Peter Schjødt, 225–61. Lund: Nordic Academic Press, 2012.
Suzuki, Seiichi. *The Meters of Old Norse Eddic Poetry: Common Germanic Inheritance and North Germanic Innovation.* Berlin: De Gruyter, 2014.
Svanhildur Óskarsdóttir. "Dáið þér Ynglinga? Gróteskar hneigðir Þjóðólfs úr Hvini." In *Sagnaþing—helgað Jónasi Kristjánssyni sjötugum*, vol. 2, edited by Sigurgeir Steingrímsson, Gísli Sigurðsson, and Guðrún Kvárán, 761–68. Reykjavík: Hið íslenska bókmenntafélag, 1994.
Sverrir Jakobsson. "Erendringen om en mægtig Personlighed: Den norskislandske historiske tradisjon om Harald Hårfagre i et kildekritisk perspektiv." *Historisk tidsskrift* 81 (2007): 213–30.

———. "The Early Kings of Norway." *Viator* 47 (2016): 171–88.
Sverrir Tómasson. "Nýsköpun eða endurtekning? Íslensk skaldmennt og Snorra Edda fram til 1609." In *Guðamjöður og arnarleir: Safn ritgerða um eddulist*, edited by Sverrir Tómasson, 1–64. Reykjavík: Háskólaútgáfan, 1996.
———. "Konungs lof. Nóregs konunga tal í Flateyjarbók." *Skírnir* 176 (2002): 257–67.
———. "'Nikulám skulu vér heiðra hér . . .': Spjall um annan málfræðinginn, kveðskap og musik." In *Til heiðurs og hugbótar: Greinar um trúarkveðskap fyrri alda*, edited by Svanhildur Óskarsdóttir and Anna Guðmundsdóttir, 79–112. Reykholt: Snorrastofa, 2003.
Sweetser, Eve. *From Etymology to Pragmatics: Metaphorical and Cultural Aspects of Semantic Structure*. Cambridge: Cambridge University Press, 1990.
Taplin, Oliver. "The Shield of Achilles within the 'Iliad.'" *Greece & Rome* 27 (1980): 1–21.
Thacker, Alan. "Membra Disjecta: The Division of the Body and the Diffusion of the Cult." In *Oswald: Northumbrian King to European Saint*, edited by Clare Stancliffe and Eric Cambridge, 97–127. Stamford: Watkins, 1995.
Thompson, Marie. *Beyond Unwanted Sound: Noise, Affect and Aesthetic Moralism*. New York: Bloomsbury, 2017.
Townend, Matthew. "Knútr and the Cult of St Óláfr: Poetry and Patronage in Eleventh Century Norway and England." *Viking and Medieval Scandinavia* 1 (2005): 251–79.
Tranter, Stephen. "Divided and Scattered, Trussed and Supported: Stanzaic Form in Irish and Old Norse Tracts." In *Metrik und Medienwechsel/Metrics and Media*, edited by Hildegard L. C. Tristram, 245–72. Tübingen: Narr, 1991.
———. *Clavis Metrica: Háttatal, Háttalykill and the Irish Metrical Tracts*. Basel: Helbing & Lichtenhahn, 1997.
———. "Medieval Icelandic artes poeticae." In *Old Icelandic Literature and Society*, edited by Margaret Clunies Ross, 140–60. Cambridge: Cambridge University Press, 2000.
Trier, Jost. "Heide." *Archiv für Literatur und Volksdichtung* 1 (1949): 63–103.
Truitt, E. R. *Medieval Robots: Mechanism, Magic, Nature, and Art*. Philadelphia: University of Pennsylvania Press, 2015.
Tulinius, Torfi H. "Milli skriptanna, spengr af gulli: On the Conversion of Gold and Other Valuables in Sagas and Skaldic Poetry." In *Gold in der europäischen Heldensage*, edited by Heike Sahm, Wilhelm Heizmann, and Victor Millet, 264–74. Berlin: De Gruyter, 2019.
Turville-Petre, Joan. "On Ynglingatal." *Mediaeval Scandinavia* 11 (1978–79): 48–67.
Vance, Eugene. "Seeing God: Augustine, Sensation and the Mind's Eye." In *Rethinking the Medieval Senses: Heritage, Fascinations, Frames*, edited by Stephen G. Nichols, Andreas Kablitz, and Alison Calhoun, 13–29. Baltimore: Johns Hopkins University Press, 2008.
Van der Sanden, Wijnand, and Torsten Capelle. *Götter—Götzen—Holzmenschen*. Oldenburg: Isensee, 2002.

Van Nahl, Jan Alexander. "The Skilled Narrator: Myth and Scholarship in the *Prose Edda*." *Scripta Islandica* 66 (2015): 123–41.

Vansina, Jan M. *Oral Tradition as History*. Madison: University of Wisconsin Press, 1985.

Van Waesberghe, J. Smits. "The Musical Notation of Guido of Arezzo." *Musica Disciplina* 5 (1951): 15–53.

Vauchez, André. *Sainthood in the Later Middle Ages*. Cambridge: Cambridge University Press, 2008.

Vikstrand, Per. "Ortnamnet Hov—sakralt, terrängbetecknande eller bägge delarna?" In *Sakrale navne: Rapport fra NORNAs sekstende symposium i Gilleleje 30.11–2.12 1990*, edited by Gillian Fellows-Jensen and Bente Holmberg, 123–139. Uppsala: Norna-Förlaget, 1992.

———. "Skúta and Vendil. Two Place Names in *Ynglingatal*." In *Namenwelten: Orts-und Personennamen in historischer Sicht*, edited by Astrid van Nahl, Lennart Elmevik, and Stefan Brink, 373–387. Berlin: De Gruyter, 2004.

Vogt, W. H. "Bragis Schild." *Acta Philologica Scandinavia* 5 (1930): 1–28.

Von Carnap-Bornheim, Claus. "Der 'Helmbeschlag' aus Domagnano—Überlegungen zur Herkunft des 'Vogel-Fisch' Motivs." In *". . . Trans Albim Fluvium:" Forschungen zur vorrömischen, kaiserzeitlichen und mittelalterlichen Archäologie: Festschrift für Achim Leube zum 65. Geburtstag*, edited by Michael Meyer, 223–238. Rahden: Leidorf, 2001.

Von Friesen, Otto. *Rökstenen: Runstenen vid Röks kyrka, Lysings härad Östergötland*. Stockholm: J. Bragges Söner, 1920.

Von See, Klaus. *Germanische Verskunst*. Stuttgart: Metzler, 1967.

———. *Kontinuitätstheorie und Sakraltheorie in der Germanenforschung: Antwort an Otto Höfler*. Berlin: Athenäum, 1972.

———. "Polemische Zitate in der Skaldendichtung: Hallfrøðr vandræðaskáld and Haldórr ókristni." In *Edda, Saga, Skaldendichtung*. Heidelberg: Winter, 1981.

———. "Snorri Sturluson and the Creation of a Norse Cultural Ideology." *Saga-Book* 25 (2001): 367–93.

Von See, Klaus, Beatrice LaFarge, Katja Schulz, Simone Horst, and Eve Picard, eds. *Kommentar zu den Liedern der Edda*. 7 vols. Heidelberg: Winter, 1992–2019.

Waite, William G. "Johannes de Garlandia, Poet and Musician." *Speculum* 35 (1960): 179–95.

Wamers, Egon. "Von Bären und Männern: Berserker, Bärenkämpfer und Bärenführer im frühen Mittelalter." *Zeitschrift für Archäologie des Mittelalters* 37 (2009): 1–46.

Wandhoff, Haiko. *Ekphrasis: Kunstbeschreibungen und virtuelle Räume in der Literatur des Mittelalters*. Berlin: De Gruyter, 2003.

Wang, Haicheng. *Writing and the Ancient State: Early China in Comparative Perspective*. Cambridge: Cambridge University Press, 2014.

Warner, Michael. "Uncritical Reading." In *Polemic: Critical or Uncritical*, edited by Jane Gallop, 13–38. New York: Routledge, 2004.

Watkins, Calvert. *How to Kill a Dragon: Aspects of Indo-European Poetics*. New York: Oxford University Press, 1995.
Webb, Ruth. "Ekphrasis Ancient and Modern: The Invention of a Genre." *Word & Image* 15 (1999): 7–18.
———. *Ekphrasis, Imagination and Persuasion in Ancient Rhetorical Theory and Practice*. Surrey: Ashgate, 2009.
Weber, Gerd Wolfgang. "'Intellegere historiam': Typological Perspectives of Nordic Prehistory (in Snorri, Saxo, Widukind and others)." In *Tradition og historieskrivning: Kilderne til Nordens ældste historie*, edited by Kirsten Hastrup and Preben Meulengracht Sørensen, 95–141. Aarhus: Aarhus University Press, 1987.
Weigel, Sigrid. *Genea-Logik: Generation, Tradition, und Evolution zwischen Kultur- und Naturwissenschaften*. Munich: Fink, 2006.
Weijers, Olga. *Le maniement du savoir: Pratiques intellectuelles à l'époque des premières universités (XIIIe–XIVe siècles)*. Turnhout: Brepols, 1996.
Weiskott, Eric. "Saint Kenelm in an Imaginative Illustration." *Notes and Queries* 64 (2017): 217–20.
Wellendorf, Jonas. *Gods and Humans in Medieval Scandinavia: Retying the Bonds*. Cambridge: Cambridge University Press, 2018.
———. "The Æsir and their Idols." In *Old Norse Mythology in its Comparative Contexts*, edited by Stephen Mitchell, Pernille Hermann, and Jens Peter Schjødt, 89–110. Cambridge: Harvard University Press, 2018.
Wenzel, Horst. "Imaginatio und Memoria: Medien der Erinnerung im höfischen Mittelalter." In *Mnemosyne: Formen und Funktionen der kulturellen Erinnerung*, edited by Aleida Assmann and Dietrich Harth, 57–82. Frankfurt: Fischer, 1991.
———. "Die 'fließende Rede' und der 'gefrorene Text': Metaphern der Medialität." In *Poststrukturalismus: Herausforderung an die Literaturwissenschaft*, edited by Gerhard Neumann, 481–503. Stuttgart: Metzler, 1997.
Wessén, Elias. "Om kuida i namn på fornnordiska dikter." *Edda* 4 (1915): 127–41.
———. *Runstenen vid Röks kyrka*. Stockholm: Almqvist & Wiksell, 1958.
Whaley, Diana. *Heimskringla: An Introduction*. London: Viking Society, 1991.
———. "The Fury of the Northmen and the Poetics of Violence." In *Narration and Hero: Recounting the Deeds of Heroes in Literature and Art of the Early Medieval Period*, edited by Victor Millet and Heike Sahm, 71–94. Berlin: De Gruyter, 2014.
Whitehead, Anne. *Memory*. London: Routledge, 2009.
Widmark, Gun. "Vamod eller Vämod." In *Nordiska orter och ord: Festskrift till Bengt Pamp på 65-årsdagen*, edited by Göran Hallberg, 210–212. Lund: Dialekt- och ortnamnsarkivet, 1993.
———. "Tolkningen som social konstruktion." In *Runor och ABC: Elva föreläsningar från ett symposium i Stockholm våren 1995*, edited by Staffan Nyström, 165–175. Stockholm: Stockholms Medeltidsmuseum, 1997.
Williams, Henrik. "Runstenarnas sociala dimension." *Futhark* 4 (2013): 61–76.

Williams, Howard. "The Sense of Being Seen: Ocular Effects at Sutton Hoo." *Journal of Social Archaeology* 11 (2011): 99–121.

Williams, Raymond. *Keywords: A Vocabulary of Culture and Society*. London: Fontana, 1983.

Winthrop-Young, Geoffrey. "Cultural Studies and German Media Theory." In *New Cultural Studies: Adventures in Theory*, edited by Gary Hall and Clare Birchall, 88–103. Edinburgh: Edinburgh University Press, 2006.

Wirth, Karl August. "Von mittelalterlichen Bildern und Lehrfiguren im Dienste der Schule und des Unterrichts." In *Studien zum städtischen Bildungswesen des späten Mittelalters und der frühen Neuzeit*, edited by Bernd Möller, Hans Patze, and Karl Stackmann, 256–370. Göttingen: Vandenhoeck & Ruprecht, 1983.

Wolf, Kirsten. "The Color Blue in Old Norse-Icelandic Literature." *Scripta Islandica* 57 (2006): 55–78.

Wolfram, Herwig. "Frühes Königtum." In *Das frühmittelalterliche Königtum: Ideelle und religiöse Grundlagen*, edited by Franz-Reiner Erkens, 42–64. Berlin: De Gruyter, 2005.

Wolfson, Harry Austryn. "The Internal Senses in Latin, Arabic, and Hebrew Philosophic Texts." *The Harvard Theological Review* 28 (1935): 69–133.

Woolgar, C. M. *The Senses in Late Medieval England*. New Haven: Yale University Press, 2006.

Zachrisson, Torun. "Ärinvards minne: Om runstenen i Norra Sandsjö." In *Om runstenar i Jönköpings län*, edited by Jan Agertz and Linnéa Varenius, 35–54. Jönköping: Jönköpings läns museum, 2002.

Zernack, Julia. "Vorläufer und Vollender: Olaf Tryggvason und Olaf der Heilige im Geschichtsdenken des Oddr Snorrason munkr." *Arkiv för nordisk filologi* 113 (1998): 77–95.

———. "Hyndlulioð, Flateyjarbók und die Vorgeschichte der Kalmarer Union." *Scandinavistik* 29 (1999): 89–114.

Zielinski, Siegfried. *Deep Time of the Media: Toward an Archaeology of Hearing and Seeing by Technical Means*. Translated by Gloria Custance. Cambridge: MIT Press, 2006.

Zumthor, Paul. *La Poésie et la voix dans la civilisation médiévale*. Paris: Presses Universitaires de France, 1984.

———. "The Text and the Voice." *New Literary History* 16 (1984): 67–92.

Þorgeir Sigurðsson. "The Unreadable Poem of Arinbjǫrn: Preservation, Meter, and a Restored Text." Ph.D. diss., University of Iceland, 2019.

INDEX

1 Corinthians, 122

Aachen, 35, 74–75, 77
Aaron (Biblical figure), 120–21
aðalhending, 149–50, 152
Alberic of Monte Cassino, 171
Alexander III, Pope, 128
Alexanders saga, 86–87
Alfífuson, Sveinn, 42
Alhacen, 112
alliteration, 158–59
alphabet, 161–62, 168–69
Altuna stone (U 1161), 104
Aquinas, Thomas, 47
Arinbjarnarkviða, 1–2, 10–11, 18, 40, 56–57, 109, 123, 191
Aristotle, 5, 108–9, 112, 114
Ari Þorgilsson, 59
Arnórr Þórðarson, 150–51
Ars versificatoria (Matthew of Vendôme), 170
Ashbery, John, 88
Ásmundar saga kappabana, 87
Aspa stone (Sö 137), 22
Assmann, Aleida, 17
Auerbach, Erich, 9
Augustine, 111, 113–15

Bacon, Roger, 165
Baltic Sea, 28
battle, soundscape of, 139–43
Beck, Heinrich, 117
Bede the Venerable, 171
Belting, Hans, 81
Benjamin, Walter, 189
Bergsveinn Birgisson, 33
Bersǫglisvísur, 136
Berudrápa, 106–7
Bettini, Maurizio, 167–68
Beuerle, Angela, 161, 180
Bevers saga, 86

Bevis of Hampton, 86
Blair, John, 25, 73
blood, 26, 61–62, 71
blue, 34–35
Blumenberg, Hans, 4
bodies, 20–21, 24–28, 110–11, 123
Boethius, 172
bookprose/freeprose debate, 4
Borró, 23
Bradley, Richard, 28–29
Bragi Boddason, 35, 82, 94, 106, 127
Braunmüller, Kurt, 161
Brenner, Oskar, 161
Brink, Stefan, 23
Brogan, T. V. F., 152–53
brooches, 93–94
Búadrápa, 128
Bugge, Sophus, 36–37
Butler, Shane, 187–88

Casey, Edward, 20
catena, 17–18, 47, 56, 70
Chanson de Roland, 141
Chappell, Sophie Grace, 135–36, 138–39
Charles the Bald, 34–35
Christ, 5–6, 44, 91, 110, 129–30
Christianization, 4, 9, 17, 42, 44, 71, 73, 110–11
Cináed ua hArtacáin, 25–26
Civilization and Its Discontents (Freud), 186
Clanchy, Michael, 7
Clári saga, 120, 150
Clunies Ross, Margaret, 117, 151–52
Codex Aureus of St. Emmeram, 34
Codex Regius, 175
Codex Upsaliensis, 118, 120, 161–62, 178–81, 183
Codex Wormianus, 123, 161–63, 166–69
colors, 34–35
Comestor, Peter, 121

common sense (*sensus communis*), 111, 114, 116
Confessions (Augustine), 114–15
Consistori del Gay Saber, 170–71
"creation of world" typescene, 34–35
Culler, Jonathan, 152

Davidson, Hilda Ellis, 54
De anima (Aristotle), 109
De arte metrica (Bede the Venerable), 171
death, 40–44, 49–51, 54–55
Debray, Régis, 10
De imagine Tetrici (Walahfrid Strabo), 74–75
De musica (John Cotton), 166
Denmark, 38–42
Derrida, Jacques, 187
De sensu (Aristotle), 112
Deutsch, Diana, 159
diagram, 160–62, 164, 178–82, 189
Dietrich of Bern, 75
Diomedes, 165
dróttkvætt, 18–19, 137–40, 143–44, 151

echo, 154–58
Egill Skallagrímsson, 18, 37, 67, 86, 106, 109, 123
Egils saga, 86–88, 107, 143, 150, 191
Einarr Skúlason, 123, 127, 154
Eiríks saga víðforla, 69, 71
ekphrasis, 84–85, 88–89, 91, 102–3, 105–6, 111
Elucidarium (Honorius Augustodunensis), 108
Empson, William, 152
enargeia, 88–91, 93, 97–99, 106
epiphany, 89, 102, 106, 127, 131, 186
Erfidrápa Óláfs Tryggvasonar, 153–54, 157
Eriksgata, 23
Ermoldus Nigellus, 35–36
Etymologies (Isidore of Seville), 108–9, 120, 152, 165, 178, 187
Exodus, Book of, 120–21
Exodus, Old English, 140
extramission, 111–13
eye, 111, 113–16, 124; inner, 113–14
Eyvindr Finnsson, 18, 37, 51, 58, 63–64

Færeyinga saga, 86
Fagrskinna, 46–47
Fassler, Margot, 171
Felski, Rita, 7
figura, 9–10
Finnegan, Ruth, 7
Finnur Jónsson, 48–49, 124, 161, 191
Flateyjarbók, 69–70, 121
flesh, 62, 70–71
Foote, Peter, 170
fornyrðislag, 18, 37, 45, 76, 144, 158
Francia, 73, 75, 185
Frank, Roberta, 135
fratricide, 27–28, 52
Freud, Sigmund, 186
Futurism, 140

Gade, Kari, 65, 67
Gamla Uppsala, 29–30
Gautreks saga, 27–28
Geisli, 70, 128
genealogical poetry, 56–58, 71
genealogy, 56–65
generational place, 17, 20–21
Geoffrey of Vinsauf, 170
German media theory, 6
Gesta danorum (Saxo Grammaticus), 27, 40–44
Gjekstad, 23
Glælognskviða, 18, 42–44, 47–48
glory, 135–37
Glymdrápa, 143–48, 153–55
God, 118–21
Golgotha, 6
Goody, Jack, 7
grace, 6, 114, 128, 130
gravesites, Viking Age, 23–24
Green, Richard, 25
Gregors saga, 113
grid, 162, 178–79, 186
Griffith, Eric, 188
Guðrúnarkviða III, 75
Guðvarður Már Gunnlaugsson, 69
Gumbrecht, Hans Ulrich, 7
Gunnell, Terry, 55
Gustavson, Helmer, 72
Gylfaginning, 96, 118, 120, 125, 130, 170

Hákonarkviða, 18, 37, 49, 65–69
Hákonar saga Hákonarsonar, 65, 67–70
Hákon IV Hákonarson, 65
Halbwachs, Maurice, 17
Háleygjatal, 18, 40, 51, 55–56, 58, 63–64, 67
Hallfreðr Óttarsson, 136, 145, 153–54
Hallr Þórarinsson, 128
Halraldr hárfagri, 33, 37, 46–47, 59, 62, 64, 143
Haraldr harðráði Sigurðarson, 64, 90–91
Hárbarðsljóð, 8
Háttalykill, 128
Háttatal, 65, 125, 138, 143, 145, 151, 164, 170–78, 180–82, 186
Haustlǫng, 37, 83, 101–3, 124–28, 130–31
Havelock, Eric, 7
Heffernan, J. A. W., 84–86
Heimskringla, 15, 41, 57, 61, 143
Hel, 49–50, 53–55, 67
Helgi *Hundingsbani*, 55, 99
Heller-Roazen, Daniel, 174
hending, 11–12, 149–54
Hiarnus, 40
Hildr, participant in the Hjaðningavíg, 82, 94, 98–99, 106, 127
Historia de antiquitate regum Norwagiensium, 59
Historia Norwegie, 46, 59, 61–62
Hǫfuðlausn, 150
Holmberg, Per, 72
Holtan, 23
Holtsmark, Anne, 117
homilies, 109–11, 113, 115, 121–22, 129
Honorius Augustodunensis, 108
Hørdum stone (NJy 30), 104
Hovrengaellis, 100–102
Hrynhenda (Árnorr Þórðarson), 150–51
Hulda, 70
hurdy-gurdy, 160, 162, 179–80
Húsdrápa, 83, 103–5, 123
Hyndluljóð, 58, 70–71

icons, 6
images: ekphrasis and, 89; gods and, 100–103; media and, 81; mediality and, 81–82; mental, 81; politics of, 81; in puzzle pictures, 93–94; on shields, 93; visuality and, 90–91. *See also* ekphrasis
information transfer theory, 5
Ingelheim, 35–36, 39
In honorem Hludovici (Ermoldus Nigellus), 35–36
intromission, 112
Ireland, 63
Isidore of Seville, 108–9, 165
Íslendingabók (Ari Þorgilsson), 59
Íslendingadrápa, 128
Íslensk hómilíubók, 115–16
itineraries, 22–24

Jansson, S. B. F., 22
Jn dedicatione tempeli, 113
John Cotton, 166
John of Garland, 170, 172
Johnson, Christopher, 61
Jómsvíkingadrápa, 128
Jón Þórðarson, 69–71
Joshua, Book of, 140–41
Jünger, Ernst, 139

Karlamagnús saga, 75
Karlevi stone (Öl 1), 151
Kenelm, Saint, 24–25
kenning, 11–12, 53, 65–66, 94–97, 110, 123, 142–43, 146–50, 153–54, 157–58, 192
kinship, 60–62
Kittler, Friedrich, 6
knowledge, 31, 44, 82, 108–10, 116–19
Köbele, Susanne, 143, 152
Kolbrún Haraldsdóttir, 69
Konungsannáll, 121
Krag, Claus, 36–37
Kristján Árnason, 149
kviðuháttr, 11, 18, 40–44, 47–49, 53, 56–57, 65, 67, 75, 185

landscape, 20–26, 28–29, 32
Laxdœla saga, 83
Legendary Saga of St Olaf, 190
Lie, Hallvard, 84
light, 113, 128–30
Líknarbraut, 128–30
Lilja, 9, 170

listing, 56–57
Litla Skálda, 123
Ljungkvist, Johan, 29–30
Loki, 32, 49, 53, 83
Lönnroth, Lars, 50
Loptr Sæmundsson, 53–54, 65
Lord, Albert B., 7
Lothar I, 35
Lothar II, 35
Lotmann, Jurij, 152
Louis the German, 35
Louis the Pious, 35
Ludwigslied, 171

MacIntyre, Alasdair, 136
Magnús Þórhallsson, 69–70
Mainistrech, Flann, 25
Malsta stone (Hs 14), 58
Marius Victorinus, 165
Máríuvísur II, 112
Marold, Edith, 37, 49–50, 175
Mary, Virgin, 34, 112
Matthew of Vendôme, 170
McKinnell, John, 27
McLuhan, Marshall, 6–7, 187
media, 5–7; images and, 81–82; imaginary, 161–62; nonverbal memory, 16–17; of vision, 111–13
mediality, 7–10; images and, 81–82; kenning and, 94–97; of memory, 16–17
mediation, 5–6, 39–40, 110–11, 118
mediology, 4, 10–12
medium, 5–7, 10
Meissner, Rudolf, 141
memorial place (*Gedenkort*), 17, 20–21, 28–30
memorial poem, 48
memory, 32, 58, 77; bodies of water and, 28, 42; death and, 18, 26; lists and, 56, 70; locational, 17–18, 21, 23, 28–29, 38, 42–44, 178; mediality of, 17; metaphors of, 2–4, 47; monumental, 15, 73–74; poetry and, 3, 11, 37, 44–45, 48, 65, 128, 136, 156; religious, 17, 25; rhyme and, 150, 155, 158; transmission and, 12, 51, 150; visualization and, 89
Metaphysics (Aristotle), 108

meter, 18, 40–44, 47–48, 137–38
Micillo, Valeria, 165
milieu, 10
Minnesänger, 143
modernist poetry, 88
Mogk, Eugen, 161
Moretti, Franco, 6–7
Morginsól, 123–24
music, 162–70, 180–81
Myhre, Bjørn, 20
Myrvoll, Klaus Johan, 37

narration, in visual art, 81, 89
Njáls saga, 7
noise, 169–78
noise words, 141–43
nonverbal memory media, 16–17
Nora, Pierre, 17
Nordal, Guðrún, 67
Noreen, Erik, 49
Nóregs konungatal, 37, 49, 53–54, 56, 64–65, 69–71
Norr, Svante, 29
Norra Sandsjö stone (Sm 71), 58
Nunberg, Geoffrey, 188

Oddi inn litli Glúmsson, 18, 43–44
Óðinn, 54–57, 102, 150
ofljóst, 10, 53–54, 65, 153, 158
Ólafr inn helgi Haraldsson (St Olaf), 42, 128
Óláfr IV Hákonarson, 70
Óláfr Tryggvason, 69, 100, 136, 153–58
Óláfr Þórðarson, 151–52, 172–73
Óláfs saga helga, 47–48, 69, 150
Óláfs saga Tryggvasonar, 69, 90–91
Ong, Walter, 7
optical illusions, 118–22
Origen, 111
Orkneyinga saga, 90
Orms Eddu-Brot, 123–24
Oswald of Northumbria, St., 24–26
Ottarshögen, 22

Parikka, Jussi, 161–62
Parisiana poetria (John of Garland), 170, 172, 177–78, 182

INDEX 295

Parry, Milman, 7
Pastoureau, Michel, 33–34
Paul, Jean, 152
Penda of Mercia, 24
perception, 114–15, 121–22
Peter, St., 108
Pharaoh (Biblical figure), 120–21
phonaestheme, 143
Physiologus, 179
picture poems, 82–85
picture stones, Gotland, 98
place(s): bodies and, 20–21; death in, 40–44; generational, 17, 20–21; memorial, 17, 20–21, 28–29; naming, 29–31; in *Ynglingatal*, 22–24
Plato, 108
Poetic Edda, 168
Poetria nova (Geoffrey of Vinsauf), 170, 172
politics of image, 81
Poole, Russell, 35
Portrait in a convex mirror (Parmigianino), 88
positivism, 85
Posner, Roland, 6
Priscian, 165
Probus, 165
Prose Edda, 85, 111, 116–18, 130–31, 137, 143, 158, 161, 170, 185
psychology, 115–16
puns, 151–53
puzzle pictures, 93–94, 107

quatrain organization, 11, 16, 41, 76
Quintilian, 88–89

Ragnarsdrápa, 35, 82, 84, 94–98, 124–25, 127
Ralph, Bo, 72
Raschellà, Fabrizio, 161
Rheen, Samuel, 100–101
rhyme, 11, 137, 143–45, 149–64, 169, 172–77, 180–82
rithmica, 150, 164, 171–74, 177–78, 183
Rǫgnvaldr, in *Ynglingatal*, 16, 32–34, 36–39
Rök stone (Ög 136), 15–19, 41, 72–77

Runby stone (U 114), 158
Rundkvist, Martin, 28
runhent meter, 172–73, 175–78, 180
runic inscription, 15, 58, 73–75, 92, 138, 151

sacral kingship, 51–52
saints, 25–26
Sapp, Christopher, 37
satire, 50–51
Saxo Grammaticus, 27–28, 40–42
scale, in music, 168–69, 180–81
Schneider, David, 61
Schück, Henrik, 72
Secgan, 28
Second Grammatical Treatise, 160–61, 163–70, 178, 180–82, 186
Sedgwick, Eve, 7
Self-portrait in a Convex Mirror (Ashbery), 88
senses, 109–10, 114–15, 122–23
Serres, Michel, 140
Shakespeare, William, 152
shields, 65–68, 81–88, 93
sight, 82, 108–9, 111–16, 118–19, 122–24, 128–30. *See also* images
Sigvatr Þórðarson, 136
Simeon the God-Receiver, 110
sjónhverfing. *See* optical illusions
Skálda saga, 143
Skáldatal, 37, 125, 189
Skáldskaparmál, 82–84, 117–18, 122–29, 170, 189
Skírnismál, 153
Skjaldardrápa, 107
skothending, 144, 149–50, 154
skrýða, 9–10
Skúli jarl Bárðarson, 65–69
Smith, Mark, 113–14
Smith, Peter, 63
Sneglu-Halla þáttr, 90, 92
Snorri Sturluson, 15, 65
Sonatorrek, 18, 40–44, 49
sonic patterning, 143–45
sound, 164–69
soundscape, of battle, 139–43
Spiegel, Gabrielle, 47, 61–62
Stenholm, Ann-Mari Hållans, 21

Stewart, Susan, 152
Stjórn, 121
Storm, Gustav, 37
Sturla Þórðarson, 18, 37, 49, 65
Styrmir Kárason, 190
Suger, Abbot, 34
Summa musicae, 180–81
Summulae dialectices (Bacon), 165
Sundqvist, Olof, 51
Sverrir Jakobsson, 62
Sverrir Tómasson, 181–82
Sverris saga, 69, 190
Sweetser, Eve, 110

Theoderic the Great, 74–75
Theodoricus, 59
Third Grammatical Treatise, 151–52, 165, 172, 178
Thomas of Capua, 172
Timaeus (Plato), 108
touch, sense of, 109–11
Tranter, Stephen, 175

Úlfr Uggason, 83
Uppsala, 17, 20, 22, 29–31, 60–61
Útfarardrápa, 190

Vadstena Abbey, 7
Vafþrúðnismál, 8, 125
Valhǫll, 54–55
Vansina, Jan, 57–58
Vauchez, André, 25
Vendel Period, 17, 21
Viken, 15, 18, 23, 26–27, 31–32, 36–38, 44
Vikstrand, Per, 22
Vilhjálms saga, 87

Vincent of Beauvais, 119
vision, 82, 108–9, 111–13, 118. *See also* ekphrasis; images
visuality, 82, 90–91, 116–18. *See also* images
Vǫluspá, 7–8, 125
Vorticism, 140
vox, 163–167, 187

Walahfrid Strabo, 74
Wang, Haicheng, 65
Watt, Ian, 7
Weber, Gerd Wolfgang, 117
Wenzel, Horst, 138
Wessén, Elias, 47–49, 72
Widmark, Gun, 73
Wieland, C. M., 152
Wolf, Kirsten, 33

Ynglinga saga, 15–16, 60–61
Ynglingatal, 185; dating of, 36–37; editions, 16; as genealogical poetry, 71; Hel in, 49–50; as map, 20; mediation in, 39–40; places in, 22–24; quatrain organization in, 76; Rök and, 15–19, 72–74; royal succession in, 31–32; as satire, 50; Uppsala and, 17

Zumthor, Paul, 7, 163, 187

Þjóðólfr Arnórsson, 91–92, 97
Þjóðólfr of Hvin, 37, 83
Þórarinn loftunga, 18, 42
Þorkell Gíslason, 128
Þórr, 82–83, 90, 94–96, 100–102, 104–5
Þórsdrápa, 124–26, 130–31
Þrymskviða, 101, 104–5

Kate Heslop is an associate professor in the Scandinavian Department at the University of California, Berkeley. Her research focuses on memory, mediality, and the senses in Old Norse textual culture. Recent edited volumes include (with Jürg Glauser) *RE:writing. Medial Perspectives on Textual Culture in the Icelandic Middle Ages* and (with Klaus Müller-Wille and others) *Skandinavische Schriftlandschaften / Scandinavian Textscapes*.

FORDHAM SERIES IN MEDIEVAL STUDIES

Ronald B. Begley and Joseph W. Koterski, S.J. (eds.), *Medieval Education*
Teodolinda Barolini and H. Wayne Storey (eds.), *Dante for the New Millennium*
Richard F. Gyug (ed.), *Medieval Cultures in Contact*
Seeta Chaganti (ed.), *Medieval Poetics and Social Practice: Responding to the Work of Penn R. Szittya*
Devorah Schoenfeld, *Isaac on Jewish and Christian Altars: Polemic and Exegesis in Rashi and the "Glossa Ordinaria"*
Martin Chase, S.J. (ed.), *Eddic, Skaldic, and Beyond: Poetic Variety in Medieval Iceland and Norway*
Felice Lifshitz, *Religious Women in Early Carolingian Francia: A Study of Manuscript Transmission and Monastic Culture*
Sam Zeno Conedera, S.J., *Ecclesiastical Knights: The Military Orders in Castile, 1150–1330*
J. Patrick Hornbeck II and Michael van Dussen (eds.), *Europe After Wyclif*
Laura K. Morreale and Nicholas L. Paul (eds.), *The French of Outremer: Communities and Communications in the Crusading Mediterranean*
Ayelet Even-Ezra, *Ecstasy in the Classroom: Trance, Self, and the Academic Profession in Medieval Paris*
Kate Heslop, *Viking Mediologies: A New History of Skaldic Poetics*

www.ingramcontent.com/pod-product-compliance
Lightning Source LLC
Chambersburg PA
CBHW042345300426
44110CB00030B/161